JIMMY CARTER

The University of Georgia Press *Athens & London*

KENNETH E. MORRIS

JIMMY
CARTER
AMERICAN MORALIST

© 1996 by Kenneth E. Morris
Published by the University of Georgia Press
Athens, Georgia 30602
All rights reserved
Designed by Richard Hendel
Set in 10.5 on 14.5 Janson by Graphic Composition, Inc.
Printed and bound by Edwards Brothers
The paper in this book meets the guidelines for
permanence and durability of the Committee on
Production Guidelines for Book Longevity of the
Council on Library Resources.

Printed in the United States of America
00 99 98 97 96 C 5 4 3 2 1
Library of Congress Cataloging in Publication Data
Morris, Kenneth E.
Jimmy Carter, American moralist / Kenneth E. Morris.
p. cm.
Includes bibliographical references and index.
ISBN 0-8203-1862-0 (alk. paper)
1. Carter, Jimmy, 1924–   . 2. Presidents — United States —
Biography. I. Title.
E873.M67 1996
973.926′092 — dc20
[B]   96-6350

British Library Cataloging in Publication Data available

In memory of Michael Alan Snyder

For Halie Francesca Morris

"I think you are

a very bad man,"

said Dorothy.

"Oh no, my dear;

I'm really a very

good man; but I'm

a very bad wizard . . ."

L. Frank Baum, *The Wizard of Oz*

CONTENTS

ACKNOWLEDGMENTS

It is difficult to imagine having written this book without the help of Randolph C. Smith. Randy helped me check facts, fetch sources, and — most important — clarify every interpretation that eventually found its way into the book (and reject many that did not).

Homer Cooper, Beth Hardaway, Rick McIntyre, Henry Perry, Deb Sommer, Burt Sparer, and several others contributed reactions and/or source material. Joe McCrary analyzed the election returns and exit polls that ultimately found their way into the notes of the book. Ann Wintrode and Lisa S. Williams provided able copyediting. Kelly Caudle guided the manuscript through publication with thoughtfulness and good will.

Early in my research two of Carter's associates, Pat Caddell and Bert Lance, graciously gave up afternoons to answer my questions. Although I came away from Lance's country office charmed by the immensely likable and mostly unfairly maligned man, I came away from Caddell's Santa Monica home with a feeling of special satisfaction. I remain convinced that Caddell's ideas, or something like them, are very close to correct in their diagnosis of the nation's ills. Since he almost alone among Carter's associates has remained reticent about opening his papers to researchers or otherwise going public with "memoirs," it was especially helpful to be able to talk with him in person.

With respect to other source material, I am doubly indebted. First, the staff of the Jimmy Carter Library went out of its way to be helpful and friendly. Indeed, among my few regrets in finally finishing this book is that I will no longer have an excuse to stop by the Carter Center. My second debt is to Betty Glad. After realizing that even the wealth of material available at the Jimmy Carter Library combined with published sources was insufficient, I asked Glad to use the interviews she undertook when writing her benchmark biography of Carter during the late 1970s. She agreed, and I came away with more than a hundred interviews — many of which would have been impossible to obtain otherwise. Although as a condition of using these interviews I had to agree not to identify anyone who had not given Glad express permission to use his or her name (thus explaining the numerous "anonymous" citations in the notes), Glad's sources enabled this biography to be more authoritative than it would have otherwise been.

My agent, Sheree Bykofsky, went to bat for me long after I assumed she would give up, and both she and her associate Janet Rosen provided more than a few good readings of early drafts. Janet also left me one encouraging phone message at a particularly discouraging time. Later, when these functions were taken over by Karen Orchard and her associates at the University of Georgia Press, I remained pleased — but Sheree and Janet got the ball rolling.

My only institutional support came indirectly from a National Endowment for the Humanities seminar at the University of California–Berkeley during the summer of 1994. Whereas the fellowship was not intended to support the book per se but was oriented toward a more general study of biography as a literary genre, I decided to take the busman's holiday. I'm glad I did. My colleagues were warm, intriguing, and supportive while our director, James E. B. Breslin, was a true inspiration and helpful guide. My only regret is that Jim died before seeing his imprint on my book.

Along with those who contributed substantively to this book, it is also appropriate to thank those who have long stood ready with a word of encouragement (or letter of recommendation). Terry Doran, Barry Schwartz, and Raymond Yang come especially to mind.

The realization that my daughter entered and then completed elementary school between the times I started and finished this book helps me appreciate why authors so often thank long-suffering family members. Halie understandably doesn't care much for Jimmy Carter or think that her dad should write another book. Still, for enduring it, she deserves credit.

But just as I was sure that I would dedicate the book to Halie, news arrived that my old friend Mike Snyder died. Since Mike and I spent most of the 1970s playing in one or another band and scarcely a page of this book was written without my thinking of the people and songs of that time, his death forced me to confront the visceral fact that our — Carter's — era is now history. It therefore seemed fitting that the dedication be shared between the two generations: one that lived it, the other that inherits it.

JIMMY CARTER

CHAPTER I

NTRODUCTION: THE MALAISE OF THE CARTER YEARS

On Sunday evening, July 15, 1979, Jimmy Carter emerged from ten days of seclusion to deliver the most startling speech of his presidency. Expected to speak on energy policy, the subject the White House had announced, the president had ample reasons to address the issue. The second OPEC oil embargo of the decade had once again constricted supplies, forcing Americans to endure erratic but widespread gasoline shortages. In March, a near-catastrophic nuclear accident at Three Mile Island ominously co-incided with the release of a film, *The China Syndrome*, about just such an accident. Popular fears about the prospects for a safe nu-clear alternative to petroleum-based energy were thereby dramat-ically stimulated. Earlier in the year, the decade's spiraling "stag-flation" (simultaneously high unemployment and inflation) was exacerbated by sharp spikes in the inflation rate, produced partly by the doubling of crude oil prices. Coupled with the recent pain-ful legacies of the Vietnam War and Watergate, the resurgent en-ergy crisis and galloping inflation fostered a climate of foreboding resignation that many felt clung like a thick fog to the nation. When the president canceled his previously scheduled energy speech to retreat to Camp David for a ten-day "domestic summit" at which he reassessed his administration and its objectives, Americans' fears were personified. Accordingly, when Jimmy Carter finally spoke to the nation in the televised July 15 address, his speech was watched by more than sixty-five million Ameri-cans — twice the number who had bothered to view his recent speeches.[1]

But in the weeks preceding the speech, Carter had come to the conclusion that more than energy policy was at stake for the nation's future. His fight for energy policy had grown increasingly frustrating. For the entire two and a half years he had been president, Carter had made the achievement of a comprehensive national energy policy the cornerstone of his administration's domestic agenda. Yet with the exception of a few piecemeal legislative victories late in 1978, he had failed to extract the necessary congressional support. Just as disheartening, the public seemed indifferent to both the challenge and his effort to meet it. Polls showed that fewer than a third of Americans ranked energy among even the top five national problems.[2] Meanwhile, viewership of his speeches on energy had fallen off, and comedians had successfully reduced his claim that energy policy was the "moral equivalent of war" to its acronym — MEOW. Carter's approval ratings put the story of these and other failures in stark numerical form. By June fewer than 30 percent of the public approved of his leadership; a solid 56 to 59 percent majority disapproved of it.[3] The president was thus understandably reluctant to deliver yet another address on energy policy, which by then would have been his fifth. In fact, he was beginning to conclude that a deeper problem needed to be addressed first.

While these concerns prompted Carter to cancel a scheduled vacation in early July and return to the White House, they also convinced him to cancel his earlier scheduled speech in favor of the "domestic summit" at Camp David. With his administration in disarray, his influence evaporating, and the course of the nation uncertain, he invited some 130 ministers, friends, intellectuals, reporters, business and labor leaders, civil rights activists, and government officials to critique his administration and recommend changes in it. He also made impromptu visits to "ordinary" families in Pennsylvania and West Virginia — as he so often had during his 1976 campaign — in order to find out whether the citizens agreed with the experts. Through these and other means he hoped to understand the conundrum of American despair that seemed to be thwarting his every effort to confront the nation's huge but solvable problems. And he also hoped to prepare a rhetoric response adequate to the challenge of that despair.

The whole tenor of the president's retreat was vehemently opposed by several of his key administration officials. Vice President Walter Mondale and senior domestic policy advisor Stuart Eizenstat were especially adamant in their opposition to it. They maintained that Carter should take swift and decisive action on the gasoline shortage, as well as on other policy fronts, and forget about his more nebulous cultural worries. As drafts of the July 15 address that focused on just these worries began to circulate,

Mondale, for one, was so incensed that he threatened to resign. Later, when Carter followed the speech by firing several of his disloyal cabinet secretaries, the vice president eagerly accepted a trip abroad and claimed he never felt "happier" to leave the country. Indeed, for Mondale, "it went from sugar to shit right there." But Eizenstat was equally vehement in his opposition to the president's squishy spiritual sentimentality. When even he had difficulty getting "any damn gas" for his car so he could chair the daily White House meetings on energy policy, he declared the whole focus of the administration's reflection "bullshit." In exasperation, and off the top of his head, the domestic policy official even rattled off the policy speech that he believed the president should give on July 15. Yet, while Eizenstat's policy speech was ultimately included in the speech, it was appended somewhat illogically onto the end of an altogether different one. The compromise enabled Carter to keep a tenuous peace while still saying what he wanted to say.[4]

Urging Carter to focus on the cultural despair, however, was his twenty-seven-year-old maverick pollster, Patrick Caddell. Widely regarded as a brilliant interpreter of public opinion after he served (while still a Harvard undergraduate) as the chief pollster for George McGovern's 1972 presidential campaign, Caddell's talents lay in blending polling data with a broader reflection on cultural themes. Drawing from both poll results and a host of contemporary interpreters of national life, including especially Berkeley sociologist Robert Bellah and Rochester historian Christopher Lasch, Caddell arrived at the alarming conclusion that America was in the throes of a massive crisis of confidence. The magnitude and importance of this crisis could not be ignored. Caddell concluded that nothing less than the historic American faith in a tomorrow that would be better than today — the essence of the American dream — was collapsing. Attending that collapse, moreover, was the disintegration of the bonds of civility that had formerly united the diverse nation in pursuit of their shared individual dreams. Caddell therefore pleaded with Carter to address this "big picture" of America's despair in his July 15 speech and enlisted others (including Bellah and Lasch) to help him present his case. Indeed, the pollster believed that unless Carter addressed the crisis of confidence both his presidency and, ultimately, the nation would fail.

In a rare sign of approval he reserved almost exclusively for Caddell, Carter responded to his pollster's spring 1979 memorandum warning of the crisis of confidence with a note that declared it a "masterpiece."[5] Indeed, while Carter liked and respected both Mondale and Eizenstat, he reserved for Caddell the privilege of becoming the only non-Georgian admitted into his inner circle of informal advisors. Separated by a generation, a region, and a religion (Caddell was Catholic), the affinity between the two was based on a common understanding of the nation's moral creed. For, no less than Caddell, Carter believed that the nation rested primarily on faith. Indeed, he once summarized the meaning of his 1976 presidential victory by saying it was about "faith."[6] Three years later, as that faith withered, Carter agreed with Caddell that he should address the crisis of confidence.

Carter did have difficulty appropriating the intellectual traditions that Caddell urged him to absorb. Although he was noticeably intelligent and had enormous capacity for information, little in his mostly technical education or his practical background as a naval officer and agri-businessman equipped him to grasp the synthesis of abstract ideas that is the hallmark of social and cultural interpretation. The evidence even suggests that, while he invited advice from social critics like Bellah and Lasch and read portions of their works, he was either unpersuaded by or just uninterested in their larger theoretical schemes. He rejected the language of Bellah's theory of American "civil religion" and expressed no enthusiasm for Lasch's synthesis of Freud and Marx. Indeed, perhaps it was the talent that Caddell possessed for just this kind of abstract intellectual meandering that attracted the more practical-minded executive to him. Whether it was or not, Caddell remained virtually alone as the administration's point man for ideas, and Carter welcomed his contribution.

Carter's sympathy for the intellectuals' moral arguments was of a more visceral sort. The product of southern populism and then the civil rights movement, as well as a born-again Southern Baptist, Carter was trebly immersed in modes of thinking that accentuated morality in public life. Both of the political traditions from which he drew were as much moral crusades as they were political movements. His more private Christian faith was naturally also a prod to inject morality and faith into public life. Coupled then with a presidential campaign that had emphasized faith and the urgings of Caddell, Carter was easily persuaded. He agreed that America's greatness rested primarily on its morals and ideals — not on its policies — and concurred that in the summer of 1979 it was time to speak to these ideals more than to policy.[7]

So the July 15 speech that Caddell later likened to a "camel" for its compromised blending of disparate themes focused only partly on the energy crisis. Its main focus was what Caddell, perhaps borrowing from Christopher Lasch, called the "crisis of confidence."[8] Indeed, the new title of the Caddell-Eizenstat speech, honed further by Carter as well as his speechwriters, was "Energy and the Crisis of Confidence."

Speaking to the nation on that Sunday evening, Jimmy Carter said that the energy crisis was only a symptom of a more pervasive "moral and spiritual crisis" in America. Americans who could not solve their energy problems also expressed a "longing for meaning," yet more doubt about the meaning of their lives than ever before. Less optimistic than previously, "too many" were "worship[ing] self-indulgence and consumption," losing the "idea that founded our nation." Never before, the president said, had Americans experienced such a collapse of "national will" or "crisis of the American spirit." Not least, the speech warned that attention to energy policy, inflation, recession, or any other national problem would be fruitless until Americans "faced the truth" of their "much deeper" crisis. "All the legislation in the world can't fix what's wrong with America," he said. Fixing these problems required a rekindling of faith: "faith in each other, faith in our ability to govern ourselves, and faith in the future of this nation."

The nation was stunned. Although Americans had long vaguely understood their nation to rest on faith — a belief in national progress, in the American dream — few were prepared to admit its collapse. The weight of the nation's history, except for the Civil War and perhaps other periods of crisis, denied this possibility. Whether through the transcendentalism of Emerson and Thoreau or the positive thinking of Mary Baker Eddy and Norman Vincent Peale, Americans have always been unequivocally optimistic and bereft of a sense of the tragic.[9] Yet on July 15 Carter signaled concern about Americans' long-standing affirmative faith when he plainly stated: "This is not a message of happiness or reassurance."

Most Americans were not prepared to hear this kind of spiritual rhetoric, even from Jimmy Carter. Although he was widely understood to be among the most religious occupants of the Oval Office, few understood how he distinguished his private faith from his public morality.[10] Part of the fault may have been Carter's. Previously his faith, which his chief campaign strategist, Hamilton Jordan, had dubbed a "weirdo factor" in 1976, had been subdued and benevolent, expressed publicly primarily in a somewhat sentimental populism. In his inaugural address, for instance, he had been persuaded by aides to substitute the less challenging Mic. 6:8 ("What doth the Lord require of thee, but to do justly, and to love mercy, and to

walk humbly with thy God?") for his harsher first choice, 2 Chron. 7:14
("If my people, which are called by my name, shall humble themselves,
and pray, and seek my face, and turn from their wicked ways; then I will
hear from heaven, and will forgive their sin, and will heal their land").[11]
In this and other ways in which his public morality seemed but a hodge-
podge of uneasily connected moral maxims, Carter poorly prepared
Americans for the more sustained challenge of addressing the basic problem of a national faith that his July 15 speech posed.

Also, the case can be made that in times of national despair Americans
do not want or expect to hear such criticisms from their president. The
seemingly successful optimistic rhetoric of presidents like Ronald Reagan
or Franklin D. Roosevelt — no less spiritual, but far more optimistic —
suggests that presidents are most popular when they confront crises with
optimistic denial. Jimmy Carter therefore surprised his listeners not
merely by speaking of the spiritual but by speaking of it as a public problem. For these reasons, if not more, when journalist Theodore White later
assessed the speech he commented, "No president since Abraham Lincoln
had spoken with such sincerity to the American people about matters of
spirit."[12]

Today "Energy and the Crisis of Confidence" is Carter's best-
remembered speech — although it is not known by its original title. Renamed by opponents (some allege by Senator Edward Kennedy) the "malaise speech," this is the title that has stuck (although Carter never said the
word "malaise").[13] But by whatever name, the address is remarkable. It has
unquestionably had what more than a decade later Caddell considered an
astonishing "half-life."[14] No other of Carter's speeches has merited such
singular attention, and few speeches by any president are as well remembered.[15] Moreover, the speech is intimately linked with the person and
presidency of Jimmy Carter. Bert Lance considers it "vintage Carter,"[16]
while as late as 1992 speakers at the Republican National Convention reminded listeners of the "malaise of the Carter years." The same year, the
television cartoon *The Simpsons* showed a statue of Jimmy Carter with the
inscription "Malaise Forever."

Yet the speech — like the man, his presidency, and his times — is not
so easily assessed. Immediately after it was delivered (though this is not
well remembered) public reaction was favorable. Some 61 percent of

Americans surveyed reported that the speech made them feel optimistic, White House mail was overwhelmingly enthusiastic, editorial reaction was mostly supportive, and Carter enjoyed an average dozen-point bounce in the polls. But no sooner did this reaction appear than it dissipated. Within weeks — and after the speech was assailed as the "malaise speech" — media assessment of it turned critical, and Carter's approval rating plummeted. Yet, as the years have worn on, scholars have provided appreciative interpretations of the address, many have revised upward their estimation of Carter's presidency, and Carter himself has soared in the polls. Today, it is simply not clear where assessment of the speech with the astonishing half-life rests.[17]

The intrigue of Jimmy Carter mirrors, it seems, this most memorable of his speeches. On one hand, he was elected president against all early expectation in 1976 in a campaign based primarily on faith, enjoyed historic highs of popularity early in his term, and rose dramatically in popular opinion during the late 1980s and 1990s, owing to his singular humanitarian accomplishments. On the other hand, he suffered the lowest approval ratings ever recorded for a president, was soundly defeated in his 1980 reelection bid, and endured bitter public hostility during the first years after he was turned out of office. Like his July 15 speech, the "half-life" of his reputation is astonishing, but it is by no means clear of what this reputation consists or where it will rest.

THE GOAL OF THIS BIOGRAPHY

The enigma of Jimmy Carter, illustrated perhaps most vividly by his July 15 speech and public reaction to it, has long centered on his role as a public moralist. It follows that the goal of this biography must be to construct a portrait of Carter that attends primarily if not exclusively to his moral outlook and moral influence.

Three interrelated objectives follow. One is simply to describe Carter's public morality in a manner similar to that which would propel the intellectual biography of any comparable moral leader. Although Carter has himself generally neglected any systematic articulation of his moral ideas, this neglect does not make the secondary explication of those ideas any less important. Indeed, it makes it more important. Since Carter is obviously propelled by powerful moral passions, yet has not bothered to articulate them clearly, it is all the more important that others do so. We want to know not only that Carter is a moral leader but what kind of morality he embraces, where it comes from, and where it is heading. An obvious source for Carter's moral ideas is his evangelical Christian faith. This faith must be understood.

However, it is important to ask whether Carter derived the gist of his public morality from his private religious faith or from some other sources. Carter's personal Christian faith may have been only one influence among many. Along with it, Carter drew freely from southern populism and the universalistic sentiment expressed in the civil rights movement. Further, he attuned his moral ear to the popular-culture moral sentiments of Bob Dylan and others. The result was a synthesis that was at once evangelical, southern, universalistic, contemporary — and quintessentially American. The challenge of this biography is to disentangle this synthesis in order to show how Carter's private religious faith evolved into his public morality.[18]

In addition to explicating Carter's moral ideas, a second objective of this biography is just to tell Carter's "story." Toward this end, the book is structured narratively, and no major episodes or events in his life are omitted. However, because the quest for biographical comprehensiveness is largely illusory — all biographers must restrict and arrange what is included, making the quest for completeness largely a biographical El Dorado — the benefit of the doubt has been extended to brevity rather than comprehensiveness. Seeking to tell the whole of Carter's story, this biography resists the pretentious claim that it tells all of it completely. Even so, the balance of completeness with brevity should be welcomed by those who want to know about Carter's life as well as his ideas.

The objectives of general biography exist in some tension with those of intellectual biography. Whereas an intellectual biography is typically satisfied to find the roots of a person's ideas in previous thinkers, a general biography also seeks to trace those ideas to their roots in lived experiences, which nowadays are often understood to be psychological. In fact the two best previous biographies of Carter have been essentially psychobiographies, even agreeing more or less on the same "diagnosis" (narcissism).[19] The presence of these previous works, coupled with the general biography's mandate to portray its subject from the "inside," forces at least some attention to be directed to Carter's psychological profile here as well. However, since the larger goal of this biography is not psychological diagnosis but moral explication, the temptation to engage in anything more than rudimentary psychological speculation is resisted. In place of it I employ a more general social psychological perspective (symbolic interactionism) that, while not inconsistent with many schools of psychological and psychoanalytic thought, avoids engagement with most disputes in psychological theory in favor of an emphasis on description.

A third objective, finally, is to evaluate Carter's public morality. This objective must not be ignored. To note that Carter is a moralist, after all, is not to conclude that he was the right kind of moralist for his times. As Nietzsche most famously argued, morality is relative to the group expressing it. This moral pluralism must be taken seriously in the study of Jimmy Carter. For at issue in the story of a "representative man" and moral exemplar is not merely whether he is good in some abstract metaphysical sense but whether he is good for us.[20]

The criteria for moral evaluation are admittedly nebulous, but they are not completely relative. Required is to juxtapose Carter's public morality with the challenges of his times. And, while this juxtaposition must be presented at a number of different junctures in Carter's life, surely the central juncture occurred during his presidency — specifically, on July 15, 1979. Was Carter's brand of moral uplift on that evening adequate to the challenges posed by the American malaise?

The evaluation of Carter's public morality should thus begin with a description of the culture that fostered the moral crisis to which he most famously responded. Directing attention to this culture of malaise offers another advantage as well. For if such observers as civil-religion theorist Robert Bellah and James Davison Hunter, chronicler of America's "culture wars," are correct, the onset of America's continuing moral crises may be traced to the 1970s.[21] By briefly reviewing the culture of this time, the stage may therefore be set for an appreciation of the challenges that once confronted Jimmy Carter — and still confront us.

A DECADE OF MALAISE

The 1970s were, by most accounts, as dismal a decade as America ever experienced. Labeled the "me decade" by journalist Tom Wolfe, later writers called the 1970s the "runt of the decades," the "Bangladesh of the decades," and the period of the "nowhere generation."[22] Although this cultural definition of the 1970s minimizes its many noteworthy developments — the spawning of the modern environmental, women's, and gay rights movements; the massive economic transformations attending the transition from a manufacturing to a post-industrial economy; the energy crisis; post-Vietnam foreign policy; post-Watergate politics; and other events — it does signify a cultural self-conception that few doubt to be characteristic of the times.

A cursory review of popular entertainment during the 1970s illustrates this inward turn and despondent tone of the decade's culture. The most distinctive 1970s film genre, for example, was probably the disaster film. Movies like *Jaws* (1975, sequels in 1978 and 1983), *The Poseidon Adventure* (1972), *Airport* (1970, sequels in 1975 and 1977), and *The China Syndrome* (1979) seem to reflect a cultural foreboding more pronounced than in other eras. The decline of the traditional socially conscious film heroes, epitomized by the classic Western,[23] and the concomitant rise of film heroes lashing out in violence against an ineffectual society (*Billy Jack* [1971, sequel in 1974], *Dirty Harry* [1971, sequel in 1976], *Taxi Driver* [1976], *Walking Tall* [1973, sequels in 1975 and 1977, followed by a television movie and series], the spate of Charles Bronson and "kung fu" movies, etc.) seem likewise to suggest a zeitgeist mistrustful of a social ethic and reverting to selfishness and violence.

Television displayed similar cultural themes. The two most watched situation comedies of the decade were *All in the Family* and *M*A*S*H*. The first reveled in the cultural conflict of the decade, while the second epitomized a generation's attitude toward the authority structure of their society: it was not so much wrong or unjust as it was simply absurd. By 1978 the collapse of shared mores and traditional heroism paved the way for the debut of *Dallas*, a drama focusing on a family's struggle for power and money in a milieu governed not so much by right as by might. Three weeks after Carter lost the White House to Ronald Reagan (who would quote Clint Eastwood's famous line from *Dirty Harry*, "Go ahead, make my day," to much applause), more Americans (83 million) watched the famous "Who Shot J.R.?" episode of *Dallas* than had watched any television show in history (including Carter's July 15 speech) — a viewership exceeded only by the final episode of *M*A*S*H* in 1983.[24]

City life, long the carrier as well as the metaphor for civilization, gave concrete expression to these cultural trends. Although a 1965 blackout in Manhattan resulted in "a night of jovial inconvenience" that, with 59 arrests, resulted in the lowest crime rate of the year, a similar blackout in 1977 produced fear and paranoia — and some 4,000 arrests.[25] Occurrences like these blend imperceptibly into social trends. Rising fears of crime matched soaring crime rates, a burgeoning underclass became entrenched in city centers, and intellectuals worried about a breakdown of "civility."[26] City dwellers who could afford to moved their homes and, increasingly, their jobs and leisure activities to suburban and exurban enclaves.[27] A tiny minority even moved to rural areas, turning around a century-long population movement away from the country. The exodus helped to erode the urban tax base, which forced many mayors to turn to the federal government for unpopular assistance. The exodus may also have been symptomatic of a larger shift in social mores. Bestsellers such as *Winning through Intimidation* and *Looking out for #1* seem to suggest that for many Americans an ethic of selfishness was replacing a commitment to the public good.[28]

Examples like these do not substantiate a cultural interpretation of a decade, and for each a counterexample can be found. If the decade witnessed the eclipse of the traditional film hero, for example, it also embraced his (e.g., *Rocky* [1976, sequels in 1979, 1982, 1985, and 1990]) or her (e.g., *Norma Rae* [1979]) return; if television reveled in conflict and social satire, it also celebrated perceived traditional values (e.g., *The Waltons*) and thoughtful dramatic history (e.g., *Roots*); if the middle class fled the cities, some also returned to "gentrify" former slums. Indeed, in perhaps the most positive development of the decade, the 1970s saw a renewed appreciation of history, illustrated by the sharp rise in popularity of country and folk musics, movements for historic preservation, and the like.

Even so, on balance the culture seemed to drift closer to the pessimistic than to the optimistic end of the continuum. And, as illustrated by urban-to-suburban population shifts, this drift was not limited to the culture realm. Beneath these despairing cultural currents, after all, were real events. Chief among these were the economic restructurings of the decade. The failures of the 1970s to produce the rising standard of living that Americans had come to expect dashed the material component of the American dream for many. Median family income peaked in 1973 and did not attain that level again until 1987. Between 1977 and 1984 a full 90 percent of American families realized a decline in real income. As the inflation-adjusted median price of first homes doubled between 1975 and 1987, these same years witnessed a decline in home ownership for families with annual incomes under $35,000 — most Americans.[29]

The material components of the American dream were not the only ones threatened. So were the emotional components of the dream embedded in ideals of family life. A rising divorce rate hit its peak in 1979, while a "baby bust" in intact families resulted in the lowest fertility rate ever recorded. The combination of increasing female employment, the explosion of day care centers, and changing definitions of gender roles made marriage and family more troublesome for more Americans than ever before.

Alongside these economic and family woes were a spate of other worries. A cold war still raged, though post-Vietnam Americans were divided in their posture toward it. The energy crisis threatened America's reliance upon the full-size automobile fueled by cheap gasoline. And a series of Supreme Court decisions gave substance to the growing tensions in American culture. *Alexander v. Holmes* (1969) and *Swan v. Charlotte-Mecklenburg County* (1971) established school busing as the means by which public-school desegregation was to be achieved, setting off storms of protests by angry parents throughout the nation. *Roe v. Wade* (1973) established a woman's right to abortion and touched off escalating waves of protest and turmoil. *O'Connor v. Donaldson* (1975) upheld the civil rights of the mentally ill, reversing the long-standing practice of involuntary institutionalization and contributing to the number of homeless and hopeless on the nation's streets. Not least, the 1978 *Bakke* decision upheld claims of "reverse discrimination" against the counterclaims of "affirmative action," casting doubt upon America's progressive self-conception on matters of race relations. These decisions, perhaps meritorious in their own rights, nevertheless led to schism rather than consensus. Along with other events, they gave form and substance to an often noted but little understood cultural travail.

In view of these events, it is no wonder polls tracking Americans' confidence in their country, trust in their institutions, and faith in the future failed to show the upward surge most experts predicted would follow the lows of the late 1960s. Indeed, during the 1970s measures of public confidence and optimism dropped even further. Nor is it any wonder that Patrick Caddell, as Jimmy Carter's pollster, was alarmed by these trends and urged him to respond. If Caddell's pleadings with the president were thought by some to be overly alarmist — his 1979 memorandum on the subject was dubbed by White House staffers the "Apocalypse Now Memo" after the film he had helped to produce — the trends were real ones. Although he would later be variously described as "a man of table-pounding tirades" and "the mad genius of perpetual insurgency," events may have warranted the angry outbursts.[30]

What has never been entirely clear, however, is why these despondent trends arose and persisted, or what they signaled about American culture during the 1970s.

A number of explanations have been offered for the cultural despair of the 1970s.[31] The explanation favored by most of the public as well as some intellectuals — and the one preferred by Jimmy Carter — accounts for it in terms of a reaction to the traumatic events of the 1960s and early 1970s. The defeat in Vietnam, the assassinations of Martin Luther King Jr. and the Kennedy brothers, the aftermath of the excesses of the youth culture, the disgrace of Watergate and other events like the energy crisis and inflation all placed such pressure on the culture that it eventually simply lost its will to survive.[32] This explanation is plausible and is to be favored for its unflinching attention to real historical events rather than to presupposed theories superimposed on those events. Yet, by itself the event-driven explanation proves insufficient. Mainly, it fails to explain why similar series of events in other historical periods did not produce similar results, or why so many of the alleged catastrophic events had delayed cultural responses. Indeed, like most piecemeal explanations, it suffers from circularity. It presumes what it proposes to explain — a widespread cultural despair — and then seeks to tease out the events that were the likely causes of this despair.

The alternative is to do what Jimmy Carter also did and blend an event-oriented explanation with a broader cultural assessment. In Carter's case, the assessment was spiritual. Although this explanation does not replace others, it does lend meaningful form and historical coherence to otherwise disparate events and puzzling trends. Not incidentally, it was also the interpretation advanced by Tom Wolfe. He did not stop at labeling the epoch a "me decade" but proceeded to describe it as a period of America's "third great awakening." According to both the president and the journalist, America was in the throes of spiritual crisis.

Evidence for a spiritual dimension of the cultural despair of the 1970s is strong. While the country's established mainline Protestant churches continued to decline in membership, participation, and influence, novel forms of religiosity grew dramatically.[33] Evangelical Christianity emerged as a potent religious and cultural force, and church growth in these often independent evangelical enclaves more than offset its decline in established denominations. By 1978, when viewership of "televangelists" peaked, the political "New Christian Right" had also coalesced.[34] At the same time, evangelicals spearheaded the decade's biggest educational movement by founding a spate of private Christian schools that often as not appeared to be motivated by genuine religious impulses rather than by mere opposition to public-school racial integration.[35]

But religious ferment was not limited to the evangelical right. A fledgling evangelical left arose in places like Berkeley and Philadelphia, and "Jesus freaks" appeared throughout the nation, blending countercultural exuberance with evangelical Christianity. Meanwhile, positive-thinking preacher Robert Schuller built his Crystal Cathedral in southern California. "New religions" — whether imported intact from other cultures, modified for American experience, or created willy-nilly by any prophet commanding a following — abounded. Growing numbers of Americans turned to Islam or Buddhism for spiritual sustenance; Transcendental Meditation, modified for American tastes into a spiritual technique, crossed the continent; clusters of college students and dropouts sought meaning by chanting "Hare Krishna"; and young people soliciting for the Reverend Sun Myung Moon's Unification Church littered the airports. Alongside these more or less overtly religious groups were the quasi-religious psychotherapies — EST, Rolfing, Primal Screaming, etc. — and countless emergent cults. The culture was alive as rarely before with spiritual experimentation.

The spiritual strivings of the era are illustrated by the mass-market paperbacks that dominated the decade. Robert M. Pirsig's *Zen and the Art of Motorcycle Maintenance* became a campus classic, as did the series of alleged enthnographies by Carlos Castaneda on the philosophy of a Yaqui Indian sorcerer. The affinities between Western science and Eastern mysticisms were popularly probed in *The Tao of Physics*, while, beginning with *Another Roadside Attraction* (in which the body of Jesus is discovered), novelist Tom Robbins wove quasi-religious motifs around stories of counterculture characters. Even highbrow writers dabbled in the mystical. Annie Dillard's Pulitzer Prize–winning *Pilgrim at Tinker Creek* bore the subtitle *A Mystical Excursion into the Natural World*, and the translation into English of Gabriel Garcia Marquez's Nobel Prize–winning *One Hundred Years of Solitude* had critics talking about "magic realism." Death, supposedly the "last taboo," came under scrutiny as college courses on "death and dying" emerged and popular paperbacks and magazine articles reported on supposedly actual "after death" experiences by people who had come back to life to tell about it.[36]

While popular paperbacks probed religious and mystical themes, similar themes were not absent from other mass media. The 1970s, after all, witnessed the gospel story set to rock music in both *Jesus Christ Superstar* and *Godspell*. Meanwhile, in a more discrete market, Christian rock emerged as an alternative to secular popular music. But again, popular culture's religious stirrings were scarcely limited to Christianity. Ex-Beatle George Harrison's classic 1970s album *All Things Must Pass* included the repetitive "Hare Krishna" chant, and Led Zeppelin's "Stairway to Heaven" (thought by some to be occult-inspired) became perhaps the most played song of the decade.[37]

In a somewhat more respectable vein, the decade also witnessed the growing popularity of "religious studies" as a university and even a high-school offering. More young people, however, were attracted to psychology, where, despite the ascendance of behavioral paradigms, the line between the psychological and the mystical became blurred. With rising undergraduate enrollments, the spawning of the magazine *Psychology Today*, and clinical psychology doctoral programs boasting more stringent admission requirements than medical schools, the culture absorbed not only the musings of a former divinity student, Carl Rogers, but also the radical psychology of R. D. Laing — who declared that psychosis was an experience of transcendence.[38] "The psychological society" slipped ever more perilously into a religious society.[39]

Although spiritual ferment abounded, Wolfe was perhaps incorrect to label the decade a "Great Awakening." For the notion of a religious awakening implies that the culture moved toward a spiritual consensus. Yet, unlike earlier religious awakenings, the country's spiritual experimentation during the 1970s did not seem to produce consensus. Instead, religion seemed to produce as much discord as unity, as much foreboding as solace. The specter of the Manson Family murders stimulated deep fears about cultlike activities, and the ordeal of Patty Hearst raised worries of brainwashing. Parents hired professional "deprogrammers" to kidnap their children from cults and redirect them into mainstream society, and annoyed patrons in airports and other public places asked whether religious proselytizers might be barred. On the cusp of the decade, the U.S. Supreme Court decided more church/state cases during the ten years between 1967 and 1976 than it had in the twenty years before, but experts agree that the decisions were far from consistent.[40]

Worse, much of the spiritual rumblings of the 1970s had a fearful, even apocalyptic cast. The best-selling nonfiction book of the entire decade was Hal Lindsey's fundamentalist tract *The Late Great Planet Earth*. But the book's subject was anything but upbeat. It was Armageddon, the end of time.[41] Likewise, while hardly a genre unique to the 1970s, films like *The Exorcist* (1973, sequels in 1977 and 1990) riveted moviegoers with depictions of the demonic and sparked comment and discussion among worried parents, religious leaders, talk-show hosts, and mental health professionals. More concretely, late in the decade Americans saw from a distance the consequences of Islamic fundamentalism in the Iranian revolution — consequences that included calling the United States "the great Satan," public defilements of the American flag, and a year-long hostage crisis. Closer to home the biggest religious news story of the decade was the mass suicide in 1978 of some 900 members of the Reverend Jim Jones's People's Temple. Spiritual stirrings, it seemed, knew no ethical boundaries. The more Americans tinkered with religion, the more ominous and foreboding it appeared to be.

An abundance of evidence attests to an American culture more or less as Carter described it in 1979: as a nation locked in spiritual crisis. Whereas the spiritual ferment of the decade may have been overplayed by the media, and other decades can claim their own religious interests, there are ample indicators of religious ferment in the 1970s. Moreover, the religious stirrings seem more diffuse and fragmentary than in other epochs — spanning the revival of American fundamentalism, Eastern mysticisms, and various quasi-religious psychotherapies — and appear to be matched by real economic, social, and political challenges. These spiritual stirrings could not have failed to impact the political culture. A nation that centers its creed on a notion — however vague — of God and his providence cannot fail to be affected, perhaps even disturbed, by widespread religious ferment. Neither could these stirrings have failed to attach themselves to the nation's most visible leader, the president.

The significance of Jimmy Carter thus resides not only in what he said but also in the culture to which he said it. Were there not an affinity between the two, it would be difficult if not impossible to account for the election of so self-consciously religious a president in 1976 — much less account for the tumultuous popular reception of his July 15 speech. Understanding Jimmy Carter's significance therefore requires not only describing his public morality in the context of his private life but also assessing how it fitted with the spiritual travail of his times. Even more, it requires evaluating whether Carter's response to the cultural malaise was adequate. But before proceeding, it is well to pause to consider another possible dimension of the story.

A LINGERING MALAISE

If a relevant life-and-times of Jimmy Carter must attend to the development of his public morality in this milieu of cultural despair, a larger problem lingers. It is the course that this despair has followed subsequent to his presidency.

Through the 1980s popular opinion seemed to suppose that the "crisis" Carter identified in 1979 was remedied by the election of Ronald Reagan. Reagan unquestionably brought a new euphoria to the nation, and there was much talk and some evidence of a "new patriotism." Indeed, in developments that could never have arisen during the 1970s, singer Lee Greenwood had a repeat hit in "I'm Proud to Be an American"; Reagan's 1984 reelection campaign boasted "It's morning again in America"; and the term "liberal" cursed the presidential campaigns of both Walter Mondale and Michael Dukakis. Although the underlying strength of the economy during the 1980s is still in dispute, the culture did seem willing to announce renewed economic prowess. The term "yuppie" was coined to refer to the growing numbers of "young urban professionals" who made a lot of money and seemed to enjoy it.[42]

Even so, little evidence can be advanced to show that this cultural renewal was either widespread or lasting. Instead, the evidence points to a bifurcation of public attitudes and social behavior during the 1980s: Some Americans did become more buoyant in their attitudes, more successful in their jobs, more nationalistic in their outlook; other Americans, however, had precisely the opposite experience. Their attitudes grew more despairing, their livelihoods more threatened, their opinion of their nation more cynical. Indeed, for all of the alleged euphoria Reagan brought to the nation, his own approval ratings tell a different story. After the initial honeymoon period, his approval ratings were consistently above 50 percent for only the three years between late 1983 and late 1986; the rest of the time he governed with minority support. Conveniently high at the time of his reelection campaign, his overall pattern of approval was lower than Richard Nixon's. Measures of public confidence, which also peaked in and around late 1984, similarly languished before and after.[43]

Worse, the supposed cultural renewal of the 1980s did not endure. By the summer of 1992, when it looked like another southern Democratic governor might win the White House and George Bush was also seriously challenged by independent candidate Ross Perot, conservative thinkers themselves turned to an indictment of American culture not unlike that advanced by Carter in his "malaise speech." On the basis of a series of essays by a dozen conservative intellectuals in a special edition of *Forbes* magazine, syndicated columnist Mona Charen concluded that George Bush's problems in 1992 had little to do with his leadership. President Bush's plummet rather had everything to do with "our culture" — namely, "a moral crisis tearing at the heart of our people." But importantly, this indictment of "our culture" was not one that proceeded along the predictable lines of the right's position on the culture wars. That indictment of course persisted — exemplified by Patrick Buchanan's fiery address on America's "culture wars" at the 1992 Republican Convention. But the tone of the Charen column and the *Forbes* essays was quieter and more reflective; it was less distinctly partisan, more diffusely spiritual — and more like Jimmy Carter's speech in 1979.[44]

It can be argued that the Republicans' turn to a cultural explanation of their impending defeat in 1992 was produced by the same motives they had accused Carter of embracing in 1979: to deflect responsibility away from the failures of their president and place them instead on a more diffuse cultural malaise. Although possible and perhaps partly accurate, the conjecture is surely too cynical. Absent contrary evidence, it is probably wisest to take the thinkers at their words.

Nor does the dismissal of the cultural explanation as mere political machination explain the return of America's malaise during the administration of Bill Clinton. After a brief flurry of interest in a "politics of meaning," the Clinton administration endured a mid-term electoral assault that eliminated Democratic majorities in both houses of Congress for the first time in a generation. Yet only the most partisan of Republicans considered the 1994 turnover a purely partisan victory. Most, rather, considered it an attack on the political system itself, which many found sinking even deeper into malaise than it had been in 1979.

When one looks today at the course of American culture since the 1970s, it is not altogether clear that it has been so different from the one Carter sketched on that July evening in 1979. It might even be maintained that Carter showed uncanny prescience in foretelling the nation's future. If so, Carter's warnings in 1979 take on truly prophetic significance. In the conclusion of his July 15 speech, Carter warned that America stood "at a turning point in our history." Choosing one path, he advised, would lead only to "fragmentation and self-interest" and "a mistaken idea of freedom." "True freedom," "common purpose," and "restoration of American values," he claimed, required following another path altogether.

But neither is it clear that Carter's words were adequate to the crisis he identified. Were they the words of an unheeded visionary charting a course not taken out of the morass of meaninglessness, or were they the words of an accomplice in the malaise, whose very lack of vision enabled it to fester and grow? Indeed, did he adequately chart the alternative course or simply hope it existed?

Opinion remains divided. On one side are those like Theodore White, who judged that "what Carter had said was true, and long overdue in the saying." But on the other side are those like Robert Bellah, who judged what Carter said as "pathetic" for its failure to promote a "social vision" that might connect America's tradition of moral individualism with the new requirements of national community.[45]

Both sides, importantly, agree that Carter is a good and decent man, even a supreme public moralist. Both also agree that Carter's diagnosis of the nation's malaise was essentially accurate. Where the sides disagree is in their assessment of Carter's remedy. The disagreement permits no compromise. What is at stake is not merely the reputation of Jimmy Carter; at stake is the future of the nation.

CHAPTER 2

FAMILY AND PLACE

"My life on the farm during the Great Depression," wrote Jimmy Carter in his 1975 campaign autobiography, "more nearly resembled farm life of fully 2,000 years ago than farm life today."[1] The remark, which might appear to be characteristic of Carter's lifelong penchant for hyperbole, is substantially accurate.

The Carters lived in a simple three-bedroom farmhouse in a remote region of southwest Georgia. In the early years of the Great Depression, when Jimmy Carter was a child, the home lacked both electricity and running water. Muscular, mostly illiterate men tilled the surrounding fields with mule-drawn plows. Women cooked on woodburning stoves, washed clothes by hand, and joined the men in the fields during the busy seasons. Families salted meat for winter storage, counted fish caught or game hunted part of their dietary staples, and substituted an autumn hog slaughter for Thanksgiving celebrations. All spoke a rural southern dialect nearly incomprehensible to outsiders and, in that biracial society, sometimes to each other. Radio, initially powered by batteries, offered glimpses of the modern world outside — of prize fights, political conventions, big bands, and children's programs — but its impact was muted by the persistence of folktales. Adults scared children with stories of bogeymen and roving spirits, of the magical fish that could not be eaten because it was caught on a Sunday, of the house that was haunted. Jimmy Carter's own father consulted a fortune-teller in the hope of finding a lost hunting dog, one of a man's most valuable possessions in that backwoods, bygone era.[2]

How the Carters came to reside in that remote farming region, and what it was like to grow up there, is a story that begins with one Wiley Carter.

THE CARTERS OF SOUTHWEST GEORGIA

Wiley Carter was the first Carter to settle in southwest Georgia.[3] Prior to his arrival in 1849 the family tree branched eastward and northward. Previous generations of Carters had been farmers in eastern Georgia, North Carolina, and Virginia. Indeed, the Carters had been in the New World for nearly three centuries, arriving from the English village of Kings Langley, where presumably their name was bestowed in consequence of an ancestor's enterprising wagoneering.[4] But so many generations over so many years had produced hundreds of branches on the Carter family tree. The branch that grew southwestward along Georgia's plantation swath began with Wiley Carter.

The land that Wiley Carter settled in the 1850s was still largely frontier. The railroad, which together with the cotton gin and slave labor that made the cotton kingdom possible, had not yet snaked its way to the state's southwestern hinterland. Only a decade before Wiley's arrival, the land was still Indian territory. That changed only in 1838–39, when the south Georgia Creeks were marched together with the north Georgia Cherokees to western reservations along the infamous "trail of tears."

Wiley Carter settled in what was then Sumter County, but is now Schley County, or about twenty miles north of where Jimmy Carter grew up in present-day Sumter County. (Like many of Georgia's counties, Sumter was later divided because of the enormous political power Georgia invested in its counties.) The area is below what Georgians have come to call the "gnat line," or the fall line that separates north Georgia's piedmont region from south Georgia's coastal plain. Below this line, which runs roughly from Augusta through Macon to Columbus, Georgia, the climate and terrain change noticeably. And the sweltering heat and humidity of south Georgia produces — among other things — an annoying increase in gnats. Even so, the geographical differences are less important to Georgians' understanding of the gnat line than are the political and cultural differences. Above the line are Atlanta, the state's major universities, the majority of its population, the state's financial and industrial centers. Below it the population is largely rural and provides the base for the state's traditional conservative outlook. To this day, statewide political contests are sometimes said to be determined by where one draws the gnat line —

the balance of power being nearly equal between the two regions. In Jimmy Carter's day there was little question about which side had the most clout. It was rural, south Georgia — counties like Sumter and Schley.

But most of Georgia's political culture was in the future when Wiley Carter settled in the region. Indeed, there is no record of Wiley Carter's having given a second thought to politics. His interests, rather, were wholly material. When he arrived in the subtropical climate that nurtured dense thickets, abundant wildlife, and the promise of profits for any white man who owned enough slaves to reshape the forest into farms, his eye was on the land's profit potential. Like others before and after him, Wiley Carter and his slaves pushed southwestward along Georgia's plantation belt to battle an inhospitable environment in the frank hope of making money.

Such men were a rough lot. They boasted little in the way of education or refinement, but much in the way of grit, determination, and a readiness to violence. One of the few written records of Wiley Carter's life shows that, ten years before he arrived in southwest Georgia, he shot and killed a man over the theft of a slave. Wiley had staked out the man's home all night waiting for him to emerge in the morning. When he did, the two men fired simultaneously. Wiley's shot turned out to be the true one — but he was acquitted of murder because both men had fired. When a dozen years after his settling in Sumter County the infamous Civil War prison was established in nearby Andersonville — the place where so many Union soldiers met emaciated ends far worse than they might have experienced on the battlefield — the death camp was not completely out of character with the culture. Men who butchered animals, ran Indians off in a death march, whipped slaves, and murdered one another over trifles were not unaccustomed to violence. They were rough men used to rough ways.

Frontier men like Wiley Carter were also restless. Whatever reality lurked beneath the myth of an American past of stable, democratic towns where neighborliness flourished and communities pulled together for their common good, that reality was largely for a more settled breed than the men of the frontier South. There men thought nothing of severing bonds to a community — if indeed they ever had any — and pushing forward in the private quest for profits. Wiley Carter's disposition was, if anything, more independent than most. He did not even move to southwest Georgia until after he had sired a dozen children and lost his wife to a mature if still early death. Perhaps, if a tender interpretation be allowed,

Wiley Carter's grief over the death of his wife motivated his move. Family was just about the only community such men knew. But maybe he would have pushed on, anyway. Whatever his motives, Wiley Carter's commitment to place was not as strong as his quest for profits. Fittingly, he died in a barely established land but left an estate that included more than a quarter of a million dollars, 2,400 acres of farmland, and thirty slaves.

Among the wealthiest five or ten percent of the state's population at his death, Wiley Carter left his heirs not only a nest egg with which to start but, equally important, a legacy to emulate. Subsequent generations of Carters might have wished for a different legacy. For, while all pursued paths of prosperity, the next two generations of Carters (Jimmy Carter's great-grandfather and grandfather) also embraced the legacy of violence — and met untimely deaths as a result.

One of Wiley Carter's sons was Littlebury Walker Carter, Jimmy Carter's great-grandfather. After service for the Confederacy he returned home, married, fathered four children, and pursued the amalgamation of farming and other business interests that was becoming the Carter family trademark. One of his business ventures, the invention of a kind of merry-go-round, turned sour. In 1873 he was murdered by his business partner in a drunken squabble over their joint profits. The guilty partner fled to South America, and the bereaved widow, it was said, died the day of the funeral, leaving their four children to fend for themselves.[5]

Then one of Littlebury Walker Carter's sons, William Archibald Carter (Jimmy Carter's grandfather), met a similar end. He farmed, ran sawmills, and dabbled in business until 1903, when he too was gunned down in a business dispute. The dispute evidently erupted over an argument about which of the two business partners rightfully owned a desk. Judging from this cryptic summary of his demise, he was apparently no better than his father had been in building bonds of trust when profits or goods were at stake. And like his grandfather's altercation with the man over the theft of a slave, the violence was mutual. Three attempts to convict William Archibald Carter's killer therefore resulted in mistrials.

By the turn of the century, the frontier was gone. The railroad had long before made its way into the region, and soon came newspapers, the radio, the telephone, and even the automobile. Towns sprang up where only fields, farms, or woods had been before. One of these towns was Plains. So, when William Archibald Carter's sixteen-year-old son, Alton Carter (Jimmy Carter's uncle), was forced as the eldest male of the family to decide upon his family's course of action following the death of his father, he chose to move the family to Plains. Established in its present location in 1888 and incorporated in 1896, it seemed as likely as any other town to become a bustling trading and cultural center. The choice was a considered one. Wishing to leave Rowenao, Georgia, where the absence of natural drainage made malaria commonplace, the family had just moved to Cuthbert, Georgia, about 25 miles north of Rowenao, when the murder occurred. But in Cuthbert the widowed mother attracted an unwelcome suitor.[6] Alton therefore decided to move to Plains, some twenty miles east. So it was that in 1904 or 1905 — the exact year is lost to memory — the Carters settled in Plains, and Buddy, as everyone called Alton Carter, established himself and his family.

THE CARTERS OF PLAINS

Turn-of-the-century Plains, like many tiny towns that dot the rural landscape, existed primarily to provide a transportation and commercial hub for rural farmers. The railroad, so essential to the farmers at the time, made half a dozen daily stops in Plains. Originally, Plains was founded a few miles to the north in present-day Magnolia Springs, but when the railroad came the town was promptly moved to accommodate it. With passenger as well as freight service available, Plains citizens could take the train to Americus in one direction or Columbus in the other. They could also ship their chief products of the time — peaches, cotton, and watermelons — to markets elsewhere. Outlying farmers who traveled mostly by foot or mule found Plains a more convenient destination for shopping, merriment, or church than the county seat of Americus nine miles east. With a peak population of less than 700 — dwindling during the 1930s to only 300 or so — Plains's clay streets were nevertheless packed most Saturdays when the droves of farmers came into town, making it "the muddiest town you ever saw."[7]

But by the 1920s Plains had a unique advantage over other similar-sized towns. The Wise brothers, three prominent local physicians (Thad, Sam, and Bowman), settled in Plains in 1921 and established a small hospital. Although it is difficult to judge the caliber of medical treatment available at the Wise Hospital, locals were proud enough of their hospital to dub it "the little Mayo Clinic." It was also of sufficient stature to become a training center for nurses, who could complete most of their training in Plains and finish it with only a short supplementary residency in a larger hospital elsewhere. The availability of the nursing curriculum was what brought Jimmy Carter's mother to Plains in the early 1920s. Clearly, it was the kind of economic and scientific asset that could set Plains apart from countless similar towns. Indeed, in addition to sustaining thriving medical practices for the Wise brothers (and later, their sons), Plains supported another physician unaffiliated with their clinic, Dr. Logan. Called the "Saturday Night Stitch-'Em-Up" by the residents, Dr. Logan performed the less prestigious emergency medical procedures and took his patients to the nearby Prather Clinic in Americus. To add to their pride as a thriving medical center, Plains voters passed a bond referendum to build a new high school in the same year the Wise Hospital was established. The town was thriving.[8]

But for Alton Carter, who moved his mother, brother, and sisters to Plains a generation after it had been established, the town had another distinct advantage. The original city fathers were aging, and ample opportunity existed for young men with a knack for business to prosper.[9] So, true to his entrepreneurial heritage and seizing his opportunity, Alton Carter followed a brief stint as a clerk in a department store with the opening of his own general store on Main Street, which he called Plains Mercantile. The store became a huge success, allowing Alton eventually to buy out his rival. It also provided a stable base for Alton to pursue other businesses (especially mule trading before mechanized farm machinery began to appear in the late 1940s)[10] as well as avocations like baseball (his passion) and wine making (though he himself rarely drank). Alton and his family also joined the Plains Baptist Church, the largest of the town's three white churches (the other two were the Methodist and the Lutheran). He became prominent enough to serve intermittently as both mayor and county commissioner. After the death of his father in 1953, Jimmy Carter spent many hours visiting with his Uncle Buddy — soliciting advice, tracing the family tree, or just talking. Even during his childhood, Jimmy often tagged along with his cousins as Alton took them all to baseball games or other outings. When Jimmy became president, which Alton Carter lived just long enough to see, Alton continued to sit in his rocker at the old Plains Mercantile and talk with passersby. By that time, however, the store had become an antique shop, the prevalence of the automobile having made a department store no longer viable in Plains.

The "Carters of Plains" — about whom so much was written during Jimmy Carter's 1976 campaign and presidency — were mainly Alton Carter's family. He, his two wives (Annie Laurie, who died in 1940, and a second wife, Betty), and his boys Donnel and Hugh were respectably rooted in the community (though Donnel eventually left for a career in

journalism). Together with them, Ethel, one of Alton's sisters, also remained, married Jack Slappey, and had a son, Willard (who moved away
after he grew up). Until her death in 1939 Nina Pratt Carter, Alton's
mother and Jimmy Carter's grandmother, was a town resident, too. But
two of Alton's sisters as well as his brother moved elsewhere. Neither one
of Plains's founding families nor an especially prominent one, the Carters
could not prevent the dispersal of some of their members to opportunities
elsewhere. Indeed, they were the sort of rough businessmen and farmers
who might even have encouraged it. And the brother who moved just far
enough outside of town in pursuit of new opportunities to cause his children to feel like strangers in town was Jimmy Carter's father.

EARL CARTER

Born in 1894, James Earl Carter — or Earl, as he was called — was five
years younger than Alton. Those years and the corresponding relief from
his brother's responsibilities brought Earl more liberties than his brother
enjoyed. Instead of being forced to quit school as soon as he was old
enough to work, for example, Earl was able to attend school in Plains
and later in Gainesville, Georgia, some 200 miles away. Completing an
unparalleled ten years of schooling (the most education a Carter of recent
memory had achieved), the younger brother, exempted from his older
brother's responsibilities for the family, moved to Texas to work as a cowboy. But Earl may not have had Wiley Carter's restless spirit, or maybe
the short, squat man with failing eyesight just made a poor cowboy. Whatever the reasons, Earl returned to Sumter County after only a couple of
years away. Although a brief stint in the army again took him away from
home in 1917 (he was drafted but got out as soon as he could after a few
months), when he returned he directed his attention to the goal that would
define his life from then on: making money in southwest Georgia.

From the beginning, when Earl clerked in his brother's store, "it was
obvious he wanted a career and business of his own."[11] Assisted by his
brother, he therefore quickly opened a succession of businesses that included an icehouse, a commercial laundry, and a small grocery store.
The grocery, called J. E. Carter's, carried the few goods — chiefly fresh
meats — that his brother's store did not, so the brothers avoided competing directly with each other. The businesses all turned out to be profitable,
partly because of Earl's personality. Although a sister remembered his having "more temper than Buddy had,"[12] outside the family most people remembered him as extremely likable, even jovial, and scrupulously fair.

Indeed, townsfolk later had difficulty seeing much of Earl in Jimmy because, they said, Jimmy just did not smile as often as his father did.[13]

But personality aside, it was no secret what it took to prosper in and around Plains during the 1920s. Most of the county's population was black, barred by custom and law from participating equally in economic enterprises. Ambitious white men understood that the key to profits was squeezing as much value as possible out of the subjugated population. Almost every Plains business of any consequence was owned and operated by a white Protestant family. (There were no Catholics in Plains, and only one Jewish family is remembered to have lived there. That family's presence was recalled only by the lingering nickname of the building in which their store was located, called the "Jew store" by longtime residents.)[14] Yet many customers, especially on busy Saturdays, were black. Although being a white Protestant male was no guarantee of success in those bleak times, it was a prerequisite. Meeting the prerequisite, Earl Carter added shrewdness and a personable disposition to the equation and did well.

But if Earl Carter had no qualms about profiting from blacks — and few whites did — he wanted more for himself than the life of a small-town businessman operating in the shadow of his older brother. Especially after he married in 1923 and began having children (Jimmy, his firstborn, arrived October 1, 1924, and Gloria in 1926), the burden of growing financial responsibility weighed heavily on him. Hoping that his family would grow even larger, Earl realized that he needed a proportionate income and home. His dreams extended beyond managing a few small businesses from a rented apartment in Plains.

So, he turned his attention to the rural areas. Earlier, in fact, he had managed to buy a few hundred acres of farm land in adjacent Webster County. It was, many remembered, the only time he ever bought anything on credit. Managing that land along with his Plains businesses, Earl realized that real prosperity was to be found in agriculture. Again, it was largely a matter of successfully exploiting blacks. At the time, most blacks lived in the country, but few owned their own land. Black men were therefore forced to work white-owned farms while their wives and children provided whites with cheap domestic help. At the same time, many rural whites as well as blacks were suffering from the ravages of the boll weevil, which, by the 1920s, decimated cotton production. The entire region had entered a rural economic crisis, ultimately sensationalized in Erskine Caldwell's 1934 novel *Tobacco Road* and recognized by President Franklin Roosevelt, who declared that "the South is the nation's number one economic problem."[15] Indeed, as early as 1926 — well before the rest of the nation slipped into depression — the Plains bank failed, leaving many residents penniless.[16] The crisis persisted until the late 1940s, when mechanization enabled southwest Georgia farmers to shift to the more profitable peanut crops. (Many blacks and some whites also migrated north during the period.) The upshot during the 1920s and 1930s was a region containing a large, landless, and desperate rural population willing to provide the manpower for the primitive, labor-intensive farming that was still practiced. Availing themselves of this labor, prudent landowners might still make money. With this in mind and desiring a home for his growing family, Earl Carter bought another farm in the summer of 1928. Located in the nearby African American settlement of Archery, two and one-half miles from Plains (and between his Webster County farm and his Plains businesses), the 350-acre Archery farm was an ideal location for Earl to settle. There the family joined one other white family (the Watsons) just in time for the birth of their third child, Ruth, in August of 1928. Jimmy, their eldest, was not yet four.

From his Archery base, Earl Carter prospered. He worked upward of 200 laborers and sharecroppers on growing landholdings at the same time he continued to dabble in dozens of other businesses. Not one to miss any opportunity to profit, he opened a commissary next to his house to provide neighboring blacks with staples and a few luxuries. With regular store hours beginning at noon on Saturdays, when the five-and-a-half-day work week ended, commissary hours coincided with payday. Laborers lined up to receive their pay at the commissary, where Earl Carter generally managed to see that more than a fair portion of the dollar-a-day wages he paid to field hands was returned to him. "For Daddy," Jimmy Carter remembered when describing the store, "it was a fairly lucrative thing."[17] His assessment may be an understatement. Commissaries were "a license to steal," commented one longtime Plains resident, "because the prices [were] about three times as high as they [were] in town."[18]

For some time, Earl Carter also kept his Plains grocery store, which doubled as his office. (Only years later did he open the Carter warehouse in Plains that his sons would inherit.) There, milk, syrup, or ham from the farm could be sold at retail, and inventory from the grocery could move to the commissary or vice versa. There too, Earl found ways to squeeze maximum profits from minimum goods. In learning "how to sell," Gloria remembers her father teaching her to pour chocolate milk into bottles in such a way that they looked fuller than they were.[19] Ingenuity knew few limits in Earl Carter. When he invented a new plow, he sold the patent to the Rome Plow Company and made more money.[20] Then, closing the laundry and icehouse, he bought a fire insurance company in 1939. All the while, he continued to reap substantial profits from the land: buying it, selling it, mortgaging it, insuring it, and managing it. By some estimates, his land holdings grew to more than 4,000 acres.[21]

The Carters' growing prosperity was reflected, naturally, in their lifestyle. Although Earl Carter was notoriously "tight" with money, he made enough to spend a lot. After his initial land purchase he paid cash for everything and kept a cash box on hand. The house that was originally without running water soon had a windmill. Although the plumbing remained rudimentary and frequently broke, tenants used to say admiringly, "If you're one of Earl Carter's tenants you can shit in the house."[22] Then, during the mid-1930s, Earl was appointed to the local board of the Rural Electrification Administration. Electricity was immediately brought to his farm, much sooner than it came even to his white neighbors.[23] Before long he managed to have a clay tennis court constructed outside his home and made a pond by damming a creek a little farther away. Then, at the pond he built a three-bedroom pond house outfitted with pool and Ping-Pong tables, as well as a jukebox for his children and a big patio and grill for his own fish fries. Although his children went barefoot much of the year, it was more a result of custom than of need. They also had bicycles and horses, hunting and fishing gear, dolls and toys. The senior Carter kept his family supplied with books and radios and later bought the very first television in the area. Earl drove new Oldsmobiles and kept trucks on the land. On one occasion he even ordered a tailor-made suit.

Before the birth of his last child, Billy, in 1937, Earl even teased his wife by offering her $1,000 cash if she could produce twins. When he took her and the baby boy home from the hospital in his 1937 Oldsmobile, the tight but well-to-do father gave his wife $500 cash for the one child she had delivered.[24] Finally, after two decades in Archery (after Jimmy was grown and gone), Earl Carter had the cash to build a new home in Plains. He may have had the cash even earlier. In those days men with Earl's outlook did not necessarily consider their house to be their chief status symbol or even their home. Status and "home" were rather found in the expanse of one's holdings and the depths of one's friendships. And the Carters had long had two houses instead of one. Nevertheless, when Earl died there four years later, his worth — like Wiley Carter's before him — was estimated at a quarter million dollars.[25]

Marveling over his brother's penchant for profiting, Alton is said to have often remarked that Earl just had a "Midas touch."[26] Others must have agreed, for his nickname slowly changed from "Turtle" to "Turk" over the course of his life.[27] Small, paunchy, and balding, Earl Carter looked a bit like a turtle. But as his affluence increased, a more flattering nickname reflective of his economic prowess may have been required. Some even considered him "rural royalty."[28]

Given his father's prosperity, some have suspected exaggeration in Jimmy Carter's description of his austere childhood. He was by no means poor. Still, there was truth to his recollection. The Carters' prosperity came gradually, and when Jimmy was young he enjoyed few of the benefits that came as he matured. (He would have been about twelve when electricity was brought to the farm.) His father's frugality also made it likely that Jimmy was unaware of the extent of the family's growing affluence. But perhaps most important, Jimmy Carter's childhood experiences were of an entire, impoverished, and primitive farming settlement — not merely of his father's cash box. Although his family was the wealthiest in the area, they lived not much differently from those around them. Worse, to the extent that Jimmy understood his position of privilege, he also understood that he was separated by it from those surrounding him. That too was a kind of poverty.

CULTURE AND CHARACTER

Earl Carter's success and temperament enabled him to fit easily into the white male world of Sumter County. His work was mostly people work — buying, selling, managing, coordinating — and most people liked the always affable, ever-grinning Earl. With rare exception, he also liked people. As a result, Earl Carter maintained an active social life. He regularly joined friends for a morning hunt or an afternoon of fishing and annually took a week-long, all-male fishing trip to some outlying location. In the evenings and usually on weekends, Earl joined friends for parties, dances, card games, or other forms of rural and small-town entertainment. On these occasions, the wife with whom he shared regular before-supper drinks and nightcaps remembered with probable understatement, "he liked to have several drinks."[29] For when he hosted parties at his pond house the revelry would sometimes last into the wee hours of the morning and, if rumors are to be believed, occasionally evolved into drunken debauchery, complete with entertainment by black prostitutes.[30] On Sundays, Earl was sufficiently religious to take his children to the Plains

Baptist Church, where he attended the men's Sunday school class, but he usually slipped out before the service in order to visit with the other un-churched men at the service station or drugstore. A smoker of hand-rolled or Camel cigarettes and a regular drinker, Earl enjoyed habits that were frowned upon by the more sanctimonious in his community. Those same habits, however, may have enabled him to fit in better with others in the community who agreed with him in taking religion with a grain of salt.

But in terms of character, Earl Carter was known to be more than fun-loving, honest, and likable; he also had a reputation for charity. When a school teacher still lacked twelve dollars for a piano after mothers had done their best to raise the funds through bake sales and the like, she remembered that Earl Carter "just handed it to me, you know, like that," prompting her to describe him as "unselfish," "nice," and "big-hearted."[31] When a Plains widow could not afford coal one winter, Earl secretly arranged for regular supplies to be delivered at his expense.[32] Striking a private agreement with a Plains woman, Ida Lee Timmerman, Earl was alerted when school children could not afford a suit or dress for gradua-tion and anonymously donated the funds to allow them to buy what was needed.[33] When a friend took too ill to work, Earl sent a monthly stipend to tide the family over.[34] Diagnosed with terminal cancer in 1953, he came home and canceled mortgages for struggling debtors he thought deserv-ing.[35] And every Christmas he hosted a Christmas party at the Americus Elks Club at which every child received a present.

Even among blacks, Earl Carter was known for his honest tempera-ment and kind heart. Although he was a strict segregationist, his tenants recalled that he was the sort of landowner who would make sure they had a good mule and plenty of fertilizer and sent their children to primary school instead of forcing them to work.[36] He also paid for any necessary medical supplies his wife needed when nursing the tenants and may have even arranged for hard-working blacks to buy their own land. When the two-week-old child of one of his tenants died, the child's sister remem-bered that Earl Carter "just took it on himself to make one of the most beautiful little old boxes [caskets] and Miss Lillian, she lined it with white . . . silk."[37] His own daughter Gloria remembered the same incident but added that "he had tears in his eyes" while he was working.[38] In his com-missary, he kept a candy jar, but his children were forbidden to eat the chocolate lollipops so they could be given to the sons and daughters of his tenants who rarely enjoyed such luxuries.[39] Many of Earl Carter's tenants stayed with him a lifetime, attesting to their loyalty, and more than a few slipped into the back of the Plains Baptist Church to pay their respects when he died.

Only by appreciating how firmly entrenched Earl Carter was in the system of racial segregation of his time and place is it conceivable that he may have participated in lynching a black man. No evidence exists that he did — and no direct evidence exists that the lynching even took place. What is known is that Alice Ruth Timmerman, a young woman Earl dated before marrying Lillian in 1923, was killed in a traffic accident in 1926. The driver of the other vehicle was a black man who had been running moonshine whiskey. Immediately the papers and townsfolk called for finding the man and bringing him to justice. But there is no story about the man being found, there was no trial, and just as quickly as the episode was aired it was forgotten. "Something happened to him because it was hushed up," reflected a longtime Plains resident. "The nigger that was driving the whiskey car that killed Alice Ruth, you see, he ran. . . . They hunted for him awhile. . . . But it wasn't wound up in court and I don't believe that they just dropped it that quick. . . . I never was close to any lynchings but you know they went on in the South. I know one went on over in this section . . . but I guess I was just a tiny little thing and I didn't know about that then."[40]

Townsfolk, in short, assumed the matter had been handled with the vigilante violence that white men used for such matters in those days. Earl, an up-and-coming young Plains businessman at the time who had been close to the deceased woman, would surely have been privy to the details if not actively involved. Indeed, he was moved enough by her death to name his second daughter, Ruth, after her in 1928.[41] Never a member of the Ku Klux Klan or, in his own words, the kind of white man who would "abuse a nigger,"[42] he nonetheless accepted, profited from, and perhaps even helped to enforce the racial segregation and exploitation of his era. Within the strictures of that system, he was fair and even compassionate — but he never doubted the system or hesitated to defend it. "He was not a racist," explained his wife years later. "Those were the days when there wasn't such a thing. It was just blacks and whites."[43] Practically, too, most Archery blacks were "good nigger people" in the opinion of a neighboring white farmer of Earl Carter's generation, and racial tensions were not normally expressed openly.[44]

It followed from Earl Carter's growing prominence and stature in the region that he moved easily into positions of civic leadership. He was welcomed into the county's more powerful Americus-based cliques even more readily than his brother Alton. He joined both the Rotary and Elks clubs in Americus, the two leading men's clubs in the county at the time. Moving in such circles, he was easily elected to the Sumter County Commission, appointed to the school board, and tapped for other leadership positions (like the local Rural Electrification Administration). In 1952, he was prodded to run for the Georgia House of Representatives, a close, countywide race he won against an Americus-based incumbent, J. Frank Myers, largely on the basis of a 250–16 vote in Plains that tipped the scales in his direction.[45] Throughout the county he was esteemed; in Plains he was loved.

But Earl Carter was not especially ambitious politically. Had he been, he might have risen higher than he did. Some remember him as naturally shy,[46] usually a liability for a politician, and no one recalled his having been especially outspoken or original in his political thinking. Indeed, what most remember about him is that he seemed to reflect rather than to shape the political culture of his times. When he was asked to run for the state legislature in 1952, the request came from the governor himself, Herman Talmadge. The incumbent representative, J. Frank Myers, had angered Talmadge, who sought a replacement for him. As a popular county leader and loyal acquaintance of the governor, Earl was asked to run against Myers. Earl agreed on the condition that he would not have to campaign, and he did not.[47]

To understand Earl Carter's politics — and the political culture in which Jimmy Carter was raised — the role the Talmadges played in Georgia's political history must be appreciated. Eugene Talmadge, first elected governor of Georgia in 1932 (subsequently in 1940 and 1946), and later his son, Herman Talmadge (governor 1948–54 and U.S. senator 1956–80), represented more than a political dynasty in Georgia politics; they symbolized an entire rural culture that expressed itself in politics. Men like Earl Carter considered themselves "Talmadgites."

Eugene Talmadge, nicknamed the "wild man from Sugar Creek," was perhaps the perfect political heir to Tom Watson, Georgia's renowned populist leader of the late nineteenth and early twentieth centuries. In the 1890s Watson had rallied both black and white farmers with a resounding call for rural empowerment in opposition to the planter and urban business elite. This elite, dubbed "Bourbons" after the epithet used for the French aristocracy a century earlier, held most of the state's population in economic dependency and cultural deprivation.[48] Populists, first joined together in loose "farmers' alliances," demanded that the Bourbon hold on the state be broken. Fueled by the fiery oratory of Watson and others, the farmers were initially successful. But Watson, elected to Congress in 1890, was cheated in his 1894 reelection campaign and sent home to his farm in rural Georgia. There, though he was the vice presidential nominee (with William Jennings Bryan) in 1896 on the Populist ticket and subsequently the Populist presidential nominee, Watson stewed in bitterness. In a process that still remains a mystery, Watson's bitterness soon found a scapegoat in Georgia's ethnic minorities, chiefly Jews and Catholics, though also blacks. By 1906 he returned to the Democratic party and supported successful gubernatorial candidate Hoke Smith's antirailroad and antiblack platform. (Under Smith, blacks were formally disenfranchised.) Continuing to promulgate his blend of populism and prejudice, Watson was ultimately rewarded with a seat in the U.S. Senate in 1920. But in 1922 he died — leaving one of the most baffling legacies in Georgia's political history.

Eugene Talmadge picked up the pieces of this legacy in 1932. Launching one of the state's most memorable gubernatorial campaigns by promising a cheaper license plate, lower utility rates, and a reduction in property taxes, Talmadge spoke the language of rural populism. And spoke it well. Rural politics at the time were dominated by the infamous all-day barbecues and rallies. Hogs were slowly roasted in earthen pits, gallons of sweet tea mixed, and moonshine smuggled in as hundreds (sometimes thousands) of farmers and small-town men gathered for a day of "speechifying." Snapping famous red suspenders and railing against any ill-defined force that oppressed the simple farmer — the Atlanta power structure, blacks, the federal government, whatever — Talmadge whipped the crowds into a frenzy of moral fervor equivalent to or even surpassing that of a religious revival. Borrowing a call-and-response pattern (ironically, of African origin), Talmadge confederates, strategically stationed throughout the crowd, egged him on with such refrains as "you tell 'em, Gene," or "tell the one about the rich men in Atlanta." Soon the crowd joined in, and men like Earl Carter, who loaded up his flatbed truck with every white man and boy he could find to attend these rallies, had a ball. Gulping moonshine between bites of barbecue at a political rally was just about as much fun as a white man could have. Or, to put it negatively, as one Sumter County resident did, politics was the only leisure-time activity available to affluent white men besides "chas[ing] women and drink[ing]," and the latter at least could be mixed with politics.[49]

But the political brilliance of Talmadge was to quietly support the economic interests of state and county elites at the same time he railed against them.[50] His famous 1932 promises of tax and rate reductions aided mostly Georgians affluent enough to drive automobiles, have utilities, and own land — in practice, large trucking companies, textile mills, and planters. He also so vehemently opposed Franklin Roosevelt's New Deal that he worked to sabotage it in Georgia and even flirted with the idea of challenging Roosevelt for the Democratic presidential nomination in 1936. In these and other ways he subtly blended pro-business Bourbonism with populist sentiment. And when the blending became strained, he could always resort to race-baiting to shore up his rural white constituency located mainly below the gnat line.

But, importantly, the blend of Bourbonism and populism did not have to be chicanery to appeal to men like Earl Carter; they, like Talmadge, had a foot squarely in both camps. Earl Carter certainly never considered himself one of the planter elite. Despite his prosperity, he worked hard and could never really think of himself as anything other than a small farmer and businessman. He was therefore a natural populist sympathizer. But compared to most others, Earl Carter was economically privileged. He therefore naturally supported the pro-business, Bourbon policies that catered to his economic class. Not least, a product and profiteer of the South's apartheid racial system, he was not immune to the rhetoric of race. Feeling like a populist while behaving like a Bourbon and believing himself a member of a superior racial caste, Earl Carter was a natural "Talmadgite." So he was thrilled to welcome Herman Talmadge into his home overnight after the young governor delivered a speech at Plains High School, and when the governor tapped him to run with his blessings for the state legislature in 1952, he agreed.

It followed that Earl Carter shared many of the Talmadges' conservative political views. "He was a real conservative, an ultra-conservative, so conservative that he's the one who gives some of the conservatives a bad name," claimed a neighbor who knew him. In particular, "he was opposed to the New Deal from the beginning."[51] Jimmy Carter suspects that his father never again voted for a Democratic presidential candidate after 1932. But, like any aspiring Bourbon, Earl Carter found a way to profit even from programs he opposed. He not only got electricity brought to his farm but also bought land from distressed owners at ten dollars an acre, ran one string of wire around it, and pocketed the federal windfall of eight dollars an acre that the New Deal offered farmers to fence their meadows.[52] Even though he profited from the New Deal, as a matter of conscience and philosophy Earl Carter could never support it. When President Truman made motions toward supporting racial equality, Earl Carter's opposition to the national Democratic Party intensified. Chances are that he voted for the Dixiecrat ticket in 1948, led in part by Georgia's segregationist Senator Richard Russell.

On attendant social views Earl Carter was similarly conservative. He had little sympathy for, for example, strong, independent women. Some reported that he loathed Eleanor Roosevelt even more than he did FDR. Once, when he was angry at his independent-minded wife, he called her "Eleanor" to register his contempt for both.[53]

Yet these views were tempered by populist sympathies and a habit of charity. Ruth Carter Stapleton suspects that her father approved of the great populist achievement, rural free mail delivery. Also, as a legislator Earl Carter worked hard enough in his single term to improve the higher education of his constituents to have the library at Georgia Southwestern College in Americus named after him. Public education, like rural free delivery, was the kind of lingering populist issue that even a diehard conservative like Earl Carter could endorse.

At the same time, and despite his disapproval of government welfare, Earl Carter practiced charity. When he died in 1953 and the stories of his charity were repeated among the mourners, Jimmy Carter broke down and cried. The twenty-eight-year-old naval officer who had left home a decade earlier realized at that moment how badly he wanted to become a man as good as he believed his father had been. And, although he claims to have learned lessons opposite to those his father intended to teach him when he was squeezed into the back of the flatbed truck and taken to the Talmadge rallies, he was convinced that he would see his father in heaven.[54]

THE GORDYS AND LILLIAN CARTER

Jimmy Carter's mother, Bessie Lillian Gordy — who, like her husband, went by her middle name — was also a descendant of generations of southwest Georgians. Of the Scottish ancestry that is typical of the South, her family had settled in and around Chattahoochee County, a little northwest of Sumter County (close enough to Columbus, Georgia, to be included today in its metropolitan statistical area). Born in 1898 in the middle of eight children, she was raised in the small town of Richland (in Stewart County), about twenty miles from Plains.

The Gordys were not the kind of rough rural farmers and business people the Carters were. Instead, they settled in towns, took middling jobs, and sometimes pursued advanced education. One of Lillian's uncles was a physician. No Carter could boast a similar accomplishment. Other Gordys were not as successful, but most of them preferred the respectability of even a lower-middle-class occupation in town to the rougher, if sometimes more lucrative, careers in business and farming. Fitting their status aspirations, the Gordys were also Methodists rather than Baptists, generally a telltale sign of slightly elevated social standing in the South.

Lillian Carter told interviewers that her father exercised the most influence over her. "I was Papa's favorite and he was my favorite," she said.[55] She spoke highly and often of James Jackson Gordy (called "Jim Jack"). And, when she and others did, Jim Jack's political enthusiasm was normally emphasized.

Jim Jack Gordy was the Richland postmaster for twenty-one years, most of the time Lillian was growing up. Later he served four years as a revenue officer, eight as a U.S. deputy marshall, and ultimately as a doorkeeper at the state capitol. The jobs earned the family a certain middling respectability, if never quite enough money or security. After leaving the post office in Richland, the Gordy family was forced to move around a bit — even living briefly during the 1930s near Archery, where Jim Jack tried his hand (unsuccessfully) at farming. While Lillian was growing up, however, the family was settled and secure in Richland. There the family took pride in Jim Jack Gordy's career, which was always understood by them to reflect his keen political interests and acumen. Most of the jobs Gordy held were patronage appointments, including his job as postmaster, and his ability to get and retain them through successive administrations was thought to illustrate his "nimble political footwork." Jimmy Carter, who often repeated this family assessment of his grandfather, likened him to a political pollster without polls. (Later, when Pat Caddell extrapolated larger cultural themes from his polls, Carter may have seen some of the same skills in him that he had learned to admire in his grandfather Gordy.) His grandfather, Carter writes, could forecast election results, often within five votes of the outcome.[56] The skill enabled Gordy to be involved in the world he loved — politics.

The family assumed that Gordy's political influence extended beyond his own ability to retain patronage jobs. They even credited him with having suggested the idea of rural free mail delivery to Tom Watson. Gordy's role in rural free delivery is doubtful, and his relationship with Watson seems to have been little closer than that of thousands of other Georgians who admired the populist leader. He merely sent occasional letters to Watson, received perfunctory replies, and volunteered to be the district coordinator for his 1920 Senate race. Watson did visit Gordy once in person, but that was probably during the 1920 campaign, and there is no evidence of another meeting between the two.[57] Even the fact that Gordy named a son after Watson is scant evidence for genuine closeness, since many Georgians were sufficiently enamored with Tom Watson to name babies after him. But the exaggeration of Gordy's influence shows how the family felt about Jim Jack Gordy. They thought of him as being in Watson's league, even if he probably was not.[58]

What Jim Jack Gordy's politics were — and, by extension, Lillian Carter's — is more difficult to ascertain. The problem is that the shrewd Gordy often kept his views to himself while using his political knowledge to further his career. Many thought that he was a Republican. He may have been, or, equally probable, he may have feigned Republican loyalty to retain his patronage position at the post office under Republican presidential administrations. Lillian Carter said that her father "liked Gene Talmadge," but then added, puzzlingly enough, "don't tell anybody" and explained that he simply liked "controversial people."[59] The equivocation suggests — as does Gordy's entire career — that he was not a "Talmadgite" in the same way Earl Carter was. He may have "liked Gene Talmadge" but was embarrassed about it for some reason.

Nor is it reasonable to assume, as one biographer did, that Jim Jack Gordy's job as doorkeeper at the state capitol meant that he was a "bodyguard" for Herman Talmadge. By the time Gordy served as doorkeeper, he was quite elderly, hardly suited to serving as anyone's bodyguard. The confusion may have arisen, however, from the turmoil in Georgia politics in 1947 when Herman Talmadge first claimed the governor's mantle following the death of his father. After the death of Eugene Talmadge, who had been elected governor but who died before taking the oath of office, a dispute arose over who should serve as governor. Herman Talmadge, eventually supported by the majority of the legislature, asserted a claim to the office against the others. Although violence was averted, Talmadge forces did forcibly seize the governor's mansion and most men carried pistols during those tumultuous months. In the midst of the fray, Jim Jack Gordy likely armed himself too. Since the legislature supported Talmadge, his role could be construed as supportive. But to call the old man who died the next year a "bodyguard" is probably unwarranted.[60] More telling about Gordy's politics is that even in the last years of his life he found a way to be in the middle of the state's most exciting political goings-on.

What is known about Jim Jack Gordy's political convictions is that he was a populist in the tradition of Tom Watson. He did exchange letters with the populist visionary, did name a son after him, and did volunteer for his 1920 campaign. But he did not follow Watson down the path of racist demagoguery. Lillian, who freely admitted her husband's racism, was clear on this point. Watson, she admitted, "hated blacks," but "my father did not."[61] Indeed, she reports that her father instilled in her the comparatively "liberal" views on race that she and her son, sometimes alone in their community, expressed.

Jim Jack Gordy's occasional identification as a Republican may even have stemmed in part from a commitment to racial equality. Prior to the defection of some southern Democrats from the national party during the Roosevelt administration, Republicanism in the South was almost exclusively black Republicanism. (Roosevelt and Truman grafted African Americans into the Democratic coalition by supporting selective policies that promoted racial equality and economic fairness. Kennedy and Johnson completed the process by advancing the modern civil rights agenda.) Gordy's Republican sympathies may well have been a reflection of his sympathies for black southerners. During Hoover's administration, even Lillian Carter was rumored to be one of three Republicans in the area, probably for the same reason. (The other two were the postmaster, a patronage appointment, and Johnny Grimm, "a progressive, well-educated Negro who had a mercantile business.")[62] It is unlikely, however, that she ever voted Republican. In 1964, the first year that Republicans won a congressional and presidential victory in Georgia, she worked in Lyndon Johnson's campaign and was a Johnson delegate at the national convention. She was probably mistakenly identified as a Republican because of her well-known liberal views on race.

Also revealing of Jim Jack Gordy's racial views was his apparent friendship with a locally prominent African American leader, Bishop William Johnson of the African Methodist Episcopal Church. The two were close enough friends for the bishop to be remembered visiting Gordy in his home, generally a strict violation of Jim Crow custom at the time. Some even remember that the two men, sharing both an interest in politics and

Methodist enthusiasm, not only talked as friends but also sang hymns together in the privacy of the Gordy home (perhaps after a drink or two too many). Their friendship seemed to be genuine. The very same bishop, living much nearer to Earl Carter, was forbidden to approach the Carters' front door and was never welcomed inside in a spirit of friendship.

Taken together, it would appear that Jim Jack Gordy's tenuous connection to Tom Watson is to his historical credit. He named his son after the populist leader when Watson was still supported by a biracial coalition, and before Watson promulgated his later anti-Semitic, anti-Catholic, and racist views. (Indeed, the son Gordy named Tom Watson was free enough of anti-Semitic prejudice to marry a Jew years later.) An assessment of his comparatively liberal views should probably not be pushed to extremes, however. There is no evidence that he took any concrete action to support oppressed minorities, and abundant evidence that he acquiesced to the race-baiting demagoguery of the Talmadges. But, on balance, Jim Jack Gordy seemed to stand apart from his fellow white southerners in many if not all of his political views. Chances are — liking "controversial people" — he harbored not a few controversial opinions himself.

The political legacy Jim Jack Gordy left to his daughter was therefore more of liberal or progressive populism than was embraced by the Carters. In no way a Bourbon and not a politician himself, Jim Jack Gordy's love of politics rested on the belief that politics is — or at least might be — a force for moral improvement. Certainly most rural Georgians felt this way about Tom Watson's populism. For them, politics was more than the efficient management of public affairs — more even than rural entertainment. It was the vehicle for expressing the spirit of the people, the forum for hammering out the collective good. Men like Earl Carter may have vaguely appreciated this sentiment, but they governed the way they ran businesses: efficiently, ably, and usually with an eye toward their own advantage. Men like Jim Jack Gordy (who never ran a business) were fascinated by another dimension of politics. For them it was not so much a means of managing public affairs as it was a forum for shaping and expressing the people's moral purposes. Explaining this conception of politics to an interviewer, Lillian Carter asked, "Did you know politics had religion?"[63]

By the early twentieth century, then, Georgia families like the Gordys met Georgia families like the Carters on the common but amorphous ground of populism. Unsurprisingly, *populist* was therefore the only political label that Jimmy Carter allowed to be applied to his political sentiments. But, equally important, by the early twentieth century populism was so vague that it could be split into at least two uneasily allied branches. One, epitomized by Earl Carter, subordinated populist moral fervor to more conservative Bourbon ends. The other, epitomized by Jim Jack Gordy, retained its moral thrust as paramount. Insofar as practical politics was grafted onto this latter branch of populism, the source was mainly the then emergent progressive tradition.[64] In Georgia, the conservative group became Talmadgites and the progressive group became the anti-Talmadgites — even if both held positions in a Talmadge administration.

Politically, Jimmy Carter would mature very much a Gordy — the product of his mother's and grandfather's influence — more so than a Carter. He could never countenance Talmadge demagoguery and was deeply embarrassed when the Georgia governor's controversy erupted in 1947 while he was a young naval officer. He openly supported Truman for president in 1948 and Johnson in 1964 — both instances in which he stood virtually alone among his peers in supporting the liberal Democratic candidate. Indeed, with his mother he stood up in the Plains Baptist Church in open support of welcoming black members, the only members of the congregation to do so. Neither he nor his mother were liberal ideologues — and both might have done more in support of the cause of racial equality that branded them as southern liberals — but both were progressive, independent thinkers. Jim Jack Gordy would have been proud of them.

Yet, while Lillian molded many of her son's political views, her influence over other areas of his life was subordinate to her husband's. Indeed, Jimmy's embrace of his mother's political views may have been largely a result of his seeking an alternative to his father's views when he sought leverage for rebellion against him. For in growing up closer to her father than her mother, Lillian Carter seemed comfortable with a similar arrangement in her own marriage and family. Indeed, in an odd reversal of custom, Earl Carter assumed most of the parenting responsibilities while Lillian did more or less as she pleased elsewhere. When neither parent was available, which seems to have been frequently, the care of the children and management of the household was relegated to nannies and housekeepers. Of course, Lillian may have had other reasons to absent herself from the Carter household, not least of which was the strained relationship with her husband. With the exception of a momentary and perhaps forced infatuation, she seems to have married Earl Carter mainly for money.

Only years later, as the nation openly debated the Equal Rights Amendment and her son was president, did Lillian Carter admit that she should have been a doctor.[65] As a young woman growing up in rural Georgia in the early twentieth century, such an aspiration was unimaginable. Except for marriage (in which women often helped in their husbands' work), there were really only two occupations open to white women: teaching or nursing. No free-spirited woman would choose teaching if she could help it. Poorly paid, teachers were supervised thoroughly and they were even forbidden to marry. (When a teacher decided to marry, she was dismissed.) That left, for Lillian Gordy, only nursing. Whereas in retrospect Lillian thought she might have been happier as a doctor, nursing was as close as she could come.

Even becoming a nurse was not easy for Lillian. Her father at first forbade her to enter nurse's training. The problem was the reputation nurses had for sexual promiscuity at the time (which, compared with school teachers, at least, was probably justified) and Jim Jack's apparently stern puritanical views on such matters. But with the first world war came a cry for nurses; government training programs arose to train them, and their reputation began to improve. So in 1918 Jim Jack relented and gave his consent. However, just as Lillian was to enroll in training, two things happened: a sister died of the flu and the war ended. The combination of family tragedy and the war's end delayed her training three more years. But with her father's permission and her increasing maturity, Lillian once again applied for admission to nursing school, this time in the civilian program at the Wise Hospital in Plains. She enrolled in 1921, enjoyed most of the work, and found a rewarding vocation she would practice throughout her life.

Jim Jack's fears, however, were probably well-founded, for when Lillian took up residence in Plains she quickly earned a reputation "as quite a swinger."[66] Even years later a Plains resident recalled that, in Lillian's younger days, the rumor circulated that she was "fast."[67] Whether the reputation was deserved or not, even in the context of the times, is not known. (Perhaps others just shared Jim Jack's prejudice about nurses.) But it is clear that Lillian was something of a free spirit and eagerly participated in what apparently was a revelrous medical community in Plains. The times being what they were, young women who could afford to sometimes led comparatively independent social lives. It was the age of the suffragists and a decade known as the "roaring twenties," in which the most popular song may have been "Yes, We Have No Bananas." The Plains area doctors and nurses were on the cutting edge of this social upheaval in southwest Georgia and were well known for parties that stretched or even broke the boundaries of moral propriety. Lillian, whose lifelong habits of smoking and drinking were either acquired or reinforced in this social setting, happily joined in.

But it was Dr. Sam Wise who took Lillian's future to heart by offering her advice that would change her life. Dating different men, going to parties, and generally enjoying herself, Lillian was not particularly attracted to Earl Carter. "I didn't like him at all," she later remembered. "I didn't like his looks. I was liking somebody else."[68] But Dr. Wise took her aside one day and told her in no uncertain terms that she should get serious with Earl Carter. "He's going to be worth a lot some day," the doctor said of his friend.[69] Although Lillian's initial response was to say, "I can't stand him,"[70] she soon reassessed her options. Dating casually, she introduced Earl to her family, and they were "crazy" about him. "They knew he was good, and he was going to be successful, and he was everything they had wanted for me."[71] So, by the spring of 1923 and with just the summer to go before earning her nursing license, Lillian Gordy agreed to marry Earl Carter.

There may well have been genuine love between the two — but practical considerations ruled. Earl insisted that the wedding be postponed until September to allow Lillian to finish her training (which required her spending the summer in Atlanta studying at Grady Hospital). The practical-minded Earl Carter no doubt saw value in the possibility of a second income, even if it meant the couple would spend the months before their wedding apart. Then, when the two were married on September 26, 1923, by the pastor of the Plains Baptist Church, they kept the ceremony simple — and cheap. "They didn't have a wedding," remembered Earl's sister. "They just went to the preacher's home and were married."[72] Few friends were invited and there was no reception. Even the honeymoon was skipped, though not for financial reasons. When Lillian developed a painful boil on her posterior, which made sitting uncomfortable, the newlyweds canceled the scheduled honeymoon train ride and remained in their Plains apartment where, presumably, Lillian could avoid irritating the troublesome boil.[73]

Uniting the couple initially was the lively Sumter County social life and, perhaps, Prohibition. Both Lillian and Earl, after all, were drinkers. Neither seems to have developed problems as a result of the habit, but both drank daily. Meanwhile, Prohibition had made the habit illegal during the 1920s and early 1930s, which in turn forced drinkers to imbibe in at least semiprivate. During the early years of their marriage, then, Earl and Lillian generally enjoyed before-supper drinks and nightcaps together at home. But the up-and-coming businessman and his nurse wife also had an active social calendar of weekend parties and dances, when they drank and carried on more liberally. Earl, Lillian remembered later, "could dance better if he got a little high."[74] The extent to which she shared his proclivities is left to inference. She "drank Blue Ribbon beer when we had a party," remembered Gloria, "but never in front of the children" — although the children "peeked." She did, however, smoke in front of the children and "always had an ashtray."[75] When one of these parties was hosted at home (probably before the pond house was built), Jimmy Carter distinctly remembers the adults being so noisy that he went out to his tree house to sleep.[76] Later, when the pond house became the preferred party location, Jimmy remembers having to help his father tow cars out of the pond the next day. Apparently, the drunken partiers sometimes misjudged their driving ability, their alcohol tolerance, or both and drove right into the pond.

Also uniting the couple were their children. Exactly nine months after the couple's first New Year's Day together, their first child was born. Named James Earl Carter Jr., the future president was born October 1, 1924, at the Wise Hospital in Plains. Gloria followed two years later, and Ruth two years after her. After three children roughly two years apart, a final child, Billy, completed the family in 1937, some thirteen years after the first.

But the evidence suggests that, beyond their children and social life, Earl and Lillian Carter were united by little more than the reciprocity of a rural marriage. The distance came mostly from Lillian. The daughter of Jim Jack Gordy, she shared few of her husband's interests and values. Indeed, she had not entered marriage expecting to share such things with her husband. She married partly for money, and her mother also advised her against seeking happiness. Upon learning of her daughter's marriage plans, Mary Ida Gordy took Lillian aside and explained how she had managed her own married life. Each week, she told her daughter, she had set aside an hour when she could be alone and scream as loudly as she might, "Damn! Damn! Damn!"[77] So advised and remembering the "little tiffs" her parents endured,[78] Lillian may not have expected her life with Earl Carter to turn out differently.

But instead of cursing the wind weekly as her mother had advised, Lillian chose to do more or less as she pleased daily. Since her interests normally entailed spending Earl's money, a running battle quickly erupted between the two. Lillian tried to spend what she could, Earl denied her the funds, and she needled him for being tight. "If my husband ever finds out he can't take it with him," she once explained in exasperation, "he ain't going!"[79] Sometimes, she even devised schemes to get money from her husband undetected. But in behavior typical of Earl Carter, he simply allotted her the pecan grove. Any money she could make from it was hers to spend as she wished, but no more.

Earl Carter did cover many expenses for his wife that might be considered luxuries. Lillian, remembered a next-door neighbor, "couldn't cook hot water" when she first married.[80] Later Lillian admitted, "I despise cooking."[81] Earl therefore soon arranged for her to have a full-time cook. And, although "she loved auctions" and bought most of her nicer tableware at auction prices, "she always had maids out there to polish" the pieces.[82] She also always had full-time, sometimes round-the-clock, nannies to help care for the children. "She always had somebody to look after the kids, to baby-sit them," commented Jimmy Carter's cousin Willard Slappey.[83] Nor was she interested in other traditionally feminine activities, like sewing. "My mother never sewed until much later in her life," remembered Gloria. "She decided she wanted a sewing machine — bought one and hemmed some towels on it. And that was all."[84] Later, when the pond house was built, she used it so regularly that the family thought of it as her private retreat. She also had her own car, usually a new Cadillac, which she described as "the only luxury I want."[85] If the Archery home was simple and the area primitive, she wanted for little in the way of material goods.

Despite the tensions over money, Lillian usually had plenty of time and enough money to pursue her own interests. Although she had many interests, they did not include staying abreast of her husband's career. She seemed oblivious to it. When he died in 1953, for example, she declined the invitation to serve out the remainder of his term in the state legislature on the grounds that she "didn't know a thing about it" and claimed that

Jimmy had to come home to take care of the businesses because she didn't know anything about them, either.[86] Her interests were simply different from her husband's.

Lillian's chief interest was reading. A regular *Life* magazine subscriber and member of the Book-of-the-Month Club (who generally bought and read the featured selection as well as others every month), she spent many of her days lying face down on the bed with her head just over the side and the book she was reading placed on the floor. This was, her children remembered, the most comfortable position she had found for reading, and the one in which they usually found her (if she was home) when they came in from school or play.[87]

But daytimes in bed were not the only circumstances under which Lillian read: she also regularly read at the table during mealtimes. All of her children followed her in this habit, which made mealtimes in the Carter household strange indeed. Visitors were astonished to learn that "talking was forbidden at the table, other than the saying of the blessing," while mother and children read.[88] "We weren't allowed to talk at the table," remembered Gloria. "We had no conversation at the table whatsoever."[89] Only Earl Carter, his eyesight too poor to read comfortably, did not read while eating. But since everyone else read, he was left with no one to converse with and fell silent.

Lillian also continued nursing, for pay or as a volunteer, throughout her marriage. Although she later claimed she did not work very much, a remark intended to counter the impression given by her children and others that she did, others remembered differently. Jimmy Carter remembered, "Mother nursed a good bit when I was a child." Lending credibility to his recollection is that he remembered her specific twelve- and twenty-hour shifts.[90] Willard Slappey similarly recalled: "Aunt Lillian was always, she was always on a case. Well, she didn't like to keep house. She'd lot rather nurse than to keep house."[91] Explained Jimmy, "Mother used to deny how much she nursed."[92]

The truth about how much Lillian worked is probably complex. Earl may not have approved of his wife working, or she may have decided to work only after her husband denied her more money than the pecan grove provided. In any case, her career was likely a symptom of marital discontent that she preferred not to emphasize at the time or to remember later. Also, much of her work was volunteer. "I didn't do nursing for money," she later said before recalling an occasion she did work for hire, "I want that understood."[93] Essentially providing all medical services for Archery's black families, this volunteer work may have led her family to remember her nursing more frequently than she remembered. Not least, the possibility that nursing was an excuse used to explain her regular absences from the home in a socially acceptable manner cannot be overlooked. Lillian, who may have preferred sitting and reading at her pond house to being with the family, appears more nurturing if her absence is explained by nursing. Both she and her family may have seized upon this excuse rather than admit the painful truth: that she was unhappy at home.

Perhaps Lillian Carter would have been happier if she had been a doctor. As it was, nursing seemed to provide her with her most satisfying identity. It allowed her to express nurturance in a way she appeared unable to express fully in her family. The identity also merged eerily with her unique social and political self-conceptions. Drawing upon her years of nursing Archery's blacks, Lillian joined the Peace Corps in 1966 with the stated desire to help black people, adding that she wished herself to be black. Assigned to India, Lillian considered the local Indian population black — and found solace.[94] Somehow nursing and nurturance melded with the causes of civil rights and racial equality to enable Lillian Carter to construct a curiously unique but perhaps troubled identity. It was, however, an independent identity, which in part defined her in opposition to the traditional roles as mother and wife.

Regardless of the explanation for Lillian's nursing and her frequent absences from the home, there are indications that the estrangement between her and her husband ran deeper than has generally been reported. "Lillian sometimes needed to have a little control over her," recalled a neighbor, "and Earl did it."[95] Whether this control was physical or just verbal the neighbor did not say, but the implication is clear. Lillian herself recalled, "My husband was the boss. I never did anything that he didn't want me to do. If I did, I had to apologize — or I was in trouble. I've apologized to him many a time when I felt like it was his fault."[96] The frank comment even many years later suggests genuine antipathy.

The Carters also waited eight years after the birth of Ruth in 1929 to have their final child, Billy, who slept in their bedroom for five years. Since Earl Carter went so far as to offer his wife money to have more children, his desire was clearly for a larger family. While the physical passions that resulted in three children in six years would understandably decline, it is possible that there was disagreement on this subject as their marriage withered. Indeed, when Lillian told Earl she was pregnant in 1936, his reaction was to say, "I know it's not mine."[97] Although he is said to have made the remark in jest, beneath it may have been more than a kernel of truth.

Most ominously, Earl also showed a pronounced and perhaps unhealthy affection for his favorite daughter, Ruth. "She was Mr. Earl's little girl," remembered a neighbor.[98] And about the daughter he named after his former girlfriend who died tragically in the car wreck he used to say, "She's so much prettier than Shirley Temple."[99] Yet the problems, insofar as they arose, came later. Still liking to dance, Earl took Ruth instead of his wife as his escort. Ruth seemed to substitute for Lillian in Earl's affection, a fairly common dynamic in families in which the marital relationship is strained. Sometimes such substitutions become a precondition for incest.[100] Whether or not the relationship between Earl and Ruth ever went to such extremes is not known. Lillian, however, did die with memories "too personal to share" about a time when Ruth was sixteen and her "life was the blackest."[101] Ruth herself described her father's affection as "not altogether healthy" and as the source of the emotional pain that led her to become a faith healer.[102] Other family members simply recalled that "her father's affection for Ruth" was "especially close."[103]

But if being Earl Carter's wife did not offer Lillian the meaning she needed in her own life, she seemed to have nowhere else to turn. Unlike her husband, she made few close friends and was not especially popular. "I couldn't get elected to anything in Plains," she confided, and "in my church, I'm sure there are a lot of people who'd be so happy if I'd go to another church."[104] (She preferred to skip church services.) She did join the local Stitch and Chat Club and other women's groups, like the Missionary Society and bridge clubs, but the extent of her participation was minimal. Lillian often found sitting alone at the pond house preferable to mingling with others. Her eccentricities were tolerated in the way they are in rural communities, but she was known to be eccentric — perhaps even Republican — and she did not win close friends. Nor could she have found special companionship with local blacks. Although she nursed them and otherwise participated in their lives — she may have even occasionally violated Jim Crow custom by welcoming some to her front door[105] — the planter's wife who was "Miz Lillian" to her tenants and employees could not have been completely accepted by them, either.

Nor does it alter this portrait to note that upon the death of her husband Lillian Carter displayed prolonged depression for which she required medication.[106] So extreme a reaction to the collapse of the life she had made with her husband is not necessarily an indication that her life with him was especially full or rewarding. It may instead indicate a pre-existing malaise. From other quarters indications of underlying psychological troubles may be detected. Her children, for example, remember that she so regularly rearranged the furniture in the house that they could not describe it to historians who wanted to reconstruct the president's childhood home.[107] The behavior may suggest an underlying uneasiness with the way her life was arranged. Later in life Lillian herself admitted to psychological problems by confessing to "getting nervous over things" and "wrecking my health."[108] In other words and regardless of the quality of her marriage, Lillian Carter's emotional health seems to have been precarious. Yet, insofar as her life possessed a stable center, she no less than her children, tenants, and laborers found it in a patriarch she both loved and loathed, needed and resented. And she descended into depression when he died.

Inspiring such admixtures of love and resentment, white men had long ruled the rural South. They — and the system they maintained — were hated and feared. Yet they were also capable of being kind and compassionate, and the men and the system were sometimes defended against all reason. It was, perhaps, the way much of rural life had transpired for many, many years. Jimmy Carter, inheriting his father's businesses in the 1950s, yet the son of Lillian Gordy, would be among the generation that dismantled the old system.

ISOLATED BUT NOT LONELY

Despite the remoteness of the region where Jimmy Carter lived, his childhood was a busy one. His father, Carter remembered, "was very committed to the proposition I ought to stay busy and so he was a little bit uncomfortable when there wasn't some job for me."[109] Beginning by carrying water to the thirsty field hands, Jimmy went on to mop cotton (a laborious procedure intended to protect the plant from the boll weevil), boil peanuts, tend livestock, clerk in his uncle's and his father's stores, and perform many of the various never-ending chores of farm life. "As soon as Jimmy got home from school," his mother remembered, "his daddy put him right to work."[110] Indeed, as long as he lived at home, Jimmy had regular responsibilities as well as additional occasional chores. He was responsible, for example, for managing the commissary in the evenings. When a neighbor came by seeking a nickel's worth of snuff or a bit of sugar during the evenings, Jimmy would get up, unlock the commissary, and handle the sale. The benefits of having his own pony also translated into the responsibilities of exercising her daily. Together with her, Jimmy also took regular charge of livestock. Additional chores were added to these, depending on need and season.

There was time for recreation. Sometimes Jimmy worked on inventions — once a Ferris wheel that, despite careful planning, was never built well enough to work. He also played tennis with his father, baseball with Archery's blacks (using a homemade ball one of the mothers made),[111] and skinny-dipped in a walled-up portion of the creek that doubled as a baptismal for the African Methodist Episcopal Church. Sometimes, Uncle Buddy took him to minor league baseball games in Americus, and once a year in the summer he joined his father on a fishing trip. Once, his mother took him to Atlanta for the premiere of *Gone with the Wind* (though they happened to miss the show). On weekends his father or uncle might take him to the movies in Americus or, when he was a little older, he would hitchhike or drive there himself. (On the farm Jimmy started driving when he was twelve.) Children missed circuses no more frequently than fathers and sons missed political barbecues. And, in winter, children sometimes played board games at the dining room table after homework was done but before their 8:00 bedtime. Typically, too, they listened to one of their favorite radio programs. The children also followed their mother's example and became inveterate readers.

But mostly life in Archery spilled outdoors. Jimmy, who built his daughter a tree house at the White House, spent many boyhood hours in his own tree house. (His sisters had on-the-ground playhouses.) He also hunted and fished — sometimes with his father, more often with local blacks. Rachel Clark, one of his nannies, was an expert fisher and took him often; Jack Clark, the family's handyman, took him on all-night raccoon hunts. Other times he just went by himself, spending the night on a riverbank fishing. As a result, he grew to love the outdoors and to seek solace in nature well into his adulthood and older age. After spending a final 1981 weekend at Camp David, for example, he and Rosalynn stopped by a camp where he and his father used to fish on their way to Plains from Washington.[112] Previously and during his reelection campaign, Hamilton Jordan worried privately that the press would realize that Carter had spent the equivalent of an entire year at Camp David during his administration, more than any other president; they did not, however, and Carter was spared having to defend his frequent retreats.[113] Understandably, he wrote happily about his childhood outdoors in his *An Outdoor Journal* and in 1994 confided that this was his "favorite so far" of all the books he had written.[114] The love of nature had been instilled in him early — as a boy who spent long shirtless and barefoot summers romping through woods and streams.

During the rest of the year, school kept Jimmy Carter busy. Plains schools (for whites) provided the kind of education that inspired boys like Jimmy to aspire to great things in spite of their small-town and rural origins. (Jimmy's entire school class included only a couple dozen students; other classes were not so large and had to be combined in multigrade classrooms.) The school day began with mandatory chapel and prayer, followed by the singing of patriotic songs, and then classes. Every boy was required to participate in sports, which, given the size of the school and the need for children to help out on farms during the spring and fall, meant that most boys played basketball, the winter sport. Jimmy played forward on the basketball team and also ran track. He joined the debate team and Future Farmers of America. The school superintendent (who also taught English), Julia Coleman, made a practice of singling out students with special abilities or needs for extra assignments tailored to their unique needs. One of those she selected was Jimmy Carter. She urged him to supplement his reading of *Tarzan* books with *War and Peace* over the summer of his twelfth or thirteenth year, and otherwise supplied him with extra challenges. The kind of dedicated teacher who planted a tree in the school yard for each child, Julia Coleman was eventually praised by the president of the United States in his inaugural address. The president's classmates and other townsfolk agreed that the praise was well deserved. And while Carter omitted mention of Mr. Sheffield, the school principal who had inspired others, it was probably not because he was the one who administered corporal punishment in the school. Jimmy took many whippings from his father, too.

Town life centered on school and church. It was unthinkable for parents to miss PTA meetings; likewise, plays and assemblies filled the gymnasium — the only building in the area large enough to house a community gathering. Second to the school, the churches served as community focal points. For a time the Baptist and Methodist churches even alternated weekly services so they would not compete with each other. Most of the white community attended one of these two churches (or both), a few attended the Lutheran church. The children often returned on Sunday and Wednesday evenings for youth programs. Later, when the children were high-school age, the churches sponsored "prom parties." These were well-supervised social gatherings for the teenagers, where there was no drinking or smoking. Misbehaving teenagers usually did no worse than steal a watermelon or play hooky from school in order to catch a movie in Americus. Jimmy at one time or another did both. (Once when he stole a watermelon, his ignorance of the extent of his father's landholdings was revealed, for he unwittingly "stole" one of his own family's watermelons.) Playing hooky denied him his standing as valedictorian of his class and cost him a whipping from Mr. Sheffield. For casual dates, a drugstore soda fountain was available. For intimate, less well supervised outings, nearby Magnolia Springs boasted a pavilion and jukebox — and plenty of private areas.

But school and church were both in Plains. And the Carters lived in Archery. Jimmy Carter, like other farm boys, spent more of his time on the farm than in town. Only as he got older did he begin to feel comfortable in Plains. But by that time, and inspired by the uncle who had been named after Georgia's great populist leader, Uncle Tom Watson Gordy, he had already determined to bypass Plains for the romance and excitement of a naval career.

Jimmy Carter's childhood may have the outward appearances of an idyllic one. But the appearance is more romantic than real. As he described it, he was "isolated but not lonely."[115] The juxtaposition is intriguing — and might be an apt metaphor for his mature character. For Jimmy Carter was ever isolated, but always too busy to be lonely.

CHAPTER 3

AN IMPERILED SELF AND SEARCH FOR COMMUNITY

When Jimmy Carter burst on the national scene in 1975 and 1976 as a candidate for the presidency, he described himself in the following terms:

> I am a Southerner and an American. I am a farmer, an engineer, a father and a husband, a Christian, a politician and a former governor, a planner, a businessman, a nuclear physicist, a naval officer, a canoeist, and, among other things, a lover of Bob Dylan's songs and Dylan Thomas's poetry.[1]

The introduction sounded a discordant note in a political culture accustomed to candidates presenting more singular identities. Jimmy Carter's complex presentation of himself made him appear more multifaceted than most men and more difficult to pin down than most candidates. As a result he was often called an "enigma" in the press and remained a "mystery" well into his presidency.[2]

As the public became better acquainted with Carter, some of his disparate identity claims were naturally challenged. He was not, for instance, a "nuclear physicist" in the strictest sense of the label. He had completed only a year-long course in the field as part of his post-Annapolis naval training, but had earned no degree. Still, the challenges were directed primarily to the magnitude rather than the substance of his claims. He was, after all, really trained in nuclear physics. Meanwhile, as Carter's hyperbolic claims were challenged, others emerged. It turned out that he was a fan of stock-car racing. Campaigning among stock-car racers, Carter had no need to feign interest or enthusiasm for a sport he actually knew about and appreciated. The situation was similar with motorcycling, classical music, art history, bottle collecting, Western square dancing, bird-watching, genealogy, wood-working, painting, and a host of other avocations and interests. At one time or another Carter had acquainted himself with all of these hobbies and grafted them into his personality. Although he was obviously not expert at so many things, the sheer range of his interests was great. He was a genuinely multifaceted man — seemingly an enigma.

But the mystery surrounding Carter's varied interests soon centered on the way these several interests seemed to reflect different selves. For Carter seemed not only to have several interests, at times he even appeared to *be* different people. "He was a friendly fellow you couldn't size up instantly," wrote Norman Mailer in a long piece that indeed failed to size him up. "It was irritating," confessed Mailer, "to have so incomplete an idea of Carter." But to the self-appointed heir to Hemingway machismo Carter "actually said the famous four-letter word that *The Times* has not printed in the 125 years of its publishing life." Charming this interrogator with a sailor's vocabulary, Carter left the interview with Mailer's endorsement.[3] Yet the same candidate moved easily in very different social circles, including the kinds of Christians who were appalled by his use of the milder word "screw" in a *Playboy* interview, but who would still pull the Democratic lever for him in record percentages. Similarly, while Carter's southern identity was obvious to all, William Lee Miller thought he "exhibit[ed] instead the clearest Yankee and 'Puritan' virtues" and labeled him "the Yankee from Georgia."[4]

Those closest to Carter also observed discrepancies in his identities and sometimes willingly commented upon them. Senior advisor Charles Kirbo, for example, told *U.S. News & World Report:*

> He's an unusual fellow with respect to people. He never finds anybody worthless that he deals with or talks with. During the campaign he'd come in and say he met this guy and talked with him, and he's a very great fellow. "I believe we're going to carry that county down there. Get in touch with him," he'd say. Well, we'd get in touch with him, and he'd turn out to be what we'd call a bum or jackleg carpenter who'd give you a lot of talk. But they turned out to be helpful in the campaign.[5]

Another early campaign aide, Joe Andrews, remarked: "He lives in a multiple world. He can be intense on [one subject] and then assign it to another compartment, while he turns intensely to [another]."[6] Still another aide, Peter Bourne, made the same point by way of anecdote. Describing a 1975 campaign party in Anchorage, Bourne recalled that, instead of identifying the "half-dozen most influential people in the room and spend[ing] the evening trying to nail down their support," Carter "set out systematically to shake hands with and speak to every one of the three hundred and fifty people present." By proceeding in this fashion Carter exposed "very little of his real self" and "did not establish a single deep relationship." But most of the party-goers "left the encounter with the sense that he really cared."[7]

The public at large, though perhaps initially charmed by Carter's empathic self-presentations, soon sensed a worrisome inconsistency in his multiple self-presentations. So often did he adopt different identities and embrace disparate views that no clear persona or political message emerged. "If he could make government come alive," forecast Mailer, it would be only "because he worked over the problem like a piece of broken machinery," not because he was guided by any overarching political philosophy.[8] Indeed, even Bourne confessed that Carter "had clear views about very little else than human rights."[9] The result was a widespread public perception that Carter was "fuzzy" on the issues. Accordingly, the summer polls that showed Carter beating Gerald Ford by a two-to-one margin gave way to November election results that gave Carter the thinnest majority in half a century — and even that on the basis of the lowest voter turnout in the history of presidential elections.

While the "fuzziness" dogged Carter's campaign, it assaulted his presidency. Accused of trying too much too quickly, the Carter administration was soon found to be lacking "focus."[10] Contributing to the perception was the "spokes-of-the-wheel" organizational scheme developed in the Carter White House. Carter preferred to have advisors with different viewpoints all report directly to him, rather than to insist upon ideological consistency among advisors reporting to a chief of staff. Fitting a temperament that thrived on diversity, the plan was politically disastrous. The administration, even insiders said, did not speak with a single voice. This left the public confused and made the administration appear to be "adrift." Two years into Carter's presidency, the public echoed the pundits in agreeing by a whopping 67 to 17 percent margin that the administration initiated "too many new programs" with "no follow through."[11]

By early 1979 (when media experts were engaged to bring "focus" to the administration and after which the "spokes-of-the-wheel" organizational plan was abandoned), polls showed that only 39 percent of the public agreed with the statement, "Jimmy Carter has the vision to provide solutions to the country's problems," down from a high of 69 percent toward the beginning of his term.[12] More practically, Carter's wide-ranging agenda and nonideological orientation earned him little consistent loyalty from any constituency in Congress or the public. He even had little use for his own political party. "Once I got the nomination and had the trappings of the party around my shoulders," he later admitted, "I felt a handicap rather than a new strength."[13] A near majority of loyal Democrats reciprocated by finding him a handicap. Led by Senator Edward Kennedy, many embarked upon the almost unprecedented attempt to deprive their own president of their party's renomination. Then, in his 1980 reelection campaign, Carter's pollster wrote the president plainly: "You suffer because you are held to have no vision, no grand plan."[14]

Although these criticisms are important politically and will be returned to in that context, here it is important to note that many of them center on his diffused foci and malleable self. Echoing Mailer, many reporters found Carter to have the mentality of an "engineer."[15] Inordinately intelligent and equally disciplined, Carter's intellect ran in a decidedly instrumental direction, mastering means but seemingly oblivious to ends.[16] Devouring detail, he seemed to lack the ability to synthesize it into coherent administrative objectives. And by 1978 the public was genuinely alarmed by this aspect of Carter's character. In that year pollster Louis Harris interpreted his results to show that "public concern about President Carter is clearly beginning to center on his personal capacities."[17] By the next year Carter's former speechwriter, James Fallows, went public with the widely cited complaint that "Carter believes fifty things, but no one thing," adding that "Carter thinks in lists, not arguments" and that "Carter did not really know what he wanted to do in such crucial areas as taxes, welfare, energy, and the reorganization of the government." The former speechwriter also jumped to the jugular of character. "[T]he subject that most inspired him [was] not what he proposed to *do*, but who he *was*." Defining, or perhaps redefining, a malleable self struck this speechwriter as Carter's chief source of "gusto."[18]

But on the matter of character the critics may not have pressed their views to their logical conclusions. It was easy to assume that a man who dwelt on his identity actually had one. Even Peter Bourne, who was a trained psychiatrist,[19] assumed Carter had a "real self" that he simply neglected to "expose." But neither Fallows nor Bourne — nor anyone else — ever described Jimmy Carter's "real self." Could it be that he did

not have one? Or — to put the matter as Carter did in his famous introduction — could it be that all his selves were real?

The idea that Carter possessed a singular "real self" that he either neglected to expose or — worse — purposely concealed for political advantage has long provided fertile ground for psychological speculation.
Guided mostly by psychoanalytic theory, the vast majority of these psychobiographers have followed this trail only to alight upon the diagnosis
of "narcissism."[20] Although the details and implications of the diagnosis
vary from author to author, all are in accord that Carter's multiple self-
presentations, coupled with his obvious drive for power and admiration,
are quintessential traits of the narcissist.[21]

The issues that this convergence of diagnostic interpretation raises are
profound ones for a psychoanalytic understanding of Jimmy Carter. Yet
the issues may not be terribly important for a more eclectic understanding
of Carter's story. On one hand, it is reasonably clear that the diagnosis of
narcissism does not fit all the facts of Carter's life equally well. On the
other hand, another theoretical orientation is capable of explaining the
assembled facts better.

The limitations of the narcissistic interpretation of Carter are clearest
when Carter's moral commitments are considered. On the depth and certainty of these moral commitments there has always been agreement.
Although he marveled over Carter's fuzzy ideas and multiple self-
presentations, Peter Bourne specifically exempted human rights from his
overall charge and maintained that Carter had "very clear ideas" about
this. (Whether or not he was right to follow this with the conclusion that
Carter is "psychologically one of the soundest people I know" is naturally
more debatable.)[22] Mailer also detected a moral center in Carter. He concluded, in sheepish admiration, that "Carter was somewhere within range
of the very good and very decent man he presented himself to be." Fallows
likewise tempered his criticism with moral endorsement. "I fully believe
him to be a good man," wrote the speechwriter while praising Carter's
"moral virtues" and "sound values."[23] And again, the public at large agreed.
Asked in 1979 if "Jimmy Carter is a good man but he isn't really able to
take charge of the government," 59 percent answered in the affirmative —
twice the percentage who approved of his performance.[24] Since narcissists
are presumably incapable of making and maintaining such external moral

commitments, the fact that Carter did casts doubt on the unmodified diagnosis.

But secondly, there may be a more suitable theoretical perspective that, while admittedly less precise than psychoanalysis, nevertheless more comfortably handles both the facts that psychoanalysis explains and those it does not. This is symbolic interactionism, particularly as developed by George Herbert Mead and modified by Erving Goffman and others.[25]

According to this theoretical orientation, the self is not so much a thing as it is a process. As a process, the self arises and is maintained (or changed) through social interactions. Others interact with us and we respond, we interact with them, and so on in an ever-shifting dialectic of self and others. It follows, importantly, that whereas "it has been the tendency of psychology to deal with the self as a more or less isolated and independent element, a sort of entity that could conceivably exist by itself," the symbolic interactionist views the self as "essentially a social structure" that "reflects the unity and structure of the social process as a whole."[26] From this line of reasoning it further follows that "we divide ourselves up in all sorts of different selves with reference to our acquaintances," a consequence of which is that "a multiple personality is in a certain sense normal."[27]

Although this brief sketch of a symbolic interactionist framework cannot possibly do it justice, it should already be apparent how the perspective might alternatively interpret evidence others use to allege narcissism. Symbolic interactionists might see a malleable (even "parasitic") self as a sign of adaptation to social disruption or change rather than as a sign of pathology. Moreover, the framework offers a partial resolution to the problem of Carter's possession of multiple selves coupled with his singular moral commitment. For, as Mead maintained, the "voice of the community" may occasionally be overruled by "setting up a higher sort of community" drawn from "the community of the past and the future," which, in turn, is the essence of reason.[28] Jimmy Carter may well have possessed multiple selves simply because he inhabited multiple and sometimes conflicting communities; but his selves might also have been unified, at least in part, by collective adherence to larger moral principle. Indeed, the unifying theme may have been sounded so loudly precisely because the pieces it brought together were so disparate.

Interestingly, whenever Carter felt called upon to explain himself he invariably pointed — as a symbolic interactionist might — to his social roots. In a campaign headquartered in Plains and involving nearly all of his family members, Carter seemed to proclaim that in order to understand him one must understand his family and community. In his campaign autobiography and again in his *An Outdoor Journal*, he writes freely and mostly frankly about both. Then, in his 1992 book, *Turning Point*, he specifically links his own development with that of his rural community (in this case his state senate district) — its subtitle declaring that the story is one of "a state, a nation, and a candidate" simultaneously coming of age. What Carter seems to be saying is that who he is can be best discerned by examining the social forces that shaped him.

The convergence of a theoretical orientation with Carter's view of himself, of course, is no evidence of its value. Still, the convergence may be more than accidental. For the story of Carter's childhood, it turns out, is not one of a self securely rooted in a stable family and organic community, but one of a self very much imperiled by a fragmented family and divided community. It also turns out that the story is one of Carter's grasping for a moral principle that promised to bring order out of the emotional chaos.

Of course, it can remain an open question whether or not Carter's unusually malleable self was symptomatic of underlying pathology, as it might be construed by another theoretical perspective. It should also remain an open question whether or not the moral principle that Carter adopted is a truly satisfactory response to the collapse of organic community. Indeed, the real tragedy of Carter's childhood may not have been that he developed disparate selves but that the moral principle of universalism he adopted to unite them is a poor substitute for the loss of cohesive community. Consideration of this latter issue, however, must await the first: the story of Jimmy Carter's developing selves.

A "DISENGAGED" FAMILY

Billy Carter, the brother thirteen years younger than Jimmy, could generally be counted on to tell the truth about his family as he saw it. He once quipped, "I got a mama who joined the Peace Corps when she was 68. I got one sister who's a holy roller preacher, another wears a helmet and rides a motorcycle, and my brother thinks he's going to be president. So that makes me the only sane one in the family."[29] The Carter who intimates say took after his good-natured father more than Jimmy did thus described his unusual family.

The description, moreover, is substantially correct. It might even be enlarged. Lillian Carter, as has been shown, often chose the isolation of reading over the fellowship of friends or family — and indeed often preferred to be by herself at the pond house rather than at home in Archery. There are also indications that Lillian did not always make these independent choices happily but sometimes in a spirit of reluctant bitterness. Indeed, when she joined the Peace Corps, some thought the primary motive was spite. Having threatened to join because she was feeling useless at home, she hoped her children would try to dissuade her. When they did not, she was forced to join to save face.[30] If true, even Lillian's atypical act of beneficence cloaked a more despondent motive. Perhaps the motives that prompted her to nurse far more frequently than she recalled were similar.

Billy Carter was also right about his sisters Ruth and Gloria. Although a slightly more respectable interpretation might be placed on Ruth Carter Stapleton's career than the one Billy suggested — she might be considered to have been a lay Christian psychologist rather than a "holy roller preacher" — she did establish and head a ministry of "faith healing." By her own admission, she was beset with emotional problems stemming from her childhood relationship with her father and spent much of her adulthood in a quasi-religious quest for "inner peace."

Gloria's life seemed equally troubled, but in a different way. The "only girl who would put out" as a teenager, Gloria reputedly drank heavily, used drugs, married a man who died in prison, and was a general "fuckup" in the words of her son.[31] Her son subsequently became, among other things, a homosexual prostitute and convicted felon. By the time his uncle became president, he was incarcerated in a California prison. From her second husband, Walter Spann, Gloria acquired a taste for motorcycles and was photographed with members of a Hell's Angels–style motorcycle gang to which she belonged. Neither of the sisters — nor their mother — led a placid, predictable life.

And Jimmy, of course, did aspire to the presidency when few thought he had a chance. (Earlier he had aspired to governor with similarly bleak chances.) But Billy disingenuously exempted himself from ribbing. He too was far from typical. If nothing else the self-styled redneck who became a cottage industry all to himself during his brother's campaign and administration was a confessed alcoholic. But he was also a millionaire businessman, a voracious reader, and a "good old boy," all before his brother offered for the presidency. His life, too, was neither placid nor predictable.

Confronted with this odd and seemingly troubled collection of Carters, it explains little to conclude that the family members were all "insane" as

Billy Carter alleged. Although Billy obviously meant the accusation humorously (and insanity is a legal rather than a psychiatric term), it is important to recognize the limits of a psychological explanation for a family so differently troubled. For all family members expressed their troubles in different ways. It is doubtful therefore that they were united by repeated instances of the same individual malady, which would presumably have resulted in more similar symptoms among them. The better conjecture is that a common social experience propelled each to curiously different reactions.

Such variable reactions to a common social experience have been described by family therapists as characteristic of "disengaged" families. In such a family, members exhibit pronounced independence, with truncated experiences of intimacy. Although the families are typically intact — they live together — members tend to keep to themselves, talk only perfunctorily, and share little of themselves. Independence is more than encouraged; it is mandated. As a result, members appear quite different from each other and develop different "personalities." Yet the independence is founded in large part on emotional impoverishment and social isolation. Beneath it are, therefore, profound dependency needs and cravings for companionship, while the independent identity remains superficial and one-dimensional. Yet it is not as if the independence is feigned, for beneath the independent self is no truer self. Beneath the independence is nothingness, the nonbeing of social isolation. Moreover, just as the disengaged family produces a multiplicity of different and independent members, so also it can produce in an individual a multiplicity of different and independent selves. Rooted in the absence rather than the presence of common experiences, little common memory exists among selves to show one that another is phony. They all may be real.

The Carter family has been described as disengaged, and the evidence for the description is strong.[32] With Lillian nursing or alone at her pond house and Earl gone to oversee his farms and businesses or socializing at one of the men's clubs he belonged to, the household was essentially run by a succession of hired maids, nannies, and handymen. Mealtimes, when the family might be expected to be together, were infrequent occasions for sharing. Breakfasts were typically grabbed on the run, the rural noontime dinner excluded the children for much of the year when they were in school, and suppers found the family silently reading around the table. On Saturday nights, when the cook was allowed to be off and Lillian took charge of the evening meal, not much was made of supper. The children remember that a typical meal was hot chocolate and buttered toast.[33] On Sunday mornings Earl Carter cooked the breakfast himself, but then the family separated as Earl took the children to church while Lillian stayed home and he visited friends after the men's-only Sunday-school class. Lillian regularly cooked only Sunday dinner, usually fried chicken, which the family devoured while reading. Other times, when many of the family members might convene around the radio in the evening, they similarly did not communicate. "You didn't talk when the radio was going," remembered Gloria.[34] Actually, they did not talk much at all. And when they did, the communication patterns were curiously oblique and passive. Earl Carter never ordered Jimmy to do something, for instance; he rather "asked" him.[35]

But if sharing was infrequent around the dining-room table or in the living room, so also was argument or confrontation. Disengaged families not only avoid pleasant intimacies; they also avoid unpleasant ones. "If there was anything wrong with the food, you didn't say it," remembered Gloria. "You sat there and you enjoyed your food. . . . We just weren't used to talking at the table."[36] Unsurprisingly, then, typical misbehavior for Gloria — the only child who sometimes "stood up" to her father — was to run away from home. "Forever getting mad," she would go to the Watsons' house and refuse to come home.[37] Jimmy misbehaved similarly, if less dramatically. When he became angry or upset he just went to his room and read. Once when this escape was impossible, he spent the night in his tree house and refused to come down. But family arguments, like family togetherness, were rare. To argue would have required more communication than the Carters typically displayed.

On holidays or other occasions when families normally come together, the Carters did not. Ruth, for example, twice published accounts of the Carters' Christmas.[38] Both accounts tell of the year (before Billy was born) when all three children were quarantined with the measles in a dark bedroom. The point of both stories seems to be how Lillian surprised the children by convincing the host of a children's radio program to wish the children merry Christmas over the air. Yet another point is conspicuous by its absence: Ruth's father is not mentioned. Nor did any Carter remember a Christmas when the whole family was together. We learn, rather, that Earl Carter hosted an annual Christmas party at the Americus Elks Club without Lillian, and went bird hunting on Christmas Day.[39] The only story of a Christmas involving both Earl and Lillian came from Gloria, who remembered a Christmas when "Daddy gave Mother a dozen shirts. . . . We always wondered about that — a dozen shirts that fit him."[40] After responsibly providing toys for the children, and perhaps shirts for himself, he simply left the house. Christmas Day was not a time Earl Carter intended to spend with his family, any more than any other day.

Nor was Thanksgiving celebrated at the Carters. Substituting for a late autumn holiday was Earl's annual hog slaughter, which the children were forbidden to watch and an activity in which Lillian had scant interest. On Thanksgiving Day, Earl again went hunting. The only holiday when he stayed home was Independence Day, for that was the day he hosted an annual barbecue for his Archery neighbors, employees, and tenants. It was, however, remembered as Earl's barbecue and a party for his employees, not as a family gathering.

The family members also usually took separate vacations, two or three at a time or sometimes one or more with other friends or relatives. Earl went on an annual fishing trip, sometimes taking Jimmy or, later, Billy with him, while the others stayed home. The children sometimes visited the Gordys in Columbus or joined their Carter grandmother for a trip to her former home in South Carolina. Jimmy, in fact, was sent to his grandmother's in Plains one or two nights a week, a schedule that reflected a rotation among the Carter cousins who took turns keeping their grandmother company. But no one ever remembered a time when the entire family vacationed together. Later, when Jimmy was a student at the Naval Academy, his father generally visited him alone — without Lillian. Indeed, even Saturday nights in the Carter household found Earl taking Ruth instead of his wife to Elks Club dances. And, in a region where family reunions were regular events — the Gordys and the Smiths (Rosalynn's family) held them — the Carters never got together.[41] Comparing her family with the Carters, Rosalynn was heard to remark that hers "likes to gossip; his just goes on right after they eat — to do something."[42]

From the standpoint of the children, too, there is little evidence of family togetherness. "I think all my children are individuals," said Lillian later in understatement.[43] Only two photographs were "ever made with the four children in the same picture," commented Gloria.[44] Pointing to one of these "rare pictures" on another occasion, Jimmy embellished, "we rarely got together, as a matter of fact."[45] Gloria, two years younger than Jimmy, was for most of their childhood bigger than he. Both remember their relationship as moderately antagonistic and mostly indifferent. From Jimmy's standpoint Gloria was such a "tattletale" that he had to shoot her once with his BB gun. But at least he could trick her out of a penny by convincing her to plant it so it would grow into a money tree. (He then promptly dug up the penny and pocketed it.) Ruth, two years younger yet, might have bonded better with Gloria had she not been chosen as her father's favorite, while Gloria was chosen as her mother's favorite. Whether for this reason or others, the sisters developed independent of one another, each with a distinct personality and a different circle of friends. Four years younger than Jimmy, Ruth could not become close to him until adulthood. Then their closest moment seems to have been in middle age when the two talked frankly about their respective emotional pain born in their oppressive family. Even that tenuous bond, however, never seemed to link Jimmy with Gloria or Billy. Gloria alone called him "Jim," distancing herself from the informality of "Jimmy," while Billy never reconciled himself to a brother who fate had decreed would determine much more of his life than he would have preferred.

The constellation of the Carter household therefore combined with distant parental relationship and the isolated Archery settlement to produce a family in which members shared little beyond economic ties. Despite the many recollections of the members, none describes a single occasion when the family was physically together (except for infrequent mealtimes when all but Earl read). Most — including Lillian, Jimmy, and Billy — seem to have developed more open relationships with their black neighbors and tenants than with family members. Yet these cross-caste relationships were necessarily limited and superficial. The result was a family that fostered independence at the price of interdependence.

Given this family life, it is no wonder that the first identity Jimmy Carter forged had nothing whatsoever to do with his immediate family. Inspired by postcards from his uncle Tom Watson Gordy, who had become a career sailor, Jimmy rather imagined a career in the navy. Everyone's earliest memory of Jimmy Carter, stemming from his early childhood, is that he planned to attend the U.S. Naval Academy and become a naval officer. Plastering his uncle's postcards around his room and keeping a three-foot model ship on his mantel, Jimmy dreamed of a different future self that would give his life meaning.[46] It was an odd ambition for a boy who would ultimately inherit his father's farm and celebrate the virtues of small-town life — but not so odd for a boy so isolated that an identity could only be crafted in the imagination. Perhaps, too, he imagined in the self-contained world of military regimentation a coordinated social life of interdependence that he did not experience at home.

But to make his way to the navy (and then, abruptly, to change his plans) required more than imagining an alternative to his fragmented family life. For within that family was the domineering force of his demanding father, unbuffered by the largely absent maternal affection. Meeting the demands of his father and finding ways to cope with his distant mother were psychological detours of the first order.

FATHER'S INFLUENCE

"My daddy was the dominant person in our family and in my life," wrote Carter some years after leaving the presidency. "I worshipped him."[47] The comments, together with other evidence (like the greater space Carter devotes to describing his father than his mother in his books), show what others have observed about Carter's parental influence. "His daddy had more influence on his life than anyone else," said a classmate, adding that "because Miss Lillian is still living . . . people would like to give her credit. . . . But in my opinion I don't think Miss Lillian had anything to do with his success."[48] And, admitted Lillian, "He was a more affectionate father than I was a mother."[49] Reflecting her admission, the children called him "Daddy," while they reserved the more formal "Mother" for Lillian. Although as an adult Carter adopted many of his mother's values, his father exerted the deeper influence on him.

Earl Carter, the patriarchal family head, was an easy man to admire. A self-made man in a region of poverty, he towered over most of his peers. His achievements, moreover, were augmented by strong character and widespread community respect. And insofar as his family had a center, he was it. Although he did not display affection freely, was demanding in his expectations, and devoted little time to his children, he was the center of his children's world. Earl arranged for the children to get to school, planned for their lunches in town, assigned chores for them after school, and helped with their homework at night. "Daddy helped us with our lessons," Gloria remembered.[50] On weekend afternoons he took them to movies in Americus or on other outings, and on Sundays he made their breakfast and took them to church. He instructed them in values, taught them how to work with hands and brains alike, and assumed responsibility for their discipline. Sometimes, at night, he even told them silly stories. A favorite, which the children heard "about twice a year" while their father peeled a grapefruit, was of the time he bought "the biggest orange he had ever seen" for "a whole dime" and it turned out to be his first grapefruit.[51] In person as in station, he loomed large in the eyes of his children — perhaps too large.

By all accounts Earl Carter's demands on Jimmy were excessive. Noting "[M]y father shaped my life more than anyone else as far as my work habits and ambitions were concerned," Jimmy Carter added, "his standards for me were extremely high."[52] Others agreed. One who did was Edgar Smith, the town mechanic and Rosalynn's father. "My husband used to say that his daddy worked him too hard," recalled Rosalynn's mother, Allie Smith.[53] One of Jimmy's classmates likewise remembered, "Jimmy had more chores than I did."[54] More regularly than his peers — and without as much need — Jimmy had to exempt himself from extracurricular activities in order to get home where his assigned duties awaited. Reflecting his high expectations for Jimmy, Earl nicknamed him "Hot Shot" — and Jimmy was called "Hot" until he left for college and insisted on "Jim." (The informal "Jimmy" would come much later.)

Perhaps the best example of Earl's expectations for Jimmy comes from his Saturday morning lessons in entreprencurship. (The lessons were daily during parts of the summer.) Beginning when Jimmy was only five or six years old, Earl required him to get up early, boil and bag peanuts, and take them to Plains to sell on the street corners. Doing so, of course, was part of a more general Carter family tradition of teaching children about business, and when he grew older Jimmy joined his older cousins Hugh and Willard to sell hot dogs, hamburgers, and ice cream in a makeshift concession stand next to Alton Carter's store. Then, still under his father's tutelage, Jimmy invested proceeds from Saturday sales into cotton, held it until prices rose, and sold at substantial profit. These profits were in turn invested in land, which was rented out for steady profits. In this way, by the time he was in high school Jimmy was himself leasing land and sharecropper shacks for a Depression-era $16.50 per month.

These experiences enabled Jimmy Carter to absorb his family's entrepreneurial legacy and prepared him to succeed in business on his own later. But the experiences were not without moral importance. First, Carter learned implicitly his role as a white man in the rural South and how to leverage it for profits. "Most of our trade was the colored people there," said his cousin about their Saturday hot-dog stand, and "we called them 'niggers' then."[55] Jimmy's tenants were also black. But he also learned a more general moral lesson. His earliest moral recollection, he wrote, was to consider those who bought his wares "good" people and those who did not "bad." To this childish reasoning was soon appended a more mature moral austerity. In both his campaign autobiography and his 1992 book, he shows contempt for "checker players and other loafers" — men whose primary flaw was to prefer a morning of relaxation to profiting.[56] Like his father, Jimmy considered it wrong to while away idle hours when work could be done. If these lessons anticipate William Lee Miller's description of him as a "Yankee from Georgia," the emphasis needs to be placed on both of the nouns. For Jimmy Carter not only absorbed Yankee entrepreneurial traits but also learned them in a caste society.

And if his father instilled in him entrepreneurial lessons appropriate to a caste society, he also arranged for his play to perpetuate the lessons. Playing primarily with the black children of Archery, Jimmy found that he won almost every game. The reason was simple: Earl Carter had ordered the black children to lose. Jimmy never admitted knowing about this practice, but Ruth reported it straightforwardly.[57] Jimmy's best childhood friend, A. D. Davis (who later became the "overseer" of the children), agreed. Jimmy "always liked to be the star," he admitted. "He always had to be the head of it. When they played baseball out in Archery, Jimmy had to be the pitcher."[58]

Members of ruling castes, however, must also learn responsibility, and Earl's lessons extended to that as well. Outfitting Hot with first a slingshot, later a BB gun, and finally shotguns, Earl Carter used firearms as occasions to instruct him in responsibility. When Jimmy shot Gloria with his BB gun, his father whipped him — just as he did when Jimmy stole a penny from the church collection plate. Another time, when Jimmy shot his first quail and eagerly ran to tell his father, his jubilation was shattered when the elder Carter asked where he had left his rifle. Having dropped it in his excitement, Jimmy's thrill of success quickly evaporated when he and his father returned to search for the lost gun.[59] Jimmy also distinctly remembered his father teaching him to hunt only what he might eat. Responsible hunting, given carnivorous practices, required that wildlife not to be consumed be protected.[60] And stewardship of the outdoors was easily generalized to integrity in other areas.

Jimmy learned these lessons well. Indeed, he had so internalized them that he found it difficult to violate them even when he might with impunity. Ordered to "pick up squares," or gather boll weevils from the ground between rows of cotton before they hatched, the children were paid twenty-five cents per hundred squares. Some children found it easy to augment their numbers (and their pay) by pulling squares off the plants themselves, though this was not supposed to be done. Jimmy refused to cheat in this way and even confronted other children who did. "No sir, you don't do that," he said. "You don't pull off the squares, you have to pick them up." The conclusion of the other children was clear: "Jimmy's . . . just as honest as the day is long." Worshiping his father and trying to please him, Jimmy did not cheat even when he could and others did.[61]

Internalizing his lessons was aided by his father's habit of repeating any punishment he found that Jimmy received in school. "When I was punished at school on occasion by Mr. Sheffield, who would use the paddle with extreme force on our rear end, instead of getting sympathy from home, I got a spanking from my daddy too." One such paternal spanking was apparently delivered as late as Jimmy's senior year in high school.[62]

Yet, no matter how hard he tried to meet his father's expectations, Jimmy could not. His father's demands were simply unmatched by enough approval or affection to enable Jimmy to feel successful by meeting them. When Jimmy did well, his father remained silent; remarks were reserved for reprimands. Nor could Jimmy succeed in direct competition with his father. Engineering success for his son, Earl nevertheless reserved for himself the right to best him. He had a "wicked serve" that he did not restrain when challenging his son on the tennis court.

The senior Carter did not even devote much time or attention to Jimmy. "Daddy was not at home during the time we were there on the weekends," Jimmy Carter recalled. During the week "he left . . . quite often before daybreak and would come home late in the afternoon."[63] He also remembered that when he climbed in the back of the truck with the other men and boys en route to the campaign barbecues, he felt that he was there simply to fill up the truck — not because his father particularly cared about him.[64] Even regarding the outdoor activities that father and son might be expected to share, Jimmy remembered that he and his father "usually went our own separate ways in the woods and on the streams . . . and I more frequently would go with my black friends."[65] His nanny, Rachel Clark, was also his chief fishing teacher. Yet when he did get to go on a fishing trip with his father, he revealed how much it meant to him by proudly repeating the men's risqué stories to his mother and sisters when he returned. Similarly, he remembered feeling especially proud cleaning his gun the night before a hunt with his father, or being a little late for school after a morning hunt with him. But Earl Carter more frequently fished and hunted with friends, leaving Hot at home.

Worshiping his father and trying to please him, Jimmy Carter tried ingratiation. When his father missed a shot when hunting, Jimmy fumbled for excuses on his behalf with a remark like, "They're sure flying high this morning."[66] But ingratiation also failed to win him the approval that merit could not gain. Indeed, much later in life when he turned his attention to writing poetry, Carter shocked even himself by the depths of the pain his poem about his father revealed. "I despised the discipline," he wrote, about "a pain I mostly hide." But "even now" he expressed "hunger for an outstretched hand/a man's embrace to take me in/the need for just a word of praise."[67]

Two of Jimmy Carter's most distinctive mature personality traits — his tendency to exaggerate and his ever-present grin — can probably be traced in part to these childish attempts to please his father. His lifelong tendency to exaggerate (as well as its less frequently observed but equally ubiquitous inverse, the fear of embarrassment) was often explained as merely "cultural." Excusing his boss's proclivity for hyperbole, for instance, Press Secretary Jody Powell explained that in rural Georgia one did not simply have a good mule but had "the best damn mule in the whole state." The explanation, however, does not tell the whole story. Hamilton Jordan — who shared the same cultural background as Carter and Powell — confessed that Carter's tendency to exaggerate was a personal quirk so firmly entrenched in his character that the repeated pleadings of advisors to curtail it failed.[68] If so, chances are strong that it sprang from a youthful habit of accentuating his accomplishments to a father who generally minimized them. Similarly, the persistent fear of embarrassment — the one painful emotion Carter regularly admitted to experiencing and one undoubtedly related to his tendency to exaggerate — may be attributed partly to the understandable shyness of a rural southerner. But surely it too sprang in part from his unsuccessful childhood attempts to win his father's approval. Trying to please his daddy, Jimmy developed the habit of exaggerating his accomplishments — and experienced melting embarrassment when his father challenged his exaggerations.

A similar but more complex origin of Carter's famous grin is likely. "Jimmy got his grin from his daddy," recalled a classmate.[69] But in Jimmy the grin seemed neither as easy nor as frequent as it did in Earl. Zbigniew Brzezinski, Carter's National Security Advisor, whose access to power depended solely on his ability to understand Carter, explained the discrepancy this way. Carter, Brzezinski observed, actually had three different smiles, only one of which was an easy, genuine one, rarely glimpsed by those who were not intimates. The most common Carter smile was a second one, which Brzezinski described as somewhat forced but essentially polite and ingratiating, often used when he wanted to please others. A third smile masked anger. When Carter was angry, Brzezinski observed, he also smiled — but "only if one knew him well did one sense that behind the mask was unadulterated fury."[70] It is easy to speculate that if the first smile was passed directly from father to son, the other two were produced by the son's reactions to his father. Yearning for his father's approval and affection, Jimmy probably flashed his ingratiating smile often. Denied the approval and affection, he still smiled — to mask his fury.

By the time Jimmy reached young adulthood, the smile that masked his rage had become a fixed habit. "My problem," Carter wrote in his diary the first year he was at Annapolis, "is that I smile too much." The assessment came after an upperclassman had ordered him to "wipe the smile off" his face and the angry Carter could not. The angrier he became, the more he smiled — and the more abuse he took from his senior.[71] No doubt Carter had grinned just as stoically for his father many times before.

Some theorize that Carter's mature personality was characterized by repressed rage, stemming from his relationship with his father and expressed obliquely in both his habit of exaggeration and his infamous grin. Political cartoonists seized these linkages in 1976 and gravitated to caricatures that exaggerated his toothy smile and suggested the bite of aggression.[72] Then, when he was president, at least one psychobiographer wrote that he detected in Carter an underlying rage so profound that he was certain to lead the nation into war.[73] After his presidency others agreed with Carter that restraint of aggression was among his main accomplishments.[74] These suspicions were advanced, moreover, without their authors knowing how strongly Earl Carter elicited rage that required repression.

If Jimmy developed a smile that masked his rage over inability to please his father, Earl's disappointment with Jimmy was expressed more directly. In 1937 when his long-awaited second son, Billy, was born (and Jimmy was twelve), Earl confided to friends and family that he had "failed" with Jimmy. He thought he had been too strict with Jimmy and should raise Billy more leniently. The conclusion was undoubtedly beneficial for Billy, who enjoyed a closer relationship with his father than Jimmy had (and by most accounts grew up to become more like his father). Yet it could not have had the same effect on Jimmy. Struggling to please his father, Jimmy must have been wounded by his father's judgment, even if it is unlikely that his father expressed it to him directly.[75]

Beyond his doubts about his own strictness, why Earl Carter thought he failed with Jimmy is undisclosed. Puzzling is that, on the face of it, Jimmy displayed few signs of failed parenting. He worked hard, made money, displayed integrity, excelled in school, and was well liked. Except for a few slight infractions, he was also well behaved. "Jimmy was the type you'd like for your sister to go with," recalled a classmate. "He just didn't have any bad habits."[76] Most fathers would have been proud of such a son — not deemed him a failure. What might be concluded, then, is that Earl's judgment about his son was based either on the quality of their private relationship or, perhaps, on some never reported misdeeds.

Ruth hinted at the poor quality of the private relationship between Jimmy and his father. Writing that both were "powerful men" with "potent personalities," she observed that they were simply destined to have "their clashes" being "two streams [that] couldn't possibly flow in the same channel."[77] Yet she offered no specific examples of their "clashes." Mentioning obliquely that his father "was kind of hot tempered," Jimmy once cited an incident when his father hurled a saltshaker against the fireplace because the salt had become damp and would not come out.[78] But he volunteered no examples of violent arguments erupting between the two of them. Perhaps there were violent outbursts between Jimmy and his father that good taste (or political considerations) prevented anyone from describing. Or maybe some of Jimmy's rebellious misdeeds were too unflattering to report (or perhaps unknown to others) but served as the basis for Earl's assessment. Lending credibility to this last possibility is that Jimmy specifically remembered receiving six whippings from his father but reported the reasons for only four. Perhaps the reasons for the other two might reveal why his father thought he had failed. These reasons, however, are undisclosed and are left to speculation.[79] So in the last analysis, we do not know why there was so sharp a rift in the father/son relationship — only that there was one.

Whatever the reason for the faltering father/son relationship, Jimmy's behavior anticipated it. Initially, he just kept small areas of life free from his father's dominance. Like other boys, for example, he collected arrowheads. But unlike others — and in behavior that puzzled his cousin Hugh — Jimmy refused to trade his away.[80] Perhaps in his arrowhead collection he found an area of life that he might keep free from the Carters' usual demands for profiting through trade. Later in life Carter embraced many such impractical interests — from the religious faith he left surprisingly free from his usual relentless mental probings to bottle collecting, classical music, and even bird-watching.[81] Although each interest was threatened by his driving need to master and dominate, his initial attraction to them seemed to be to escape from just these compulsions.

Also, Jimmy Carter increasingly gravitated toward his mother's values — especially when they opposed his father's. He joined her in attending the black funerals that his father refused to attend (and once even took a high-school date to a black church service). Doing so, of course, suggested at least subtle defiance of his father's racial views. He also adopted Lillian's habit of reading. But most important, he used her family as a model for his own career plans. Unlike the Carters, he determined that he would not spend his life as a farmer and businessman. Instead, he decided to follow the example of his Uncle Tom Gordy and become a sailor. More than this, he opted to do so by attending the U.S. Naval Academy to receive the kind of college education that had so far eluded the Carters, but which fitted the Gordy family's more professional values.

The possibility follows that Jimmy's increasingly firm plans to attend the naval academy (coinciding more or less with Earl's announcement of failure in raising his son) allowed a kind of truce to be broached in their antagonistic relationship. The substance of the truce would be that both would work toward a future in which they might be satisfied but separated. Preserving their nominal independence, they might then coexist in relative tranquillity. If such a pact was effected, each did his part. Earl made biannual contributions to his congressman, Stephen Pace, in order to smooth the way for an eventual request for a congressional recommendation for his son's appointment. Jimmy memorized most of his dog-eared copy of the academy's admissions catalog and did what was required for acceptance. He studied hard, made good grades, and worked to develop the kind of character that would win him acceptance into the academy.

Yet the combination of announced failure and decision to separate could not have completely satisfied either party. Jimmy, especially, was not without insecurities suggesting that his ambitions were infused with doubts arising from his relationship with his father. Specifically, he worried about his slight stature (he weighed only 121 pounds when he enrolled in the academy and was reportedly several inches shy of his mature height of 5'9"), his flat feet, and a deeply personal problem — the inability to urinate without leaving a few drops behind. (The latter fear resulted from his misunderstanding the academy's policy of disqualifying applicants who suffered from "urine retention.") Focusing on perceived limitations of stature, feet, and penis, the easy and persuasive psychological interpretation is that his feelings of inadequacy in the eyes of his domineering father slipped easily into more diffuse doubts about his masculinity and ability to "measure up." Such doubts would be understandable.

Nevertheless, as the product of Earl's stringent demands Jimmy did not allow his doubts to overwhelm him. Instead, he used them as prompts for action. In addition to applying himself to his schoolwork he ate bananas to increase his weight, rolled his feet on Coke bottles to improve his arches, and presumably tried similar but unreported methods to correct his problem with "urine retention." Doing so, perhaps, he revealed how much he wanted to escape his father. But at the same time he showed how desperately he hoped to prove himself in the kind of man's world in which his father was so much a part — a world from which he had been excluded.

Jimmy Carter made it to the naval academy. But whether attending it or establishing a successful naval career afterward helped him make peace with his father is doubtful. Evidence indicating that it did not includes his abrupt resignation from the navy and return to southwest Georgia immediately after his father's death — behavior suggesting that his naval career may have been an unsatisfying ten-year escape from his father. But between his departure and his return, another incident linking father and son indicates that real independence had not yet been secured.

The incident was an argument that erupted during the Christmas holidays in 1950–51, while Jimmy was visiting home some seven years after he had left. Jimmy told his father about his ship's crew being invited to a party by the British governor-general of Jamaica, who added that the black crew members were not welcome to attend the segregated affair. The white crew members promptly voted to decline the invitation and conveyed their displeasure over the governor-general's racial views in salty language. Proud of his crew's decision, Jimmy expressed that pride to his father, who became livid. Earl Carter supported racial segregation, approved of the governor-general's policy, and was upset by his son's rejection of these views. The last and most bitter argument between father and son thus erupted on the issue of race.[82]

It has always been politically convenient for Jimmy Carter to tell this story, for it has the effect of sharply distancing him from his father's racism. The effect is appropriate. If not as quickly or as forcefully as he sometimes implied, Jimmy Carter did ultimately embrace full racial equality.

Yet it is doubtful that in 1950 he had completely conceded the integrationist cause. Indeed, an abundance of evidence shows that he only gradually came to support civil rights for blacks during the 1950s and 1960s. It is also puzzling that Jimmy would have bothered to mention the incident to his father — unless, of course, he intended to spark an argument. For he surely anticipated the argument that would ensue. "Jimmy and his father didn't discuss politics when he came home from the navy," remembered Rosalynn, "because they disagreed so much."[83] Since Jimmy knew his father's opinions and normally avoided confrontations with him, the conjecture arises that Jimmy initiated this argument. Why he did so may reveal more about the father/son relationship than about his emerging racial views.

If the 1950 argument between father and son was not the clear-cut ideological dispute that it appears to be today, its importance may lie in its use by Jimmy Carter as a pretext to assert moral independence from his father and to achieve an identity partially independent of his father's domineering influence. Seizing the one issue on which his father was demonstrably wrong, Jimmy Carter hammered home the counterview. The substance of his view, although obviously important, may not have been as important as the assertion of independence itself. Indeed, in the heat of the argument Jimmy may have found himself committing more deeply to the cause of racial equality than he had previously. But by challenging his father, Jimmy may have achieved his aim: to become his own man. If so, from that time forward any certainty of self he possessed would include an abiding commitment to racial equality.

Also important is that Carter's support for racial equality in this vignette springs not merely from his own opinions but from the collective decision of an entire crew. The usually overlooked subtext in this story is that it was a community's solidarity on behalf of human rights and not merely an individual opinion that prompted the egalitarian decision. When race threatened to fracture the ship's community — as it had his childhood world — Carter was proud and happy that it did not. Perhaps this too was the moral lesson he tried to convey to his father.

Two years passed without visits or real communication between the two. Then, in early 1953, Earl Carter was diagnosed with cancer. Jimmy used his accumulated leave to be at his dying father's bedside. The two talked more intimately than they had in years. When the end came in July, Jimmy cried. His daddy, the man he had worshiped, died.

And then, mysteriously, Jimmy Carter came home. Surprising even himself, and over the determined opposition of his wife, he resigned his commission and returned to take up where his father had left off. As he put the inexplicable: "I began to think about the relative significance of his life and mine. He was an integral part of the community, and had a wide range of varied but interrelated interests and responsibilities. He was his own boss, and his own life was stabilized."[84] By comparison, Jimmy Carter's life paled. It always had.

The legacy Earl Carter left for his firstborn son was therefore a profound and ultimately paradoxical one. From him Jimmy Carter learned ambition, hard work, shrewdness, and frugality — the traits that would propel his later success. Yet he also learned kindness and charity. From his father, perhaps, he also acquired his habit of hyperbole and his famous grin — telltale signs of the severity of his father's instruction. Then, in opposition to his father, Carter developed an equally fierce commitment to racial justice and human rights.

As he wrestled with the many paradoxes of his father's legacy, it is no wonder that Jimmy Carter gravitated to the social theology of Reinhold Niebuhr. Concluding that his father was a good man and in heaven, Jimmy Carter found himself attracted to Niebuhr's distinction between "moral man and immoral society."[85] Earl Carter, his son concluded, had been a good man corrupted by an evil society. Pondering the contradictory legacy of the father whose life he hoped to emulate, Carter concluded the obvious: that, insofar as he could, he would reform society. Again Niebuhr's words echoed. "The sad duty of politics," Carter often quoted him, "is to establish justice in a sinful world." But ironically, the reformist impulse would never replace what Earl Carter enjoyed so naturally without it: the sense of just being at home in a community despite its injustices. For Jimmy Carter, moral reform would have to substitute for the more visceral security that his father — and ultimately his community — denied to him.

THE MATERNAL LEGACY

When Carter was an adult and joined his sister Ruth to look through some of their old family furniture, they chanced upon an old black-stained hardwood desk that used to sit in their Archery living room. Upon seeing the desk Jimmy said, "Oh, hello Mother." Ruth burst out laughing. She knew as only siblings could that the desk represented their absent mother. As she explained, when the Carter children came home from school or play, often as not they were greeted not by their mother but by a note from her left on the desk excusing her absence.[86] So frequent were these absences that the children took to calling the desk "Mother." "[T]his was Mother over here," corroborated Gloria, pointing to the desk. "It seems now in retrospect that my mother [was gone] every afternoon."[87]

Others, perhaps not knowing about the desk, remembered Lillian's frequent absences. "Lillian used to be away from home pretty much," recalled the children's cousin Willard Slappey.[88] A classmate who occasionally spent the night at the Carters' remembered that the nanny "used to cook us breakfast" because "Jimmy's mother would already have to be up and gone."[89] The children's second nanny verified that "she'd go whenever she took a notion," adding that "she wasn't going nowhere." As a result, said Rachel Clark, "I took the house over. I cooked, I washed, I ironed and I fed Jimmy and the children. I done it all."[90]

Ruth Carter Stapleton freely admits being emotionally wounded by her mother's absence.[91] Gloria Carter Spann's recollection that "Mother cooked Sunday dinner; that's what was so great about it" testifies to her similar reaction.[92] Only a child yearning for maternal affection would find her one meal a week "so great." Jimmy Carter, no less than his sisters, was likely pained by his mother's absences. Once it almost cost him his life. When he was two, his mother left him in the care of his ten-year-old cousin Willard, who "sort of forgot" Jimmy and allowed him to wander onto the railroad tracks. Alerted by the horn of the oncoming train, Willard barely rescued Jimmy in time. A nurse at the hospital who had observed the incident mentioned it to Lillian and advised her to choose a more responsible baby-sitter. Instead, Lillian just "cussed out" Willard.[93] Recalling similar outbursts, a neighbor commented, "Miss Lillian, she had a temper."[94] As for Jimmy, escaping the train, he was later run over by a bus, breaking both feet, and twice broke other bones in childhood accidents.

Most psychologists account for Carter's apparent good relationship with his mother in adulthood as a "reaction formation," a psychological defense by which an emotion is turned into its opposite.[95] Although it is equally possible, as Carter said, that his mother "really blossomed forth much more after my father's death in 1953,"[96] he seemed to have reason to be insecure about his mother's affection when he was a child. All reports of the Carter household do indicate that Lillian Carter was frequently physically absent and, when present, was emotionally distant. Moreover, there is evidence that Lillian actually belittled Jimmy and equivocated in her affection for him. When he confided in her that he intended to run for president, she asked, "president of what?"[97] Then, when he became president, she commented that "so far" his performance was only "pretty good."[98] Indeed, she made it plain that her favorite child was not Jimmy. He was, she said, "not complex at all" and thought Gloria, whom she favored, her smartest child.[99] (Suiting the psychological distance between the parents, Gloria was the child Earl Carter favored least.)[100]

The enduring consequences of Lillian Carter's distance from her son are probably impossible to gauge. The usual interpretation was expressed this way by Betty Glad: Since Lillian Carter "did not provide the kind of nurturance that would have balanced her husband's demands" (an amount that would have had to be great), Jimmy Carter succumbed to a narcissism not unlike his mother's — projecting an "idealized self-portrait" yet "sensitive to criticism."[101] This may well be true, but it overlooks the strategies that Carter used to compensate for his missed maternal affection.

Jimmy Carter could compensate for missed maternal affection by establishing close relationships with mother substitutes, and the evidence suggests that this is precisely what he did. He was deeply attached to his nannies, for example, particularly Rachel Clark. He maintained a warm lifelong relationship with her and later described her as "a special person in my life."[102] In the first grade he was so smitten with his teacher, Eleanor Chambliss (later Eleanor Forrest), that he offered to give her his mother's diamond ring. That it was his mother's ring suggests that Carter was also rebelling against his distant mother, whom he wanted to replace.[103] Later, in his inaugural address, Carter singled out Julia Coleman, the Plains High School principal and English teacher, for special praise. Although others shared Carter's affection for this spinster who devoted her life to the children of the area, Carter was among those especially enamored of her. He also regularly spent one or two nights a week with his grandmother Carter, usually sleeping in the same bed.[104] Not least, he was perhaps able to bridge the distance between him and his mother by adopting many of her values and developing fondness for her father and brother, Jim Jack and Tom Watson Gordy. (That these alliances served him well in his rebellion against his father could not have been inconsequential, either.) With respect to maternal affection, then, Carter seems to have found it easier to compensate than he did with respect to excessive paternal demands.[105]

Jimmy Carter's marriage to Rosalynn Smith on July 7, 1946 — when he was just twenty-one and she eighteen — also appears to have had elements of maternal compensation. Carter dated only casually in high school and college. One girl dated him until he was twenty-one when she — not he — ended the relationship. Another dated him off and on while he was home on breaks from the naval academy.[106] But Rosalynn, remembered a classmate, "was the first serious girl and that was in Jimmy's navy career."[107] In fact, Jimmy became "serious" with Rosalynn after their first date, which took place over Christmas break in 1945–46. Deciding immediately that he wanted to marry her, through letters he convinced her to agree in time for a ceremony the following summer. Why Rosalynn attracted him so deeply and immediately may have elements of maternal compensation.

Rosalynn Smith was Ruth Carter's best friend. No stranger to the Carter household, she had been a frequent visitor since she was thirteen, when her father, Edgar Smith, died. Earl Carter welcomed her into his home to ease her family through the tragedy. (He also sent money to the bereaved widow.) And, although it is not necessarily unusual for a boy to find himself suddenly infatuated with a friend of his sister who had been around unnoticed for a long time, if he were seeking a mother surrogate there was no more ideal candidate than the best friend of Earl Carter's favorite daughter. Rosalynn, after all, came as close as any woman could to the kind of woman his father might love, for his father showered affection on her. The possibility that such motives prompted Carter's sudden infatuation and speedy marriage to Rosalynn Smith cannot be overlooked.

And, as if to symbolize just this linkage between his need for his mother and his love for his new bride, Carter defied tradition and allowed both Rosalynn and his mother to pin his insignia on him at the U.S. Naval Academy's graduation ceremonies. Customarily, the honor was reserved for only one loving female.[108] Later, though both denied it, there was some suspicion that Lillian Carter did not approve of Rosalynn, and many whispered that the two women developed a rivalrous dislike for one another.[109]

If a psychological scenario of this sort helps to explain Jimmy Carter's marriage to Rosalynn Smith, the ploy was successful. The marriage blossomed into a lifelong friendship that Carter admitted was so good that he could barely understand why others did not find similar satisfaction.[110] Despite the occasional "lust in his heart" (which at least Zbigniew Brzezinski reveals extended to not a few neck-craning episodes when the president and national security advisor spied sexy women), Rosalynn seemed to diminish in him any concerns about connecting well to women.[111]

Henceforth he could bear the burden of his distant mother and even grow into a mature and loving relationship with her.

Compensating successfully for feelings of rejection by his mother, Carter was also able to enlist her aid in his struggle with his father. He embraced her values over his and used her as an ally in his contest with his father. Indeed, insofar as Earl and Lillian Carter experienced marital tensions, Jimmy Carter threw his weight on the side of his mother. Doing so did not forge his character to the same degree that his relationship with his father did, but it provided him with a set of alternative values to embrace when he rebelled against his father.

A SUMMARY PARABLE

As governor and later as a candidate for the presidency, Carter at least twice related an incident from his childhood that he considered meaningful.[112] The incident is of an occasion when his mother had baked cookies. "Honey," Jimmy remembered his mother calling, "would you like some cookies?" But Carter remembered hesitating. He had just returned from the railroad bed where he had picked up handfuls of pebbles to be used as ammunition for his slingshot. To accept the cookies, he explained, meant having to drop the pebbles. He remembered an agonizing "15 or 20 seconds" of not knowing whether to accept the cookies and drop the pebbles or reject the cookies and keep the pebbles.

Both times this story was recorded Carter interpreted it as a parable of his native state. The cookies, he said, represent the goals of racial integration and social justice, while the pebbles represent segregation and injustice. His stated interpretation was to consider himself foolish for wanting to hold onto the pebbles he called "worthless" rather than accepting the cookies — and to consider white Georgians similarly foolish for wanting to hold onto racial segregation.

Yet, on the face of it, the story is a poor vehicle for conveying this lesson. It is not clear why holding onto the pebbles (which suggest initiative and forethought) is bad, or why cookies (which lead only to temporary satiation) are good. Nor do the associations between pebbles and segregation or cookies and integration fit well. Not least, the listener or reader is just not gripped by the dilemma Carter implies. Why not just drop the pebbles, eat the cookies, and then pick up the pebbles again? Without Carter's forced interpretation, those hearing the story are at a loss to explain its meaning or understand its drama.

Chances are that Carter, who was not an especially gifted writer or public speaker, just cobbled together the best story he could and did not do a very good job of it.[113] But for a man who would eventually write almost a dozen books and who cited *War and Peace* and diagrammed the poems of Dylan Thomas, this explanation lets him off the literary hook too easily. For if Carter was not blessed with literary gifts, neither was he so awful as to have failed to notice that his story fitted his interpretation poorly. The conjecture arises, therefore, that the story was not merely ill chosen by someone who did not know better. Chances are stronger that it conveyed a personal dilemma for Carter that, in its cryptic expression, others miss.

The most obvious interpretation of this story is that it is Carter's metaphor for his rebellion against his father. He does not say so in this story, but elsewhere he relates that his father had made him the slingshot and used it to teach him to hunt.[114] Nor does he say that a plate of cookies baked by his mother, who rarely cooked, was a special occurrence. Add that Carter's own interpretation of the story linked the pebbles with racism and injustice, while the cookies were linked with racial equality and justice, and the biographical meaning is plain: His own commitment to racial equality and social justice occurred when he rebelled against his father and adopted his mother's values.

Yet this meaning of the story does not quite complete its biographical interpretation. Still missing is an understanding of the dilemma Carter intended the story to convey. The movement from pebbles/father/injustice to cookies/mother/justice is accounted for, but not the dilemma of choice prior to this movement. For again, the reader or listener does not experience the movement as a dilemma, because the better choice is obvious. The dilemma must therefore spring from something in Carter's own life that he imputes to the story.

The dilemma arises plainly from the fact that the man who claimed to have rejected his father's ways and embraced his mother's values was also a governor and presidential candidate. Certainly he had not completely foregone pebbles of initiative for cookies of justice in his life. As a matter of assent to moral principles, Carter had indeed chosen his mother's way. But he had arrived at that position only in rebellion against his father. If "he thought more like his mother," intimates who said so were nevertheless "not sure" whether his mother or father exerted the stronger influence over him.[115] His values were his mother's, but his character was his father's. The personal dilemma in this otherwise flat story is therefore the dilemma of his own mature personality. Two very different and sometimes antagonistic parents, each with a strong personality, raised him. In some combination of rejection and embrace of both he found his swirling moral center.

Nor should the occasion pass without noting the emphasis that Carter places on his paralysis in the story. Many times, particularly when he was president, Carter would be accused of being indecisive and otherwise weak as a leader. Among his strengths was surely his ability to empathize with multiple viewpoints, and perhaps even to embrace contradictory ones in different modes of his self. Among his weaknesses was being unable to commit decisively to a singular course of action or to display a certain self — unless, of course, that certainty hinged upon the moral universalism that alone infused them all.

Carter's parable of the cookies and pebbles summarizes perhaps better than any other vignette the dual influence his parents exerted on him. Yet parental influences, as important as they are, are only part of the forces that shape mature identities. Especially when a child is immersed in an isolated milieu, other forces are also influential.

BLACK ARCHERY AND THE SEARCH FOR COMMUNITY

When Jimmy Carter entered the first grade at the Plains grammar school he thrust forward his right hand for a handshake and said to his future classmates, "Hello, I'm Jimmy Carter." Jimmy's cousin Hugh Carter, who reported this incident, did so because of the foretaste it provides of the future politician.[116] So often did the adult Carter introduce himself to the world this way that it became perhaps his most well known line. Fittingly, he opened his acceptance speech at the 1976 Democratic Convention with it to good-natured laughter, and used it subsequently in speeches to similar effect.[117]

But the classroom introduction reflects more than the budding politician. It also suggests a certain formality, perhaps a product of good training and perhaps masking shyness, that is nevertheless uncharacteristic of children. Few children resort to formal handshakes and announcements when introducing themselves to other children. But more important, the introduction reveals something that is often overlooked in Carter's story: He was not already acquainted with his classmates; he had to introduce himself.

Carter is generally thought to have grown up in Plains. This view, as has been shown, is mistaken. Although he was born there, visited frequently, and attempted to settle in Plains for a decade or more during his middle years, he was never fully a part of Plains society. His childhood home was rather the outlying farm near Archery, two and one-half miles west of Plains. Carter himself has written, "During my childhood I never considered myself a part of the Plains society, but always thought of myself as a visitor when I entered that 'metropolitan' community."[118] When he enrolled in the first grade in Plains, then, he was a stranger. Nor did his seven months a year of schooling or periodic visits to town enable him to meld comfortably into "Plains society." His sister Ruth recalled that "we rarely went into town,"[119] and no one remembered his making close friends with anyone in Plains. "I hate to say," confided a neighbor, but "he didn't have too many friends."[120] Part of the reason for this was surely personal. "Jimmy was a selfish boy," explained his nanny. "He liked to be with himself. That's the way he was."[121] Or, as a classmate more politely described his disposition: "Jimmy was a bookworm. He played basketball, but not very well. . . . He spent most of his time trying to get a good education."[122] But part of it, too, was a consequence of his living on a farm outside of Plains. "The country people were not as close as the kids who lived in Plains," recalled classmates.[123] Another, who became one of Carter's closest friends in school, began his interview by explaining: "I was a city boy. I guess Jimmy lived two and a half or three miles outside town." They did not see each other "too often" or have "too much social activity" together, because farm boys "had to go home and do a lot of work."[124] Reflecting this town-and-country division, Rosalynn Carter remembered that "Jimmy always teased [her] about being a city girl because he lived out in the country 2-1/2 miles."[125]

Carter never melded into the Plains milieu. As soon as he was able to, he left Sumter County for a naval career. Returning in late 1953 (just before the Supreme Court *Brown* decision), he refused to join the white Citizens' Council. As a result, his business was boycotted and he was ostracized by the community. Nearly a decade later, after tensions had subsided and he had earned some community respect through volunteer service on a variety of local boards, he nevertheless barely won a 1962 election to the Georgia state senate. Despite his family's prominence, and in sharp contrast to the easy victory his father had won ten years earlier, Carter had to claw his way into positions of leadership that had been his father's for the asking. By the 1963 legislative session he was living part of the year in an Atlanta hotel and generally stayed through the Friday sessions that most of his colleagues skipped. About this time an acquaintance remembered that "Jimmy really didn't show interest in the place" and was overheard saying that "he'd outgrown Plains."[126] Then, from his first 1966 run for governor through his campaign travels for the 1970 race and his tenures in Atlanta (1971–75) and Washington (1977–81), Carter was less frequently in Plains than elsewhere. Indeed, after the presidency Carter was more likely to stay in his Atlanta apartment or his north Georgia cabin than in Plains. "We're home so seldom now," commented Rosalynn Carter in 1988 while showing an interviewer around Plains.[127]

The notion of Carter hailing from Plains was a purposely created myth. In one of the first presidential campaigns to appeal to "values," Carter campaign strategists decided to celebrate the value of community. Nominally headquartered in Plains, the campaign was actually run out of its larger Atlanta office, particularly after the primaries. The Plains headquarters (in a railroad depot) was "totally inadequate" for serving as anything more than a "national symbol . . . and a rallying point" for the campaign, according to one of its principal organizers.[128] Carter agreed. "Symbolically and visibly it represented the essence of a small town."[129] The symbol, moreover, was a potent one. According to an aide who handled some of the Carters' correspondence, people "would write and pour their hearts out" because coming "from a small town" and becoming president "reinforced the idea that this is the American dream."[130] A Florida State professor of religion wrote in 1977 that "Plains, Georgia, is now duly consecrated as the most recent entry in the American civil religion's list of sacred places."[131] But, as with many symbols, reality was sharply different.[132]

Summarizing the real influence of Plains on Jimmy Carter, nanny Rachel Clark observed: "Oh, the town didn't produce him. He was himself and that was it."[133] Carter agreed. Asked by a National Park Service historian what aspects of his childhood community he thought should be preserved, Carter said:

> You know, for someone to be born in a house and then live there 'til he's 4 years old and then move away to a different home or to a different community I think would leave that birthplace as relatively insignificant except as a curiosity. . . . I don't think that would be nearly as significant as a place where the President's own attitudes and priorities in life, moral standards or work habits were shaped.[134]

Plains, in other words, was a "curiosity" — symbolically important but not the place where Carter's "attitudes and priorities in life, moral standards or work habits were shaped." That place was Archery.

Outside of his immediate family, then, Jimmy Carter was the product of Archery's African American world. All of his playmates were, accordingly, black. The chance constellation of the settlement and the Carter household made this experience even more pronounced. Carter's nearest siblings were girls, two and four years younger than he, and Billy was a dozen years his junior. The Watsons, the other white Archery family, had children much older than he. If Jimmy Carter was to play with other boys, then he would have to play with blacks. And he did. His mother recalled, "He had all black friends. . . . There was no white child within miles of our house."[135]

Despite Earl Carter's practice of arranging these friendships, at least one of the friendships appears to have been genuine. Jimmy Carter baffled critics during his 1976 campaign by recalling that his black childhood friend, A. D. Davis, had fourteen children. Suspecting that they had caught the candidate in an embellishment of his friendship for political gain, critics pointed out that Davis had only eleven children. Davis cleared up the confusion, however, when he pointed out that Carter was counting the two children who had died and the one he had sired out of wedlock.[136] Carter had indeed kept up with his childhood friend. Although life took them in different directions — Jimmy to naval, business, and political careers; A.D. to prison for manslaughter and then release to labor at a sawmill — the friendship appears to have been genuine.

By contrast, Carter mentioned only one white friend from his childhood in his campaign autobiography, Rembert Forrest. Others have supplied the names of a few additional white acquaintances, but intimates like his nanny mention only Rembert Forrest and his cousin Willard Slappey as his white friends, and even them as only infrequent visitors. "They'd come out to see him," remembered Rachel Clark, "but he never was so much for going to see the other fellows. . . . He wasn't very close to nobody."[137] In family recollections neither Forrest nor any other white friend appears significant; all, however, remembered Davis. Carter himself said that Forrest lived a full five miles away from him and was only an occasional playmate, and Hugh Carter recalled that Lillian Carter actually had to force Jimmy to play with him because the boy's mother had died, he himself was ill, and Lillian thought he needed a friend.[138] Similarly, although Carter's cousin Hugh Carter wrote a colorful book about their childhood escapades, the two were not very close. Hugh Carter was four years older than Jimmy and lived in Plains; the cousins mostly teamed up for their Saturday street-corner sales. (Later, when the adult Jimmy Carter moved to Plains, the cousins took opposite sides in local political battles.) Asked whether Hugh was "around a lot," a neighbor said "no."[139]

But along with black playmates, Carter was surrounded in youth by black domestic help. With their father almost always gone and their mother frequently gone, the Carter children were raised by black nannies. Indeed, since this help was cheap (nannies were paid a dollar a week), Earl and Lillian Carter generally retained their services even when they were home. The black cook arrived before the family woke up, in time to fix their breakfast, and on chilly mornings a black handyman built fires in the stove and fireplaces before morning so the family could wake to a warm house.[140] All recognized the subtle racial etiquette of the period that forbade black visitors from approaching the front door of whites' homes but allowed black domestics to come and go through any door at any time of the day or night to perform their services for the family. The result was not only a household in which children were frequently in the sole care of blacks but also one in which black domestic help moved throughout the house regularly and at all hours.

In other ways, too, Jimmy Carter was immersed in an African American world. If he was spared the roughest of the farm work, he often worked side by side with the field hands, or at least fetched water for them at thirsty intervals. Sometimes the black men would even take him on an all-night raccoon hunt — game hunted by blacks but not by whites in his youth. Mentioned already was his taking a high school date to a black church service and his recollection of Rachel Clark having been his main fishing instructor.[141] He also regularly accompanied his mother to the funerals of neighboring blacks, which his father refused to attend. Their stories and songs, outlook and dialect, were absorbed by this precocious boy who knew little of any other social world.

Carter also grew up to realize that, while his father was the economic and political head of the tiny settlement, he was by no means its cultural leader. That mantle fell to Bishop William Johnson — the sometime visitor to his maternal grandfather, Jim Jack Gordy. Johnson was the regional bishop for the African Methodist Episcopal Church, pastor of Archery's AME congregation, insurance company owner, and head of a small "industrial college" for blacks located in Archery. Blacks came from hundreds of miles to study with this man, who was probably the most learned man in the settlement. Bishop Johnson was also one of the more financially comfortable of Archery's citizens. His two-story house was larger than the Carters', and, while Earl Carter managed to buy a new Oldsmobile regularly, Bishop Johnson employed a driver for his car. The bishop even maintained his dignity in the white-dominated world. When business dealings brought him to the Carter home, instead of bowing to custom and knocking at the back door or flouting it by approaching the front, Bishop Johnson would send his driver to the back door to announce his presence and ask Mr. Carter to speak to him in the yard. There the two would converse, preserving the dignity of each within the strictures of racial etiquette of the time.

Jimmy Carter plainly remembered Bishop Johnson as "the most prestigious person in the community." Embellishing this recollection is Carter's memory of the bishop's funeral in 1936. Carter remembered it as "the most important event which ever occurred in Archery" and reported that he had been "amazed at the stream of big black Cadillacs, Packards, and Lincolns which had come from other states" to pay their respects to this eminent man.[142] Although Carter "worshipped" his father and enjoyed considerable affluence as a result of his father's expanding farms and businesses, on different occasions his Archery childhood taught him that his father was not the important man he usually took him to be. In the black community in which he was raised, in fact, Earl Carter was just another rich white man — and an outsider.

Jimmy Carter periodically caught other glimpses of the African American life that surrounded him in boyhood. One such occasion was the famous 1938 Joe Louis/Max Schmeling fight. Joe Louis had become a symbol of black pride; Max Schmeling, the Aryan, of that racial doctrine. Gathered around the yard of the Carter house where Earl Carter had allowed neighboring blacks to listen to the fight on one of his radios (few of Archery's blacks could afford a radio), Louis's knockout punch was delivered quickly, in the first round. Knowing that the Carter patriarch favored the white Schmeling, the field hands deferentially thanked "Mr. Earl" for allowing them to hear the fight and then went quietly on their way. Before they were out of earshot, however, their cheers rang out. Their spontaneous revelry left Jimmy Carter with a lasting impression of black pride.[143]

So immersed were the Carter children in southern African American life and culture that they grew up "bilingual" — speaking both black and white southern dialects. The speech patterns of the rural blacks were so different from those of the whites that it took special skill to converse in both. Because Jimmy had lived in Plains during his earliest years he did not have the same problem his younger sister Gloria had. By school age she embarrassed him by speaking only the black dialect and learning the white dialect only with considerable difficulty. Jimmy simply grew up knowing both.[144]

Given his childhood in an African American community, his severance from the white society of Plains, and his emerging racial liberalism, it is tempting to derive from Carter's Archery childhood only a richer appreciation of the grounds for his later commitment to racial equality. This conclusion would be only partially accurate. True, when Carter embraced the cause of civil rights in his native region, he could do so on the basis of personal acquaintance with the African Americans who had suffered without such rights. Yet it is naive to believe that because Jimmy Carter was raised among blacks he grew up to empathize with their plight. Generations of southern whites were raised in intimacy with blacks and did not grow up to question the caste system that kept them superior and blacks inferior. Like them, remembered a black tenant who knew Jimmy Carter well in childhood, when "he growed up to be teenagers, I didn't see him too much. But when he was growing, you know, up into boy-manhood, we separated."[145] Explained one white classmate: "Now, it's not friends in the same sense that he and I were friends, social. But we played with them, you'd normally play as you got to about fifteen, their social life and your social life was different."[146] Prejudice, discrimination, and apartheid were thus maintained in spite of closeness in childhood.

Worse, Jimmy Carter was raised to accept the caste system of his region — and admitted that he unthinkingly did. He never questioned the basis for his repeated victories over his friend A. D. Davis or the legitimacy of the different careers the two would follow. Nor did he give thought to school segregation, even as he was bused to his white school while his black playmates trudged on foot to their black school. He admitted that it was not until he was on the school board during his thirties that he ever realized the extent of inequality that existed between the black and white schools of his home county.[147] If his father encouraged blacks to send their children to primary school, the only person who signed the release for her interview at the Jimmy Carter Presidential Library with an X was Rachel Clark; she could not sign her own name. Or, when Jimmy and his friends decided to ride some of his father's horses, it did not seem to occur to him that his father "always had some tenants there that would catch them, of course, and put on a bridle." This was just one of many marks of his caste privilege and their caste servitude.[148] Indeed, by the time he was in high school, Jimmy Carter was by his own admission a white landlord to black tenants. In countless other more subtle ways, too, he absorbed the endless evidence of racial inequality — the deferential "Mr." and "Miss" (or "Miz") blacks used to address whites, for example, versus the, at best, "Aunt" and "Uncle" whites used to address blacks. And his embarrassment at his sister's African American dialect revealed how deeply entrenched his sense of racial superiority had become by the third grade. By all outward indications, Jimmy Carter was raised to accept the apartheid system of his region without question.

Conversely, it is difficult to imagine Archery's blacks welcoming Jimmy Carter fully into their midst, and there is no evidence that they did. As warm and intimate as relations were between the two races in Archery, the relations still crossed caste boundaries. The subordinate caste could simply not risk too great a familiarity with the ruling caste. Jimmy Carter — soon to be "Mr. Jimmy" — could not have been completely trusted. And Carter revealed this distance from his black neighbors in his memories of both Bishop Johnson's funeral and the Louis/Schmeling fight. In both instances Carter was surprised to learn of the extent of black prominence or pride. He was fully acquainted with neither. As a white living in an African American community, he could still never really be a member of that community.

When Jimmy Carter bypassed Plains society for the U.S. Navy, and then rejected his father's racism, he paid a price few pay willingly. That price was to ensure that he would never enjoy the experience of community. Black Archery — not white Plains — was his boyhood home. As the son of the white planter in Archery, however, Carter could never be fully accepted by that community. But when he escaped into the navy and then rejected the racial views of his father and of the white community, he ensured that he would not be fully accepted by the white community, either.

Perhaps the chief irony in Jimmy Carter's story is that, as presidential candidate and as president, he symbolized for so many the values of community. Plains itself was overrun by tourists seeking to glimpse the roots of a candidate they took to be representative of a mythical time when America was comprised of communities and the values that attend them. But Carter himself never experienced that mythical community. And if his childhood left him — as most psychobiographers claimed — emotionally impoverished, that impoverishment was as much social as psychological. Humankind's most basic need — to belong to a community of others — was denied him. As a result, Jimmy Carter never developed the kind of unified self that grows naturally from a community that sustains it. Instead, his selves were many and fragmented, like the fractured communities that formed them.

The boy who extended his hand to first-grade classmates and said, "Hello, I'm Jimmy Carter," concluded his high-school career similarly. One of four graduates selected to deliver a speech during graduation ceremonies, Carter's was entitled "The Building of a Community."[149] In the handshakes and the speech is nestled his lifelong quest. His greatest achievements would be to build bridges of reconciliation in the torn communities of black and white, Arab and Jew, China and the United States, and in countless Third World nations around the globe. The quest was also the cornerstone of his "very clear ideas about human rights." For "the essence of diplomacy, of negotiation," he remarked in 1984, "is to recognize that your adversaries are human beings."[150] That recognition, however, and the communities that spring from it, was precisely what was wanting in his childhood home and region. Its absence prompted the central moral imperative of his character and career.

THE QUEST FOR LEADERSHIP

Lillian Carter vividly remembered how she and her husband re-acted on the summer Saturday in 1943 when Jimmy left for Annapolis.[1] After saying good-bye to their son when his train departed just before noon, the couple rode the nine miles from the Americus train station to Archery in silence. As soon as they arrived home, Lillian got out of that car, went straight to her car, and drove to her pond house, where she spent the rest of the afternoon alone, fishing and crying. Earl sped away in the opposite direction, to a friend's pond, and spent the rest of his afternoon fishing and drinking. Both parents grieved and both parents fished; but they could not do so together. Nor did either bother to visit with their other children, who were left in the care of a nanny.

Had Jimmy Carter known how his parents reacted to his departure, he might have had earlier and more serious reservations about his hoped-for career in the navy. For in the estranged relationship of his parents was the kernel of the moral challenge that, left to simmer for a decade, would ultimately pull him back home. This challenge — how to unite different and sometimes antagonistic people — found few parallels in the low and middle ranks of the navy where Carter found himself. Yet southwest Georgia offered ample instances of this challenge, one of which was the icy relationship of his own parents.

But another instance of the moral challenge that would come to define Carter's career arose from the strange legacy of his uncle, Tom Watson Gordy. So often did Carter tell the story of this uncle who had inspired his naval career that his uncle's influence over him cannot be disputed.[2] Yet the story of Tom Gordy was not a usual one or, as it turned out, the story Carter thought it was in 1943. Had he known the real story in 1943, he might have questioned his naval career earlier than he did.

Stationed in Guam during 1941, Tom Gordy was reported missing in action soon after the outbreak of hostilities. Informed of his disappearance, Gordy's wife, Dorothy, and their children moved from San Francisco to southwest Georgia in order to be near the Carters and the Gordys during those uncertain times. Not long afterward, however, certainty arrived in the form of Red Cross notification that Gordy was dead. There being no further justification for remaining in Georgia, Dorothy returned to San Francisco and, after an appropriate interval, remarried.

Carter began his naval career with the understanding that the uncle who had inspired it had paid the ultimate price for his service. If this understanding helped personalize the diffuse apprehensions about the war which were then widespread among Carter's classmates,[3] it did so in a predictable manner. Gordy, who had opted for a sailor's life, had paid the price exacted by that life. If unfortunate or even tragic, his was a soldier's and perhaps even a hero's fate not unlike that suffered by tens of thousands of others at the time.

But at war's end Carter and his family learned that Gordy's fate had not been what they had assumed. Gordy, it turned out, had not been killed but had been interned in a Japanese prison camp for the duration of the war. The revelation of Gordy's survival, however, could hardly be received cheerfully by the family. For not only was Gordy himself in horrible shape — he weighed less than 100 pounds, railed incessantly against the "dirty Japs," and had to be hospitalized for both physical and mental rehabilitation — but he also returned to learn of his wife's remarriage. Although Dorothy offered to have her new marriage annulled, Gordy declined. Still, he could not help but succumb to a depression that concluded, with some justification, with the feeling that it would have been better if he had died.

The anguish of Gordy's fate reverberated throughout the family for a long time and became a staple in family lore. Yet little moral sense could be made of the story. Carter remembered that most family members leaped to the easy moral conclusion, which blamed Dorothy for remarrying, but that he considered this judgment too harsh. Certainly, thought Carter, Dorothy could not be held responsible for remarrying, when authorities had reported her husband dead. Yet, if Carter could not join others in blaming Dorothy, whom could he blame? The truth is that he could blame no one — and so the story of the uncle who inspired his naval career became a kind of paradoxical parable of the collapse of family and community for which no one was individually responsible. Overlying the experience of his own disengaged family and racially divided community, the story of Tom Gordy ultimately inspired his career in a way that he could not anticipate when he bid his rural home good-bye at the Americus train station on June 26, 1943.

But in the summer of 1943, the not quite nineteen-year-old Jimmy Carter evidenced scant appreciation for the moral challenges that would draw him back to southwest Georgia. At the time his youthful hopes were pinned on a different future in a different place. Perhaps, to the extent to which he sensed the challenges of his childhood and home, they even intensified his desire to leave. The son of Earl Carter may have wanted the opportunity to prove himself independent of his family and his father. For a southern boy with much to prove, there was no surer route to independence and stature than a military career by way of an academy education. And Carter had already languished a year at Georgia Southwestern Junior College in Americus and another at the Georgia Institute of Technology in Atlanta while waiting for an appointment to the academy. He was therefore eager to get on with the future he dimly imagined. So, as the train snaked its way up the eastern seaboard, Jim Carter (as he would insist on being known during his naval career) recorded in his diary that he was "nervous and excited."[4]

THE EDUCATION OF A LONG-DISTANCE RUNNER

The nervousness Carter felt en route to Annapolis is puzzling. For it was not diffuse but specific, and it centered on concerns that had little basis in reality. He was worried, he plainly confided to his diary, about passing his physical examination. With the test scheduled for the first day of arrival, Carter feared that he would fail this final requirement for academy admission.[5]

The worry was without objective basis, for Carter was in near-perfect health. He had long before developed the habit of exercise that, combined with a hardy constitution, led to good health. In addition to his active life on the farm, he elected to play basketball and run track for his required extracurricular athletic activity in high school. Although the 1941–42 year he spent commuting to classes at Georgia Southwestern seemed an exception, his next year at Georgia Tech continued the tradition of mandated exercise as part of his formal schooling. With classes scheduled to begin by 8:00 six mornings a week (including Saturdays), Georgia Tech's all-male student body was awakened by 6:00 A.M. for mandatory before-breakfast calisthenics. Physical training was then interspersed throughout a day that included morning classes and afternoon labs, with "lights out" by 10:00 P.M. Tech's physical education program even required "survival swimming" — which amounted to throwing students into a pool with hands and legs tied.[6] By the time Carter enrolled in the academy, he was in top physical condition; he had to be. And, during his first year at the academy, he thoroughly impressed his cross-country coach and helped lead the team to an undefeated 1943 season.

Carter's habit of strenuous physical activity might even be considered excessive. Twice during childhood, rough play led to broken bones. Although perhaps not unusual for an athletic farm boy, the accidents attest to an occasional willingness to take ill-advised risks in physical activities. (These two incidents of broken bones were in addition to the time the school bus ran over both his feet.) Later, as an adult living in Plains, Carter performed regular physical labor while managing his businesses, yet still made time for softball games, hunting trips, fishing expeditions, square dancing, and other similarly demanding avocations. During this same period he also adopted the practice of taking catnaps at his warehouse during busy seasons so that he could work as close to twenty-four hours a day as possible. When, following his first campaign for elective office in 1962, he slept for twenty-four consecutive hours after thoroughly exhausting himself and dropping eleven pounds from his already slight frame over a two-week period, he simply showed that he had applied his willingness to push himself to, if not beyond, his physical limits to political campaigning.[7] Later, his penchant for exercise seemed to border on addiction. Engrossed in difficult negotiations in 1978, for example, he reported that he "craved intense exercise."[8] And at least once, as president, the lifelong jogger collapsed in exhaustion in the midst of a run. He was not ill; he had just demanded too much of himself. Throughout his life Carter maintained an active program of physical exercise and near-perfect physical health; throughout it he also displayed the tendency to push himself too far — to stretch or even exceed his ample limits.

If the results of Carter's lifelong penchant for physical exercise were to produce what an interviewer later described as "one of the healthiest looking 65-year-olds I've seen"[9] — and much earlier resulted in his easily passing the physical examination required for academy admission — the motivation for physical fitness appears not to have been so narrow. For in his diary at Annapolis and in his excesses throughout life, Carter showed doubt about his physical condition. His penchant for exercise and willingness to push himself to the point of injury and exhaustion suggests an underlying fear of physical inadequacy. Yet, since any physical inadequacies he possessed were perceived, not real, Carter's apprehensions about his physical condition must have functioned as a metaphor for some other, more diffuse doubts about his character and abilities. Finding the real basis for these doubts promises to unlock the secret motivation of Jim Carter in the navy — and to go a long way in explaining the steely determination apparent in the more mature Jimmy Carter.

One thing is certain: Any doubts Carter had about his abilities — at eighteen or throughout his life — did not attach themselves to his intellectual competence. Although some who enrolled in the academy had reason to worry about its academic rigors, Carter did not. He never showed any signs of concern over his academic abilities, and never was there reason for concern. Indeed, at every school he attended Carter always stood near the top academically. Even the fact that he never ranked number one in his classes — but always fell just below it — may not indicate that he was not the brightest. Instead it may indicate that he preferred to minimize his academic prowess by purposely slipping out of first place in order to avoid being stigmatized by his peers.

At Plains High School, for example, Carter may have missed being named valedictorian of his admittedly tiny class on purpose. Some of his classmates did say that Carter was just not the best student in the class, but Carter himself attributed his drop in rank to punishment meted out to him for playing hooky one day just before graduation. Hugh Carter further conjectured that Carter purposely gave up top honors so that the scholarship that went with them could be bestowed upon a less financially fortunate classmate.[10] While Hugh Carter's conjecture of magnanimity is farfetched, the suspicions of those in a position to know were often that Carter's failure to graduate as the valedictorian of his class was voluntary. Equally important, everyone remembered him as at least one of the best students in his class.

While the truth of Carter's high-school ranking is lost to memory, his records at Georgia Southwestern and Georgia Tech suggest strong ability. Remembered as a high-school "bookworm" who "naturally got good grades," he went on to impress a classmate at Georgia Southwestern as "extremely intelligent" and another as "extremely smart in chemistry."[11] While at Georgia Southwestern, Carter was also inducted into an honorary fraternity, IFT ("Ingenuity, Fidelity, and Trustworthiness") and merited a part-time job as a lab assistant in chemistry after his first college course. At Georgia Tech there is no direct testimonial evidence of Carter's performance, but there is evidence that the curriculum was rigorous. "The grading was very tough," recalled a classmate, who also remembered that in chemistry "every test except the final was a pop test." Then, as now, Georgia Tech also admitted only the most promising students (though then promising African Americans and women were excluded). Carter's roommate, for example, went on to become president of Lockheed of Georgia.[12] That Carter maintained a strong academic record there is evidenced by his admission to the naval academy the following year.

Carter's academic performance at the academy was also near stellar. Drawing on two years of college before the academy (some classmates had as much or more, though), a fellow student remembered that "he got good academic grades easily and naturally."[13] A roommate recalled that Carter "had an especially agile mind for math" and found the coursework so "easy" that he often used mandatory study time to do outside reading or listen to music.[14] But if math, like chemistry, came easily to him, his Spanish instructor at the academy was no less impressed with this "outstanding student" whose "progress was phenomenal."[15] Graduating in the top ten percent of his class of 822 with room to spare (Carter actually made the top eight percent), he did miss top honors. But since he performed well with apparent ease and even chose to forgo studying sometimes in order to read or listen to music, it is not implausible to suppose that he semiconsciously chose to miss top ranking in order to avoid the stigma that sometimes attaches itself to the academically gifted. Secure in his academic abilities, Carter felt no urge to perform better than near best.

Despite his obvious ability and strong performance, it might be mistaken to conclude that no criticisms of his intellectual accomplishments are valid. A criticism that has often circulated is that he never became an intellectual or fully appreciated the life of the mind. When he was denied a Rhodes scholarship in 1948 for which he was a finalist, for example, he did not appear to understand why an applicant who specialized in Elizabethan poetry was selected rather than him. To Carter, who specialized only in what he called "current events" (learned mostly by reading news magazines), an academic specialization in something like Elizabethan poetry was an unnecessary extravagance. When telling the story of the Rhodes scholarship competition later in life, he even appeared to mock his successful competitor and derive a certain satisfaction by adding that the person who received the scholarship later succumbed to mental illness. Too much should not, perhaps, be made out of this single incident. But the observation that despite his mental precocity Carter did not develop a full appreciation of the life of the mind probably stands.[16]

The fault — if it is one — may not have been Carter's. Despite his rigorous training, little of it promoted genuine intellectual activity. For example, Georgia Tech, which became a top academic college, was at the time Carter attended so oriented toward "fundamentals" that students "were taught to use their hands in wood shop, machine shop, smith shop, etc."[17] At the U.S. Naval Academy similar practical foci dominated the streamlined curriculum. (The formerly four-year curriculum was compressed into three during the war.) Except for required courses in English and history, as well as an elective foreign language, the entire course of studies was devoted to math and applied engineering. By the last year of the three-year program "every course was devoted to some aspect of naval engineering."[18] If this coursework was augmented by such mandatory activities as after-dinner speaking, it did not include academic corollaries, such as rhetoric. A formal education that mandated morning calisthenics, "shop," and after-dinner speaking may therefore have deprived Carter of much — even if it fitted his practical inclinations and goals at the time.

Despite these potential criticisms, by the standards of the education he did receive there was never a justification for Carter to doubt his academic ability. Explanation for his self-doubt — which he himself wrote centered on his physical rather than his mental fitness — must be found elsewhere.

The intellectually questionable curriculum at the academy was justifiable, however, in light of its objective: to graduate leaders. Academy graduates could also be intellectuals, but the objective of an academy education was to produce officers who could manipulate men, not ideas.

So, in addition to academics the academy curriculum included training and evaluation in leadership. The student body was divided into companies that mirrored the hierarchical authority structure of the navy and sought to foster experience in leadership. Companies of 100 to 150 men were formed with approximately equal numbers of members from each of the three classes, and within each company upperclassmen exercised authority over underclassmen. Faculty then evaluated students on their leadership abilities and assigned the most promising to different formal leadership positions in their company. Meanwhile, students chose their own informal leaders and were keenly aware of who they were.

"Carter did not score high in his leadership grades," remembered a classmate, who added that Carter "was viewed more as a follower than a leader."[19] The informal assessment, apparently, followed the formal one, for Carter was not even widely known, much less esteemed, outside of his own small company. "Few classmates outside our company were able to recall Carter," remembered a member of his company, and those who could were "amazed" when he became governor of Georgia and "positively astounded" when he became president.[20] Others admitted that Carter had made "no impression" on them or that they just "did not know him that well."[21]

Carter had not merited a genuine leadership role in his past, either. Although he served as class president in the ninth grade, he held no class office during the next two years (despite a class that numbered only two dozen students). Classmates at Southwestern likewise remembered Carter as serious, intelligent, and friendly — but not as a leader. And it was not because they had not chosen leaders. They *had* voted on class leaders (among those identified was Garland Byrd, one of the candidates who would oppose Carter in the 1966 gubernatorial race);[22] Carter was just not among them. Nor is there evidence of Carter displaying leadership at Georgia Tech. Few of his classmates and instructors even remembered the future president when asked about him some thirty years later.

Did Carter want to be a leader? The evidence suggests that he did. Not only is it safe to assume that any applicant to a military academy desires to become a leader, but there is also direct evidence of Carter's desire for leadership and his pain at being passed over. Bobby Logan, perhaps Carter's closest friend at Georgia Southwestern, remembered that he and Carter used to mock the college leaders. The mockery suggests envy, for Carter accused Southwestern's student leaders of lacking "high moral standards" and criticized them as "goody-goodies."[23] Since they could not be both, the criticisms probably reflected an underlying envy instead of real objections. More telling, the mockery reveals that on a junior-college campus of a couple hundred students to which he temporarily commuted for classes, Carter deemed the subject of class leadership important enough to mock.

And there is evidence from his years at the academy that Carter not only suffered from his inferior position but also retaliated against it when given the opportunity. The suffering took the form of hazing, of which Carter endured more than his share from upperclassmen.

Hazing usually took the form of either acceding to an upperclassman's demands — no matter how ridiculous — or suffering the punishments of a paddling, doing forty-seven push-ups (for the class of '47), "shoving out," or eating a "square meal." "Shoving out" entailed "sitting" at the dining hall table without a chair; having to eat a "square meal" meant that each forkful of food had to be made into a perfectly square shape before being eaten. Many times, particularly in the beginning, Carter was paddled, forced to do push-ups, to "shove out," or to eat a "square meal." So intricate were the rules and so outlandish the demands that a good underclassman met punishment daily; inept ones, more often. Carter endured the hazings with more than typical frequency. The smile he could not control (and which brought on more hazing) was only one reason.

Another reason was that Carter was a southerner. Southerners were routinely required in some way to embarrass themselves and their region. Many remember the occasion when Carter willingly endured additional hazing rather than betray his native region. Ordered by an upperclassman to sing "Marching through Georgia," Carter refused. The southerner and future governor of his state would simply not be forced to bring dishonor upon it. He would rather be, in effect, tortured. And he was.[24]

But Carter retaliated. Although his diary concludes after his first year and his classmates generally report that they did not perpetuate the traditions they had to endure, in a later interview Carter obliquely admitted to having perpetuated the hazing. Describing a part of a mule-drawn plow commonly used in his youth, he mentioned that as an upperclassman he used to ask underclassmen to identify the part and its usage. When they were unable to answer the impossible question, Carter presumably met the failure with the requisite hazing, whatever it might have been.[25] There is also evidence that Carter retaliated against his aggressors with relish during his first year. The opportunity came on the "100th night" celebration, a Halloween ritual in which the underclassmen and upperclassmen temporarily reversed positions. Carter's longest diary entry describes some of the more innocuous aspects of this celebration. A classmate reported as "hearsay" that Carter was "seen 'having a ball' paddling the posteriors of the more obnoxious members of '45 with an aluminum bread tray."[26] That the "hearsay" includes the instrument of aggression lends credibility to it. And in the opinion of his superiors, who gave him more demerits than most, Carter was not always pleasant and accommodating.

In his first year he ranked in the bottom half of his class in "conduct," suggesting some forms of frequent misbehavior.[27] Certainly, he endured much with control and restraint; but he also had impulses that he needed to control and restrain.

While Carter found a leadership position elusive, he may have suspected that there was a simple explanation for his failure. It was his stature. Still inches and pounds shy of a mature height (5'9") and weight (155 pounds) that were themselves smallish,[28] Carter simply could not "measure up" to the standards of the bigger, beefier males at the academy. And the standards mattered. The person who *was* Carter's high-school senior class president remembered Carter as "small for his age" and concluded, "[W]hen you're short, red-haired and freckled all you can do is grin."[29]

At the academy the situation was similar. Within his company, one classmate, Donald Whitmire, had earned a reputation for leadership largely by playing football. Outside his company, the most prominent of his classmates at the academy was Stansfield Turner, who had also earned his reputation on the football field. Indeed, Turner was "extremely prominent at the academy," even though he was judged to be "not as smart as Carter."[30] Then, perhaps, even more so than now, physical stature was a prerequisite for leadership. (The pattern also obtains in presidential politics, making Carter's victory over Gerald Ford in 1976 one of the rare occasions that the shorter candidate defeated the taller.) In the currency required for leadership, Carter was poor — and he knew it.

Carter's worry on his train ride to Annapolis about passing his physical examination — and then his lifetime of pressing his physical capacities to their limits — may therefore have arisen not so much from a concern with physical fitness as from a concern over physical size. Size and attendant prowess may have both represented and been the precondition for the mantle of leadership to which he aspired. Despite his intelligence, which he may have purposely deemphasized, and his other abilities, most notably his friendliness, Carter may have been denied his chief goal simply because he was small. Accordingly, he may have worried about — and resented — it.

☆   ☆   ☆

As in high school and at Georgia Tech, the academy required students to participate in extracurricular athletics. Carter chose, among other sports, cross-country. If not as prestigious as football, the sport suited Carter's size and, perhaps, his temperament. And the academy's cross-country coach, Captain Ellery Clark, may well have understood Carter's doubts and dreams — as well as his abilities — better than anyone.[31]

"Long-distance runners are a breed of their own," Clark said when recalling Carter. They are "generally thin, somewhat introverted, friendly as a group, dedicated to self-improvement, [and] intelligent." Clark substantiated the last point by showing that Carter's cross-country team stood on average in the top third of their class. (Carter's rank was the highest.) Observing that "a cross-country runner has great determination, stamina, and consistency," Clark added that "Mr. Carter is a fine example of all three." Indeed, Clark considered Carter "exceptionally interested in and dedicated to excellence" and noted that he was especially "adept at making good finishes, often nosing out a competitor or two near the finish line."

Clark's generalizations about cross-country runners may be overblown. But they do fit the facts here. Stansfield Turner — the football star and class leader for whom everyone expected great things — did go on to make admiral and ultimately to become director of the CIA. The surprise was not that Turner made it so far, but that he received his appointment from President Carter. Carter, although "somewhat introverted" and enduring much anonymity in his school years, clearly possessed "great determination" and was "adept at making good finishes." Indeed, after "nosing out" Gerald Ford in the presidential race, Carter sent Clark a note thanking him for his cross-country coaching. But in the mid-1940s the story was different. Far from the finish line, Carter languished in obscurity while others merited the accolades.

While the dominant theme in Carter's college years may have been his frustrated quest for leadership, symbolized by his stature, a deeper frustration lingered in the background. This was his inability to fit in, to make friends, and to enjoy the community and camaraderie of his social surroundings. Although Carter was generally regarded as friendly by those who knew him — and more than one incident shows him to have been keenly attuned to the values of community — he was also considered to be an outsider.

Out of more than 800 academy classmates (and over two dozen in his company) who experienced three years of fraternity-like camaraderie in relative isolation from the outside world, Carter made few, if any, genuinely close friends. After graduation he exchanged Christmas cards with several classmates and, still later, tapped two or three to help in his presidential campaign. But he named no one, and no one named him, a close friend. None could recall discussions with him about politics, religion, or anything else that might be construed as personal. One assumed that "he ran around mainly with southerners," but no southerner surfaced as a close friend.[32] Another simply could "not recall his closest friends" because "we had no close mutual friends."[33] Except for Rosalynn (whom one classmate incorrectly identified as his "high school sweetheart"), no one could remember the name of anyone he dated or even whether Carter was present at significant academy social functions. And, when he married immediately after graduation in the summer of 1946, none of his classmates is on record attending the ceremony or serving as "best man."

Perhaps Carter's frustrating quest for leadership prevented his forming close attachments with others whose friendship might not further his ambitions. Suggestive in this regard is that Carter may have been as close to Stansfield Turner as he was to anybody at the academy. Introduced by a classmate to classical music, Carter and Turner, together with one or two others, would sometimes listen together at a graduate student's apartment.[34] Carter could have opportunistically calculated that a friendship with Turner would boost his stature with others. But if his motives were these (and it is a harsh conjecture), they were frustrated. No one, including the principals, remembered Carter and Turner as being especially close. Carter was close to no one.

But remaining a loner at the academy did not mean that Carter was ostracized or especially unpopular there. To the extent to which he was known, in fact, he was liked. Classmates who did remember him later generally recalled him as pleasant, helpful, and possessing a friendly smile. No one reported disliking him. And one classmate, Albert Rusher, remembered an especially revealing positive experience with him. Rusher, who admitted to knowing Carter only superficially while at the academy (they became closer when stationed together in Virginia), nonetheless recalled how he came to be Carter's roommate. Rusher's previous roommate had committed suicide during their senior year by jumping to his death from a dormitory tower. After the death Carter suggested that Rusher move in with him and three others so he would not be alone. The move, said Rusher, was "Carter's idea" and he had to get special permission. By proposing it, Carter showed a sensitivity to the need for community that was, ironically, largely unmet in his own life.[35]

Another incident suggests the same sensitivity. On October 30, 1943, in a meet against Baltimore City College, eight academy runners, including Carter, tied for first place. "As sometimes happens in cross-country when one team dominates a race," explained Ellery Clark, "these eight Navy runners chose to finish in line abreast, as an indication of team unity and solidarity."[36]

These incidents hinted at the future that lay in store for Carter — as they also recalled his past. But at the time, they were just incidents. Jim Carter wanted nothing more than to become a leader, yet found his dreams eluding him. For he was just "a slim fellow, always having an alert bright smiling face," but not the sort of young man who stood out as a leader.[37] However, since he was also no one's trusted friend, he was especially fortunate to have convinced Rosalynn Smith to marry him immediately following graduation. He would, after all, ultimately achieve his goals of leadership. But except for Rosalynn, his would be a lonely quest.

WHY NOT THE BEST?

Carter never openly admitted to suffering from depression. Yet the psychiatrist who served in Carter's Georgia and Washington administrations, Peter Bourne, suspected that he regularly battled tendencies toward malaise. The doctor further surmised that Carter's habit of restless, relentless activity — most of it optimistically oriented toward self-improvement — was his chief defense against depression.[38] By keeping himself busy with activities that promised an improved self, Carter kept the demons of depression away. Occasionally, however, the demons surfaced. One such time was 1953, just before he resigned from the navy and moved to Plains.

The battle against depression may have been especially difficult during the first two years (1946–48) of his career as a commissioned officer. The problem was that there was little opportunity for self-improvement. Scaled back after the long war, the navy, Carter concluded, was "in bad shape." Worse, his service began with two years of mandatory sea duty, with assignments determined by lot. Carter fared poorly in the lottery and was assigned to the USS *Wyoming* at Norfolk, Virginia. The ship was so decrepit that it was quickly scrapped for a vessel in little better shape, the USS *Mississippi*. Both ships were known informally as the "Chesapeake Raiders," an epithet suggesting the limited scope of their activities. Carter, trying to look on the bright side, said that he found the work "interesting." But in the same sentence he frankly admitted that "the duty was terrible."

Indeed, his experience at Norfolk was so "discouraging" and "demoralizing" that, he admitted, had he not been an Annapolis graduate obligated to serve, he would have resigned immediately.[39]

Since he was at sea all week, as well as every third weekend, the newly wed Carters had little time to develop a satisfying marriage to offset the drudgery of the duty. Remembering herself to have been "the total wife and mother" during those years, Rosalynn described her life in terms of the then prevalent stereotype: "I washed and ironed, I cooked and cleaned, mopped floors. . . . I bought women's magazines and clipped recipes and household tips. . . . And I knitted argyle socks for my husband while I waited for him to come home on weekends." The stereotypical relationship, moreover, involved a strict demarcation between his and her activities. Rosalynn plainly recalled, for example, "[W]e had bought a new record player so Jimmy could listen to the collection of classical records he had accumulated" and "[W]e added a sewing machine for me." Listening to music was not yet a shared activity — and of course Jimmy did not sew. And, while Jimmy read widely, Rosalynn distinctly recalled devotedly studying her manual, *The Navy Wife*. Except for weekends (when Jimmy was not out to sea), the couple shared little with each other.[40]

It was not a happy time. When pregnant with their first son, John William Carter (called "Jack"), born in Norfolk on July 3, 1947, Rosalynn claimed that she was "miserable, sick not only in the morning, but afternoon and night as well." When Jack turned out to be the kind of baby who "slept little and cried a lot," Rosalynn "cried with him" out of "exhaustion and loneliness." Jimmy was kind and considerate, but he "had, and still has, no patience with tears, thinking that one makes the best of whatever situation — and with a smile."[41]

But Jimmy too was growing frustrated with his attempts to make the best of his assignment at Norfolk. It was his desperation for a new challenge that prompted his application for the Rhodes scholarship. When his application was denied, he took the rejection hard (and not with a smile). Years later a perceptive interviewer even observed that Carter linked the 1948 denial of his Rhodes scholarship with his defeat in the 1966 governor's race — an emotional connection that suggests the magnitude of the perceived failure in 1948.[42] And, since the one time Carter did admit to depression was following his 1966 defeat, it can be surmised that in 1948 he was losing the battle against depression.

But there may have been a more fortuitous juxtaposition of Carter's personal malaise and his later political career than that suggested by a link between depressive episodes. For 1948 was a dramatic year in politics. Underdog incumbent Harry Truman defeated Thomas Dewey in an upset presidential race — after the Dixiecrats had bolted from the Democratic party. Carter, an avid follower of current events, was captivated by the political drama. He was a staunch if somewhat solitary supporter of Harry Truman (most of his fellow officers were Republicans) who, throughout his life, regarded Truman as a model of presidential leadership. Perhaps the coincidence of Truman's surprisingly victorious presidential campaign in the same year that Carter languished in Norfolk and was turned down for a Rhodes scholarship inspired him to consider politics as a means to achieve the success that he had not yet found. If so, it was with apt biographical resonance that some twenty-eight years later he recalled Truman's famous 1948 gesture by holding the headline "UDALL WINS" high over his head when, in the wee hours of the morning, the Wisconsin primary barely went for him.[43]

But by the fall of 1948 circumstances were beginning to improve for Carter. The improvements arose as a consequence of two related developments. One was Carter's acceptance into the navy's submarine corps and the other was the beginning of his and Rosalynn's habit of mutual studying, which would soon define their marriage.

Although not as prestigious as a Rhodes scholarship, submarine duty was as challenging and elite a service as the scaled-back Navy offered. Most who applied for the duty were refused, and of those accepted only about three-quarters successfully completed the training. Correspondingly, success in the field was one of the few avenues the navy offered for rapid advancement. Carter's obvious ability and ambition were therefore finally acknowledged — and subsequently demonstrated — when he was accepted into the submarine force in the fall of 1948.

Carter found the service surprisingly satisfying. He later described it as "one of the most interesting and enjoyable periods of [his] life," a remark only partially heightened by his characteristic hyperbole and the requirements of an optimistic campaign autobiography.[44] Indeed, since he "never wanted to get too old to learn new things,"[45] submarine duty provided him with the intellectual and practical challenges that had been unavailable in Norfolk. Six months of classroom and practical training in New London, Connecticut — followed by assignments in Hawaii, San

Diego, and back to Connecticut — stretched Carter's abilities, yet never so far that he could not master the challenges. Since the assignments were prestigious and predicted to lead to advancement, Carter's restless quest for self-improvement leading to leadership also finally promised to be satisfied.

A serendipitous benefit arose in tandem with the submarine assignment. The transfer to New London allowed Carter to keep regular hours and to be home at night for the first time since his wedding. He and Rosalynn could therefore join others in the backyards at night for refreshments and cookouts, go to discounted base movies, visit the Officers' Club, or just talk. Rosalynn was "no longer lonely" as she and her husband began developing a relationship that soon transcended the era's stereotypes.[46]

Breaking the stereotypes occurred quite accidentally. A fellow officer who had been previously stationed in New London had ordered a home-study course in commercial art, which arrived by mistake at the Carters'. Instead of sending it back, however, the couple decided to take the course together. At the same time, another couple who were stationed in New London spoke Spanish as their first language. This gave Jimmy (whose progress in Spanish at the academy had been "phenomenal") and Rosalynn (who had taken two years of Spanish at Georgia Southwestern) the opportunity to practice their Spanish in conversation. These two shared pursuits — though lasting only the six months the couple was stationed in New London — provided the foundation for what would become an unusual marriage partnership. Likely born of Carter's penchant for activities promising self-improvement, the activities were readily shared by Rosalynn, and their marriage became characterized by mutual study. Even though the frequent and sometimes long separations resumed when the couple moved to Hawaii in 1949, the habit of studying together had by then become a firm bond in their marriage.

Meanwhile the Carters' marriage was cemented in a more traditional way. Their second son, James Earl Carter III (called "Chip"), was born in Hawaii in April of 1950; their third, Jeff Donnel, after they were transferred back to Connecticut in 1952. Although the couple, who wanted a daughter as well as three sons, were disappointed when physicians informed them that having another child would pose a severe health risk for Rosalynn, on balance their family life was rich and rewarding. Rosalynn was contented beyond expectations, and Jimmy, when he was transferred to Groton, Connecticut, for additional training, found the work — predictably — "intriguing."[47] He also qualified for command of his own submarine (but did not receive one, owing to lack of seniority) and was promoted on schedule to full lieutenant.

Yet the upturn in Carter's life between 1948 and 1952 was not without its unsettling undercurrents. Mainly, Carter's loneliness and search for community grew from a minor discomfort into a major if dimly perceived frustration. Secondarily, after the initial excitement of the new challenges had diminished, he began again to doubt his ability to become a leader.

Carter gave a surprising explanation for his enjoyment of submarine duty: "The crew and the officers lived in intimate contact with one another, depending upon the quality of each man and his knowledge of the ship to provide safety and effectiveness for us all."[48] Or again: "There was a closeness just among the men which I liked."[49] In other words, alongside the challenge and prestige of submarine duty, Carter also relished the community that necessarily developed in the self-contained undersea ship.

Despite this stated reason for enjoying submarine duty, the striking thing is how incapable Carter was of participating openly in that enclosed social world. When he was stationed in Hawaii and assigned to his first submarine, the USS *Pomfret*, for instance, he spent the winter of 1949 in a long Pacific voyage along the China coast. Yet even during that long voyage Carter failed to form close attachments with fellow crew members. As he had at the academy, Carter earned the respect and good will of his peers — but not their friendship. One recalled that Carter was "bright," "very capable," and willing to take "extra effort" (evidenced by his voluntarily tutoring shipmates). But the *Pomfret*'s engineer and communications officer also remembered that Carter "remained very reserved about many of his beliefs."[50] Another, who observed that the officers were "a tightly knit group," said that Carter displayed "exceptional capabilities," was "well liked," and possessed a "balanced character." Adding the "vivid" memory of Carter's exceptional "ability to express himself," this fellow officer nonetheless specifically remembered that Carter had "no political affiliation."[51] Apparently, Carter felt neither close enough nor comfortable enough with his peers on the *Pomfret* to share his political opinions with them during a voyage of several months.[52] Similarly, during his 1949 voyage Carter was washed overboard during a severe storm and came as close as he ever had to death. At such times, among crew members afraid and alone in a violent sea, one might be inclined to talk about personal matters. Carter apparently did not. None of the interviews with his fellow crew members found anyone even remembering the incident (though some said it was a fairly common experience that may well have happened). Escaping death by a near miracle, Carter evidently did not share his feelings about this experience with others.

The social reticence extended to his relationships on land. Another *Pomfret* colleague, remembering that the two often went to parties at other officers' houses and frequented the Officers' Club, noted that Carter had "no political affiliation" and "never talked about religion."[53] A similar impression was left with a classmate from submarine school in New London. Remembering that they used to play cards, attend movies, and drink "a little grocery store beer," Roth Leddick "became friendly but never intimate friends" with Carter, who struck him as "not being anxious to form close relationships."[54]

Of course, there were exceptions. A colleague reported that he had discussed politics with Carter and understood him to be a conservative who had difficulty reconciling some of his liberal views with his conservative philosophy.[55] This specific (and likely accurate) recollection suggests at least some open discussion between the two. However, the specific recollection is the sole exception among over a dozen interviews that offer no memories of Carter revealing his private political views. Also, no interviewee remembered anything about Carter's religious or other opinions; none named him as a best or even close friend. The exception may therefore be of the sort that proves the rule. Liked and respected, Carter was genuinely close to no one.

Interviews with two crew members on the next submarine to which Carter was assigned (based in Connecticut), the USS *K-1*, repeat the familiar story. "As hard as it is to believe about anyone in the navy," summarized the executive officer of this ship, "there are no sea stories about Jimmy Carter." He was just a loner. Carter was remembered by one as "a fine officer" but "quiet" and by another as a "conscientious officer" with whom he "did not have many nonbusiness talks." Neither recounted the incident in Jamaica, which Carter used as the pretext for his final argument with his father, or reported any other personal knowledge of him. As before, Carter seemed to blend in so well that he did not stand out. He was, summarized one, "no better and no worse than what was expected."[56]

It is also likely that Carter once again began to battle depression during his time on the *K-1*. The challenges that had temporarily satisfied him after 1948 naturally began to lose their luster as the years passed. Meanwhile, although he was advancing satisfactorily in the navy, he was not rising any faster than was expected. Not least, the horrible argument with his father had erupted over the Christmas holidays in 1950–51, just after he had been assigned to the *K-1*. If he was shaken and depressed, the feelings were understandable. And the worst part about the argument with his father may have been that it had solidified his commitment to a career in the navy at the same time that prospects for real advancement seemed dim.

There were also allegations made by associates on the *K-1* that were absent from the recollections of his associates on the *Pomfret*. The two fellow officers independently took offense at Carter's "stretching the truth" about his service on the *K-1* in his campaign autobiography, *Why Not the Best?*, and pointed to faults in his performance. They claimed that Carter was not the senior officer, as he stated, but a junior officer, and one added that Carter's command thesis was actually suggested to him and developed by others. (The implication was not that Carter plagiarized the work of others but that he took credit for more originality than he deserved.) These interviewees were also quick to point out that Carter was not a nuclear physicist, as he claimed to be, and in fact was less well trained in the field than were several associates. Indeed, one added that Carter so fouled up the submarine's motors and generators that it took others six months to repair them.[57]

If these critical recollections are true — and the two do corroborate each other — it appears that in his quest for the presidency Carter embellished his accomplishments on the *K-1*, which in fact included at least one major failure. But puzzling about these allegations is that they were made by members of the *K-1* but not the *Pomfret*. Many more colleagues were interviewed from the *Pomfret* than from the *K-1*, yet none from the *Pomfret* reported any similar exaggerations or mistakes. Without discounting the corroborated recollections of the two *K-1* officers, the conjecture that must arise is that on the *K-1* Carter *did* perform more poorly and, whether intentionally fabricated or not, he later remembered that performance as better than it was. If true, the chances are strong that the depression was once again beginning to descend.

☆   ☆   ☆

The navy offered Carter only one more challenge. It arrived in the form of a person, Hyman Rickover; a program, nuclear propulsion; and a question: Why not the best?

Hyman Rickover, once described as "a gnome-like figure," was the immigrant son of an Austrian Jewish tailor who had manipulated both the navy and Congress into ceding to him virtually unaccountable power over the navy's nuclear submarine program. By the 1960s his power was so entrenched that neither President Johnson nor Secretary of State Henry Kissinger could remove him, although both tried. By the 1970s the commander of naval operations, Admiral Elmo Zumwalt, simply regarded him as a "complication" who had to be placated.[58] Yet, from Rickover's point of view, his position was both crucial and justifiable. An ardent believer in the role nuclear power could play in national defense, Rickover was also convinced that the society was "basically oligarchical — that is, dominated by wealthy businessmen and other special interests."[59] It followed that one did what one had to in order to carve out a position of power vis-à-vis the oligarchs. When Jimmy Carter met him in 1952, Rickover was well on his way to carving out this power position.

The key to Rickover's power may be that he never made the mistake of overestimating either it or his own abilities. Enormously intelligent, he considered himself "dumb" — "just dumb enough to know he has to use his wits." To compensate, he purposely surrounded himself with "people who are smarter than I am" and whom he counted on "to keep me out of trouble." He also held the conviction that "the only way to make a difference in the real world is to put ten times as much effort into everything as anyone else thinks reasonable." If his conception of himself as "dumb" was doubted by subordinates who "knew we were not as smart as he was," his capacity for work was only slightly exaggerated by his goal of ten times the amount thought reasonable. Countless recollections — including Carter's — reveal a Rickover who regularly carried a heavier work load than his subordinates — themselves able, ambitious, hardworking, and younger.[60]

Ultimately Rickover's personal philosophy grew into a social philosophy (applied primarily by him to educational reform). He believed that "the price of progress is the acceptance of . . . more exacting standards of performance and relinquishments of familiar habits and conventions rendered obsolete. . . . To move but one rung up the ladder of civilization, man must surpass himself. . . . That is the never-ending challenge."[61] The philosophy perfectly extended the one Carter appropriated from his beloved high-school teacher and superintendent. In words that Carter repeated in his inaugural address as president, Julia Coleman had taught her students to "adjust to changing times and still hold to unchanging principles." Omitted from his inaugural address, however, was the Rickover addition: that to adapt to changing times "man must surpass himself." This addition was the message that inspired the twenty-seven-year-old lieutenant in search of a fresh challenge.

The first, and perhaps primary, challenge that Rickover posed to recruits was the interview. Carter was not alone in recalling his interview with Rickover as one of the most memorable aspects of his service in the program. For the Rickover interview — second only to the man himself — was the most remarkable feature of the service.[62] Elmo Zumwalt was so outraged by his experience of being interviewed by Rickover that he made a near-verbatim transcript of the ordeal and published it in his memoir.[63] The reason for Zumwalt's outrage (and almost everyone else's vivid memory of the interview) was that it was patently abusive. Interviewing prospective recruits only after they had been approved by previous interviewers and made the preliminary cuts, Rickover's interviews were frankly designed to find out "how they will behave under pressure." Convinced that he could not discover this "with routine questions," he endeavored to "shake 'em up."[64]

Tactics varied somewhat from recruit to recruit, and there is some discrepancy in reports. (One discrepancy concerns the length of the front legs of the chair on which the interviewee was ordered to sit. Some recall that the front legs were sawed shorter than the back legs, which forced the interviewee to slip perpetually forward and remain literally as well as figuratively off balance. Others either sat in a regular chair or failed to notice the differing lengths of the chair legs. Carter was one who did not mention the chair.)[65] But variations were minor, and the interview evolved into one with a predictable structure. First, the interviewee was fatigued and angered by having to wait hours, sometimes days, in a waiting room informally called "the tank" before being called in for the interview. Some concluded that "the tank" was secretly monitored and that behavior there was part of the selection process. Next, upon being ushered into Rickover's sparse office, the applicant was ordered to sit across the desk from Rickover while an ever present aide sat nearby. No sooner did the questions begin than the applicant's answers were ridiculed, sometimes by Rickover directly, other times by Rickover addressing the aide and, shaming the applicant, saying something like, "Get him out of here. Let him go and sit until he's ready to be interviewed properly."[66] After this initial badgering (which was sometimes repeated over days of follow-up interviews when applicants had been sent back to "the tank"), the interview proceeded with Rickover allowing — as Carter also recalled — the applicant to choose a subject for discussion on which he considered himself informed. Then, Socratically (and drawing from a wealth of knowledge in a number of fields), Rickover would ask a series of questions on the subject until he had demonstrated to the applicant that he was not well informed about the subject after all. Finally, questions would turn to the applicant's performance in college. Since all had done well and were justifiably proud, all reported strong performance. To this Rickover would retort: "Did you always do your best?" Invariably, the applicant would slink back and murmur "No, Sir." Rickover then asked "Why not?" and the interview was over.

From the verbal assault that substituted for an interview, no one knew how Rickover chose the officers he did — or why he rejected most of those who were similarly qualified. All anyone knew is that Rickover insisted upon deploying these offensive interviewing tactics and, in the process, made his decision. But Rickover once implied an explanation for his autocratic tactics that fitted his developing social philosophy. When an aide asked him to explain the apparent discrepancy between his abusive interviews and his devoted attention to minor personnel matters for his existing staff, he explained:

> These are *my* people. . . . Did you ever really look at the kind of people I've brought in here?. . . Our senior scientist . . . is also an ordained Orthodox Rabbi. . . . Our senior metallurgist is so highly regarded by the Mormon church that I'm afraid they're going to pull him out of here for a top position in Salt Lake City. . . . One of our chemical engineers is a leader in the Church of Our Savior. . . . And now I've got a request from one of our people for six weeks off so that he may make the pilgrimage to Mecca required by his faith. These are very spiritual people. They're not just technicians; they are highly developed human beings.[67]

Perhaps the Rickover interview was intended to discern whether an applicant had a bedrock of spiritual commitment that would sustain him in times of trauma. If this indeed were the motive lurking behind the Rickover interview, Carter may have been chosen because he possessed the requisite search for spiritual fulfillment — however underdeveloped it may have been at the time.

In any event, while an officer who served with Carter on the USS *K-1* during 1951 and 1952 considered Rickover to be an "offensive bureaucrat,"[68] and Admiral Zumwalt proudly remembered having withstood Rickover's interview only to refuse to accept the position offered, Jimmy Carter endured the interview, was offered a position, and accepted it proudly. Indeed, Rickover wound up influencing him more than anyone except for his own parents and, when he later ran for president, it was the infamous question that Rickover used to conclude his interviews that Carter used to entitle his campaign autobiography: Why not the best?[69] Clearly, Rickover had provided Carter with not only his final challenge in the navy but also the inspiration to continue to challenge himself throughout life.

The influence that Rickover exerted over Carter — an influence that other equally capable officers abhorred and rejected — had many possible bases. A few likely ones stand out. First, in Rickover Carter may have discovered the only authority figure who rivaled his father in domineering expectations. Coming as it did in the aftermath of the final argument with his father, the Rickover relationship may have filled a deep void in the young lieutenant. But a second source of attraction, not unrelated to the first, might also be detected. Foundering about in search of a new challenge, the Rickover question — Why not the best? — spurred Carter on at just the time he was ready for the spur. If the long-distance runner wanted to edge others out at the finish line, time was growing short. Already in his late twenties, his career had progressed solidly but not remarkably. To excel, he needed to apply the last ounce of effort. Rickover promised to inspire this effort. Third, there was a similarity of personal philosophies and emotional outlook between the two men. The "gnome-like" Austrian Jew thought of himself as an outsider in an oligarchic society and was determined to beat the oligarchs through superior intelligence and harder work. The equally slight Southern Baptist was also an outsider whose immersion in populism had taught him something about oligarchs. His quest for leadership would require his outsmarting and outworking entrenched powers. Carter would not remain with Rickover long enough to absorb and appreciate the whole of his philosophy — but its basic emotional outlines fitted his temperament and background well.

Despite the affinity between the younger and older man, however, there was not closeness. The fault was not entirely Carter's. "Rickover rarely talked to anyone except the senior people," claimed a fellow officer in the program, who was "dubious that Carter had much personal contact with him."[70] Another simply said that Carter "had little contact with Rickover."[71] But "to be categorized as 'close' to Rickover needs explanation," claimed one who was in his service a long time. It meant that one was still treated as a "pupil" in a "never-ending process of educating and training."[72] So, when Carter became a viable presidential candidate, it is no surprise that Rickover had to have Carter's personnel file pulled in order to refresh his memory about this former subordinate who, some concluded, was publicizing the philosophy of the crusty old admiral. And, since Rickover's "perfectionist" demands were "impersonal," some also suspected, paradoxically, that the "lack of relationship was, in some way, the bond."[73]

Such a paradoxical closeness was perhaps the only kind that Carter was capable of experiencing, anyway. Again, peers in the program remembered Carter as a loner. A fellow officer who had known him for three years and lived in the same apartment complex (in Schenectady, New York) could not recall Carter's "closest friend." Whereas another had guessed that it was Bill Lalor, Lalor said it was not. Carter was rather "quiet, polite, very pleasant, and smiled often," but was not a particularly close friend.[74]

No sooner did Carter join the nuclear program, however, than the news arrived of his father's illness. He took leave time to be by his father's bedside and then, at his death, wrestled with "the relative significance of his life and mine." His conclusion was that his father's life as "an integral part of the community" was the superior one.[75] So, violating the understood rule that an officer was obligated to serve two years for each year of training he received, Carter took his year of training and promptly resigned. Rickover, that "offensive bureaucrat," was not pleased.[76] Perhaps as Carter headed back to southwest Georgia in 1953 to replace his father in Plains, he felt a certain subconscious satisfaction in knowing that he had defied Rickover.

The decision had not been an easy one. Sometime during his last year in the navy, Carter tried his hand at landscape painting. One who saw the painting reflected upon its "overwhelming greyness," which, he thought, suggested "utter despair."[77]

PLAINS, CIRCA THE 1950S

If the move to Plains was prompted by the final ascendance of Carter's desire to become the "integral part of the community," the crisp autumn drive down the eastern seaboard in 1953 revealed that his other ambition, the quest for leadership, had only slipped into a close second place. For the family (which included three small children, the eldest a first-grader) stopped to vacation in Washington, D.C. Although Carter later explained this stop as one in which he said farewells to colleagues with whom he had worked in the nation's capital, the explanation is dubious. Carter was especially close to no one in Washington, he reported stopping nowhere else to say good-byes, and he ended up taking the perfunctory tours and listening to the standard speeches normally arranged by congressmen for visiting constituents.[78] Moreover, although it was the slow season for agribusiness in Georgia and the Carters were not destitute, the comparatively expensive Washington vacation could hardly be justified when the family, who would move into public housing upon their arrival in Plains, faced an uncertain economic future.

Years later Carter admitted what was apparent from his otherwise inexplicable Washington visit in 1953: "I had given some private thoughts to running for the U.S. Congress."[79] The plan, of course, was vague — so vague that either he did not emphasize it in his argument with Rosalynn about leaving the navy (she wanted to stay) or she found the goal too wistful — and, though Carter nearly did run for Congress in 1966, the ambition never quite materialized. But the vague plan does betray the double motives that really drew Carter back to Georgia. Partly, it is true, he wanted to experience the life in a community that he had not yet enjoyed. But he also aspired to the positions of leadership, which he had also failed to attain. Carter hoped that Plains would provide him with the experience of community; but whether it did or did not, he reasoned that it would offer him the geographic base necessary for a political career.

☆   ☆   ☆

There was much, however, needing to be done before Carter could think about politics. Mainly, he needed to earn a living — and ideally one high enough to make political ambitions realistic. This was initially no easy task. Although Carter had once remarked on his father's "plantation" when he agonized over leaving the navy — and Earl Carter did die a comparatively wealthy man — the truth was that, between the senior Carter's death-bed magnanimity and the division of his estate among several heirs, there was little left over for Jimmy to inherit. Much of Earl Carter's wealth had been in IOUs — and many of those he "forgave" before dying. His most lucrative business, his fire insurance company, was willed to the secretary, Nellie Walters, who actually ran it (so an inheritance that most thought deserved). Remaining were the houses — in which Lillian and Billy still needed to live — acres of cheap land, miscellaneous assets, and a fledgling peanut warehouse. Once this remainder was divided among the heirs, Jimmy ended up with the peanut warehouse, a little land, and the U.S. savings bonds that he had faithfully purchased over his years in the navy.

So the Carters moved into public housing (Carter was the only U.S. president to have lived in government-subsidized apartments for the poor) and applied themselves to the challenge of building a successful business out of the warehouse. With Rosalynn studying accounting to manage the books, and Jimmy availing himself of his local extension agent and the county library to learn what he could about agriculture (mostly the seed business, as it turned out), the family barely broke even during their first year. It was a good thing, the politically aware and staunchly Democratic Carter must have thought, that Franklin Roosevelt had been president. Under Roosevelt low-income housing had been built and the agricultural extension service that was crucial to farmers and business people unacquainted with scientific advances in farming had been greatly expanded. Private charity of the sort Earl Carter had practiced would not have provided the support his son needed during his first years on his own.

Even so, the challenges were not as severe as they seem. Although the Carters technically qualified for public housing owing to a nonexistent initial income, the truth was that there was nowhere else for them to live. Plains was the kind of town in which families built homes for their own use and passed them down through the generations. Rarely was a house ever put on the market for rent or for sale, and no one (besides the government) thought to build apartments. The Carters' temporary residence in public housing was more a consequence of the limited real-estate market in Plains than an indication of their poverty.

Similarly, Carter's ignorance of agriculture should not be overstated. Raised on a farm and a lifetime member of Future Farmers of America, he was also superbly trained in just the kinds of scientific and technological subjects that lent themselves to an understanding of agriculture. Nor were his risks large. Carter's advanced training in nuclear engineering provided him with a standing offer from a private firm for civilian employment that, though he preferred not to accept it, eased any financial insecurities he might otherwise have experienced. Not least, however small, he *had* inherited his business outright. His risks were negligible and, with his family's good name, his opportunities great.

Since the challenges were more apparent than real, Carter was quickly able to parlay his willingness to work hard into substantial success. He was also "tight." Business associates remembered that "down to the last dime, he'll fight you over it."[80] As a result of these combined factors, the Carters' poverty-level 1954 income rose twentyfold in 1955 and nearly doubled again in 1956. Since this 1956 income was nearly twice the salary Carter had earned as a full lieutenant in the navy,[81] the Carters were quickly comfortable financially.

So the family did not live long in public housing. After about a year they found a house to rent. The next year a better house — a lumbering 100-year-old farmhouse on the outskirts of town — became available and they moved to it. Although rumors were that the house was haunted (which may have helped to explain its availability as rental property), the Carters loved the house enough to ask the owner to sell it to them. When the offer was declined, they set their sights on what most other aspiring middle-class families seemed to desire at the time: a custom-built ranch home on a large lot. The widespread preference for ranch houses, as opposed to traditional southern styles of architecture, may have been a way for southern families like the Carters to symbolize their desire to be seen as Americans who had overcome their provincial southern roots.

Whatever their mixture of motives, the Carters chose a two-plus-acre lot adjacent to downtown Plains on which they built a rambling ranch house that announced their growing prosperity. Although similar homes were springing up for equivalently successful Sumter County families, the Carters were the only ones rumored to have hired professional architects to design theirs. Jimmy, meanwhile, insisted upon such stringent standards of craftsmanship that he allowed the use of no molding to disguise even slightly mismeasured boards, and Rosalynn ordered a large chandelier for the dining room. When the Carters moved into their new home in 1961 it was therefore one of the nicest new homes in the area — even if it remained essentially middle-class — and was, said Carter later, "what we wanted at the time."[82]

Rising financial success was matched by an apparently satisfying social life. The Carters regularly socialized with other up-and-coming couples, chiefly John and Marjorie Pope (later, John and Betty Pope, his second wife) of Plains and Billy and Irene Horne of Americus, both couples with husbands in the construction business. (Billy Horne was also an engineer.) The three couples — sometimes only two of them; other times additional couples were invited — regularly went to dinners or dances together, invited one another to their houses, bowled, played tennis, or took trips to Atlanta, the Florida beach, or the Daytona 500. By late 1955, the Carters even made the Americus newspaper's society page after hosting a dance at their pond house.[83] They joined the Sumter Squares, a group that enjoyed modern western square dancing, and enrolled in both ballroom dance lessons and a great books discussion group.

Although it is unclear whether the Carters ever formally joined the whites-only Americus Country Club, John Pope was certain that they did, since they could not have socialized there so often without joining.[84] Indeed, the Carters' social life tended to be centered on nearby Americus and easily extended to the restaurants and nightclubs in the still larger Albany. To go bowling, for example, a Plains resident had to go at least as far as Americus, and the only "nightclub" in Plains was the black-owned Skylight Club (which the Carters never frequented).

But besides the Americus Country Club and, perhaps, another social club that surfaces in interviews, the Dawson Club, Jimmy Carter joined neither the Americus-based Rotary nor Elks clubs in which his father had been so active. The reason may have been that he joined the new Plains chapter of the Lions Club instead. Meanwhile, Jimmy — and he was then secure enough with himself to revert to the familiar "Jimmy," establishing its spelling with a "y" rather than an "ie" — regularly found friends with whom he could fish or hunt. And, as if to satisfy his thirst for community in ways other than friendly camaraderie, he spent countless hours with his Uncle Buddy tracing the Carter family tree.

Carter's quest for leadership was also gradually yet repeatedly fulfilled. Soon after arriving in Plains, the Georgia Power Company held a statewide "better home town" contest designed to encourage local beautification efforts. Carter volunteered to chair the Plains effort, succeeded in raising money for a public swimming pool and street pavings, and helped persuade town residents to upgrade their homes and lawns. Plains won two first-prize and two second-prize awards from the six categories judged.[85] Then, in 1955, Carter was appointed to the Sumter County School Board, rising to chairman five years later. His membership in the Lions Club also resulted in his being named chapter president immediately (and then district governor, followed by chairman of the Council of Governors during the 1960s). He also quickly joined two professional organizations, the Certified Seed Organization and the Georgia Crop Improvement Association, both associations in which he would eventually rise to president. In 1956 he was appointed to Americus and Sumter

County Hospital Authority and was named chairman of the Future Farmers and Future Homemakers of America Camp Development Committee. By 1961 he merited appointment to the Sumter County Library Board and to Chairman of the Sumter County Overall Economic Development Committee. Meanwhile, he regularly attended the Plains Baptist Church — still the largest of Plains's three white churches — where he became a scout leader, taught Sunday school, was elected a deacon, and rose to superintendent of the junior Sunday school department. "Everything he was involved with he was president, chairman or, come what may, the head of it at least by the second year," commented John Pope.[86]

The efforts, however, were almost for naught. For the racial tensions that were then sweeping the South erupted in Plains, and Carter was perceived by many to be on the wrong side of the issue. The first incident arose when members of the White Citizens' Council came by the Carter warehouse to insist that he, Jimmy Carter, join. When Carter stammered out a refusal, his fellow whites pressed the matter by offering to pay his five-dollar dues for him. Carter exploded. He took a five-dollar bill from his cash register and told the council members that he would rather flush it down the toilet than join the vigilante organization. The matter — which may not have been as dramatic as Carter later recalled — ended quickly. Carter claimed that his business was temporarily boycotted but admitted that the boycott lasted only a few months and that most of his customers returned.[87] In the eyes of his fellow white businessmen, however, the incident did brand him a racial liberal and prompted some ill will.

A second incident was like the first. While chairman of the school board, Carter supported a referendum favoring school consolidation. Although the normal arguments, pro and con, were advanced in regard to consolidation, the subtext of the issue was race. Consolidation would enable school desegregation to proceed while, opponents thought, smaller isolated schools would allow segregation to be maintained. At a time when governors Herman Talmadge and, then, Marvin Griffin were urging "massive resistance" — and desperately funding black schools in the hope of successfully defending the "separate but equal" doctrine — Carter was again on the losing side of what he considered his first political fight. Loyalties were so strained during the consolidation fight that even his cousin Hugh Carter, who led the opposition, did not speak to him again until 1966. Others called him a "race mixer and a nigger lover."[88] And the morning after the vote Carter discovered that a sign had been nailed to the front door of his warehouse, which read, "COONS AND CARTERS GO TO-GETHER."[89]

Yet Carter's support for civil rights should not be exaggerated. When in the early 1960s some white landowners threatened black tenants with eviction if they sent their children to the newly integrated school, one of Carter's tenants approached him to ask what he should do. Carter told the tenant to send his children to the integrated school, to tell the other tenants to do likewise, and not to worry because he — Carter — "would take care of it."[90] Testifying to Carter's integrationist views, the incident also revealed that Carter remained very much in paternalistic control of the black tenants who still worked his family's land. Similarly, his nephew remembered that Carter's black employees, who called their boss "Mr. Jimmy," were generally paid less than the whites and that "Jimmy wouldn't let blacks into his house, either, except for a maid, or maybe a sharecropper to talk to him in the hallway for a few minutes."[91] A leader of the neighboring Koinonia Farm, an interracial pacifist Christian community established in Sumter County in 1942, likewise failed to remember Carter.[92] Although Carter later claimed to have befriended the community, which during the middle 1950s had been riddled with bullets, dynamited, and seen a member beaten by townsmen (only to have an all-white Sumter County grand jury conclude that Koinonia's residents shot, bombed, and beat themselves), no evidence exists that his support was more than private. Perhaps, as he later claimed, he processed their seed when other Plains businesses refused.[93] If so, his support may have been real — but it was minor. And Carter's seven years on the school board — all after the 1954 *Brown* decision — moved Sumter County schools no closer to integration than those in most other rural counties of the South. Indeed, he later confessed that even as a school board member he only slowly became aware of the deplorable conditions in the black-only schools and "found various reasons" to avoid visiting them and learning their conditions firsthand. Later claiming that he "tried in every way possible to improve the county's school system," he nonetheless admitted in uncharacteristic understatement that he did nothing "heroic or economically suicidal."[94]

It also merits emphasis that Carter was not completely alone among the whites of his region in his tempered support for civil rights. Although in the mid-1950s it is plausible, as some interviewees believed, that every white Plains businessman except for Carter was a member of the town's

White Citizens' Council, by 1961 acquiescence to school desegregation seemed evenly split, at least as measured by the votes cast on the school consolidation referendum. The referendum lost by what the local newspaper called a "slim 84-vote margin," a much closer vote than a similar referendum had received in 1954.[95]

Emotions ran high on the race issue, but Carter always believed that white opposition to black civil rights was not as strong as it appeared to be. Even when he was publicly ostracized for his stance favoring civil rights, he recalled that other whites would call him privately and whisper their support. Moreover, many attributed Carter's position on civil rights to his mother's influence, which they had long accepted, and just concluded that "the Carters are like that. If they believe in something, they stand for it."[96] In this way many townspeople managed to attribute Carter's support for civil rights to an appealing trait — the propensity to stand on principle — even if they happened to disagree with the particular principle.

And on most other issues Jimmy Carter was just as conservative as his fellow townspeople. Although the race issue dominated all other political issues in the South of the time, Carter's racial liberalism could be construed as but the sole aberrant view of an otherwise conservative southerner. Quietly voting against his state's segregationist governors in primary elections, for example, he nevertheless failed to openly support more liberal Democrats. Any strong opinions he may have held regarding the 1956 and 1960 Democratic presidential elections, when Adlai Stevenson and John Kennedy were the Democratic nominees, were remembered by no one. Except for Truman in 1948, in fact, he mentioned supporting only one other Democratic presidential nominee, Lyndon Johnson. But this support was largely determined by his (and his mother's) racial views. Lillian Carter campaigned for Johnson and was a delegate to the 1964 Democratic Convention because of the former vice president's stand on civil rights issues. Carter followed his mother's lead and supported Johnson openly — though the rationale that prompted their support caused the majority of Georgia's electorate to cast Republican ballots in that year's presidential race for the first time in history. Still, on other liberal Democratic issues, like the labor issues that surfaced in nearby textile mills, Carter remained silent — and presumably in the conservative camp.

Nor did Carter's personal life reveal more than a hint of liberal sentiment. "Jimmy raised his kids like it was a military school. Very strict."

Indeed, while living in the farmhouse his three boys shared a room that his nephew called "a fucking barracks. . . . [E]verybody had his own little area. Everything . . . was laid out very neatly." Also striking to this nephew was that "we couldn't be seen naked in front of each other" — an indication, he thought, of sexual prudishness. Meanwhile, the religious atmosphere of the home was oppressively thick. In the evenings the family gathered for a circle of prayer, on Wednesday evenings the Carters hosted a community prayer meeting, and meals were begun with prayer — and "when Jimmy says grace he gives a sermon." As a Sunday school teacher, Carter was not given to very progressive methods of education either. "He would stand up there in his dark suit, white shirt and tie and he would tell us stories straight from the Bible. Then . . . he'd cite chapter such and such, verse so-and-so, and he'd ask us to look it up. The first one to get it would win." These "Bible drills" were "a race, not an attempt to understand anything." In all, concluded his nephew: "He smiles outwardly, but at heart he's a cold motherfucker."[97]

These opinions should probably be discounted somewhat, however, given that their source was an imprisoned nephew who was bitter about receiving no help from his uncle-turned-president. Indeed, the fact that during the 1950s Carter *did* try to help this nephew by giving him a job and taking him into his home offers a compelling, if partial, rebuttal to these criticisms. And elsewhere Willie Carter Spann presented a softer view. He remembered, for example, that "Jimmy didn't have the hang-ups most rednecks have, you know, where a father can't show any affection. He could and he did." And if, in a criticism reminiscent of Holden Caulfield's famous one, he regarded Carter as "a phony," he also admitted to "liking" him and "appreciating" his efforts to help him.[98]

Carter's attempts at personal charity, though not as memorable as his father's private good deeds had been, were also remembered by others. Lottie Wise Tanner recalled how her father, who farmed land that the Carters owned, suffered from a debilitating mental illness only to be released from the hospital and return to the financial nightmare that his farm had become. "He went to Jimmy and told him his problems and Jimmy took care of the matter. Jimmy has always been a person you could rely on. He has always been a good and honest person."[99] But kindness and attempts at charity did not reveal a permissive disposition. "He never boozed or smoked. . . . He never had any of the problems you might have when you're growing up . . . so he can't understand," concluded his troubled nephew.[100]

And, while few would publicly use the same phrase, others observed the aspect of Carter's character that prompted Spann to call him "a cold motherfucker." One of his closest friends at the time recalled an occasion when Carter played golf against her husband. Although Carter did not care for golf and was not as good at the game as his opponent, he won because "he's just really competitive." Her husband was upset.[101] Another remarked after Carter was elected president that he was pleasantly surprised that Carter was "not as dictatorial as I feared." Based upon his experiences with Carter in Plains, this acquaintance expected Carter to be far more "dictatorial."[102] If the Carters were the sort who would "take a stand" for what "they believe in," the trait could be construed as a commitment to moral principle — or attributed to coldness, competitiveness, and dictatorial tendencies.

Whether or not Carter ever enjoyed the community he had come to Plains to experience is doubtful. He and Rosalynn did forge deeper friendships with a few more couples than they had previously. "He's just so interested and interesting," claimed one of their closest friends of the time, "I'd rather talk to him than anybody I've ever known." But this same friend failed to remember ever talking with him about politics and confided that "Jimmy has not always been the most popular person around."[103] The remark was intended to refer to Carter's stand on civil rights, which earned him the temporary antipathy of many if not most of the whites in his community. But it stretches credulity to suppose that Carter was unpopular only because of his position on civil rights. Some, perhaps more than a few, may not have cared for his "dictatorial" tendencies either. When he ran for governor in 1966 and his closest friend from the 1950s, John Pope, actively supported his opponent, it may have been for either or both reasons.[104] Yet, during his years in Plains, Carter at least avoided experiencing the outsider status that had haunted him during his navy years. If "he was not always the most popular person around," his lack of popularity could also be explained — perhaps too conveniently but explained nonetheless — by his stand on civil rights.

So it was that in the Plains of the 1950s Jimmy Carter tried to immerse himself in a community, only to find that he remained a partial moral outsider and still longed to be a leader. Which goal would rise ascendant, the life of community or the quest for moral leadership, was revealed on the morning of Monday, October 1, 1962, his thirty-eighth birthday. Upon waking he put on his Sunday pants instead of his work khakis. When Rosalynn asked him why he was dressing up on a workday, Jimmy, who had not discussed his plans with her, replied that he intended to qualify for election to the state senate.[105]

CHAPTER 5

THE SPIRITUAL PASSION OF POLITICS

"Someone's been eatin' Marvin's barbecue and not votin' for him," quipped a campaign aide on the September 1962 night that Marvin Griffin lost his comeback bid to be Georgia's governor.[1] The remark added levity to an otherwise somber occasion. Griffin, who had served as lieutenant governor under Herman Talmadge and then as governor himself between 1955 and 1959, epitomized the rural political culture of his era. His 1962 loss to Carl Sanders, an Augusta lawyer whom even Jimmy Carter considered a "city slicker,"[2] signaled the end of that era. That at least is what Griffin concluded on the evening of his defeat. "It seems to be a trend of the times," he mused.[3]

The times did suggest change. Although in 1962 the civil rights movement met its first major setback in Albany, Georgia, where eight months of effort resulted in little tangible progress, the next year witnessed the movement's crescendo in the march on Washington and Martin Luther King Jr.'s famous "I Have a Dream" speech.[4] Meanwhile, Bob Dylan's haunting 1962 anthem of the civil rights movement, "Blowin' in the Wind," captured the imagination of many — a few of whom had joined the Freedom Rides the year before and more of whom would yet volunteer for "Freedom Summer."[5] More substantially, Georgia schools had begun to desegregate. Confronted with the choice between admitting two African American students into the University of Georgia or closing the school in January of 1961, Governor Ernest Vandiver reluctantly ordered the flagship university to remain open. The next fall four Atlanta high schools desegregated without incident, and by 1963 public schools in Athens and

Savannah quietly transferred a few black students to formerly all-white schools.[6]

Other signs of shifting trends were more subtle. John Kennedy, the youngest candidate ever elected president, lent an urbane cachet and fresh wit to an office recently vacated by Dwight Eisenhower. Since both Carl Sanders and Jimmy Carter were likened to Kennedy,[7] the suspicion arises that some Georgians' desire for Kennedy-like dynamism in their politics was strong. More subtly, the election of the first Roman Catholic president may have provided an early sign of the declining influence of the Protestant establishment in American life. As if to hurry this decline, the Supreme Court ruled six to one in the spring of 1962 against allowing prayer in public schools. The next year, John A. T. Robinson published *Honest to God*, the book that "in a real sense . . . must be credited with setting off the explosive chain reactions of new theologies that continue to fill the horizons today."[8] But by 1961 theatergoers were already privy to the difficulties of maintaining faith in the modern world, when Tennessee Williams's *The Night of the Iguana* opened on Broadway.

Faith in science was also shaken. Although in 1962 John Glenn became the first U.S. astronaut to orbit the globe, later in the year the nation came perilously close to a nuclear confrontation with the Soviet Union during the Cuban missile crisis. As if the threat of nuclear annihilation was not enough to shatter faith in science, the year also saw the publication of Thomas Kuhn's influential critique of cumulative scientific discovery, *The Structure of Scientific Revolutions*, as well as Rachel Carson's *Silent Spring*, the watershed treatise on the ecological costs of technological excesses.[9] Meanwhile, the television technology that had produced the first live coverage of a presidential news conference in 1961 found its social critic in Marshall McLuhan's 1962 *The Gutenberg Galaxy*.[10]

Popular culture captured some of the uncertainty of the transition year. In television, the futuristic cartoon *The Jetsons* premiered in 1962, injecting humor into fears of space-age technology. But it failed to stimulate much viewer interest. Instead, a more slapstick commentary on the shift from rural provincialism to modern urbanity resonated with the majority of viewers. Eclipsing the staple westerns (*Wagon Train*, *Bonanza*, and *Gunsmoke*) that had merited the top three rating positions during the previous season, *Beverly Hillbillies* became the top-rated television show of 1962–63, and went on to enjoy the highest seasonal average rating during the 1963–64 season of any television show in history.[11]

Since the first baby boomers turned sixteen in 1962, the demographic mass required for the strident youth culture of the 1960s was finally in evidence. So also was its ideology. In 1962 Tom Hayden drafted the infamous Port Huron Statement, the manifesto of Students for a Democratic Society.[12] Yet in 1962 teens bursting with hormonal angst turned more to frenetic dance than to political activism. Little Eva, an African American back-up singer and baby-sitter for songwriters Carole King and Gerry Goffin, scored the number one hit in the week of August 25 with King's "Loco-Motion." Although the dance to which the song alluded did not even exist, Eva Boyd invented one to appease fans who earlier in the summer had tired of the generic Twist to dance "The Wah-Watusi" or even, perhaps, "The Stripper," each of which had been a top-five song earlier in the summer. By the week of the 1962 general elections, however, a more foreboding youth cultural theme was innocuously suggested by a song released by the black female vocal group the Crystals. "He's a Rebel" soared to the number one chart position.[13]

Although blacks and whites usually led separate lives, they shared or, more frequently, swapped top positions on the record charts. This too was new. Before the mid-1950s, "race music" — the records of African Americans — was a separate category in popular music. Georgia's Ray Charles is credited with changing this in late 1954 with his release of "I Got a Woman," a record that so solidly crossed the color barrier that the barrier itself was shattered.[14] By 1962 Charles easily merited two top-five hit songs (one, "I Can't Stop Loving You," hit number one in early June and went on to sell a phenomenal three million copies), while other more distinctively African American songs — like the legendary "Green Onions" by Booker T. and the MGs — crept toward the top of the charts. These successes paved the way for the subsequent celebrity of other African American popular music giants from Georgia, including Little Richard, Otis Redding, and James Brown.[15] Since less distinctively African American tunes, like Nat King Cole's "Ramblin' Rose," also merited top chart positions in 1962, black artists merited a disproportionate third of all number one hits in that year.[16]

Mainstream popular music and politics, however, had not yet fused. With the exception of the theme of the role military service played in unrequited love, illustrated by songs like the Shirelles' "Soldier Boy," which went to number one in May, political protest was at best encoded even in African American popular music. After hearing Bob Dylan's "Blowin' in the Wind," for example, Sam Cooke, the legendary African

American rhythm and blues artist, realized: "I got to write something. Here's a white boy writing a song like this." So he sat down and wrote "A Change Is Gonna Come." Excluded from the released single (but included on the album version), however, was the verse that branded it a civil rights song.[17] Blacks were still subservient to whites, even when they displayed superior abilities. White fraternities throughout the South continued to hire black bands to perform at their parties even though the band members were otherwise unwelcome on campus. Sublimating the tensions, zaniness temporarily ruled. During Carter's two-week campaign for the state senate, "Monster Mash" was the number one popular song in the nation.[18]

Marvin Griffin was on the losing side of these changes. Like most successful white politicians in the South, he was a segregationist. But Griffin had pressed his white supremacist views into actions that even most of his white constituents could not countenance. As governor he tried to prevent the Georgia Tech football team from playing in the Sugar Bowl against the University of Pittsburgh, because Pittsburgh's team included a black player; he traveled to Arkansas to lend his support to that state's segregationist forces; and he equipped the Georgia Bureau of Investigation with state-of-the-art surveillance equipment while directing it to investigate, in most cases illegally, suspected integrationists — including the families of every black applicant to a white college or university. These extremist antics, combined with an administration so riddled with corruption that even the *Reader's Digest* claimed "never in Georgia history had so many stolen so much," made Griffin the distant second choice of Georgia voters in 1962. If many enjoyed his barbecues and concurred when he exclaimed that no place could match Georgia, "where the peaches are sweeter, the watermelons redder, the fish hungrier, or the girls prettier," barbecues and boosterism proved to be inadequate bases for the election of a segregationist governor in that era of change.[19]

More was at stake in the changing times, however, than just vague shifts in cultural currents. Even more was at stake than civil rights. When people like Marvin Griffin considered the changes sweeping Georgia in 1962, they normally thought first of a specific political change: the forced dismantling of Georgia's county unit system. Secondarily, when they considered the kaleidoscope of changes swirling about them, they sometimes detected a more fundamental shift in moral values. This shift was from a society still sympathetic to the values of southern particularism to one fully in favor of moral universalism. Together, these two changes gave precise political shape and tangible moral texture to an era of diffuse change and cultural zaniness.

Of most immediate importance to Marvin Griffin — and, as it turned out, to Jimmy Carter — was the dismantling of the county unit system. By Democratic party custom and then by the Neill Primary Act of 1917, Georgia had apportioned its state legislature by counties rather than by population. It had also used county unit votes instead of popular votes to determine statewide elections. Under this system, each of Georgia's 159 counties was granted at least one representative in the lower house of the state legislature and two unit votes in statewide races. Larger counties were allotted more representatives and unit votes than smaller counties, but the differences were not proportional. In 1962, for instance, tiny Quitman County (where Jimmy Carter would contest his election to the state senate) had a population of 2,432, yet merited its own state representative and two unit votes in statewide elections. This compared, for instance, to 20 representatives and 40 unit votes for Atlanta's Fulton County. Since Fulton's population of 556,326 was more than 200 times greater than Quitman's, its twentyfold increase in political clout remained far below what proportional influence would require. A vote in Quitman County carried eleven times the clout of a vote in Fulton County, and the discrepancy between Quitman and Fulton was not the largest.[20]

The county unit system thus augmented the political power of Georgia's rural counties at the expense of its urban counties. This resulted, in turn, in a legislature and statewide elected officials beholden to rural constituencies (many below "the gnat line"). Conversely, small-county bosses and their machines had even more incentive in Georgia than elsewhere to amass and exercise power. When a rural county's political clout could be magnified by a factor of ten or more, "delivering" even a tiny county — and especially a tiny county — proportionately augmented a boss's statewide power. Indeed, one of the reasons Georgia has more counties than any state but Texas is that in Georgia real political incentives existed for counties to subdivide into even smaller counties. Well into the twentieth century — nearly three hundred years after it had been settled — Georgia's roster of counties continued to grow.

But in April of 1962, the Supreme Court declared in *Gray v. Sanders* that Georgia's county unit system was unconstitutional. The court followed in May with *Toombs v. Fortson*, a ruling that required the Georgia state legislature to be reapportioned by population. Marvin Griffin was the most visible casualty of this first ruling. Elected governor in 1954 with a majority of the county unit vote, he had even then garnered only 37 percent of the popular vote. In 1962, when his political fate was decided by popular vote, he lost in a landslide. The political spoils went to Carl Sanders, the Augusta lawyer who became the first "city slicker" to live in the governor's mansion.[21]

Beneath the dismantling of the county unit system, however, lurked a more inchoate moral contest — the battle between the remnants of southern particularism and a more universalistic moral code. The linkage between these two issues is suggested by the memory of many, including Jimmy Carter, who recall the demise of the county unit system as an instance of the civil rights movement.[22] On the face of it, this memory is incorrect. Race played a negligible role in the debate over the county unit system, and blacks had little to gain by doing away with it. Although several of Georgia's urban counties were increasingly populated by African Americans, they also made up substantial minorities — and sometimes majorities — of many rural counties. Had African Americans in these counties been free to exercise their franchise and otherwise participate in political life, they stood to gain as much as whites from the county unit system. That blacks were effectively disenfranchised in these counties was therefore a different issue from the debate over the county unit system.

The linkage that Carter and others detected between civil rights and the dismantling of the county unit system, however, did exist on the more abstract plane of universalism, a moral philosophy that upholds the fundamental equality of every individual. Against universalism stood the remnants of southern particularism, a philosophy that emphasizes the social inequalities that arise from membership in different social groups and that urges differential treatment of individuals based upon their group membership. By establishing the principle of "one man, one vote," the Supreme Court decided in the March 1962 case of *Baker v. Carr* that universalism would be the law of the land. This ruling then became the legal crux of the argument against *both* the county unit system and black disenfranchisement. Upholding equal political rights of every citizen regardless of group membership, this universalistic principle provided the philosophical glue for Carter's sense of a moral affinity between the collapse of the county unit system and the rise of civil rights. Both were instances of what he would later call "human rights."

The shift away from southern particularism toward universalism had, of course, begun in a much earlier time, and by the 1960s all that was left to do was finalize it.[23] Moreover, to imply that segregationists like Marvin Griffin were moral particularists may flatter them unduly. By the middle of the twentieth century southern particularism in the hands of people like Marvin Griffin may have degenerated into little more than rank racism and political self-interest. Nevertheless, when Marvin Griffin campaigned on the slogan "segregation and the county unit system," some heard in it a final plea for particularism. Conversely, when southerners like Jimmy Carter cast their lots for civil rights and against the county unit system — and linked the two morally — the final victory of moral universalism was evident.

It is easy to favorably evaluate the changes that swept though Georgia in 1962. It is much harder to assess their costs. If it was right to dismantle the county unit system and right to grant equal access to the ballot for all, the final consequences of the underlying moral shift may be more problematic; for particularism, despite its obvious excesses, is at least a social philosophy. It presupposes the existence and importance of groups in society, and fashions standards of morality designed to preserve and enhance group life. To do this it must necessarily restrict the rights of some individuals. It also stumbles easily over the problems of deciding which groups to favor over others, under what circumstances, and why. However, the abuses of southern particularism may be traceable more to the dubious bases the region used to justify favoring some groups over others than to the moral philosophy itself. For universalism, while eliminating any and all group favoritisms, cannot from these premises envision a society that is anything more than an aggregate of equal individuals. It is hence not a social philosophy. When individuals are found to be unequal even in a universalistic society, and when these inequalities derive in part from different group experiences, the philosophy can provide no guidance for establishing a just society. Insofar as a modern complex society must meld disparate groups as well as autonomous individuals into one — and insofar as preserving and enhancing these social enclaves is desirable — universalism is devoid of moral guidance. It can conceive of society in terms no richer than that of individualism aggregated.

Perhaps Herman Talmadge, one of the leaders of Georgia's mid-century particularist faction, made the "philosophical case" for particularism best:

As members of society, we do not exist solely as individuals; we are also members of groups. We belong to families, churches, neighborhoods, fraternal organizations, political parties, and the like. A republican form of government (as opposed to a mere plebiscitary democracy) ought to reflect this diversity in its political institutions. The ancient Greeks and Romans believed that every tribe, no matter how small or how remote, deserved representation. The British still adhere to this principle in their parliamentary system. . . . [M]embers of parliament . . . represent [districts that] are very unequal in size. Each state has exactly two United States Senators, regardless of the population of that state, and the U.S. Senate is the most important legislative body in the world. As everyone knows, the Electoral College is the outfit that officially elects the President of the United States. Electoral votes do not exactly reflect the popular vote, and on more than one occasion the candidate with the most popular votes has lost in the Electoral College. And yet, for two hundred years all proposals for reforming this system have been rejected as worse than the Electoral College itself.[24]

But Talmadge did not rest his case solely on an oblique affirmation of particularism. He also pointed out that many of the so-called pluralistic strategies designed today for minority inclusion are in fact particularist strategies indefensible on the grounds of universalism. "In the Democratic Party today," he wrote in 1987, "you find all kinds of quotas based on race, sex, and God knows what else." But "liberals can't treat one man-one vote as if it were holy writ when it suits them to do so and ignore it otherwise."[25]

As the nation struggles to develop policies that support families and communities, as well as to promote minority political inclusion and economic opportunity, Talmadge may be correct: universalistic morality alone is inadequate. We also increasingly depart freely, if uneasily, from it. Whereas the departures may well be just, the point is that they are departures. Whatever the shortcomings of a particularistic moral philosophy — and there are many — a universalistic philosophy gropes in the dark for moral strategies that recognize individuals not only as discrete automatons but also as members of groups.

☆　☆　☆

For Jimmy Carter, the commitment to universalism came easily. As a Christian, he had long endorsed the spiritual universalism of his faith.

Indeed, universalism has often been traced, and perhaps should be traced, to the vision that directed Peter to open the early Jewish-Christian church to believing Gentiles. In this act, the Christian message was made a universal one.[26] Yet it is one thing to countenance spiritual universalism, which assumes only that all are equal before God, and quite another to apply it to this world. For Carter, like so many similarly inspired white southerners, the worldly application of universalism came through his commitment to civil rights. His first public stand in favor of civil rights, in fact, showed precisely this linkage. He and his family cast the sole votes in the Plains Baptist Church in favor of allowing black worshipers.

Whereas this initial act of commitment to universalistic social equality was, like so much of the early civil rights movement, an act of inclusion, Carter's embrace of universalism ultimately exacted its opposite cost. Committed to lowering the barriers of inequality that prevented community from arising, Carter failed to develop a positive vision of the community that might arise once these inequalities were removed. Indeed, like many moral universalists opposing an oppressive particularism, Carter seemed to assume that community would be an automatic consequence of individual equality. He did not foresee the opposite possibility: that equal individuals might fragment and disband as each asserted his or her own rights and claims to a meaningful life irrespective of others. Yet, arguably, this is precisely what happened as his region and the nation pressed forward solely on the grounds of universalism.

There was a certain tragedy, then, to the moral posture Carter adopted during those early years of the 1960s. In seeking to reform his community, Carter found himself endorsing a philosophy that not only thrust him outside it — sometimes as its solitary critic — but also ultimately offered him little guidance for establishing a new community. Later, as his views and others like them became the dominant ones and no new community spontaneously emerged, he remained outside of community. Indeed, after years of defending it despite its shortcomings, Carter finally even left his own church in the early 1980s, establishing with others the rival Maranatha Baptist Church. Yearning for community, the 1960s took their toll on Carter as they did on the nation: Celebrating universalism, both learned too late that it was an adequate basis only for individualism — but inadequate for common life.

Carter's moral trajectory during the 1960s, however, was propelled by experiences sharper than his vague Christian universalism and concomitant commitment to civil rights. The first of these experiences was his

1962 race for the newly reapportioned Georgia Senate. In this race Carter found himself pitted against all the forces represented by men like Marvin Griffin — and defined his political identity in moral opposition to them.

THE CAMPAIGN FOR STATE SENATE

Homer Moore won election to the state senate the old-fashioned way. A respected businessman from Richland (the Stewart County town where Lillian Carter grew up), Moore had made a success of himself in the farm supply business. At age forty-four, active in community affairs and already a member of the Richland city council, he felt that it was time he ascend to the next rung of the political ladder. That rung was the state senate. Since senate seats were traditionally rotated among each of the counties in the three-county senatorial districts, limiting senators to a single term and preventing them from accumulating significant power, the senate was considered but a small step up from local government. Real power existed in the nominally lower chamber of the Georgia legislature, the House of Representatives. But Homer Moore did not choose to run for a House seat. Since in 1962 it was Stewart County's turn to offer a candidate to the state senate, he decided to run only for that more humble office. And, selecting as his campaign manager his House representative, Sam Singer, Moore showed that he had the backing of his county's leading political clique. Unsurprisingly, he won his contested county-wide election and went on to win the district-wide primary in September.

Moore's problem, however, was *Toombs v. Fortson*, the Supreme Court ruling that required the Georgia legislature to be reapportioned by population. His September 12 primary victory therefore counted for little; the new senate districts were to be drawn later in the month and would require yet another primary election. Nevertheless, Moore had won his election — as he would later say — "fair and square" and announced that he would stand for election again from his district no matter what its final composition.

Jimmy Carter was more furtive about his political ambitions. Or he may have been simply unaware of how much he hoped for a career in politics. Although it struck an acquaintance that "Jimmy was dying to get his foot into politics," he himself later claimed that he was motivated only by a "naive conception of public service."[27] With another, he agreed that John Kennedy's election to the presidency had helped to inspire him to enter politics, an inspiration that would not have arisen until 1960 and so suggested that his 1962 political ambition was of recent vintage.[28] His acquaintances, similarly, fail to remember Carter talking much about politics prior to his 1962 campaign.[29] Since he did not even tell his wife about his ambition until the morning he announced as a candidate, there is ample reason to conclude that Carter had just not given much thought to elective office. What consideration he had given the matter, such as the occasions during the 1950s when he considered either running for Congress or, more realistically, challenging his House representative, Thad Jones,[30] seems to have been submerged beneath the responsibilities of a busy, active life.

But there were also practical reasons for Carter to repress his attraction to elective office — and then to plan secretly for it. He was by no means a political insider and, with a reputation as a racial liberal if not also as somewhat dictatorial, he stood little chance of receiving the necessary support from political insiders. His acquaintances were the more progressive young Sumter County leaders, not its older pols and power brokers. And despite a social life that took him regularly to the country club in Americus, one in his social circle reported that he "never was in with the power structure centered in Americus."[31] Indeed, as it turned out, even Representative Jones supported his opponent, Moore, in the senate race.[32] Moreover, Carter later admitted that he had calculated his odds of winning a race against a popular incumbent only to conclude, "I would not have been successful if I had."[33] However indifferent he may have been to a political career, then, the truth is that he also recognized that his chance of inaugurating one successfully was nil. He may have therefore feigned a political aloofness to mask his furtive search for a political opportunity.[34]

But the opportunity arose with the newly reapportioned state senate district, which, while including much of the old district, could be construed to be a new district in a new era. When Carter put on his Sunday pants on the morning of October 1, intending to qualify for election to the senate, he therefore hesitated just long enough to learn the composition of the recently redrawn district. Only after he studied it did he decide that a two-week campaign against Moore promised the clearest shot he would ever have to gain elective office. What he did not yet know was that the two-week campaign would last five — and define his still nebulous political sensibilities.

☆   ☆   ☆

There were no overt issues in the Fourteenth District's Democratic primary senate race, decided by special election on October 16. Voters who had already trudged to the polls several times that year and who had already elected their governor and congressmen were weary of politics. Few deemed the election of state senator, historically a minor office, worthy of much attention. And, since the entire campaign was limited to little longer than two weeks, few issues naturally surfaced.

The campaign was therefore "mainly a personality contest."[35] Moore and Carter each crisscrossed the district, shaking hands with courthouse influentials, patrons at town stores, and farmers whose fields they passed. Each advertised in local newspapers, telephoned likely supporters, and tacked up campaign posters (Carter used roofing nails) that included little more than the candidate's name, picture, and the phrase "For State Senate." With the exception of Moore's insistence that he had already been elected "fair and square" and Carter's rebuttal that he had not been elected outside of his home county, the campaign lacked substance. Carter's lengthier newspaper advertisements, when they were not rebutting Moore's claim at having already been elected "fair and square," stressed his "qualifications." These were, his advertisements claimed: graduation from Plains High School and Annapolis, attendance at Georgia Southwestern College and Georgia Tech, membership on the Sumter County School Board, experience as a businessman and a farmer, and the facts that he was a native of Plains, a Baptist, a husband, a father, and a member of the Lions Club. All the bases were covered in an issueless campaign.[36]

Yet even campaigns that are primarily "personality contests" often personify larger, if more inchoate, issues. And there was an implicit issue in the 1962 race for the Fourteenth District's state senate seat. The issue was not civil rights, or at least it was not reducible to them. Carter was known to have liberal sympathies on the race issue, and undoubtedly this knowledge cut deeply into his support. But no one spoke openly about race in the campaign, and Carter's stance on civil rights branded him no more than a "moderate" on the issue. Rather, the implicit issue in the campaign was the value changes that were sweeping Georgia, symbolized by the new senate district itself. When Moore and his supporters argued that he had already been elected "fair and square," the assertion in effect challenged the new universalistic system by which the state senate — and all other aspects of Georgia politics — were being forcibly changed. Similarly, Moore's support among established political figures, like his own and Sumter County's representatives, signaled that he was the candidate of the establishment. By challenging Moore's claims to having been elected fairly and by proceeding without the support or endorsements from established politicians, Carter signaled that he was the candidate of progressive, universalistic change. The signals were subtle and should not be exaggerated (Carter was not quite, for example, "a total newcomer to politics," as he later claimed, and he managed to merit the endorsement of the *Americus Times-Recorder* despite the general trend of establishment forces supporting Moore),[37] but, for the few who paid attention to such matters, the signals were there.

One who paid attention to these signals was Joe Hurst, Quitman County's political "boss." At the last minute, Quitman County had been added to the redrawn Fourteenth Senate District. Since it was Hurst's business to "deliver" his county to the right candidate in elections, he also made it his business to find out as much as he could about the upcoming race between Moore and Carter. After soliciting the advice of others, including Sumter County Representative Jones, Hurst decided that Moore was the candidate to support.

The decision turned out to be a tragic one for Hurst, but a fortuitous one for Carter. The events that followed ultimately sent Hurst to federal prison but supplied Carter with the one issue other than race that he could seize to define himself politically. That issue was the most classic of political crimes, election fraud. By seizing it, Carter was able to define himself as an opponent of all the wrongs that the old county-boss system represented and to position himself safely on the crest of the wave of progressive changes that were washing Georgia clean.

Why Joe Hurst felt that the election of Homer Moore was important enough to warrant obvious fraud in the Georgetown precinct of Quitman County remains a mystery. Other county bosses who felt the same way Hurst did about the election did not resort to fraud. Indeed, fraud may not have been necessary to defeat Carter. The final vote tally on the evening of October 16 was 3,063 for Moore and 2,924 for Carter, a margin of 139 votes. Although Quitman's vote tally did give Moore the race by 224 votes in a 360 to 136 count, only about a hundred votes were outright fraudulent. "Had Joe not stuffed a hundred ballots in that box," recalled the friend on whom Carter had called to verify the irregularities, "Homer would have beat Jimmy by 43 votes."[38] Why Hurst moved the precinct from the courthouse to the ordinary's office where he could personally oversee balloting that was in no way secret and then even stuffed the ballot box are mysteries he took with him to the grave. The only thing certain is that he did these things.[39]

The best explanation may be that Hurst was asked by power brokers in other counties to perform the dirty work of the election. Adept at delivering his county since he had swung it for Governor Ellis Arnall in 1942, Hurst had a stranglehold on Quitman County as strong as or stronger than that of the bosses in any of the neighboring counties. He was Quitman's state representative, held a series of simultaneous state jobs, and appointed his wife county welfare director (which enabled him to deliver checks personally to recipients who were left with no doubt about from where their largesse came). Such power, though prompting Hurst to boast that "I'll run my county like I always have," is nevertheless reciprocal. "Joe was . . . a real Robin Hood," recalled John Pope in a memory suggesting that much of Hurst's chicanery was on behalf of rather than against his impoverished constituents.[40] Indeed, the recollection is similar to the one many had of Eugene Talmadge. When Talmadge was governor and rightly accused of thievery, his reply was, "I stole, but I stole for you!" and all was forgiven.[41] Similarly, there was real doubt over whether Hurst himself trafficked in moonshine, a charge for which he was later convicted. (Although Hurst had operated a service station and beer store called the Last Chance during the late 1920s and then opened the Monte Carlo, a rural casino with hard liquor, acquaintances suspected that Hurst himself did not sell moonshine. As county boss, he simply knew where the still was and good-naturedly took the undercover federal agents to it.) The reciprocity was likewise with other state power brokers. Hosting the ongoing poker game at Atlanta's Henry Grady Hotel, where most state legislators stayed during the sessions, Hurst could not have amplified his power if the games had not been run fairly and others allowed to win. Perhaps, then, it was just the reciprocity of the state powers, combined with Hurst's firm command of his own county, that prompted others to ask Joe to help them with Homer's election. For Joe Hurst was the kind of fellow who would go along.

Whether the conjecture is accurate or not, Carter's more onerous description of Hurst strains credulity. No doubt Hurst was a county "boss" with all the negative connotation that epithet implies. Yet even Carter notes that he was also "benevolent" and "caring." But a chief anomaly is Carter's unexplained account of Hurst's rise to power in 1942 when he "delivered" Quitman County for Ellis Arnall in the gubernatorial election. Arnall ran against and defeated Eugene Talmadge in that year and went on to be regarded as Georgia's most liberal governor to date. (Historians surveyed in 1985 ranked Arnall as more liberal, more effective, and as earning a more positive national reputation than any other recent governor, including Carter).[42] Perhaps Hurst's support for Arnall against Talmadge was purely opportunistic. But if it was not, his rise to power can be attributed to political sentiments very different from those that Carter later implied. Indeed, while Hurst clearly participated in the political system as it operated in his time, his sentiments were sufficiently liberal to enable John Pope to consider him something of a "Robin Hood" in his black-majority county. Similarly, Carter's moral surprise over Hurst's "bossism" is scarcely believable. Asked how Carter could have been raised in the area and remained apparently unaware of the county "boss" system, a neighbor simply replied, "Well, you can see what you want to see."[43] Another reported that Carter had actually known that Hurst was "a political power in Georgetown" and had gone to see him to solicit his support.[44] Only when that support was denied was Carter forced to turn against him. Carter, whose own father had been a member of Sumter County's "courthouse gang" and who knew enough about his local political scene to solicit Hurst's support, chose to remember him very narrowly indeed.

It is possible that Carter's narrow memory of Hurst was rooted as much in his personal competitiveness as in moral outrage. In all but one of his subsequent campaigns, Carter showed a tendency to reduce his opponents to villainous caricatures. (The exception was 1976.) Doing so, perhaps, enabled him to attack them guiltlessly. Confronted with Hurst's election fraud, which not only threatened to cheat him out of the mantle of leadership but also, by its very essence, underscored the degree to which he was excluded from the political community of his region, Carter may have developed a strong personal animosity toward him. Yet, whatever the personal bases for Carter's harsh memory of Hurst, the encounter with him had the effect of helping him to form his somewhat vague political sensibilities into a mature political identity.

The encounter with Hurst reveals an embryonic political identity that defined Carter's subsequent career. Against men like Hurst and the paternalistic political systems they represented, Carter would stand for good, fair, universalistic government. These thematic positions could encapsulate civil rights but were not reducible to them (a convenient posture for a southern politician at the time). They would also suit a temperament that was inclined to isolation and was as uncomfortable personally as it was morally with the back-slapping and deal-making reciprocity of politics-as-usual. And, if Carter would be excluded from the political community, he would turn this social liability into a moral asset. He would become a moral reformer — the quintessential outsider whose devotion to the community is displayed in efforts to reform it.

Ironically, Jimmy Carter never really won his election to the state senate. Homer Moore just gave up. For three largely sleepless weeks Carter protested his defeat in the state Democratic party, in newspapers, and in open court. Most of his efforts were in vain. Appeals to the state Democratic party were turned back to the county party, headed by Joe Hurst; local newspapers wanted to have little to do with a candidate they perceived as a sore loser; and court victories were met by court losses.

Three factors, however, worked in Carter's favor. First, Charles Kirbo, a partner in the prestigious Atlanta law firm of King and Spaulding (who went on to become one of Carter's closest political advisors) agreed to represent him. Kirbo, whose roots were in southwest Georgia despite his partnership in the Atlanta firm, did not tally clear court victories but did keep Carter's case alive through the general election. The second factor working for Carter was John Pennington, an Atlanta newspaper reporter whose aid Carter enlisted through his cousin, Donnell Carter (then with the *Wall Street Journal*). Whereas the Columbus papers were reluctant to carry stories critical of a county boss in their circulation area, the Atlanta papers were not. Pennington wrote a number of stories about the alleged election fraud, which lent Carter's case some media credibility and appealed to the state's more urbane and progressive forces. Not least, the third and major factor that contributed to Carter's eventual victory was, simply, his tenacity.

Although a series of court and party victories resulted in rulings the weekend before the election that Carter's name should be placed on the November 6 general election ballot as the certified Democratic candidate (without Republican opposition), Moore's forces took the matter to court again on Monday, November 5, the day before the election. At midnight the judge ruled that Carter was not legally the Democratic nominee and that the next day's election should pit Carter and Moore against each other again in a special write-in election. The ruling posed enormous logistical and legal problems. Not only was it impossible for the two candidates to alert their supporters of the write-in election that very day or, as one county ordinary protested, to prepare new ballots overnight, it was also not clear whether Monday's district court ruling overruled the secretary of state's different ruling the previous weekend, or whether the state's ruling took precedence. In that ambiguous situation (in which two of the seven counties that Carter carried handsomely left his name, but not Moore's, on the ballot) it was in no way clear that the resulting 3,013 to 2,182 victory for Carter on November 6 reflected the will of the people. Nor was the election legally binding. Moore was entitled and expected to contest the election, which almost certainly would have required yet another special election. But after stewing over the matter, Moore decided to concede the race. He had had enough of politics.

Carter's victory in 1962 was therefore an ambiguous one. Indeed, the fact that he faced no opposition in his 1964 reelection campaign may be attributable as much to the reluctance of potential rivals to challenge so tenacious a candidate as it was to the caliber of his service. Joe Hurst, after all, went to federal prison as a consequence of his run-in with Carter, while the exhausted Homer Moore retired from politics. Moral tenacity rather than political acumen had catapulted Carter to office. It was a lesson he would never forget.

Yet it is by no means clear that Carter's moral victory was any less ambiguous than his political victory. Although for Carter the ordeal confirmed his commitment to universalism, in the long run the altercation in Quitman County may have served a purpose no larger than getting Carter elected and Hurst dethroned. If political success is measured not by who wins and who loses but by how the people governed fare, Carter's victory in Quitman County in 1962 may have been a dubious one.

In the same years that Carter wrote his memoir of the 1962 election, intending it as a metaphor for thirty years of progressive change in the nation, tiny Quitman County struggled against daunting challenges. The majority black county, with a per capita income only 64 percent of the national average, was the poorest in a still poor state. The poverty rate among African Americans was over 50 percent, and the county received the largest percentage of government transfer payments (29 percent) and merited the highest percentages of incomes from government employment (24 percent) of any county in Georgia. Fewer than 40 percent of its adult population possessed a high-school diploma. Its small population, moreover, continued to decline as those with ambition and the wherewithal to achieve it left.[45]

Whether the bossism of Joe Hurst, now buried in Georgetown, contributed to this deplorable situation or helped mitigate its horrors remains — or at least should remain — an open question. "The people are free now to cast their votes . . . in honest elections," concluded Jimmy Carter in his tale of the county.[46] By such measures — and by ignoring others — progressive universalism has long been justified.

SERVING IN THE SENATE

"You just dreaded to see Carter coming down the hallway in the legislative session," remembered Reg Murphy, the Atlanta newspaper reporter who was assigned to cover the state legislature in the early 1960s and who went on to become Carter's editorial nemesis in Georgia. "You never could talk about substantive issues for him wanting to point out little picayune comma faults in stories. . . . Jimmy Carter . . . will never be human enough to overlook the faults of anybody else."[47] Another reporter agreed. Bill Shipp, who later became the dean of Georgia's political reporting by writing a weekly newsletter as well as statewide political columns and television commentary, remembered that "Carter also forced me to start using a tape recorder" because he was "very bad about saying he was misquoted." To illustrate, Shipp recounted an occasion when the reporter had to play back the tape for Carter to extract an apology for his public objection to a story. Although the reporter received a quiet apology, Carter never retracted his public missive denying his remarks.[48]

The journalists' assessment of Carter's character was shared by others and was largely accurate, at least during the years 1962–66. (Later in life Carter showed more willingness to overlook faults in others, even if he continued to correct grammar well into his presidency.)[49] Propelled in part by his moralistic victory over Hurst, Carter's lifelong tendency to prideful self-righteousness was at its most pronounced during these years.

There were, however, beneficial consequences to this orientation. While Carter's "picayune" attention to the written word had its annoying side, it also made him an especially diligent legislator. Having vowed to read every bill in its entirety before voting on it, Carter did just that (despite his later realization that hundreds of bills, sometimes running hundreds of pages each, would cross his desk in a given forty-day legislative session). To do so he moved out of the rowdy Henry Grady Hotel where most of his colleagues stayed (and the poker games were held) and took a room in the quieter Piedmont. Ever a devotee of self-improvement, he also took a speed-reading course. Rising early and staying up late, Carter speed-read the bills that would potentially affect his state and voted knowledgeably on each. He even remained in Atlanta on Fridays, when most of the legislators went home for three-day weekends. The Friday sessions were devoted to approving minor bills affecting only selected regional constituencies. Having read them, Carter stayed in order to vote on these "special interest" bills. He also used the extra day to visit state department heads and others who might help him form better judgments of pending legislation.[50]

Carter's efforts won him the respect, if not always the affection, of the majority of his colleagues. Although "he did have a way of voting against things when he disagreed with them" and "was somewhat intransigent," a colleague remembered that "he was well liked by his fellow senators."[51] Another remembered his reputation somewhat differently. Brooks Pennington, one of his closest senate colleagues, recalled that "Carter perhaps alienated himself with certain senators by his philosophy of promoting his own position on matters and trading as little as he absolutely had to in order to prevail." But he also judged that "Carter would be in the top one-third of the 52 senators in the Georgia Senate at that time."[52] "His record," recalled another senator who worked closely with him, "was that of a good, hardworking, reform legislator."[53] Another, who said "it was obvious from his utterances that he did his homework," remembered him as "a dedicated senator."[54] He also secured favors from the like-minded progressive governor, Carl Sanders, and in 1966 enjoyed the support of several of his senate colleagues in his own race for governor.

Carter's diligent attention to detail did not however inspire him ideologically. Like many whose moral convictions are so firmly held that they permit little questioning, Carter saw no need to probe either ideological positions or their philosophical underpinnings. Morality was, rather, a given that needed only to be applied. Joining a reapportioned senate that brought a number of similarly progressive senators into the fold, Carter therefore generally voted with the majority on major pieces of legislation. His one stand on principle (later to be taken out of context and used against him) was to call for changing a phrase promoting religion in a proposed revision of the state constitution to one that better conformed with the Bill of Rights. (His proposal was: "No law shall be passed respecting an establishment of religion or prohibiting the free exercise thereof.") Such liberal positions extended, but did not modify, the accepted progressive consensus.

But in the political arena of the early 1960s, morality also had to be applied cautiously. Thus, although Carter spoke against the "30 questions" that were used as a means of disenfranchising black voters, he supported the bill that included modifications of those questions. His speech against the practice was also sufficiently bland to be overlooked by his constituents, despite his fears that some would seize it as a pretext to oppose him. Indeed, Carter's civil-rights activities while senator may have extended no further than his learning to pronounce the word "Negro" politely. Remembering LeRoy Johnson, the first black legislator to be elected in Georgia since Reconstruction, who joined the newly constituted senate in 1962, Carter recalled how Johnson instructed his colleagues to pronounce "Negro." Pointing to his knee and then saying "grow," Johnson taught his progressive white colleagues to say "Negro" without slurring it into something that sounded like "nigger."[55] Carter presumably benefited from the lesson in elocution as much as his moderate colleagues did. (In 1966 Gerald Rafshoon, Carter's media expert, decided "I liked this guy Carter" because "he could properly say the word 'Negro.'")[56] But, except for learning to pronounce "Negro" and opposing the most onerous form of black disenfranchisement, "Carter was not involved in the civil rights issue, as were not most of the legislators. The issue was so emotional it was dangerous to touch, so everybody left it alone."[57] His work on educational matters — his chief policy concern at the time — in fact proposed nothing that would further school desegregation. Carter was known, if at all, as "a fiscal conservative . . . with a progressive attitude."[58] Several times his "picayune" review of bills prompted him to support strategies that lessened the tax burden of, especially, rural districts, while his low-key progressive attitude kept him in good standing with his colleagues and constituents.

His diligence, combined with a practical yet moral orientation, did, however, prompt Carter to strike out independently in at least one area. During his service in the senate and then later in the decade, Carter became intensely interested in the process of planning. He helped found and later headed his regional planning commission, secured both state and matching federal funding for the agency, and maintained a conception of himself as a planner through his presidential campaign.

It is possible that Carter's attraction to planning betrayed less sanguine personality traits, not unlike those detected by Reg Murphy. The quest for "comprehensive" plans may reflect an underlying insecurity that substitutes a need to dominate a threatening process of change for a healthier desire to direct it. Planning may have also offered Carter a medium for cautiously expressing the moral dimension of his forming political personality. Historically wedded to the progressive political impulse, planning assumes that moral uplift can be accomplished through rational-scientific social engineering. Yet planning also disguises moral ambition. In planning, moral impulses are cloaked in rational garb and expected to grow to fruition only years or decades later. For one fearful of the repercussions that might meet a more immediate moral pronouncement, planning affords a way to pursue a moral agenda discreetly.

Although many who worked closely with Carter took offense at his self-righteousness, the combination of effective service, avoidance of controversy, and a high moral tone allowed his general political capital to soar. At home he even managed to get Georgia Southwestern College upgraded from two-year to four-year status. On such accomplishments often hinge political careers. When in 1964 Lyndon Johnson became the first Democratic presidential candidate to lose Georgia, and the state elected its first Republican congressman since Reconstruction, Carter was safely insulated in an uncontested senate seat. He also had the respect of many, if not all, of his colleagues. It was thus natural for him to envision moving up the political ladder.

So on March 3, 1966, just after the state senate adjourned, Carter announced his candidacy for the United States Congress. His victory in that race, the dream he had harbored since his return to Georgia a dozen years earlier, was virtually certain. Howard "Bo" Calloway, who had won the office as a Republican in 1964, was vacating it in 1966 in order to make a gubernatorial run. Carter, no longer a political outsider but a two-term state senator with a solid if not sterling reputation, was well positioned to win the congressional seat. Supporters paid his qualification fee and no one thought he could lose.

But then, on June 12, 1966, Carter made a surprise announcement: that he too would be a candidate for governor. Although his sudden shift in political goals was quickly supported by a number of his youthful colleagues (including Georgia's future U.S. senator, Sam Nunn,[59] and fellow state Senators Bob Brown, Brooks Pennington, Bob Smalley, and Ford Spinks),[60] most of his supporters were bewildered. They forecast (correctly) that Carter had virtually no chance of being elected governor and wondered why he gave up a congressional seat to try.

The best explanation for this surprising change in political ambition is not unlike the descriptions of his senate character. Proud and self-righteous, Carter simply overestimated his abilities. He may even have already had his eye on the White House. Explaining the inexplicable, Charles Kirbo later offered the opinion that Carter's switch was politically "wise" because "Congress is a very poor place to progress from. . . . If he wanted to be governor and then later president it was a good time to switch. . . . It helped him develop an organization and he gained experience and maturity during that time."[61] Other comments, like those of Senator Brooks Pennington, who recalled that "Carter discussed with me his plan to run for governor of Georgia during his last year in the senate" (a year that officially concluded the second day in March), show that prior to announcing for the congressional seat Carter had considered a gubernatorial run.[62] Clearly, by early 1966 Carter had already set his sights higher than most people expected.

But giving shape to his political ambition was an opponent whom, like Joe Hurst, Carter chose to construe as a personification of political evil. Bo Calloway, a former student at Georgia Tech and a West Point graduate of about Carter's age, had not only beaten Carter to Congress but was also the Republican front-runner in the gubernatorial contest in a year that many thought would bring a Republican victory. Perhaps because Calloway had beaten him to the congressional seat, Carter no longer cared for it. What he cared about was defeating the rival he often called, without elaboration, a "rich young Republican." Calloway reciprocated the feeling and later recalled that "there was a strong competition between us."[63] Yet, while Calloway was quick to add, "So far as I know, the competition between the two of us was never personal," Carter's actions suggest that for him it was. Later he admitted that "one of the major reasons" for his decision to enter the gubernatorial contest in 1966 was his "not especially admirable" feeling of personal "competitiveness" toward Calloway.[64]

Fueled therefore by a combination of overconfidence, self-righteousness, and personal competitiveness, Carter brashly joined five other Democratic candidates in the race for governor. But 1966 was not 1962. The progressive changes that had swept Georgia in 1962 were met in 1966 by a strong backlash. Jimmy Carter was pummeled by the crosswinds — and defeated.

MADDOX COUNTRY

Calloway could not have been more delighted by Carter's entry into the gubernatorial fray. Carter's entry promised (and proved) to be that of a Democratic spoiler. With little chance of winning outright, the only hope he had was to garner enough votes in a fractured Democratic field to merit a position in the runoff. (By Georgia law, unless a candidate achieves a 50+ percent majority in the primary election, the top two primary contenders face one another in a runoff election.) But, whether he succeeded or not, the result would be divisive for the Democrats. This divisiveness could not help but contribute strength to Bo Calloway, the sole Republican candidate in what many predicted would be an anti–Lyndon Johnson and anti–civil rights Republican sweep.

There was, however, marginal merit in Carter's strategy. The crowded Democratic field made it reasonable to predict that a second-place primary finish, and so a position in the runoff, could be earned with considerably less than a majority of votes. (As it turned out, only 24 percent would have been necessary.) A second-place finish was also ideologically feasible. The acknowledged front-runner was former governor Ellis Arnall. But he was generally considered too liberal for a state that two years before had broken out of its Democratic mold and voted Republican in the presidential race as well as in one congressional campaign. Opposing Arnall were four candidates boasting various shades of conservatism: James Gray, Garland Byrd, Hoke O'Kelley, and Lester Maddox. With the ideological middle left wide open, Carter might position himself just to the right of Arnall and take a wide swath of moderate votes. Then, with the race narrowed to two candidates, he could move to the right to defeat Arnall and be well positioned as a conservative Democrat to beat Calloway in the general election.

But it was not to be. When the returns came in, the first-place finish went, as predicted, to Arnall. Just behind Arnall's 24 percent, however, was a shockingly strong 23.5 percent for Lester Maddox. Carter, with 21 percent, came in third — and lost. He always considered that his defeat came at the hands of Maddox rather than Arnall. Ultimately he was right. For Georgia in 1966 was "Maddox country."

☆   ☆   ☆

Lester Maddox was a study in paradoxes.[65] As a Depression-era working-class boy growing up in Atlanta, he quit high school to work a variety of jobs to support himself and his family. (During the Depression, like many others, he was forced to work under the auspices of the WPA, a line of government work he later characterized as "shovel leaning.") After the war, however, a combination of hard work, improving economic conditions, and ingenuity enabled him to start a business for himself. The business, a restaurant he called the Pickrick, located on U.S. 41 in Atlanta, specialized in southern cuisine, like fried chicken, biscuits and gravy, and heaping piles of vegetables cooked in animal fat. The food was good, the prices right, and the location ideal; Maddox succeeded.

Whether the Pickrick's success enabled Maddox to develop a popular public persona or whether the persona contributed to the Pickrick's success is anyone's guess. But by about 1950 the two became fused. Beginning in that year Maddox bought advertisements in the Atlanta newspapers that began with the phrase, "Pickrick says." Personifying himself as Pickrick, Maddox wrote copy that commented upon all manner of culinary and, increasingly, political issues. To describe the views expressed in these advertisements as conservative is too simple; as populist, too vague. They were, rather, a silly blend of the two, sprinkled with the charming quirkiness of a self-described "little man." Such "little men" were essentially populist in outlook, resentful of all powers that reminded them of their smallness. But in an era of an activist federal government, populists frequently directed their resentment toward the federal government. That made them conservatives. In Maddox, with ample resources and a public advertising forum for expression, these views were united in a persona of considerable color. Indeed, in the later 1950s and into the 1960s he even took to embarrassing himself further by running and losing a series of local and state political races — defeats that were nevertheless good for business.

Then came the altercation of July 3, 1964, the day after President Johnson signed the Civil Rights Act. Three African American divinity students attempted to integrate the Pickrick. They were met by Maddox, angry and armed, in the parking lot. Although the students escaped unscathed, on their way out of the parking lot a furious Maddox grabbed an ax handle and bashed the students' car. Maddox — and the ax handle — became an overnight symbol of southern resistance to civil rights.

Maddox (who bought up every ax handle he could find and sold them for tidy profits in his restaurant) always denied that he was a racist. His claim was rather that federal government intervention, as illustrated by the Civil Rights Act, extended too deeply into the lives of small businessmen. When one considers that in order to convict him of violating the federal law prosecutors had to prove first that the Pickrick was engaged in interstate commerce — and actually did so by having witnesses from out of state testify that they had dined at the Pickrick while traveling through Georgia (leaving the food in their digestive system after they had crossed the state line) — some appreciation of Maddox's claim may be extended. Moreover, as governor, Maddox could point to more appointments of African Americans than could any of his predecessors, as well as to policies like early prison work-release that disproportionately benefited poor blacks. He was also the kind of colorful restaurateur who would occasionally interrupt his all-white diners and ask them to give the all-black kitchen staff a round of applause (and argue that closing the Pickrick would cost blacks their jobs). He simply found forced integration an intolerable federal intrusion into his rights as a small businessman and the regional way of life he had been raised to accept.

Whether or not Maddox was a racist — and it is difficult to believe that he was not in at least some form — he emerged as a symbol of white resistance and the more general populist conservatism. At the time, other southern states found such symbols in their politicians, and one may have been required for Georgia too. For the times were foreboding. In August of 1965 race riots erupted in the Watts area of Los Angeles. The neighborhood was set aflame, thirty-five people died, and profound questions were raised nationwide about the wisdom of the liberal consensus on civil rights policy. The next year Californians elected Ronald Reagan over Pat Brown as their governor. When the next summer the riots spread to Baltimore, Brooklyn, Chicago, Cleveland, Jacksonville, Omaha, and San Francisco, a race war seemed imminent to the fearful. Indeed, Martin Luther King Jr., just awarded the Nobel Peace Prize in December of 1964, was losing his grip on the leadership of the civil rights movement as more aggressive organizations like the Black Panthers emerged promoting more assertive tactics. Meanwhile, the eruption of antiwar protests on college campuses spread to the cities — and met with a decisive cultural backlash. Whereas the last weekend in March saw antiwar rallies in seven U.S. cities, the number one popular song during the month was the proud "Ballad of the Green Berets."[66] Within two years and despite the strong third-party candidacy of George Wallace (who won Georgia), Richard Nixon reaped the political windfalls from this backlash with his famous 1968 "southern strategy" and "law and order" presidential campaign. In Georgia of 1966, substantial numbers of "little people," reeling from the dizzying barrage of changes, likewise sought a leader who could personify their frustrations. So in the 1966 Democratic gubernatorial primary, 23.5 percent of them cast votes for Lester Maddox.

Maddox was no George Wallace, Ronald Reagan, or Richard Nixon. His political savvy was negligible and he never rose to be a serious national or even state leader. When he took his newfound ax-handle celebrity and crisscrossed the state in 1966 hanging up signs declaring the regions "Maddox country," few took him seriously. But his appeal was stronger than many forecast and, through a series of flukes, he became governor.

The two most liberal candidates in Georgia's 1966 Democratic gubernatorial primary, Ellis Arnall and Jimmy Carter, together took 45 percent of the vote, nearly twice the percentage garnered by Maddox. The runoff election therefore promised to be a close one that, given Maddox's more negative image, would probably go to Arnall. Relying upon anecdotal evidence, most of Georgia's political observers therefore explain Maddox's runoff win as a consequence of Republicans crossing over to vote in the Democratic runoff election for him. The thinking is that Republicans considered Maddox to be an easier opponent for Calloway than was Arnall, so voted for him in order to engineer the contest in their favor. Some Republicans may have also hedged their bets and voted for Maddox as their second choice. Whatever the explanation (though voter turnout was higher in the runoff election than it had been in the initial primary), Maddox emerged from the contest as the Democratic nominee.

Liberals were incensed; moderates uncomfortable. Neither could bring themselves to support either party's nominee for governor. A write-in campaign, called WIG (for Write In Georgia), was therefore orchestrated to elect Arnall, anyway. WIG was, predictably, unsuccessful. However, it did succeed in depriving Calloway, who received the plurality of votes, of winning an outright majority. Since Georgia law required a majority for electoral victory, the race was thrown into the state legislature. There the overwhelmingly Democratic legislators let party loyalty decide and gave the nod to the second-place, but Democratic, finisher, Lester Maddox.

Georgia thus officially became, to the embarrassment of many, "Maddox country," while Calloway was denied the office that in any other state would have been his electoral right. Jimmy Carter was partially to blame for the outcome. Not only had he acted as a spoiler in the Democratic primary, but after his defeat he refused to endorse a candidate in the runoff, as was the custom. The absent endorsement served Carter well four years later when he ran again for governor and sought to graft Maddox's constituency onto his own more moderate base, but it also may have contributed the final blow to Arnall's candidacy. As for Calloway, who had more justification than anyone for bitterness, he moved to Colorado. There he resurfaced in Republican politics and by 1976 climbed to national prominence when he temporarily managed Gerald Ford's presidential campaign against Jimmy Carter.

This, Carter's second campaign, had also been a whirlwind affair. But this time there had been no outright vote fraud and there was no pretext for protest. Carter had done better than many had expected, but he had lost. Later he would view the loss as an essential learning experience — as a necessary deflation of his growing ego — and use its lessons to fashion a more viable campaign strategy (mostly by moving to the right in 1970 and making direct appeals to Maddox supporters). At the time, however, the defeat was crushing. "I remembered," wrote Hamilton Jordan, who had joined Carter's campaign in 1966 after hearing him speak at an Elks Club, "how he had packed up his family and driven off into the night without thanking his campaign workers." The lack of gratitude may have reflected the selfish egotism that Carter himself grew quickly to loathe. But he may also have been embarrassed. Jordan wondered whether he had been crying.[67]

MAGGIE'S FARM

Two weeks after the 1966 primary, Jordan received a call from Carter. The defeated gubernatorial candidate apologized for leaving on the evening of the returns without thanking his chief volunteer but then broached the subject that was really on his mind. Would he, Jordan, assist him in his 1970 race? The request prompted Jordan to suggest that Carter consider a more realistic race for lieutenant governor in 1970. It soon became apparent to Jordan, however, that Carter had already made up his mind to run again for governor.[68] It was also quickly apparent to others. By the 1967 legislative session a reporter recalled seeing Carter "walking through the state capitol, telling everyone he saw, reporters and politicians, that he was running for governor and was going to win in 1970."[69]

But four years is a long time to plot a political campaign, especially when the requirements of work do not seriously intervene. Money was no longer a problem for Carter. (Only partially unlike Calloway, Carter was "a rich young Democrat.") Although he did have campaign debts to retire, did need to raise more funds for his 1970 campaign, and had to provide for his family, Carter's finances had by this time worked themselves out. The base he had established during his 1966 campaign, coupled with his commitment to run again, made raising campaign funds relatively easy. As for his personal finances, his business in Plains thrived under the direction of his brother Billy, who had come home to manage it during the 1966 campaign. Billy may have even been the superior businessman, for under his leadership the Carter warehouse grew to be a multimillion-dollar operation. So, while Carter continued to work at the family warehouse (where his private office and nominal campaign headquarters were also located), much of his energy could be directed as he saw fit.

Carter therefore used the years between 1966 and 1970 as an interlude for reflection. "I tried to expand my interests in as many different directions as possible," he wrote about this period in his life. Although he accepted as many speaking invitations as he could during this period — he later estimated that he delivered 1,800 speeches during his four-year campaign for governor — to prepare a single "original" speech on any one of the number of issues he was asked to address in talks throughout the state he sometimes read as many as "three or four books" for background.[70] And, without the bills he had vowed to read crossing his desk, he was also able to read more broadly, especially in philosophy and theology. He acquainted himself with the writings of Reinhold Niebuhr, Paul Tillich, and Søren Kierkegaard, as well as with more contemporary theologians like the then-fashionable "death of God" theologian, Thomas J. J. Altizer. Sequestered in a warehouse office decorated with a small ivory statue of Gandhi and a large wall map of Georgia[71] while the world in which he hoped to be a player swirled outside and beyond him, Carter read, wrote, plotted, and thought.

And he changed. The degree of the change was not detected publicly until he delivered his inaugural address as governor in January 1971. Then he shocked the state by announcing not only that "the time for discrimination is over" but also that "no poor, rural, weak, or black person should ever again have to bear the additional burden of being deprived of the opportunity for an education, a job, or simple justice."[72] Although this forthright declaration of racial equality was in keeping with Carter's long-standing commitment to civil rights, in the context of the times the statement was sensational. The *Atlanta Constitution* declared it an "end-of-an-era statement," while even Reg Murphy admitted in a signed editorial that it was "an impressive beginning."[73] Bill Shipp, in a "comment and analysis" piece, considered Carter's speech "Kennedyesque," which "in the era of the Talmadges . . . would have been denounced as the talk of wild-eyed liberals or Communists or race-mixers or worse."[74] The inaugural address was also sufficiently provocative to attract national media attention. *Time* magazine, for instance, put Carter's picture on the cover of their next issue. Carter was, the cover photograph implied, saying something dramatically new in the old South.

But Carter's changed rhetoric was not limited to supporting civil rights, despite the attention the media gave to this aspect of his inaugural address. It also included a more general call for social justice — specifically, for the "poor," "rural," and "weak," as well as blacks. If anything, this general theme of social justice was more pronounced in his rhetoric than was the call for civil rights. At smaller gatherings throughout the state, the general theme of social justice was sounded the loudest. To a Lions Club convention on Jekyll Island in May 1971, for instance, he spoke about the need for social justice and compassion. "There is," he told the assembled audience,

> a mandatory relationship between the powerful and the influential and the socially prominent and the wealthy on the one hand, and the weak, the insecure, and the poor on the other hand. . . . [I]n a free society we do see very clearly that one cannot accept great blessings bestowed on him by God without feeling an inner urge and drive to share those blessings with others of our neighbors who are not quite so fortunate as we.[75]

And, less than three years after delivering this speech, he gave the famous Law Day speech at the University of Georgia, which, with its calls for social justice, attracted the attention of counterculture journalist Hunter Thompson and won Carter the endorsement of *Rolling Stone* magazine. Among other things in that speech, he said: "I grew up a landowner's son. But, I don't think I ever realized the proper interrelationship between the landowner and those who worked on the farm until I heard Dylan's record, 'I Ain't Gonna Work on Maggie's Farm No More.'"[76]

Although Carter often reported that his favorite book was *Let Us Now Praise Famous Men*,[77] he might have become acquainted with this 1941 combination of haunting photographs and text depicting the lives of white southern sharecroppers at any time. But his discovery of Bob Dylan's

"Maggie's Farm" could have occurred only after 1965, when the song of outrage over the lot of farmworkers appeared on Dylan's album *Bringing It All Back Home*. In mentioning Dylan, Carter therefore dated with some precision his heightening social conscience. It would have been sometime between 1965 and 1971 — during his interlude of reflection.

Often it has been assumed that Carter's social compassion is traceable to his growing up amid wrenching rural poverty. He himself said as much. "I do have unique experience," he once told an interviewer. "One of the strongest and best of these is my relationship with poor people. That's where I came from. That's where I lived. Those are my people."[78] It is also likely that his parents — the liberal Lillian and the charitable Earl — instilled in him an ethic of compassion that, coupled with the populist political climate of his youth, slipped easily into a more general sensitivity to social injustice. Yet, while these experiences contributed to Carter's compassionate outlook, he plainly stated in his 1974 Law Day speech that the plight of poor farmworkers did not impress itself upon him until he listened to Bob Dylan.

Other signs indicate that Carter's social conscience grew keener during the late 1960s. Prior to then no one remembered his displaying an especially pronounced social compassion, outside of his quiet support for civil rights, and few in Plains even recalled his continuing his father's well-remembered charitable practices. Similarly, before 1971 there is no record of a Carter speech that spoke as forcefully about problems of social injustice, or as compassionately about the needs of the less privileged, as those that emerged after then. Acts of kindness and words of compassion can be discovered, but they are minor.

Beginning in the late 1960s, moreover, Carter also seemed driven to express his feelings of social compassion through actions. He volunteered, for instance, for domestic missionary service through his church. Although the service was primarily oriented toward converting the unchurched rather than toward social betterment, the assignments took him to the ghettos of northern cities in Massachusetts and Pennsylvania where he worked with the poor and disinherited. (On one such occasion his assigned neighborhood consisted mainly of poor, Spanish-speaking Puerto Ricans.) He also accepted assignments at inconvenient times. One, for example, required that he spend Thanksgiving Day away from his family. Likewise, although it was a pleasure trip, the occasion of the Carters' late 1960s vacation to Mexico touched him deeply. The thirst for learning he discovered among the peasant children became the subject of one of the first poems he ever wrote, even as a second poem, about leprosy, drew from his mother's simultaneous experience as a Peace Corps volunteer in India.[79] Clearly, by the late 1960s Jimmy Carter was touched by a deeper compassion for the less privileged than he had felt previously.

Based upon his volunteer missionary service, his poems, and many of his own statements, it seems certain that something changed in Jimmy Carter between the years 1966 and 1970. The change, of course, should not be overstated. The sharp self-righteousness and egotism so characteristic of his years in the state senate remained, even though these traits seemed tempered by a greater willingness to appreciate others' views and a deeper acknowledgment of his own limitations. Carter's political ambition also persisted, and the general outlines of his moral passions after the late 1960s built upon those evidenced earlier. In particular, it is no accident that the loner deprived of community became, by middle age, a politician compassionately devoted to bridging social divisions. Yet the detectable changes that occurred in Carter sometime during the late 1960s need to be stressed against previous biographers who, promoting psychological interpretations over others, failed to detect the changes and therefore rooted his social compassion solely in a personality forged in childhood.[80] This personality and his childhood experiences contributed much to Carter's more mature sense of social compassion. But the personality forged in childhood cannot be the whole story. For by the late 1960s there was a detectable intensification of Carter's compassionate impulses, which Carter himself attributed to an experience that could not have occurred before 1965.

The change in Carter during the late 1960s was reflected in a change in his thinking about society and social issues. Prior to then, Carter thought of society in primarily progressive terms. He conceived of it as a fairly static arena subject to incremental and rationally planned changes. But by the 1970s these progressive views were melded with a more dynamic conception of society. The view he promoted after 1970 was of a society that is essentially oligarchic, deeply divided by inequality, and fundamentally unjust. This view did not diminish his commitment to universalism, but it did prompt him to replace the progressive assumption that carefully planned improvements would lead to social betterment with the more radical assumption that fundamental social inversion would be required to achieve universalistic justice. Although Carter did not press his views to these radical conclusions — he always recommended compassion rather than revolution — his underlying image of society was strikingly similar.

Yet, it is not likely that thought alone — or the reading and study that engaged him during the late 1960s — prompted this altered view of society. As Norman Mailer observed in 1976 when he wrote that "Carter was not necessarily one of America's leading authorities on Kierkegaard," Carter's moral "decency" did not seem to be grounded primarily in intellect.[81] Carter himself admitted as much. "I obviously don't know all the answers to philosophical questions," he told Bill Moyers in a 1976 interview, adding that many of the philosophical and theological questions struck him as "contrived" so "I just accept them and go on."[82] This candid assessment of his intellectual limitations indicated that his reflections had not been especially deep. A similar verdict was rendered by a Plains acquaintance who, like Carter, had tried to stay abreast of intellectual developments. Remembering when she tried to discuss Altizer's "death of God" theology with Carter, she also recalled his response. He had said, "You can't read that thing and understand it," a comment she took to mean that "he couldn't read it and understand it." She therefore concluded, "I don't know how profound Jimmy is. My feeling was probably no more profound than I was."[83]

And later, when he became governor and then president, Carter continued to show himself bereft of a solid intellectual foundation for his political views. Basing their assumption upon his compassion for the less privileged and his view of society as unjust, many thought that he would promote a liberal agenda of social reforms. He did not. Although he approved of compassionate policies that mitigated the harshest consequences of a free market system, he remained essentially an economic conservative. As governor, his chief accomplishment was to reorganize state government — precisely the kind of reform that appealed to the business class — and, as president, he championed conservative causes like economic deregulation. Yet, ironically, Carter never endorsed the moral claims of the conservative economic agenda. He often argued that "efficiency" was not a central mandate of government,[84] railed against the consequences of unbridled competition, and gave no evidence of believing that a competitive free market economy actually provided "the greatest good for the greatest number." But, failing to embrace the moral claims of competitive capitalism, Carter also neglected to propose liberal alternatives. Indeed, he sometimes supported the very political system that at other times he declared unjust.

On the underlying values that often divide liberals from conservatives, Carter also displayed apparent befuddlement. A key instance of this is the tension between liberty and equality. Universalism, and a vague if sincere commitment to "human rights," can emphasize either. Liberty, which allows individuals to achieve goals according to merit or luck, necessarily results in inequality. Equality, which urges that rewards be similar regardless of merit or luck, necessarily curtails liberty. "These two terms," Carter's presidential speechwriter James Fallows reminded him, are "like city and country, heaven and hell; the tensions between them shape much of American society."[85] The reminders came, however, after Carter promised to bring the two irreconcilable values into "correlation."[86] How he proposed to accomplish this impossible feat baffled Fallows and indeed was never explained by Carter. Finally realizing that Carter was not "vulgarizing his ideas for the crowd" but "genuinely believed what he said," Fallows was forced also to conclude that, in terms of political philosophy, Carter had no ascendant "idea" but just "happen[ed] to believe them all."[87]

Lacking an ascendant political idea, Carter's altered image of society and intensified moral compassion are difficult to trace to intellect. Instead, they seem rooted in emotion. Once in 1977, when a member of his Sunday school class asked him bluntly whether equality or freedom (liberty) was the more important value, Carter explained: "If I was teaching this class in the ghetto of New York, they'd say 'equality.' There is a natural preference for the powerful and the rich and the good to say 'freedom,' but for many people in the world who are deprived, all they want is to be equal."[88] The explanation was an intellectual sidestep, the meaning of which was nevertheless emotionally clear. Unable to defend equality rationally, Carter defended it emotionally.

The same conclusion arises from a fuller look at Carter's 1971 speech to the Lions Club convention on Jekyll Island. There, where he called for a mandatory moral relationship between the more and the less privileged, he also admitted candidly that the relationship "is not always something that is completely understood." Indeed, in an impulse that may have owed as much to Bob Dylan as to Søren Kierkegaard, he even confessed that "I don't completely understand it myself." He rather assured his listeners, simply, that the lesson was "instilled within me and within your hearts."[89]

☆　☆　☆

Whenever Carter was asked to identify turning points in his life, he invariably mentioned the religious conversion he described as becoming "born again." This occurred during the autumn of 1966, a timing that coincides with his changed outlook. And from it can be discerned his altered conception of society rooted in emotion more than in intellect.

The experience occurred as follows. After his defeat in the gubernatorial primary, Carter reported symptoms that his later aide, psychiatrist Peter Bourne, described as a "classic description of depression." Carter said, "everything I did was not gratifying. When I succeeded in something, I got no pleasure out of it. When I failed at something, it was a horrible experience for me." He was also convicted by pride and consumed by self-loathing. "I'd never done much for other people," he realized. "I was always thinking about myself." Battling these feelings, he was prompted by a sermon to give them a religious interpretation. He realized: "I never really had committed myself totally to God. My Christian beliefs were superficial. They were based primarily on pride." Then he took an autumn walk in the woods with his sister Ruth, who had already alighted upon her own psychoreligious answer to emotional pain. Ruth explained her "total commitment" to Christ and how, by making it, her pain had eased. Jimmy listened and, somewhere in the woods of southwest Georgia, gave his life to God.[90]

The experience was transformative. In the classic mode of Christian conversion, Carter's emotional life was inverted. By "giving up" his life he was able to "find it" again. He became "at ease" with his "hatreds" and "frustrations." And, although it was "a little bit embarrassing" for him to talk about, his conversion enabled him "to accept defeat, to get pleasure out of successes, to be at peace with the world."[91] Providing respite from his punishing depression and self-loathing, the born-again experience even fortified his political resolve. A volunteer from the 1966 campaign believed that "this personal commitment Carter found to Christ helped him gather the strength to begin campaigning again right away."[92]

So transformative a personal experience was bound to have consequences for his evolving moral and political ideas. Reporters and aides believed it did. "The core of his religious and personal faith," wrote the UPI correspondent assigned to his 1976 campaign, "seems to be the core of his political philosophy as well."[93] A campaign volunteer agreed that his "political philosophy" was anchored in his religious experience. Carter believed that politics offered "a fuller implementation of his religious beliefs, of doing what he believes as right to fulfill human needs," the aide said.[94] The explanation for the intensification of Carter's social compassion as well as his more dynamic view of society may thus be found in the implications that his born-again experience held for him.

After completing a mammoth review of Christian social teachings, the influential German theologian and sociologist Ernst Troeltsch concluded: "Nowhere does there exist an absolute Christian ethic, which only awaits discovery." The history of Christianity rather taught Troeltsch that there are a variety of ways that Christians have devised, and may devise, a social vision from their faith.[95] A similar conclusion was reached by H. Richard Niebuhr in the United States, who devised a fivefold typology of the possible relationships between faith and culture.[96] Few today dispute either conclusion. The social visions of Christianity are myriad.

Yet the American evangelical tradition in which Jimmy Carter was immersed since childhood and into which he was "born again" in 1966 tends to promote a particular social — or, more accurately, *asocial* — Christian ethic. It does so because salvation, virtually the sole aim of this religious tradition, has always been construed as a fundamentally personal experience. People are saved by individually heeding the quiet call of Christ. Given this personal emphasis, it has always been difficult for the evangelical tradition to develop an acceptable doctrine of society and politics. Intensifying this difficulty in twentieth-century American evangelicalism was surely the fundamentalist/modernist controversy, which shunted evangelicals to the periphery of public life in order to make way for the march of modernism. However, at least one interpreter of Carter's faith, a medievalist historian, argued that as long ago as the "late 11th and early 12th centuries . . . [t]he central message of the evangelical movement was that the moral reform of the individual through the imitation of the gospel message of love and salvation took precedence over . . . society."[97] In other words, the very logic of evangelicalism's salvation message is usually to emphasize the individual and deemphasize the society. This logic was simply intensified in the American evangelical experience.

Although it is not a happy conclusion (and is therefore often rejected by many in the movement), the normal consequences of the evangelical tradition are to produce a fatalistic view of society and politics. Steeped in original sin, the wider society and its government are seen as irredeemable. Indeed, when grafted onto millennialist expectations of a second coming, as it sometimes is, the evangelical faith is also inclined to forecast and even to hope for worsening social conditions as a sign indicating that the end is near. But even without millennialist expectations, the usual consequence of the evangelical faith is to construe society and government as an arena of sin best to be ignored. And such seemed to be the sentiments expressed to Carter by a visiting pastor who challenged his political ambitions as early as 1962. "[W]hy don't you go into the ministry or into some honorable social service work?" the minister inquired.[98] The implication was plain: Politics is no place for a Christian.

Tempering, but not replacing, this apolitical view is, however, another widely held evangelical doctrine. This is the doctrine that the love of neighbor is on a footing equal or nearly so with the love of God. The doctrine is found in the Gospels:

> . . . a lawyer asked Him a question, testing Him,
> "Teacher, which is the great commandment in the Law?"
> And He said to him, "'YOU SHALL LOVE THE LORD YOUR GOD WITH ALL YOUR HEART, AND WITH ALL YOUR SOUL, AND WITH ALL YOUR MIND.'
> "This is the great and foremost commandment.
> "And a second is like it, 'YOU SHALL LOVE YOUR NEIGHBOR AS YOURSELF.'
> "On these two commandments depend the whole Law and the Prophets." (Matt. 22:35–40 [NAS])

This notion that love of neighbor is tantamount to love of God has therefore, and somewhat paradoxically, also long lent the evangelical tradition a strong ethic of social compassion. And, despite their apolitical views, throughout America's history evangelicals have often been in the forefront of compassionate social service.[99] Nevertheless, it is important to appreciate that evangelical social compassion does not usually derive from a larger vision of a just society. The evangelical social vision rather remains fundamentally apolitical. The ethic of social compassion makes no promises to produce a final good society but simply to ameliorate some of the harshest consequences of a perennially sinful one. In the process, compassion may also produce converts.

When Carter debated the minister who criticized his political ambition, the gist of his argument was that politics provided a forum for "service to other people." His Christian defense of his political ambitions, in other words, was couched in the language of social compassion. Absent from it, however, was any challenge to the minister's apolitical assumptions. He did not respond to the minister by offering any rationale for the special importance of politics in human affairs; he did not articulate any vision of a better society; he did not even argue that society might be better. He merely implied that politics would enable him to serve others as well as or better than he might elsewhere. By arguing as he did and failing to argue otherwise, Carter showed how deeply he shared the evangelical tradition's essentially apolitical views. He did not believe that government could be good or society better; he merely believed that through politics an individual Christian might augment his capacity for service.

Later in life, even when he was a presidential candidate, Carter conveyed no loftier political vision. Claiming that his choice of a political career had been "almost accidental,"[100] he implied that it was no better (or worse) than many other worldly careers. Then, after he had left politics and inaugurated his celebrated postpresidential humanitarian career, he often spoke of the "enormous satisfaction" that his new career offered, explaining further that its rewards far exceeded those he had found in politics. Never, in fact, did Carter articulate a vision of political action that credited it with more significance than that found in many other fields of human activity. In this neglect Carter displayed his lifelong agreement with evangelicalism's essentially apolitical views.

Much of the criticism of Carter's political career, illustrated by James Fallows's charge that he had no ascendant political "idea," finds its explanation in this understanding of Carter's evangelical moorings. Carter remained a faithful proponent of evangelicalism's social logic throughout his career. Quick to display compassion for others, he nevertheless embraced no political philosophy promising a just society. Thus he answered Bill Moyers's question about whether he considered our society to be a just one with the flat statement, "No, no I don't."[101] But then, instead of using the question as an opening to present his plan for enhancing justice, he continued, "I think one of the major responsibilities I have, as a leader and a potential leader, is to try to establish justice." Fittingly, in the same interview he also twice referred to the presidency as a way to "magnify" his personal capacities to do good.[102] For Jimmy Carter, politics was a forum in which he might augment his ability to serve others but not an arena which might be fundamentally reformed. He therefore did "happen to believe" all good political ideas moderately — and none of them absolutely. For he did not believe, ultimately, that a just society was possible.

Carter's self-directed reading — or misreading[103] — of Reinhold Niebuhr during the late 1960s intensified this apolitical orientation. Writing in the aftermath of America's social gospel movement, Niebuhr counseled Christians to resist the dreamy Christian utopianism that promised to establish the Kingdom of God on earth. Social action, he warned in his book

Moral Man and Immoral Society and elsewhere, should be more realistic. Realistic social action entailed recognizing that society is an arena of power politics in which justice would never be perfectly attained and where action would always be tainted by moral impurities. It did not follow for Niebuhr, however, that social action was unchristian or that no reorganization of society would lead to improvement. His was simply a corrective message to a movement's mystification of society. Yet, read outside of historical context, when Christian political activism was virtually nil, Niebuhr's writings permitted more pessimistic interpretations than he intended or embraced. Carter's reading of Niebuhr some thirty-five years later inclined him toward these more pessimistic conclusions which, in turn, corresponded with the sentiments of his own evangelical tradition.[104]

But while his reading of Niebuhr confirmed his apolitical evangelical social ethic, that same ethic also inspired Carter to embrace fervently the mandate for social compassion. For him, Christians have "two loves" in their lives. "One is a love for God. The other is a love for the person who happens to be in front of you at any particular moment." Moreover, he understood the love of neighbor as an active love. "Love in isolation doesn't mean anything," he said. Meaningful love "is not a quiescent thing" but "an active thing." It was translated into acts of "fairness, equality, concern, compassion, redressing of grievances, elimination of inequalities, [and] recognizing the poor are the ones who suffer the most even in our society." Hence, even though a "person should have as a goal complete agape-love," in society "the most we can accept or expect . . . is to institute simple justice." As a Christian, Carter's proximal worldly goal was therefore "the enhancement of the lives of [his] fellow human beings." As an elected official, he wanted to "do simple justice through government." Indeed, he often described the responsibility of government officials as "to speak for those who have no adequate spokesman," namely, "those who are poor, disadvantaged, rural, illiterate, without influence, [or] who belong to minority groups." More generally, he often explained the Christian role of government to be that of working "to establish justice in a sinful world."[105]

From this sincere commitment to social compassion, combined with his belief that society was unjust, arose Carter's dynamic view of society. Acts of compassion must perpetually invert the existing and unjust status quo; piecemeal progressive changes were never enough. Yet, simply because he was a critic of society did not mean that Carter envisioned its reform or replacement with a better arrangement. For while the reach of Carter's commitment to social compassion extended into government, it included no vision of a fundamentally better society. As an evangelical Christian, Carter did not believe such a society possible.

Erected on a foundational commitment to universalism, Carter's evolving Christian philosophy gave him no reason to challenge his individualistic assumptions. Neither moral philosophy prompted him to develop a social vision or political philosophy rightly named, while both intensified his commitment to moral individualism. Indeed, the closest Carter ever came to propounding a political philosophy was to call for "a government as good as its people." In this slogan the government, like the wider society, is conceived as being little more than individuals aggregated.

This individualistic and apolitical philosophy, coming as it did from a man who made it to the presidency, has long provided fodder for critics. Carter was undeniably a good man, and his weaknesses as a political leader are in large part traceable to his failure to develop a moral philosophy that transcended the individual. He therefore flitted erratically from proposal to proposal and reform to reform. Even if all were good ideas (and many were), Carter's inability to coordinate them into a coherent social vision prevented him and his administration from sounding the singular theme or articulating a central vision that might have lifted his actions beyond the realm of personal goodness to that of collective betterment.

Yet there was one noteworthy exception to this general tendency. This exception reflects a perennial temptation among evangelicals, unhappy with their impoverished social vision, to look more toward the Old Testament than the New in order to fashion from it the vision of collective redemption that their individualistic faith lacks. The temptation has arisen in many periods and many guises throughout U.S. history. And when it arises, its logic is always the same: the nation is understood as analogous to the individual so that, just as the sinful individual may be saved by faith, so also might the sinful nation be collectively saved by a common faith.

Sometimes Carter thought this way. Experiencing a conversion that relieved him of self-hatred stemming from pride, it was easy for him to think of society analogously. Wesley Pippert even considered this his "central theme." Summarizing it, Pippert explained it as meaning that "persons, and nations, are fallible and sinful and require forgiveness; that persons, and nations — perhaps especially the United States — are 'afflicted' . . . by pride and need to learn humility." Or, in Carter's own words: "People in the United States are guilty of pride." "We as individuals" and "we as a nation" must "forego pride."[106] It did not automatically follow that a society might be "born again." Carter normally avoided a too literal analogy between the person and society, preferring to identify "love" as the goal of the individual and "justice" as the goal of society. But sometimes the literalism was patent. "[W]hat a person, individually, ought to be," Carter said, "also describes exactly what the government of that person ought to be."[107]

But on these occasions Carter betrayed the inadequacy of his own individualistic evangelical philosophy. Revealing that he too wanted, somehow, to achieve the community that both faith and experience had denied to him, he succumbed to the prophetic temptation of envisioning society as an analogue to the individual and it too as capable of redemption. But in quieter and more rational moments he withdrew into his more personal and apolitical assumptions and, on the whole, failed to develop a truly prophetic political vision.

At this juncture the tragedy of Carter's developing political views becomes most alarming. For arguably the very prophetic social vision to which Carter was attracted, but from which he also shrank, provided the rudiments for precisely the political philosophy and social vision that he lacked and the nation required. Even if, as Carter believed, society should be erected on the basis of universalism, it can cohere only when its citizens adhere to a common faith and a shared creed. That alone might prevent the amalgamation of equal individuals from splintering into myriad oppositional factions. Alternatively, should the nation choose a more particularist social strategy, a shared faith is also necessary to direct its decisions concerning which groups to favor and why. In fact, the case can be made — and Carter once made it — that the United States cannot survive without a revival of faith and a shared redirection of creed. Yet, while Carter himself made this prophetic case, he himself retreated swiftly from it. He did so because little else in his thought or experience equipped him to sustain it with a social vision or political philosophy. The prophetic call, substantially accurate and sorely necessary, therefore quickly degenerated into the failed attempt of a good man to substitute aggregate "morale boosting" for "social vision."[108]

Jimmy Carter's spiritual journey, however, was not an idiosyncratic one. America was embarked upon a similar one.

America, noted Alexis de Tocqueville in a word coined to describe the new reality, is a land of "individualism." During the twentieth century the nation has also long held the record in the industrial world for the persistence of religious belief. Fittingly, the religion that has predominated in the United States has been Protestantism — a faith that places more emphasis on the individual's personal relationship to God than perhaps any other. Throughout its history, America has not wanted for a religious citizenry devoted to pursuing personal meaning.

The challenge of America, however, has always been to discern mechanisms by which individuals can be bound together into a common life. "Each man is forever thrown back on himself," observed Tocqueville about the consequences of individualism, "and there is danger that he may be shut up in the solitude of his own heart."[109] For much of its history, Americans have met this challenge with resignation. Although the United States has been the site of notable utopian communal experiments, few of them have proven durable. Often, as in the case of the social gospel, communal thinking has been so misty-minded that it is difficult to view it as more than a brief, collective delusion. Realistic thinking about community has usually given way to the more primal celebration of the individual. The nation that made the lone cowboy and private detective cultural icons has long subordinated community to the solitude of the individual's heart.

The late 1960s were different only in their accentuation of this quintessentially American preference. Part of the reason collectively, as for Carter, was philosophical. A people who had in the main come to endorse the universalistic goals of the early civil rights movement were hesitant to challenge individual liberties on any other front. Because some laws and social customs were found to be oppressive, doubt was cast on all laws and social customs. And under scrutiny, many did prove doubtful. An increasingly unpopular Vietnam War provoked a legitimation crisis so severe that thousands of draft-age men felt justified in resisting conscription by means legal and not. The government's dubious misclassification of illicit drugs prompted many to ignore the laws and use them, anyway. Laws and customs relating to marriage and sexuality, some also of questionable merit, were openly flouted. In areas both important and not — like the liberated fashions of dress and speech — the freedom of the individual was proclaimed supreme; the requirements of community confining.

Ironically, the culture also endorsed equality. Unequivocally committed to individual liberty, many also embraced equality of outcome. President Johnson successfully launched a massive "war on poverty," while even President Nixon countenanced the welfare state.[110] Driving the quest culturally, however, was not so much a social theory as it was an assumption of prosperity combined with a vague indifference to it. The economy still boomed, and wealth seemed abundant enough to finance entitlement programs painlessly. Indeed, the percentages of Americans living in poverty dropped dramatically during the late 1960s even as average incomes rose. But wealth in such abundance was no longer so valuable. In a sensational display that illustrated the contempt many in a generation felt for material prosperity, yippie leader Jerry Rubin staged a dramatic demonstration in which money was thrown into the street at the nation's financial capital, Wall Street.[111] Liberty *and* equality were thus held to be primarily personal, spiritual commodities. They could be attained by liberation from — not allegiance to — a wider social order. Henry David Thoreau, a writer in whom much interest was revived at the time, could not have made the point more eloquently.

Against the increasingly fashionable critics of this brief but crucial epoch in America's history, it must be asserted that there was much good. Minority groups were unjustly oppressed, the war in Vietnam was a tragic mistake, drug laws were (and remain) illogical, and sexual customs were unduly repressive. There is also much commendable in an era that realizes that values that transcend the economic are sometimes the most important ones. Indeed, who can doubt that liberty and equality are both important values, and that both are as much spiritual as they are material? The explosion of enthusiasm for personal expressiveness also produced innovations in popular art and music scarcely rivaled in other times. These praises, however, cannot diminish the severity of the criticisms that must follow. For in elevating the spiritual individual, the community suffered.

Two areas of common life rightly stand as testimonials to the collapse of community that became the tragic legacy of the late 1960s. These are the areas of sex and violence.[112]

Although scientific credit for the 1960s sexual revolution is normally granted to the widespread availability of the contraceptive "pill," cultural credit might be extended to go-go dancer Carol Doda. For on the evening of June 19, 1964, she was persuaded to dance topless at a North Beach nightclub in San Francisco.[113] Topless — and later, all-nude — nightclubs quickly swept the nation. Simultaneously, the pornography industry exploded, and within two years the miniskirt became a fashion rage. The same year, 1966, saw *Who's Afraid of Virginia Woolf?* become the first film "suggested for mature audiences," while the next year saw an off-Broadway musical, *Hair,* feature complete nudity. By the last year of the decade, a popular dance review, *Oh! Calcutta!,* displayed full frontal nudity, while *Midnight Cowboy,* a film partly about homosexuality, became the first X-rated film to win an Oscar for "best picture." That summer, Woodstock, the infamous three-day rock concert, flooded the nation with images of free love and abundant drugs.[114]

During those same five years, however, the divorce rate also rose 30 percent.[115] At the same time, couples began to flout convention and openly live together in quasi-monogamous unions. Marriage, if not family, was among the first social casualty of the revolution in sexual mores. But it was not the only casualty. In 1966 feminists founded the National Organization of Women (NOW). This emergence of neofeminism, while not necessarily antifamily, nevertheless articulated the wedge that divided women from men. Similarly, in 1969 New York's Stonewall Riots inaugurated the modern gay rights movement. In this liberation movement, like so many others, just grievances challenged needlessly oppressive laws and social mores. Yet the cumulative effect of such movements, like the more general underlying quest for personal liberty unfettered by social restraint, proved destructive. Sexual liberation led inexorably both to licentious individualism and to the crystallization of crisscrossing, antagonistic interest groups; the casualty was common life.

But the breakdown of social cohesion illustrated by the consequences of relaxed sexual mores can be tracked into another, more ominous area. Elevated personal passions and diminished social restraints created a context of permissiveness that allowed some to enact violent fantasies. The vast majority of Americans obviously did not take individual liberty as an excuse for violence — but only a few were required to strike fear into the hearts of many.

The customary lineage of 1960s assassinations need not be repeated here. A more insidious tale of escalating violence is more illustrative. In March of 1964, Kitty Genovese was brutally stabbed to death in broad daylight while some thirty-eight New Yorkers looked on and did nothing. The event challenged the moral conscience of the nation, which wondered how so heinous a crime could be greeted with such bystander apathy. Then, two years later, on July 14, 1966, Richard Speck was arrested for stabbing and strangling to death eight student nurses in Chicago. Two weeks after that Charles Whitman shot passersby at random from atop a tower at the University of Texas in Austin. Prior to these incidents, observed a criminologist, "mass murder was not something that was in our vocabulary."[116] Afterward the phrase was permanently planted there.

And by 1969, when rumors of a massacre of innocent South Vietnamese civilians in the village of My Lai surfaced, even the antiwar counterculture proved that it was not immune to eruptions of violence. Followers of cult leader Charles Manson went on a murderous rampage in 1969, while, at a rock concert at Altamont, members of the Hell's Angels motorcycle gang murdered a black youth during a performance by the Rolling Stones. Even the iconic Kennedy image was tarnished by the charge of murder when, in 1969, the remaining Kennedy brother was himself implicated in the drowning death of an apparent paramour, Mary Jo Kopechne, at Chappaquiddick Island. And it was not only the reactionary right who decried an escalation of violence they attributed to amorphous but cataclysmic social changes. A sympathetic left, prompted in part by Truman Capote's *In Cold Blood*, seized also on the theory that our society was, somehow, to blame for its violence.[117]

Yet solutions were not forthcoming. Resisting restraint and challenging an "establishment," a burgeoning counterculture engaged in political protest without believing in a political end. Their impetus was not so much to reorganize or redirect political authority as it was to replace it with personal authenticity.[118] This in fact was the objective spelled out in the manifesto of Students for a Democratic Society, the Port Huron Statement. "The goal of man and society," declared the statement, "should be human independence: a concern . . . with finding a meaning in life that is personally authentic. . . . We would replace power rooted in possession, privilege, or circumstance by power and uniqueness rooted in love, reflectiveness, reason, and creativity."[119] Accordingly, the slogans of the era stressed the personal. "Power to the imagination," proclaimed one. Others included "do your own thing," "turn on, tune in, drop out," and "the personal is political."

While liberation movements of every conceivable stripe arose in challenge to every sort of injustice, few were well organized or devoted to attainable objectives. Protesters at the 1968 Democratic National Convention in Chicago, for instance, succeeded not in reforming a viable national political party but in ensuring its electoral impotence. Such were, however, the protesters' objectives. For "the movement," explained a participant and later chronicler of the times, placed a "premium" on "the glories and agonies of pure existential will." This emphasis "ill equipped many of us to slog away in coalitions in a society crisscrossed by divisions" and, indeed, "was poor training for politics."[120]

Bob Dylan had said as much in 1965. Whereas David Crosby of the folk-rock trio Crosby, Stills, and Nash summarized the counterculture's political sentiments by shouting "politics is bullshit!" at a 1969 rally in San Francisco's Golden Gate Park,[121] Dylan had beaten him to the assessment by at least four years. "Politics is bullshit," Dylan told fellow folk singer Phil Ochs in 1965. "It's all unreal. The only thing that's real is inside you. Your feelings."[122] So, on the 1965 album that included "Maggie's Farm," Dylan also sketched his more popular personal vision of liberation. "To dance beneath the diamond sky with one hand waving free," rasped the bard in his surreal "Mr. Tambourine Man." That song, more than "Maggie's Farm," expressed the sentiments of a culture whose social vision was rooted in little more than collective experiences of individual ecstasy in an "Age of Aquarius."

Jimmy Carter, living in a state where civil rights remained the singular issue, may or may not have been aware of how steadily American culture of the late 1960s had drifted away from substantive concerns like civil rights to a more general celebration of individualism and political indifference. But an odd remark made to a reporter in 1969, when he was still an early candidate for governor, suggests he was attuned to these more general themes even as he was busy plotting his more narrow campaign for governor. "We talk far into the night," Carter explained about his meetings with youthful volunteers, "about what America is like and needs."[123] Whereas most gubernatorial candidates would have said "Georgia," Carter plainly said "America."

And Carter was eerily in sync with America's wider culture. Both were outraged by social injustice and yearned for social equality. But both were even more deeply committed to a liberty that was primarily personal and religious rather than political. Carter in fact echoed the Port Huron Statement when he told Bill Moyers that he never prayed for a political victory but only for his life to be "meaningful."[124] For him, as well as for the young people who increasingly gravitated to his campaign, politics provided but one forum for meaning — and by no means the only one. But if one's search was for personal meaning through politics, surely no elaborate political philosophy or precise social vision would be necessary. Indeed, one could be simultaneously prophetic and fatalistic and see in the two impulses no inconsistency. For the standard of success in politics was not a better society but enhanced personal meaning. Appealing, then, to these times, Carter could confidently announce that the words "economy" and "efficiency" are nowhere to be found in the Constitution or Declaration of Independence — and then list words like "fairness," "equity," "brotherhood," "compassion," and "love" that are not there, either.[125] The new list simply appealed to the sentiments of an individualistic generation devoted more to spiritual meaning than to political accomplishment.

It was odd, however, that Carter could envision political success outside the South as a born-again Southern Baptist. By most reckonings, including those of aides Hamilton Jordan and Peter Bourne, his allegiance with evangelicalism (and all the strict moral rules it entailed) would brand him an outcast in the licentious "Age of Aquarius." But after Bourne commented that a May 1975 *Los Angeles Times* article describing his religious beliefs "would really be damaging," Carter showed how sharply he disagreed. "You're wrong," he replied quickly. "It will help me — even in Los Angeles."[126] His political assessment may have been based on a calculation of the then woefully underemphasized evangelical political clout. But it may also have been based on an understanding that his personal Christian faith was little different in kind, even if it was in substance, from the similarly personal spiritual quests that were mushrooming all over the nation. He readily admitted, after all, to other departures from purely rational awareness. "I don't laugh at people anymore when they say they've seen UFOs," he said during a 1975 news conference, "because I've seen one myself."[127] Similarly, he later admitted to reading the *Bhagavad-Gita* with apparent enthusiasm.[128] Indeed, Carter's Christian faith was never exclusive, and he welcomed those with other faiths. (The usual evangelical doctrine that salvation comes only through Christianity seemed to be one of those "contrived" theological issues about which Carter chose not to think.) Carter thus felt at home with "a generation of seekers" whether or not their search led to the same faith as his had.[129] But often, as with Bob Dylan's own born-again experience some years later, it did. And, when during their walk in the woods Ruth had asked him if he were willing to give up everything for Christ, including politics, Carter remembered: "I thought for a long time and had to admit that I would not."[130] Perhaps that was because he understood that his faith and his politics were really of one piece — and that both resonated with a similarly disposed era.

And at some point Jimmy Carter began to reason that if only he could win the governorship of his state and then pick up the pieces of the shattered national Democratic party, his ability to personify the nation's values might well catapult him to the presidency. It was a bold dream for a man who had just been defeated in his race for governor and whose life's work consisted primarily of a peanut warehouse in southwest Georgia. But the 1960s were a time of bold dreams. And Jimmy Carter was nothing if not ambitious. He was also accustomed to miracles. After long ago resigning herself to being unable to have another child, Rosalynn was able, through advancing medical procedures, to risk having removed the uterine tumor that had made another pregnancy unsafe.[131] The Carters were thus able to have their long-awaited daughter in October 1967. Amy, who grew up to flirt with numerous activist causes while her much older brothers established themselves as lawyers and businessmen, reflected many of the values of her born-again father. The real new birth could not but help reinforce the metaphorical new birth on which Carter rested everything.

CHAPTER 6

GOVERNOR— AND BEYOND

By the beginning of the 1970s Jimmy Carter reached the plateau of personal and political maturity that would define him as a public man. The maturity was signaled by at least three simultaneous developments. One was his born-again experience, which provided him with inexplicable "equanimity" at a time of personal and social crisis and helped him solidify his faith and outlook.[1] Another was the transition in his family life. With the three sons he had raised since the early 1950s approaching adulthood, Amy promising to begin the process anew, and Rosalynn emerging as a political coequal, the Carter family evolved a new, leaner, and more flexible structure. The third development was his full-time entry into politics. Although Carter had been in or around politics for a decade or more and had planned his gubernatorial race since 1966, only in the fall of 1969 did he begin submitting to the schedule of full-time political activity that would characterize his life for the next dozen years.

An aide quickly recognized Carter's personal and political maturation. Peter Bourne, the psychiatrist who joined his administration in 1971 to coordinate the state's drug-abuse programs, remembered marveling early over Carter's psychological makeup. Although Bourne also noted Carter's remarkable ability to engage in multiple self-presentations, he sensed beneath the multiplicity an unshakable grounding.[2] Five years later, on the eve of Carter's presidential election, another aide made a similar observation even more strongly. In a phrase reminiscent of Nietzsche, pollster Pat Caddell described Carter as "a finished man."[3]

The similarity of the assessments separated by five years merits consideration. Although in 1971 Carter was just the newly elected governor of a southern state, while in 1976 he emerged as the favored candidate for president, those closest to him found in him an essential continuity. To them Carter's outward accomplishments were less singular than his inner character and, rather than registering surprise at his meteoric political rise, they expected it all along. Indeed, no sooner did Peter Bourne join Carter's gubernatorial administration than he asked him point-blank, "Have you ever thought about running for president?" Although Carter replied coyly that he had not, both knew that he had — and would.[4]

The story of Carter's governorship is thus also the story of his presidential bid. "I began considering a nationwide race in 1971 when I had only been in the governor's office a few months," he later confided.[5] The evidence indicates that he may have considered it even earlier. Equally important, his expectations were shared by his inner circle of aides and advisors. What these men were like and what they saw in the south Georgia politician explains much about the governor and future president during his peak plateau years.

THE ASSEMBLED TEAM

By 1969 Carter had already assembled the core group of aides and advisors who would propel him to the governorship and then to the presidency. In addition to Rosalynn, this initial group included Hamilton Jordan, Charles Kirbo, Jody Powell, and Bert Lance.

Jordan, who joined Carter's 1966 campaign after his junior year as a political science major at the University of Georgia, was then one of the first people Carter called to help with his 1970 gubernatorial campaign. In 1972 he drafted a blueprint for Carter's presidential campaign and went on to serve in a variety of senior campaign and administration positions up to and including White House chief of staff.

Kirbo's association with Carter began when he served as his legal counsel during the 1962 altercation in Quitman County. After that he remained a staunch behind-the-scenes supporter and strategist. Eschewing formal positions in the campaigns and administrations as well as elsewhere (he even declined Carter's offer of a U.S. Senate seat vacated at the death of Richard Russell in 1971), Kirbo was once aptly called "Carter's Georgia Guru."[6] Older, wiser, and sound of instinct, he offered the seasoned advice that only one at some remove from daily operations could dispense.

Powell, the newcomer to the group in 1969 when he took a break from graduate study in political science at Emory University to volunteer as Carter's driver, quickly became one of Carter's most trusted confidants. He went on, in the governor's mansion and then in the White House, to serve in the sensitive role of press secretary.

Lance, a banker, met Carter in 1966, supported him, and did so again in 1970. When Carter was elected governor Lance was named commissioner of transportation, a position that enabled him to help steer much of Carter's major gubernatorial legislation through the general assembly. Then, following his own narrow defeat in the 1974 governor's race, Lance joined Carter's presidential effort and, after the election, served as director of the Office of Management and Budget. Although questionable banking practices forced his resignation in the fall of 1977, he was until that time a key player in Carter's political career.

To identify these four men as the nucleus of Carter's team naturally minimizes the contributions made by many others. The circle of Carter advisors easily expanded to include others (even as it sometimes constricted to exclude them). Gerald Rafshoon, for instance, served as media advisor during Carter's four major campaigns between 1966 and 1980 and briefly held a position in the White House. Some would insist on his inclusion in any list of key Carter aides. For a time Peter Bourne, and later Pat Caddell, fitted well into this inner circle. Others like Robert Lipshutz (a Georgia supporter who rose to special counsel to the president), Stuart Eizenstat (issues director for the campaigns and domestic policy chief in the White House), and Landon Butler (an early supporter and environmentalist who served as Jordan's assistant in the White House) could be plausibly identified for their early instrumental roles in Carter's rise. Yet, when one thinks of Carter's core group of aides and advisors in 1969 — the men whose attachment to him transcended their specific professional or instrumental contributions, who served him in different capacities over the years, and who, for instance, could generally see him without an appointment after he became governor and president — the list is reasonably short. It includes Kirbo, Jordan, Powell, and Lance, but few if any others.

Drawn from two different generations and different in many ways, the men nevertheless shared certain common bonds — all were white Protestant males from small towns in Georgia. (Rafshoon's background as a New York Jew may have partially accounted for his ambiguous inclusion in the group, although the fact that he headed a separate advertising agency, retained by Carter, also explains his relative independence.) And coming from geographic peripheries of power, as Carter did, may have been their most important common bond.

Although Kirbo and, to a lesser extent, Lance, managed to rise in Atlanta-based power structures, both considered themselves to be rooted in small towns. Kirbo grew up in Bainbridge, the southwest Georgia home of Marvin Griffin, and continued even as an Atlanta attorney to drive a pickup truck. He was recruited as Carter's attorney in 1962 largely because his prestige in the Atlanta legal community was coupled with rural familiarity. Lance's roots in the north Georgia town of Calhoun were so deep that even when he served as commissioner of transportation he preferred to rise early and commute to the state capital instead of living there. Later he did buy an Atlanta mansion, but the ostentatious purchase may have said more about his desire to join the Atlanta establishment than about his inclusion in it. The effort was of no avail, however, for he soon lost the mansion and returned to Calhoun when his business dealings soured.

Powell and Jordan were also from small towns. Powell, from the tiny south Georgia town of Vienna, had chosen, as Carter had, the customary route to achievement open to such boys, by attending the U.S. Air Force Academy. But Powell's dreams were dashed when he was expelled for cheating. Struggling with a second career choice as a political scientist, he abandoned his studies when he joined Carter's campaign. Even in the White House, however, he spoke about his desire to return to Vienna and raise hunting dogs when his political career was over. (As it happened, Powell was the only one of the four to remain in Washington, where he works privately doing more or less what he did for Carter.)

Jordan, hailing from a middle-class suburb of Albany, came as close as any of the four to boasting nonrural roots. Yet the smallest of Georgia's six officially designated metropolitan areas was not, in his youth, large enough to merit the U.S. Census Bureau's "metropolitan" designation. Making his way to the University of Georgia while working odd jobs, including once (when Carter called) spraying mosquitoes in south Georgia, suggested a measure of ambition. But some at the university remember him as more interested in beer than books. And during his public career he was frequently criticized for behavior and demeanor that some considered crude for a member of high society.

Carter, James Fallows observed, often railed against those he referred to as "the socially prominent."[7] Who exactly these people were and why they disturbed Carter (when he seemed to move easily among them) eluded Fallows. The speechwriter could only conclude that Carter carried a rural chip on his shoulder that no amount of experience to the contrary would remove. Peter Bourne made a similar observation.[8] He thought he detected in Carter a certain sense of inferiority, stemming from his rural upbringing, that caused him to feel diminished whenever he was around people from more privileged backgrounds. For Bourne, this sense of rural inferiority explained much of Carter's relentless quest for self-improvement. He wanted always, the psychiatrist concluded, to prove himself the equal to, if not the superior of, those who were born to greater privilege.

Those in Carter's inner circle may have been similarly impelled by their backgrounds. Indeed, the times supplied added reason for the group — as *white* rural southerners during a period when popular media stereotyped members of their ilk as rabid racists and slow-talking buffoons — to feel shunned by "the socially prominent." Small-town boys from southern hinterlands, much maligned by the nation during the 1960s and 1970s, had no easy access to respect, much less prominence.

So, it was understandable that these men would seek through politics the inclusion they could not find elsewhere. It was also natural for their quest for political power to become a vaguely populist one. The texture of the political culture in which they were reared, populism also came as close to capturing their quixotic quest for empowerment as any creed could. Although only Powell betrayed conscious sympathy for populism (the subject of his unfinished doctoral dissertation), the others could not escape its allure.

Yet, by the late 1960s if not long before, populism had been ransacked of substance. Not since the late nineteenth century, in fact, had populism stood for an identifiable governing agenda; after that it stood for little more than empowerment of the common people regardless of what objectives, if any, that empowerment produced. But this very emptiness of populism also united the Carter entourage. For to a man each was averse to any and all political creeds — beyond the vague one of their own empowerment.

Powell was the most eloquent opponent of political ideology. "It is the handmaiden to self-righteousness and abuse of power," he wrote in 1984, "the refuge of the slow mind and faint heart. . . . We have been testing political ideologies since day one, and the only thing that proves out every time is that none of them work."[9] Earlier, in 1977, he was no less caustic in his opinion of the systems of ideas by which some people choose to envision a better society. "I reject the idea that there is some undeniably true system of political or social ideals," he said. "The greatest damage has been done by people who were less eclectic philosophically."[10]

Jordan agreed. "I probably had a political philosophy at one point," he confided in 1977, "but I don't think much about political philosophy any more."[11] Fittingly, there is no record of him and Powell, even when both were fresh from the academic study of politics, ever debating political ideas or otherwise becoming embroiled in the "bull sessions" that usually characterize the conversations of bright young men with shared political interests. Later, when both served in senior White House positions, they also helped to set the administration's decidedly anti-ideological tone. "In two years in the government," recalled James Fallows, "I had not one serious or impassioned discussion with a member of the senior staff about what all those countless government programs meant, which of them, if any, really worked, how the government might be changed."[12] Jordan and his White House deputy, Landon Butler, could not disagree. We "didn't have a lot of ideological bickering in the White House," recalled Jordan. Butler said, "I can't remember a senior staff discussion in which we talked ideologically."[13]

Kirbo, the sage of the group, was also amazingly bereft of a political philosophy. "Charlie doesn't care much about politics and he doesn't give a damn about government," recalled a lawyer who knew Kirbo throughout his career. "All he cares about is Jimmy."[14] Nor did it bother him to be unable to describe Carter "philosophically — as a liberal or conservative." When asked to do so he simply replied, "That's always a tough question," and mentioned instead Carter's drive for improvement and his compassion.[15] Some Carter supporters, Kirbo also noted, were "liberal, some conservative and some moderate." Their distinguishing feature was not their political outlook but simply that all were "involved in a personal relationship with him."[16]

Bert Lance summarized this indifference toward ideology, and even toward policy, when he replied to questions from the state transportation board about his pending appointment as commissioner. Asked whether he was well versed about transportation issues, Lance confessed he was not. But then he said, "The only things I know about are people and money, and that's all there is anywhere."[17] The remark (which Lance often good-naturedly repeated and which earned him his confirmation) was well suited to membership in the Carter entourage. Whereas few other members admitted to knowing much about money, all understood that politics was essentially about people, not ideas or policies. In the words of Jordan: "Politics is people and the need to understand their emotions."[18] A pithier expression of what the populist outlook had become could not have been offered.

Nor did another, nonpolitical creed unite the members of Carter's inner circle. Only Lance shared Carter's open religiosity. The others were either skeptics or just did not place the same importance on religion that Carter did. An other-worldly ideal united them no more deeply than did a this-worldly ideal.

Yet to extrapolate from a shared quest for power supported by no common ideal only Machiavellian motivations would be a mistake. The mistake would be to ignore, as Kirbo noted, that each man was involved in a "personal relationship" with Jimmy Carter. Although the nature of each of these relationships is elusive — Carter managed his staff as he had learned from both his father and Rickover, without praise or compliment, and his staff reciprocated by suppressing similar expressions for him[19] — it is plain that each saw in Carter moral qualities and administrative capabilities they found admirable. As Kirbo understood him, Carter was defined not by any political ideology but by his personal drive for "improvement," coupled with "compassion." Or, as Powell wrote in his 1984 memoir: Carter possessed a "quiet determination to do what he saw as right despite the consequences."[20] Through these expressions and others, it is clear that those in Carter's inner circle believed, and believed deeply, that Carter was an exceptionally good man and tremendously able executive. Indeed, they believed that in some sense his goodness transcended politics, in particular the overwrought ideological divisions of politics in the 1970s.

It is therefore a mistake to conclude that Carter's inner circle of aides and advisors were attached to him only for reasons of rank opportunism. Resentful of their exclusion from power and rejecting of ideological commitments, they were unquestionably inspired by the promise of political victory and in large part indifferent to the means they might deploy to achieve it. Indeed, to overhear one Georgia White House staffer tell another, "You know, there really ought to be a place for people like us between elections, someplace we could rest up and get ready for the next one,"[21] is to raise serious doubts about the capacity of such thoroughly political men to govern. Yet, Carter's aides and advisors were not oblivious to moral issues. They rather believed, as Carter did, that morality impacted politics through the person of the candidate. And they were persuaded that their candidate was the moral one.

Even so, as a practical matter all of Carter's aides and advisors saw Carter's chief strength as his electability. They also concurred that this strength was directly attributable to his capacity to ignore and even manipulate political ideologies. Lance conveyed this collective impression of Carter when he remembered, "Jimmy was a formidable campaigner. He was a moderate to the moderates, a conservative to the conservatives, and a liberal to the liberals. He was all things to all voters, a great trait to be able to project — and it got him elected."[22] Kirbo similarly recalled that "he was a remarkable campaigner" because "he had the capacity to deal with people who differed from him on major concerns. . . . Even though they disagreed with him they would vote for him."[23] What Powell found attractive in the nonideological populist candidate, and what Jordan found intriguing in what he first thought was Carter's "commonsense" approach, echoed their elders' assessments. Carter's political strength, all concluded, was his ability to campaign across the ideological spectrum on the strength of his personal qualities.

So twice, once in 1970 and again in 1976, this small band of Carter devotees applied themselves successfully to the task of electing Jimmy Carter. Although the campaigns differed in many ways, the thrust of both was the elevation of Carter's personal qualities above existing political ideologies. Presenting Carter this way faithfully represented both what he believed and what they found believable about him. Yet, by the more traditional issue- and ideological-driven political standards they rejected, the presentation was manipulative, even duplicitous.

THE 1970 CAMPAIGN

Borrowing more than a page from Lester Maddox's 1966 campaign playbook, Carter's 1970 campaign strove to portray him as a populist candidate of the people who, in turn, was opposed by both the state's entrenched political and financial interests. At one juncture the former naval officer and agri-businessman who supported civil rights, found worthwhile social criticism in Bob Dylan, and sometimes read poetry while listening to classical music, even described himself as "basically a red-neck."[24]

While the description of himself as a redneck was misleading personally, it also misled voters about the extent of planning and preparation that had gone into his campaign. Only later did Carter admit that they "had a very carefully prepared campaign in 1970."[25] At the time, however, he sought to minimize the sophisticated planning that went into his campaign by feigning the posture of an ignorant redneck. He admitted, for example, to only a dozen paid staff members; the newspapers counted twenty-eight.[26]

The campaign actually began, Jordan thought, in 1966 when Jimmy and Rosalynn sent handwritten Christmas cards to every Georgian with whom they were remotely acquainted.[27] About this time, and building upon this same list, Carter made it a habit to dictate names and other potentially pertinent information into a tape recorder during his drive home from campaign appearances, after which Rosalynn added the information to the master file and sent each new person a note.[28] By the summer of 1970, the master file was organized by zip codes, and booklets were prepared for each zip-code grouping, listing supporters by name, occupation, and political philosophy.[29]

Meanwhile, Carter studied election returns in every race and every Georgia county since 1952. To help him and his campaign staff discern patterns in these data — no small chore, since Georgia includes 159 counties and Carter tracked nine separate election years for each — the campaign prepared colored charts and graphs. Studying these so thoroughly that he later admitted to learning the most about "voter motivations" by comparing the different vote percentages garnered by the same candidates and issues over time, Carter entered the gubernatorial race with an expert grasp of Georgia's recent political history.[30]

But, while he studied county election returns himself and created his own file of supporters, Carter did not rely only on his own judgments. He also turned to professionals. He commissioned the Washington-based polling firm of William Hamilton and Associates to conduct a series of opinion polls for him. A poll was commissioned in the fall of 1969, one year before the election, which Carter admitted using to help him determine the issues he would emphasize in his campaign. Later polls then helped him fine-tune strategy and advertise effectively.[31]

Armed with polls, his memorized history of county elections, and briefing booklets prepared by zip code, Carter was escorted around the state by his driver, Jody Powell, and private pilot, David Rabhan. And, beginning in November 1969, his itinerary was systematically prepared in advance. Based upon a careful assessment and mathematical weighting of the many variables believed to be politically significant in different areas of the state, the Carter campaign used a computerized procedure known as "linear progression" to calculate the amount of time he should allot to each area. Two-week schedules reflecting these calculations were thus prepared for him and his family members. Then, to keep track of the location of the candidate and his surrogates, a map using color-coded pins to represent the movement of each campaigner was maintained in campaign headquarters.[32]

The campaign also used television advertisements with professional effectiveness. Rafshoon, aided by Hamilton's polls, created commercials so strong that Bill Shipp later judged the campaign to have been "the first modern media campaign" in the state. In fact, twenty years later Shipp maintained that "no other TV campaigns have matched the quality — or viciousness — of that video onslaught."[33]

Viciousness? The judgment is a harsh one. Yet for a candidate to describe himself as "basically a red-neck" and present himself as the populist underdog only to be remembered for waging a "modern media campaign" suggests a certain discrepancy, beneath which may lurk something akin to viciousness.

☆　☆　☆

In the main, Carter campaigned as he believed: on the strength of his personal qualities. Much of this campaign was genuinely populist, innocuous, and even laudable. A state senator approvingly noted that he took his campaign "directly to the people and not the so-called influential politicians" at "the county courthouse."[34] Bill Pope, Carter's 1970 campaign press secretary, also considered him "one of the most superb campaigners probably in this century" for the same reason. His success, explained Pope, was "achieved by giving the person he was talking to the feeling that he was talking to that person and that person only. There was never any of this looking around to see if he could find somebody, you know, more important and consequential. Amazing campaigner."[35] Even reporters were charmed by Carter's personal campaign skills. One recalled: "He had the same facility with newspeople as with other people — the ability to make you feel that he understood precisely where you were coming from, that he understood and sympathized with your views, and that he was talking directly with you, as one intelligent, concerned human being to another. He neither talked down nor up to me. And, even though I tried to report objectively, I felt Carter, while not exactly a friend, *knew* me to some degree and liked me."[36]

Estimating that over the course of his campaign he delivered some

1,800 speeches and that, between them, he and Rosalynn shook some 600,000 hands,[37] Carter clearly worked his personal political magic on as many voters as he could. Although the essence of this magic was his ability to engage in multiple self-presentations, it was reinforced by his religious convictions. Believing that his faith commanded him to love "the person who happens to be in front of you at any particular moment,"[38] Carter tried to empathize with — and even to love — every one of the people he met. This genuine moral imperative, however, had obvious political benefits, for the person in front of him at any particular moment also usually happened to be a voter. Empathizing with them, Carter was often also able to persuade them to support him politically — and to do so without revealing much about his own views, since the encounter was defined by Carter's empathy for their views.

Aiding Carter in his personal campaign were his wife and mother, as well as his son Chip, who took a year off from college to help his father. Often the family members traveled separately in order to maintain a personal Carter presence at simultaneous locations throughout the state. The campaign also enlisted some 200 Sumter Countians to travel the state and vouch for him. This "Hi Neighbor" strategy, as Carter called it, was the forerunner of the infamous "Peanut Brigade" that he used when campaigning for the presidency. Its idea and effect were, like his family's separate campaign appearances, to magnify the personal dimensions of a predominantly personal campaign.

Yet, while Carter campaigned on the strength of his personal appeal and strove to magnify it through the testimonies of others, he was not unaware of the favorable contrast it struck with his main opponent, former governor Carl Sanders. This darling of Georgia liberals had been elected in 1962 at the time of the dismantling of the county unit system and had a progressive reputation not unlike Carter's. In addition, however, his 1963–67 administration was regarded as a model of good governance. This made the better-known Sanders a formidable opponent. Well before Carter commissioned the polls that showed his trailing Sanders in the primary race, he realized that he needed to drive a "wedge" between his and Sanders's candidacies.[39] And one way of doing so, he realized, was to sharpen the contrast between his populist appeal and Sanders's more urbane sophistication.

The contrast began being effected innocently enough. Arriving at a county celebration wearing overalls and a plaid shirt, Carter agreed to be dunked in water and otherwise willingly participated in the day's festivities. Sanders, also attending, wore blue pants and tie with a red blazer and so refused to do more than speak. Carter won the hearts and ultimately the votes of the rural celebrants.[40]

Carter's preferred interpretation of his usual lack of newspaper endorsements was also harmless. When he received the endorsement of a newspaper, which he occasionally did, he naturally seized it as evidence of his appeal. But when, as was more often the case, a newspaper endorsed Sanders, Carter used the absent endorsement as evidence that his candidacy was opposed by the established powers and was therefore a populist one. Since Eugene Talmadge's time this strategic use of newspaper endorsements had become a populist staple in Georgia campaigns. Nor was the problem that at the same time the Atlanta newspapers endorsed Sanders — allowing Carter to stand firm in his claim that he represented the forgotten rural people — Carter quietly solicited and received a substantial campaign contribution from the newspapers' owner, Anne Cox Chambers. That too was staple campaign chicanery. The problem arose when Carter resorted to blackmail to manipulate his coverage in the Atlanta papers.

Someone mailed the Carter campaign copies of credit-card receipts in Sanders's name which showed his paying for part of a Florida vacation taken with Reg Murphy, then an editor with the Atlanta newspapers. Carter privately threatened Murphy that he would make the receipts public if his newspaper coverage was not favorable. Enraged by the blackmail attempt over receipts that most believed were innocent (Murphy explained that Sanders had simply put some group charges on his credit card, which the others paid off in cash), Murphy spared little venom attacking the candidate he already disliked in print. Although Carter's blackmail attempt appeared thus to backfire, Bill Shipp, then a political reporter for the paper, believed that the whole affair helped Carter because Murphy's attacks on Carter became so strident that Carter ended up the beneficiary.[41]

But while luck seemed to be on Carter's side in the blackmail attempt, more than luck was required for Carter to sharpen his own populist image by portraying Sanders as the antithesis. To portray Sanders as an aloof and wealthy urban politician out of touch with the people, Carter referred to Sanders as "Cuff Links Carl." Then, to reinforce this nickname, Rafshoon created the television advertisements that Shipp deemed especially "vicious." The commercials showed only gold cuff links, which viewers could be counted on to assume were Sanders's and represented everything they resented about wealthy politicians.

Even calling Sanders "Cuff Links Carl" and then reinforcing this nickname with the commercials may have been permissible campaign tactics. But these gimmicks actually only underscored more onerous allegations that Carter leveled against Sanders. From spring through summer Carter charged that Sanders had used his tenure as governor and subsequent prominence to enrich himself personally. The charges, most realized, were patently false. But, seizing McCarthy-like tactics, Carter continued to advance them while promising "proof" that would be unveiled only two weeks before the election. Meanwhile, he repeatedly refused invitations to debate Sanders in forums that might have enabled Sanders to deflect the accusations. Finally, when Carter revealed his "proof," his exaggerations were apparent; no charges were brought and few thought any warranted. But by then it was too late for Sanders to rebut the charges effectively. Carter's disingenuous accusations, reinforced by the "Cuff Links" nickname and commercials, raised enough doubts about Sanders to cut his early lead down to a second-place primary finish.[42]

To his credit, Sanders ignored the Carter tactics he believed would be discounted for what they were by an enlightened electorate. Only when the September 9 primary returns came in showing Carter almost beating him outright, with 48 percent of the vote in a multicandidate race, did Sanders discard his jacket and begin campaigning for the runoff election wearing short-sleeved shirts.

☆   ☆   ☆

Campaigning personally as much as he could, Carter had few qualms about publicly admitting that his 1970 campaign for governor would be run without benefit of a political ideology. Already in 1966, after a reporter asked him whether he was a liberal, conservative, or moderate, Carter had replied, "I believe I'm more complicated than that."[43] On the occasion of his formal announcement of candidacy in April 1970, the *Atlanta Constitution* again noted that Carter "refused to place himself on the political spectrum." He preferred, the article continued, simply to take the "issues" to the people.[44] And later, when in July he released his formal seventeen-page platform, it listed thoughtful positions on so many issues (sixty-five in all) that no overall ideological pattern could readily be detected. Reflecting his genuine intellectual eclecticism and nonideological political orientation, the number of issues and diversity of positions reinforced Carter's claim of remaining above ideology.

In an article following Carter's formal announcement, the *Atlanta Constitution* pointed out the disadvantage of this nonideological campaign strategy. The "campaign Carter has mapped out," observed the state's leading newspaper, "is a bit tricky" because he cannot "allow his image to become too all-encompassing." Yet, the piece continued, there were decided benefits in such a strategy. Carter could plan on "taking the advantages of both sides of some issues" and so augment his existing "moderate" constituency with both "the downright poor, black and white" and "conservative Georgians who normally would vote for a Lester Maddox or a George Wallace." This simultaneous appeal to both sides of Georgia's major ideological groupings was especially brazen. But Carter maintained that he foresaw "no trouble in pitching for Wallace votes and the black votes at the same time." Both groups were just "average working people" who want a governor "who understands their problems."[45]

Strategic objectives, however, may explain Carter's nonideological posture almost as well as his genuine beliefs do. For, while he was himself indifferent to ideology, he was not unaware of its political importance. In the list of potential supporters he carefully accumulated throughout his four-year campaign, for instance, he added notations that identified each as conservative, liberal, or moderate.[46] The leeway he allowed himself to deviate from consistent ideological positions was not extended by him to supporters, whom he catalogued by ideology.

The problem of ideological identification also had a practical side in the 1970 gubernatorial race. Since Carl Sanders was perceived to be as liberal as a successful politician could be in Georgia at the time, the end of the political spectrum to which Carter would have naturally gravitated was already taken. Indeed, in 1985, Georgia historians rated Carter as substantially *more* liberal than Sanders on both social and racial issues, although slightly more conservative on fiscal issues.[47] Since any honest attempt to define himself ideologically risked blurring the distinctions between him and the more popular Sanders, Carter realized the success of his campaign depended in part on his ability to avoid the ideological label that, without resistance, would otherwise be bestowed upon him.

There was also the problem of liberalism's general lack of popularity at the time. Had Carter allowed himself to be defined in ideological terms, he would have been branded a liberal at a time when no serious political observer believed a liberal would fare well in the 1970 gubernatorial race.

Maddox, the outgoing governor, was running for lieutenant governor, was expected to win, and would draw many conservative Democrats to the polls. And the signposts left by the 1968 presidential election in Georgia were even more ominous for liberals. Hubert Humphrey, the Democratic nominee, had lost Georgia badly; he came in third behind both independent George Wallace and second-place Republican finisher Richard Nixon. If Carter had identified himself ideologically, he would have risked not only having his own candidacy swallowed by Sanders but also being identified in unfavorable terms.

Political observers therefore interpreted Carter's nonideological stance as an attempt to sidestep the punishing political labels that, were they applied, would prevent him from taking a wide enough swath of votes to win. They also predicted, accurately it turned out, that despite his protestations Carter would run ideologically. Specifically, they guessed he would run "just to the right of Sanders."[48]

But what the political observers did not predict was how hard the nominally nonideological Carter campaign would work to push Sanders to the liberal left. Needing to campaign to the right of Sanders was after all made easier if Sanders could be pushed left. Doing so therefore became one of the major strategic objectives of the Carter campaign.

The strategy was inaugurated when Carter discovered that beneath some of Sanders's campaign buttons were old buttons from Hubert Humphrey's presidential campaign. Apparently, the firm that had supplied Sanders with buttons had leftover Humphrey buttons, on top of which they simply stuck "Count Me for Carl" slogans. The same April week that he formally announced his candidacy, Carter therefore ceremoniously peeled off the top of a Sanders campaign button at a press conference to reveal the underlying Humphrey slogan. Without formally charging Sanders with allegiance to the left wing of the Democratic party, Carter managed to make precisely that point symbolically. Although the press saw the issue for what it was — "just a bunch of foolishness" — the newspapers also admitted that it was "the most talked about thing" in the early weeks of the campaign.[49] Perhaps it was because Sanders was known to have supported the unpopular Humphrey in 1968 and generally to have allegiances toward the national party. By highlighting these connections, Carter, who refused to place himself on the ideological spectrum, managed to place Sanders on its least attractive pole.

Later, when summer hit and the campaigns were in full swing, Carter followed the campaign-button issue with one that was even more "foolishness." He pointed out that the registration number on Sanders's campaign airplane was 6272. Of no special significance (a point Sanders was forced to prove by producing documents showing the sequence of airplane registrations), Carter charged that the number was purposely chosen to symbolize Sanders's real political ambitions. These ambitions, Carter continued, were national. Sanders had been elected governor in 1962, which the "62" on his airplane signified. But, Carter said, what Sanders really wanted was not to be elected governor in 1970 but to be elected to the U.S. Senate when Richard Russell's term expired in 1972. The "72" on his airplane registration represented that ambition, Carter claimed.[50]

The numerological charge was patently ridiculous, and there is no way of knowing whether it helped or harmed Carter's campaign. Yet by making it Carter revealed how desperately he tried to brand Sanders a liberal. By accusing Sanders of national political ambition and implying that he opposed the enormously popular conservative Senator Russell, Carter also tacitly accused Sanders of being a liberal Democrat.

But these two episodes show Carter merely attempting to manipulate meaningless symbols for political advantage. Beneath them is a more serious charge. For Humphrey was not just a liberal and Russell not only a conservative. Each had acquired his ideological label in Georgia largely for his positions on civil rights.[51] Humphrey had been perhaps the Senate's most ardent supporter of civil rights legislation, and Russell its most stalwart opponent. The two had even been chosen by their respective camps to debate the issue on television's *Meet the Press* early in the 1960s. To imply that Sanders was a Humphrey supporter and a Russell opponent was therefore to imply that he was a *racial* liberal. This disingenuous stimulation of the race issue in the governor's race made Carter's campaign chicanery a more serious matter. And, in another page Carter borrowed from the Maddox campaign playbook, this seriousness was evident.

A few weeks before the election at a rally in Columbus, Georgia, Carter publicly criticized former governor Sanders for having refused to allow George Wallace to speak in Georgia. Carter promised that "when" he became governor Wallace would most definitely be invited to speak. Actually, Sanders had not banned Wallace from speaking in the state but only denied him permission to speak on state property. His rationale was that Wallace's early 1960s rhetoric might inflame racial tensions and potentially incite an incident for which the permissive Georgia governor would be held responsible. While Carter understood all this and did not claim to support Wallace or what he stood for, his criticism of Sanders could easily be interpreted as an endorsement of the Alabama governor's segregationist stance. Choosing his words carefully, Carter opted to portray himself in precisely this fashion.[52]

To his credit, throughout the campaign Carter continued to speak to African American audiences. Polls showed the overwhelming majority of these voters supporting Sanders, and Kirbo argued that Carter should just cut his losses and focus his energy elsewhere. But Carter persisted.[53] He also never once made a public comment that could be literally construed as racist.

Even so, the comments Carter did make were often worded in ways that implied, without directly stating, racist sentiments. In addition to implying that he supported Wallace, for example, he also forthrightly opposed school busing. Promising once to appoint blacks to policy-making positions, he qualified his promise with the insulting caveat that he would not choose "any of the so-called black leaders who have in the past taken money to deliver the black vote."[54] He also courted — and received — endorsements from acknowledged segregationists like Georgia Speaker of the House Roy Harris and even former governor Marvin Griffin.[55]

Behind the scenes, the not-so-subtle racism of the Carter campaign was more blatant. Mailed to white barbershops, beauty parlors, and Baptist ministers — and even personally distributed at a Ku Klux Klan rally — were copies of a photograph showing Sanders with two black members of the Atlanta Hawks basketball team (which Sanders partially owned) who were pouring victory champagne over the former governor. The photograph, Bill Shipp later explained, had the double negative effect of showing Sanders with alcohol and "cavorting" with blacks.[56] (It might also have had a third negative effect of showing Sanders as the kind of urban businessman-politician wealthy enough to own a professional sports team.) Although Carter and other members of his campaign denied distributing this photograph (and in fairness, the Sanders campaign retaliated by preparing a photograph linking Carter with black activist Hosea Williams),[57] there is little doubt that it occurred and that someone in the Carter campaign was responsible for it. Nor is there much doubt, given that the photograph was distributed at a Klan rally, that the intention was to appeal to white racists.

Equally ominous is the likelihood that the Carter campaign paid for the advertising of C. B. King, a long-shot black candidate in that year's gubernatorial race. With polls showing Sanders taking the bulk of the black vote, it is difficult to believe that some in the Carter campaign were not tempted to undercut that support by financing a rival. Again, no one in the Carter campaign ever confessed to funding King's campaign, but an employee of Rafshoon's advertising agency assumed that money was laundered from Carter's campaign to pay King's bills.[58]

In these ways and others, Carter's purportedly nonideological campaign nevertheless made free and frequent use of ideology when it suited their purpose — which it often did. To critics, this purpose was plainly to polarize "the electorate into rednecks, rurals, and racists versus the big city liberals."[59] As questionable as this divisive effort is when used by a candidate genuinely committed to ideology, the effort was even more questionable in Carter's hands. For Carter's polarization of the electorate misled voters about which side he was really on.

THE CALCULATED COST OF VICTORY

When the returns came in for the runoff election, Carter won a handsome 60 percent to 40 percent victory over Sanders. Then in the general election, where he faced nominal Republican challenger Hal Suit, he won by almost as large a margin. The candidate was happy; his campaign ecstatic. But the price of victory was high.

Many in Georgia and elsewhere faulted Carter for seeking to destroy the reputation of Carl Sanders with his trumped-up accusations. None of the charges Carter leveled about Sanders's business dealings ever amounted to anything, and, in perhaps the chief irony of the Carter campaign, the national ambitions Carter ascribed to Sanders were actually those he harbored himself. (Whether Sanders had an eye on the U.S. Senate in 1972 will never be known. Russell died in 1971 and Carter appointed David Gambrell, a major campaign contributor, to the unexpired seat. Sam Nunn won the office in 1972.) And, when the opinion of Georgia historians is considered, it is doubtful that Carter was the superior governor. They rated Sanders as effective (if not more effective) a governor as Carter.[60]

Carter's image as a moralist who sought to love everyone he encountered is also tarnished by the flagrant exception of Carl Sanders. Politically, of course, the explanation for the exception is plain. A campaign run on the strength of a candidate's personal qualities inevitably necessitates personal attacks against the opponent. When neither issues nor ideology distinguishes the candidates, only character remains to emphasize or disparage. A more personal explanation for Carter's exempting Sanders from his usual rule of love was indirectly suggested by Steve Ball's early inquiry into Carter's campaign strategy. "Carter," discovered Ball, "would like to equate Sanders with 1966 Republican candidate Howard Calloway."[61] In this discovered linkage Ball perhaps found what others missed in Carter: that when it came to winning, the rage he had so successfully repressed against the father who never let him win was unleashed against surrogates — especially "socially prominent" ones. Still, whether explained politically or psychologically, Carter's caricature of Sanders heavily tarnished his own image.

The price exacted by the election went beyond a depletion of Carter's personal moral capital. It included frank recognition of his duplicity. After he delivered his inaugural address, the duplicity of his racist campaign was apparent. Then when he announced that his major gubernatorial objective would be the reorganization of state government — a pledge he had not bothered to mention during his campaign — the duplicity was underscored.[62]

Lester Maddox expressed his reservations about Carter immediately after the election by saying: "When I put my pennies into a peanut machine, I don't expect to get bubble gum, and neither do the people."[63] Reg Murphy waited until the inaugural. Noting that Carter's address "did strain credibility," Murphy reminded Georgians that Carter was asking them "to forget a summer of speaking favorably of George Wallace, of deliberately splitting Atlanta off from the rest of the state," and of other rural racist tactics.[64] Even within Carter's campaign, incredulity was expressed. The producer of his television advertisements, who worked for Rafshoon, admitted: "I was not aware that Carter was far more liberal than the campaign we were waging."[65]

Some, naturally, found the change in Carter's image welcome and justified the discrepancy as necessary campaign chicanery. "I always thought he was a progressive man and had these notions," said a black representative after Carter's inaugural, "yet couldn't say them and get elected."[66] But the chicanery had been more than incidental; it had been systematic. After the election Jordan admitted to establishing dual Carter committees in selected counties — "one headed by people who supported Maddox or Wallace and one headed by a less conservative element."[67] Some, including Lester Maddox, could not forgive Carter. Charging that he "campaigned on one platform and was living on another,"[68] Maddox proceeded to spend his four lieutenant-governor years in an angry anti-Carter crusade.

A historian of Carter's gubernatorial administration blamed Carter's plummet in popularity in large part on the feud between him and Maddox. Whether or not the correct explanation, the consensus was that Carter's popularity dropped sharply after his election. Whatever Maddox's role in this drop, however, it should be appreciated that his irritation was based in fact. Beneath their feud, after all, were more than personal and political differences. Echoing Maddox's opinion that Carter campaigned on one platform but governed on another, Gary Fink noted that "Carter usually claimed the moral and ethical high ground" but "practiced a style of politics based on exaggeration, disingenuousness, and at times outright deception."[69]

Carter, as well as his closest aides and advisors, undoubtedly took comfort in the discrepancy between his campaign and his governance. For, had Carter governed as he had campaigned, the faith he placed in himself and elicited from his aides would have been shaken. But the unquestionably high caliber of Carter's administration, which prompted the historical assessment that he was "a better governor than he has led us to believe,"[70] confirmed the conviction among the Carter forces that the end of his election justified the means used to get him there.

Moreover, the drop in public support that the discrepancy between Carter's campaign and governance engendered did not worry the Carter forces much. Nor were they especially concerned about alienating Georgia voters for pursuing a major administrative objective on which they had not campaigned. These costs of Carter's duplicity were rather carefully calculated ones that the inner circle planned to pay willingly.

While the experts concluded that Carter could not be elected to statewide office again,[71] the Carter team had no intention of seeking one. Pretending to be angling for Herman Talmadge's U.S. Senate seat, Carter was actually running for president (and Talmadge was the first outside the inner circle to be quietly apprised). Pausing only to reschedule Georgia's 1976 presidential preference primary later in the year than it was in 1972 — and so at a time when Carter would presumably have momentum on his side and be able to avoid an embarrassing defeat in his home state — the Carter team calculated that Georgians who might be reluctant to send him to the Senate would nevertheless support him proudly in a presidential race. Indeed, his surprising gubernatorial initiatives were designed to substantiate future, rather than past, campaign promises.

The first open indication of Carter's presidential ambitions occurred at his forty-seventh birthday party on October 1, 1971. Bert Lance presented him with a set of commemorative coins from each of the fifty states and explained: "This gift represents your dominion over one state as governor, but from what I've seen, at some point in the future you will have dominion over all fifty states."[72] Perhaps, though neither admitted talking about it previously, the two may have already discussed Carter's presidential ambition. Or Lance may have just had experiences similar to those of Charles Kirbo, who remembered "wondering" about Carter's presidential timbre as early as 1966 and claimed that the presidential quest evolved through unspoken "osmosis."[73] However Lance became aware of the ambition, a letter from Joe A. Bacon in Plains to Janet S. Merritt in the state legislature suggests that Carter signaled it long before Lance made it public. "Jimmy Carter of Plains still has his big sign up at Plains as Georgia's next governor," noted Bacon. "I understand that he says he will be Georgia's next governor and after that he will run for President." The letter was dated January 16, 1967.[74]

Newer members of Carter's inner circle were naturally not privy to the "osmosis" that had arisen among the likes of Lance and Kirbo — but they readily sensed it. This sense was undoubtedly what prompted Peter Bourne to ask Carter bluntly about his presidential plans in July 1971. And by that time even Carter's denial contained a tantalizing subtext: "If I did," Carter said, "I'd run for four years, the same way I ran for Governor."[75] Grasping the subtext, Bourne responded in kind a year later by submitting the first formal memorandum urging Carter to run for president.[76] As Carter had requested, the July 25, 1972, memorandum arrived four years before the 1976 presidential election.

Intervening events had brought the issue to the fore. Among Carter's aides the key event was the 1972 Democratic National Convention in Miami. Convinced of Carter's presidential stature, but still vague in plans to realize it, the aides who attended the convention arrived with the surreptitious objective of securing Carter's nomination as George McGovern's vice presidential running mate. Although haphazardly conceived, the objective made a certain amount of political sense. Perceived as a liberal, the only hope McGovern had of winning the general election was to temper his leftist image, and one way of doing that was to select a more conservative southern governor as his running mate. Moreover, Carter's aides also brought with them to Miami private poll results showing that McGovern would do much better in Georgia, and presumably throughout the South, with Carter in the second spot. (The continuing commissioning of opinion polls like these also indicates the persistence of lingering if imprecise political ambitions in the Carter camp immediately after the gubernatorial election.) Although the Carter forces did not genuinely believe that McGovern could win the presidency with or without Carter in the second spot, they at least had a plausible case to make for Carter as the vice presidential nominee — even though their transparent objective was to garner much-needed national exposure for their own candidate.

But there were problems with the plan. Chief among them was that Carter was a known opponent of McGovern and was slated to deliver the nominating speech for Senator Henry "Scoop" Jackson. In addition, as a newly elected first-term governor of Georgia, Carter was hardly the strongest southern running mate McGovern could choose. That at least is what Pat Caddell concluded after finally granting Jordan and Rafshoon, Carter's emissaries, a brief meeting. The precocious twenty-two-year-old pollster, then working in his first presidential campaign for McGovern, believed he conveyed the gist of Jordan and Rafshoon's pleadings when he suggested that McGovern consider Reuben Askew of Florida for the second spot. Carter's name was never mentioned.

Spurned by Caddell, the Carter emissaries resorted to cornering South Dakota's lieutenant governor, Bill Daugherty, in the hotel coffee shop and badgering him with their idea. When he too demurred, they convinced then Congressman Andrew Young to make Carter's case for them to McGovern. When even his overtures were deflected, the aides admitted defeat. But in palpable frustration that fueled the resentment over exclusion that had drawn them to Carter in the first place, they finally asked one another, "Why can't Jimmy run for president?" None could offer a convincing rebuttal. A reporter remembered the epiphany distinctly. At about four in the morning, immediately after McGovern's acceptance speech, Kandy Stroud recalled listening incredulously at an all-night Miami Beach diner as Peter Bourne forecast not only McGovern's defeat but also Carter's victory four years later.[77]

Carter's part in these goings-on remains sketchy. Although he approved the effort to secure his selection as vice president and set the tone that enabled such ambitious plans to be launched, the indirect patterns of communication that characterized his management style enabled him to condone the plans without specifically authorizing them. All that is really known about his personal decision to seek the presidency is his claim to have made the decision during his 1971 and 1972 meetings with that year's leading presidential candidates. Unimpressed with them, he lost his "awe" of the presidency and decided to run himself.[78] However, there are hints that by the time of the 1972 convention his decision was already firm. His speech nominating Jackson, for example, included a passage that spoke otherwise irrelevantly of John Kennedy's bid to be nominated as vice president in 1956.

So, when Bourne's memorandum of July 25, 1972, arrived it was no real surprise. The time had come to make a decision. When later in the summer Peter Bourne, Hamilton Jordan, Gerald Rafshoon, and Landon Butler met with Carter to present him with what Jordan still considered the "crazy notion" that he run for president, Jordan recalled, "[W]e quickly saw that it was not an original idea with us. He didn't flinch."[79] Reaching the same conclusion, Rafshoon commented to Jordan: "The son of a bitch, he wants it."[80] The conclusion was not a difficult one to reach, for the meeting continued for six long hours during which presidential campaign strategy was thoroughly discussed.

Jordan was relieved of his other duties, based upon this meeting, and assigned the task of synthesizing the various ideas aired during it into a coherent campaign strategy. Meanwhile, Rafshoon wrote his own memorandum and Carter continued his study of "the campaign platforms of all the unsuccessful candidates for President since our electoral process began."[81] Finally, on November 4 — the day before the 1972 presidential elections — Jordan submitted his fifty-page campaign blueprint. By December the memorandum was discussed and approved. "The whole campaign," commented Peter Bourne four years later, "was like a play written in 1972."[82]

☆　☆　☆

The play was a thematic one. Although Jordan's campaign blueprint essentially addressed the mechanics of securing the nomination, the notion that Carter's candidacy would be erected on two basic themes infused the entire document and attendant planning.

Jordan was the first to articulate these two themes. "One of the things that was manifested in the McGovern campaign," Jordan observed during the six-hour late-summer meeting, "was the real need for moral leadership in the country." McGovern, Jordan believed, "understood and projected this moral leadership." Carter would be wise to do likewise.[83]

Also during that initial meeting, however, Jordan offered the opinion that McGovern's moral leadership was not adequate to secure his election. The problem was that McGovern projected an image of moral leadership without also "seeming presidential, not seeming competent." Reasoning further that "the problem-solving ability of the American government" was as much a voter concern as was moral leadership, Jordan forecast that it too would be an important theme in the next presidential race. In this way already during the first meeting Jordan identified the two themes of the Carter candidacy: morality and competence.[84]

Jordan's November memorandum returned to these themes. "Perhaps the strongest feeling in this country today is the general distrust of government and politicians at all levels," he wrote. "The desire and thirst for strong moral leadership in this nation was not satisfied with the election of Richard Nixon. It is my contention that this desire will grow in four more years of the Nixon administration."[85] Yet, while Jordan sounded this theme of moral leadership again in his memorandum, he chose to place more emphasis on the other theme of competence. Suggesting that the Democratic party's more general "preoccupation with Senators" had placed a premium on the competence that might be demonstrated by "a highly successful and concerned former governor," he urged Carter to make this his main campaign theme. Moreover, if Carter could achieve substantial reforms in Georgia that demonstrated executive competence, he could begin campaigning early and surreptitiously by promoting his views on "revitalized state government" and "making state government work." Reinforcing this emphasis, Jordan's memorandum urged Carter to heed the "excellent" advice of the separate Rafshoon memorandum. According to it, Carter's image simply needed more "depth" than was conveyed by his "hand-shaking" and "good guy brand of populism." Needed was a "heavyweight image" constructed from "heavyweight ideas" and "a heavyweight program."[86]

Although Carter's own contributions to this development of thematic strategy are unrecorded, his role in helping to generate these themes is obvious. When he wrote the campaign autobiography that Jordan's blueprint suggested, he organized it around precisely these two themes. Beginning and ending with what Carter called "two basic questions," *Why Not the Best?* asks: "Can our government be honest, decent, open, fair, and compassionate?" and "Can our government be competent?" The two questions were those identified as the most important themes during the first discussion of strategy. Perhaps, too, they were not even original with Jordan; Carter, after all, was the central figure in the discussion.

Still, it is interesting that both Jordan and Rafshoon urged Carter to attend more to competence than to morality. They may have done so because they honestly believed that the one would be more politically salient than the other in 1976. Or, as is more likely, knowing that Carter's natural inclination would be to stress morality and to minimize competence, they made the case for competence as strongly as they could. Although in the end morality did win out — Carter listed it as the first of his two questions — their concerns were unnecessary. For no sooner did Carter take the oath of office as Georgia's governor than he identified as his major initiative one that would demonstrate competence: government reorganization.

GOVERNING IN LIGHT OF THE THEMES

As Gary Fink's exhaustive study of Carter's reorganization effort in Georgia attests, the effort was an enormous one and fraught with pitfalls and potentials for failure.[87] The problem was that, while reorganization is a popular (and populist) issue, it is a low-salience issue for voters. Few who support streamlining government find the rewards exciting enough to participate actively, or even to pressure their legislators about it. By contrast, those for whom the issue is of high salience — typically the state officials most threatened by it — can be counted on to oppose it. Moreover, their opposition is likely to be shrewd and effective.

Fink therefore gives Carter an outstanding political grade for ultimately pushing the gist of his reorganization bill through a recalcitrant state legislature. The judgment has been disputed. Opponents, like the chair of Georgia's Republican party at the time, predictably claimed that "the program has been a total failure."[88] In an effort so mammoth, there is naturally no way to settle the matter. (Even Jody Powell later admitted that he had no idea whether reorganization had succeeded or failed. When asked privately during the presidential campaign how much money was saved by reorganization, Powell confided: "We say $30 million, but no one really knows how much it saved or cost. It depends on how you calculate it.")[89] Yet, while Carter's campaign claim that he "abolished" 278 unnecessary state agencies might not be taken at face value,[90] it is difficult to dismiss the effort as a failure. For again, the only full-scale scholarly study of government reorganization evaluates it favorably, on balance.

But if Carter's reorganization effort was a task so complex that a consensus evaluation of it is impossible, the question of why he even attempted it is emphasized. Having never mentioned it during his campaign — and having scant pressure placed upon him to tackle it — Carter might easily have left it alone. Seizing it and then having it dominate his administration requires explanation.

The explanation usually offered focuses on Carter's background and inclinations. For example, Robert Lipshutz explained that the initiative "gets into his overall background and training in that . . . number one he is a planner."[91] Similarly, Bill Pope guessed that "the reorganization phase is another part of his personality which is, you know, the engineer's approach to problems and efficiency and that sort of thing."[92] Undoubtedly these judgments are accurate: reorganization was precisely the kind of complex technical and administrative problem that one "phase" of Carter's personality found enjoyable and important. Nevertheless, the judgment couched in terms of Carter's background and inclinations overlooks an obvious political consideration as well: that by reorganizing the entire state government Carter would be able to claim a measure of executive competence rarely displayed by a one-term governor. Similarly, as an initiative favored by many Republicans that could be effected by borrowing executives from Georgia's leading industries to assist with the effort, government reorganization enabled Carter to earn the goodwill of those on the other side of the partisan divide as well as those in the best position to finance his presidential campaign. For a man planning to run for president on the theme of competence, considerations like these could not have been irrelevant — whatever his personal inclinations.

A similar set of explanations may be applied to Carter's other main gubernatorial reform, zero-based budgeting. According to this budgeting system, state department heads were no longer allowed to submit annual budget requests that simply repeated their previous year's budget augmented by requested increases. Instead, department budgets were annually slashed to zero and every department was forced to justify each program, whether existing or new, from scratch. By further requiring department heads to prioritize their funding requests without regard to the previous year's budget, Carter hoped to be alerted to worthwhile new programs as well as wasteful old ones. Insofar as it could be touted as successful, zero-based budgeting suggested a measure of government accountability rarely envisioned before.

No less than government reorganization, of which Carter considered it a part, zero-based budgeting had its critics. They argued that crafty department heads quickly learned to manipulate the process as easily as they had the previous one by simply placing a low priority on a much needed program and higher priorities on more frivolous ones. In this way they hoped to trick the governor and legislature into funding their entire budget, largesse and all. Whether or to what extent this manipulation occurred is anyone's guess. Suffice it to say that the process was not foolproof.

The explanations for Carter's initiatives in this area are again both personal and political. On one hand, there are voices like Lance's, who explained Carter's commitment to zero-based budgeting (which he defended) by saying simply that "Carter's cheap."[93] On the other hand, speculation might center on the way this initiative also helped to substantiate his claim to fiscal competence. But the two explanations here, as with government reorganization, are not inconsistent. Carter may well have been just as competent as he hoped to appear — indeed, most evidence indicates that he was.

☆   ☆   ☆

As Jordan and Rafshoon expected, Carter had little difficulty projecting an image of moral leadership in the governor's mansion. If anything, as perhaps they also feared, his moralism bordered on excess. Described privately by both reporters and legislators with words like "integrity," "genuine," "sincere," and "honest," he was also held to be stubbornly self-righteous.[94] "His practice of attempting to do things that he felt were right regardless of the political implications sometimes didn't sit too well," recalled a state official.[95] State senator Julian Bond complained that "he just won't give in," while Representative Grace Hamilton said "he thinks he's still commander of a submarine."[96] Considering Carter to be as "stubborn" as "a South Georgia turtle" because he did not "like to trade," many wondered how Carter could possibly be effective with old "horse traders" like Speaker of the House George L. Smith. "Virtue is on the governor's side," the *Atlanta Constitution* editorialized after his first year, "but how many votes has virtue?"[97] Indeed, when virtue did not succeed, Carter sometimes resorted to moral rebuke. He once called the general assembly "the worst legislature in the nation."[98]

Yet most concurred that Carter was surprisingly effective and that his moral high-mindedness was an asset. (Some even inferred that his reluctance to "horse trade" was itself a negotiating tactic, albeit one that enabled him to position himself normally above the fray.) One state senator spoke highly of Carter's strategy, which he described this way: "If there was an issue that was particularly important to him, he usually called you down to the governor's office," explained "the importance of the issue and the closeness of it to his heart," and "solicited your support" without "undue pressure."[99] While moral hyperbole and stubbornness diminished Carter's reputation, this sort of humane negotiating enhanced it — and his effectiveness.

Carter's personal morality was further displayed in the openness of his administration. With little to hide except his own political ambition, he supported state "sunshine laws" designed to open as much of the governing process as possible to the media and the public. Similarly and with populist flair, he occasionally moved the governor's office for a day to some outlying town or rural hamlet. He also established an ambitious "Goals for Georgia" program that held more than fifty forums throughout the state, in which citizens were invited to give input.

The one achievement mentioned by many to illustrate the open and moral tone of Carter's administration was judicial reform. He became "the first Governor in the history of Georgia," noted Attorney General Arthur Bolton, "to really use the Judicial Nominating Commission." Whereas previous governors had routinely bypassed the commission in order to appoint friends and political supporters to judgeships, Carter appointed judges only from the list of those nominated — even when they were known political opponents. In light of this, together with Carter's support for fair reforms of both the judicial retirement system and the salary structure for all statewide elected (and some appointed) officials, Carter's initially skeptical attorney general became a "convert." He concluded that, despite Carter's "anti-lawyer" reputation, "he did more to enhance the prestige of the courts of this State than any other Governor in my lifetime."[100]

Similarly, Carter was regarded as an early champion of environmental legislation. Although Rafshoon later claimed that the choice of green as a campaign color was accidental — it was the only color he had on hand in 1970 when he first needed paper for a Carter brochure, and the campaign just stuck with it[101] — the color choice was appropriate. Working tirelessly in this long-neglected area, Carter earned substantial praise from early environmentalists and, in 1976, was ranked along with Morris Udall as the most environment-friendly presidential candidate.[102] To this day, canoeists and others regard Carter highly for having reclaimed Georgia's Chattahoochee River for recreation. Prompting his interest in the river, however, was more than morality. Jimmy and Rosalynn also found time to take up canoeing and kayaking during his governorship — practicing their skills at Georgia State University's pool, where, many years ago as an ROTC student, Carter had been thrown in with hands and legs bound for a "survival swim."

SATISFYING YEARS

Later in life, long after he was defeated for reelection as president, Carter recalled his gubernatorial administration as among the most satisfying years of his life.[103] There were ample reasons for him to think so. Although the duplicitous campaign that elected him might have given him cause for concern — and his initiatives as governor were designed in part to substantiate the themes of his presidential campaign rather than to fulfill his gubernatorial campaign promises — never again would he display so enormous a capacity for work or for pleasure, or accomplish so much that was worthwhile.

His capacity for work during these plateau years *was* enormous. "He would take a stack of papers — sometimes almost a foot thick — home and go over it at night until 1:00 A.M.," remembered a state official.[104] Another judged that the pace must have "just flat wore the man out."[105] Yet little did these observers know that the pace was double what they perceived. For in addition to the work they saw, Carter was also planning his presidential campaign. This entailed not only the visible additional commitments Carter accepted — his cochairing of the Democrats' midterm elections in 1974, his membership in the Trilateral Commission, his foreign trips (ostensibly designed to enhance Georgia's international trade) — but also much that was not visible. Although slimmer and less well written than his subsequent books, Carter found secret time to write his campaign autobiography, *Why Not the Best?*, during his otherwise active gubernatorial administration. He also directed Jordan to research the party rules for every state's Democratic primary or caucus and analyze every media market in the country. Absorbing this information (often in tabular form), Carter then oversaw developing plans for his two-year presidential campaign, which, like his gubernatorial campaign writ large, assigned mathematical values to each state and region, predetermined budgets, and roughly outlined an advance schedule. Meanwhile, he made time to deliver as many speeches as he believed helpful, writing most of them himself or speaking extemporaneously. He seemed oblivious to sleep or schedules on evenings when not only national politicians but also the likes of Bob Dylan, Hunter Thompson, or even Pat Caddell were invited to drink beer and converse at the governor's mansion. At the same time he spent Saturdays searching dumps for bottles to add to his collection, arranged early morning tennis matches, and canoed the Chattahoochee. At his peak in mid-life Carter was both moral and competent — and his life was enormously full.

Supporting him in his efforts, moreover, was something Carter had never really known before: a community. The community was not what he may have initially desired. Jordan, Kirbo, Powell, and Lance — together with Rafshoon and later Bourne — were not coequals; they were subordinates. But they melded together into a team whose synergy was greater than the sum of the parts. "We knew each other so well," remembered Rafshoon years later when recalling "the strength that we had." Never was there any "backbiting" or reason for it. "I'd do my thing, Hamilton would do his thing and Jody would do his thing without consulting. We never had a meeting. . . . And nobody ever worried that the other person was usurping his territory."[106] Jordan could therefore be sent to work on the Democratic National Committee in Washington and Bourne to work with the Nixon administration's drug-abuse prevention efforts, both operating in part as undercover Washington infiltrators for the Carter effort, without worrying that their positions on the Carter team were threatened. Indeed, all acknowledged that Jordan was the de facto White House chief of staff long before he officially accepted the position (but after it had been offered thrice). Although Lance and later Bourne were both dismissed from the White House under a cloud of scandal (Bourne had allegedly prescribed Quaaludes for a staffer), when Carter announced Lance's departure reporters observed that his eyes filmed with tears. If not quite a community of coequals and more like the interdependent submarine crews in which Carter felt so secure, these men were needed by Carter almost as much as they needed him.

Carter was also propelled by a dream, which his intimates shared, supported, and helped to realize. If, as Aristotle observed, happiness is not so much a state of being as an activity,[107] Carter was happy because, together with others, he was actively in pursuit of his dream: becoming the best.

So it was that, along with "integrity," Bill Shipp mentioned "ambition" as one of his two distinct impressions of Governor Carter. Another reporter conveyed a similar opinion through an anecdote. Invited to play an early morning tennis game with Carter toward the end of his administration, the reporter recalled how he lost. Carter "took some delight in repeatedly hitting the ball toward a rosebush growing partially into my side of the court. I emerged a loser and a bit bloody from the scratches." The reporter then reflected, "Why I pass that along I don't really know." But in some inarticulate way, this episode seemed to capture something of the ambition that the nation would soon see in Georgia's governor.[108]

But, as planned, the nation saw more than ambition in Jimmy Carter. By September 1976 a Gallup poll found that 68 percent of the public believed that Carter was "a man of high moral character," while 72 percent deemed him "bright, intelligent" — adjectives that suggested competence, which was not a choice available to the poll's respondents. Except for the 72 percent who considered him to be "a religious person," a perception not inconsistent with moral character, these two traits topped the list of those attributed to him.[109] And less than two months later the people who perceived him this way elected him president.

1976 IN AMERICA

"In my travels around the country," Carter announced to a Baltimore audience early in his marathon campaign, "I have found two basic concerns." One of these was that "our government in Washington has lost its basic integrity"; the other was that "government in Washington is incompetent." Six months later in Tallahassee, Florida, Carter similarly declared, "There are two basic questions that I hear everywhere." One was "Can our government be competent?" The other was "Can our government in Washington, which we love, be decent?"[1]

The campaign themes that Carter had identified at least as early as 1972 were thus woven into his early stump speech. Although the themes were somewhat disingenuously attributed to the people, the attribution was not completely dishonest. For when he seized these themes early in his gubernatorial administration, Carter did not believe that they originated with him. Instead he believed that these really were the themes that would be of most concern to voters in 1975 and 1976. Poised to hear these themes during his campaign, he undoubtedly heard them.

Yet as Carter's campaign gathered momentum he began to evidence appreciation for the way the themes of morality and competence formed the twin pillars of a more comprehensive theme. This broader theme, which he increasingly emphasized as his campaign progressed, was simply faith. By the time he spoke to the California State Senate in May 1976, for example, he no longer emphasized morality and competence. Instead he spoke of faith. "I think that the political campaign this year is operating on two levels," he commented to the assembled California politicians. "On one level we have the tangible issues — unemployment, welfare, taxation — but on another level we have the intangible issue of the cynicism and apathy that afflict too many of our fellow Americans." Leaving no doubt about which level his candidacy addressed, he added: "If I had to sum up in one word what this campaign is all about, the word would be 'faith.'"[2]

In a speech the next week to the AFL-CIO in Ohio, Carter hinted that the larger theme of faith had really emerged ascendant only during the years since he had first identified morality and competence as his central themes. "Perhaps my campaign would not have been so successful if I had run for president four years ago or eight years ago," he conjectured, "but I think that this year my candidacy coincided with a new mood in America." Of what precisely this "new mood" consisted he did not say. However, he made general reference to "all the scandals and failures of recent years" — a phrase suggesting immorality ("scandals") and incompetence ("failures") — and then noted their political effect. "This may be the first year in our history," he said, "when it is better to run for President as a peanut farmer from Plains, Georgia, than as a United States Senator from Washington, D.C."[3] In other words, disgust over government immorality and incompetence was so pervasive that "faith" was more readily stimulated by a candidate dissociated from Washington.

This rhetoric of America's "new mood," created by "scandals and broken promises" and begging for "inspiration and hope," then became the cornerstone of Carter's acceptance speech at the Democratic convention in July.[4] In it the most massive audience of Americans ever to listen to Jimmy Carter heard his twin themes of competence and morality woven into a larger fabric of faith. Understanding this "new mood" in America, and how precisely competence and morality were related to it, therefore promises to explain much of Carter's appeal in 1976. It may also aid in understanding the challenges posed by America's political culture during a year when the nation celebrated its bicentennial with what many felt was a noticeable want of enthusiasm.

AMERICA'S "NEW MOOD"

As early as the New Hampshire primary, Elizabeth Drew warned her *New Yorker* audience against reading too much into the impending elections. "When histories of this year are written," she forecast, "there will undoubtedly be a temptation to see more of a pattern in events than there has been." Against this temptation to "overconclude," Drew advised that "there may be less meaning and more accident in what has happened than many suppose." Specifically she cautioned against accepting the view that the elections "reflect a search for spirituality, for something to believe in again." Although she admitted that "there is undoubtedly some truth to that" and — referring to Jimmy Carter — predicted that "the Democratic candidate who pitched his campaign toward the search for spirituality will probably win his party's nomination," she counseled interpretive restraint.[5]

Drew's caution is justified. Much that occurred might have occurred differently, Carter came perilously close to losing, and no one theme easily blanketed the nation. Still, the warning itself may stand as evidence to the contrary. When a Washington journalist cynically warns a sophisticated readership against concluding that an election is about faith, a reasonable inference is that faith is precisely what the election is about. And that, at least, is an inference easily drawn from both popular culture and opinion polls.

Signaling, perhaps, the angst of the years to come, Rod Stewart's guttural two-sided hit "Maggie May/Reason to Believe" soared to number one on the pop charts in late 1971. In the same year, the album on which the songs were included hit number one and *Rolling Stone* named Stewart "Rock Star of the Year." Meanwhile, "Reason to Believe" enjoyed an even wider audience as a cut on the easy-listening Carpenters' number one album, *Close to You*. Although the song did not say more than could be fitted within the standard theme of unrequited love, its lyrics were sufficiently vacuous to allow other interpretations. Indeed, as is usually the case with that theme, "Reason to Believe" directed more attention to the unbelieving self than to the never-identified object of belief.

During the same year, frankly more spiritual searches for belief were suggested by two top-ten albums, *Jesus Christ Superstar* and George Harrison's *All Things Must Pass*.[6] In both, however, the potentially hopeful message was partially negated. *Jesus Christ Superstar* told the story of Christianity's central figure largely from the perspective of Judas, the disciple who betrayed him. As such, many felt that the rock opera mocked rather than upheld the traditional Christian story. George Harrison's *All Things Must Pass*, undoubtedly an authentic expression of spiritual searching, nevertheless offered a tacit criticism of Western religion by celebrating Eastern religiosity. Its chantlike musical construction, moreover, conveyed more of a sense of moody search than of spiritual uplift or fulfillment. Together, the spiritual messages of these two albums may not have been unlike that which many might have imputed to "Reason to Believe": Western faiths had lost their power to compel, and one might just as well consider Judas's perspective or turn east.

By the next year popular music's "search for spirituality, for something to believe in" attached itself vaguely to America. Don McLean's eight-and-a-half-minute "American Pie," a song that posed ambiguous popular cultural allusions about "the day the music died" around the theme of the nation's meaning, hit number one in both single and album formats despite its noncommercial length.[7] Along with it, other songs suggesting an inchoate search for nationalistic meaning, like "A Horse with No Name," also sailed to number one in 1972. That song, together with others like it, was even released by a band that named itself simply America.[8]

As the decade matured, however, a search for either purely spiritual or nationalistic meaning seemed to recede in the most-listened-to popular songs. (Chart position, measured by sales, also determined the amount of airplay a record received on most major radio stations in the country at the time. Americans who did not buy a popular record or even like the song hence generally heard it anyway.) By the middle of the decade the rage was disco music — more or less meaningless dance tunes. Although disco was not as dominant as some recall, other strands in popular music's tapestry of sound seemed also to resist any articulation of collective meaning. Instead, it splintered into regional tributaries. Thus, for example, enormously popular folk-rock artists like John Denver, Linda Rondstadt, and the Eagles emerged to direct the search for meaning to the American West and Southwest, while country music also soared in popularity and directed attention to the American Southeast.[9] One strand of the revival, that associated with truck drivers and the citizens band radio craze, substituted the highway for a regional sense of place, while another situated itself in cities and eventuated in an "urban cowboy" craze. (A branch of country music, the southern rock revival associated with Macon's Capricorn Records and led especially by the Allman Brothers, proved to be of more than cultural assistance to Carter's presidential campaign. Several of Capricorn's bands performed benefit concerts for Carter and flooded his campaign with cash at critical junctures.)[10] Perhaps the most distinctive feature of middle 1970s searching songs taken together was the particularistic identity of place. Whereas immediately preceding songs had sometimes suggested nationalistic meaning, later ones invariably directed the quest either regionally or to lifestyle segments within the nation.

The portrait of interpersonal relationships that appears in the popular music of the early and middle 1970s is also distinctive. When the themes of the songs transcended the customary emphasis on unrequited love, they sometimes focused on personal compassion or interpersonal anger. Examples of number one songs about personal compassion include Simon and Garfunkel's classic "Bridge over Troubled Water" (1970), James Taylor's "You've Got a Friend" (1971), Bill Withers's "Lean on Me" (1972), and Billy Swan's "I Can Help" (1974). Examples of number one songs expressing less sanguine interpersonal emotions include Carly Simon's "You're So Vain" (1973), Jim Croce's "Bad, Bad Leroy Brown" (1973), "Kung Fu Fighting" (1974), and Linda Rondstadt's "You're No Good" (1975). Occasional songs, like Eric Clapton's "I Shot the Sheriff" and John Lennon's "Whatever Gets You through the Night" — both number one songs in 1974 — even smacked of nihilism. Besides John Denver's unique praise of nature ("Sunshine on My Shoulder" and "Thank God I'm a Country Boy"), number one songs conveying a positive theme other than romantic fulfillment celebrated only interpersonal compassion.[11] Equally prominent motifs, however, were anger, violence, and nihilism. More important, no top song after 1972 expressed the hope of finding national meaning.

Nor did the string of hits during the election year alter this trend. Except for Diana Ross's melancholy "Theme from 'Mahogany' (Do You Know Where You're Going To)" early in 1976, no top song appeared that raised serious, searching questions about meaning. By March and then again in May, nostalgia ruled with The Four Seasons' top hit "December 1963 (Oh, What a Night)" and John Sebastian's number one "Welcome Back." Later in May, Paul McCartney's band Wings hit number one with "Silly Love Songs" — a frank apologetic for the trivial in popular music directed against John Lennon's rival insistence that popular songs be socially relevant. By the July week of the Democratic convention, the Starland Vocal Band's "Afternoon Delight" was the number one song in the nation (and presumably reflected the preferred activity for Americans celebrating their bicentennial). Then, after almost being teased by the September top song, "Play That Funky Music (White Boy)," Carter was elected president when "Disco Duck (Part 1)" by Rick Dees and His Cast of Idiots was America's number one popular song.[12]

Although popular music conveys no one message crisply, and variety as much as consistency characterized 1970s hits, the apparent trend is suggestive. Several of the most popular early 1970s songs expressed a search for spiritual or national meaning, but they gave way to middle 1970s songs that found meaning either regionally, in a romanticized nature, in interpersonal compassion, or not at all. The trend appears to confirm Drew's dismissal of "the search for spirituality, for something to believe in again" as an interpretation of the 1976 elections to a degree that even she did not seem to anticipate. By that time the record of popular music suggests that Americans had already given up the search.

But what may have been overlooked by Drew was that Americans who had given up finding "something" to believe in may yet have harbored the dim hope of finding "someone" to believe in. The songs of personal compassion, after all, remained resilient. The middle 1970s trend toward meaningless music was also built on an immediately preceding foundation of songs that did seek spiritual and nationalistic depth. If a person, perhaps regionally identified, arose promising personal compassion, even spiritual depth, he might yet spark a kind of faith.

It was fitting, therefore, that when Carter formally announced his candidacy in December 1974 Billy Swan's upbeat "I Can Help" was the number one song of the nation. Although hardly buried beneath it in the number-four chart position that same week was a more ominous counterpoint: "Tin Man" by America reminded that "Oz never did give nothin' to the tin man that he didn't already have." Sandwiched between the two, Carter's campaign may have followed the only path available to a candidate who hoped to be successful: to promise a renewal of faith based on the personal merits of a moral and competent leader.[13]

Television told a similar story of America's withering search for meaning and mid-decade apathetic plunge. After reigning for five years as the nation's most-viewed television show, for example, the 1976–77 season suddenly found the socially conscious *All in the Family* drop to twelfth place in the ratings (just behind the sexually titillating *Three's Company*). The number one show in that election and inauguration year was the light-hearted situation comedy about life in an America before the crises of the 1960s, *Happy Days*, which was followed by its almost as nostalgic spin-off, *Laverne & Shirley*. Even the most socially poignant popular show of the period, *M*A*S*H*, which ranked fourth in the season's ratings, was ostensibly set in the more quiescent 1950s.[14]

The record of film is less precise because movies are not quite the mass medium that songs and network television shows are. Nevertheless, the observation by a professor of film studies that "the themes and motifs" of the horror film infiltrated "every area of 70s cinema" is suggestive. Even more suggestive may be Robin Wood's claim to have detected a "fragmentation" and "consciously motivated incoherence" in the era's films, which he believed is best exemplified by *Taxi Driver, Looking for Mr. Goodbar,* and *Cruising.* Ignoring the more obvious example of a film depicting societal insanity, 1975's *One Flew over the Cuckoo's Nest* (winner of that year's Academy Award for Best Picture), Wood's more aesthetic judgment is directed to films released in 1976, 1977, and 1979, respectively. His choices and evaluations suggest that film's "textual incoherence," and so the underlying social fragmentation, increased markedly after mid-decade.[15]

The connections between America's popular and political cultures are naturally difficult to discern. But it may be telling that Theodore White chose 1972 to be his last installment in his "making of the president" series and then included the next two elections in his 1982 book, *America in Search of Itself.* Similarly, it is striking that a journalist who chose to chronicle Carter's victory anticipated Carter's own diagnosis of national ills. "A deep malaise blanketed the country," wrote Kandy Stroud two years before Carter's best-known speech was given that same label. "America was in a fugue state, passing through a night of the spirit."[16]

☆   ☆   ☆

The declining "search for spirituality, for something to believe in again" is also reflected in the harder data of opinion polls. Surveys showed that during the scandal-ridden years of 1972 to 1974 the percentage of Americans who expressed confidence in the federal government dropped sixteen points. However, since that drop was from 53 to 37 percent and left only about one out of three Americans measurably upbeat about their national government, the absolute numbers are alarming. Equally alarming was the decline in confidence in the presidency. Already at a dismal 27 percent in March 1972, confidence dropped thirteen more points to settle at 14 percent in March 1974. Even the resignation of President Richard Nixon in August 1974 produced no improvement. By 1976 confidence in government was lower by four more points than it had been in 1974, and trust in the executive branch remained at lows averaging around 15 percent.[17]

Lillian Carter with infant Jimmy.
Courtesy of Jimmy Carter Library.

Earl Carter with Gloria, Ruth, and Jimmy.
Courtesy of Jimmy Carter Library.

Jim Jack Gordy.
Courtesy of Jimmy Carter Library.

Plains, circa 1925.
Earl Carter's grocery is on the left;
Alton Carter's general store, center.
Courtesy of Jimmy Carter Library.

Interior of Earl Carter's grocery. *Courtesy of Jimmy Carter Library.*

Jimmy with his pony, Lady Lee.
Courtesy of Jimmy Carter Library.

"Jim" Carter's
Annapolis photograph;
the inscription is to
Rosalynn.
Courtesy of Jimmy Carter Library.

Jimmy Carter "pinned"
simultaneously by Rosalynn
and his mother at his
graduation ceremony.
Courtesy of Jimmy Carter Library.

Rosalynn and Jimmy Carter's wedding day, July 7, 1946. *Below:* The Carters visiting with Hugh and Alton Carter in the latter's antique store (formerly Plains Mercantile). *Courtesy of Jimmy Carter Library.*

Brothers Billy (left)
and Jimmy (right) with
unidentified man.
Courtesy of Jimmy Carter Library.

One of Jimmy Carter's
first campaign posters,
1962.
Courtesy of Jimmy Carter Library.

State Senator
Jimmy Carter at
the Georgia State
Capitol. (Note the
resemblance to
John Kennedy.)
Courtesy of Jimmy Carter Library.

Carter's campaign
strategy always stressed
personal contact with voters.
Courtesy of Jimmy Carter Library.

Rosalynn and Jimmy Carter being interviewed following their victory in the 1970 gubernatorial race. *Courtesy of Jimmy Carter Library.*

Some of Carter's youthful presidential campaign aides. Left to right: Hamilton Jordan, Jody Powell, Patrick Caddell. *Courtesy of Jimmy Carter Library.*

Mondale and Carter during one of their regularly scheduled working lunches.
Courtesy of Jimmy Carter Library.

Above left: Strategists-turned-aides Jody Powell and Hamilton Jordan worked smoothly together, seemingly sharing each other's unspoken reaction to the same event. *Courtesy of Jimmy Carter Library.*

Above right: Bert Lance visits Carter in the Oval Office. *Courtesy of Jimmy Carter Library.*

Left: Stuart Eizenstat with Carter. *Courtesy of Jimmy Carter Library.*

Dr. Peter Bourne
with Carter.
*Courtesy of Jimmy Carter
Library.*

Carter and
Charles Kirbo
in the
White House.
*Courtesy of Jimmy Carter
Library.*

Hyman Rickover
visits President Carter.
*Courtesy of Jimmy Carter
Library.*

A Carter family portrait during the presidency.
Courtesy of Jimmy Carter Library.

Carter listens to Pat Caddell in the Oval Office.

Courtesy of Jimmy Carter Library.

Pat Caddell, Hamilton Jordan, Gerald Rafshoon, and Jody Powell in discussion at Camp David prior to Carter's "malaise speech."

Courtesy of Jimmy Carter Library.

Carter napping in the Oval Office during the hostage crisis, which often required him to be available for instant negotiations twenty-four hours a day.
Courtesy of Jimmy Carter Library.

Carter's last campaign appearance on November 3, 1980, in either Portland, Oregon, or Seattle, Washington. Later that evening he learned that he would lose the next day's election.
Courtesy of Jimmy Carter Library.

President-elect Ronald Reagan discusses the transition with President Carter. (Note Carter's slight stature compared with Reagan's.) *Courtesy of Jimmy Carter Library.*

The Jimmy Carter commemorative sculpture on Georgia's State Capitol grounds.

So, when Carter spoke of his candidacy coinciding with "a new mood in America," the polls indicated he was correct. But he was also overstating the case. Just as the popular culture record indicates that the collapse of faith was heightened during the years following 1972, so also the polls indicate that declining confidence in government worsened, but did not begin, during this period. According to the polls, confidence in government dropped sometime between 1964 and 1966 — the first biannual survey year in which the decline was noted — and then dropped further in both 1968 and 1970. (In 1964 about three-quarters of the population expressed faith in government; by 1970 the portion was down to about half.) Similarly, confidence in the executive branch fell from 41 percent in 1966 to 23 percent in 1971. (The surveys did not ask about confidence in the executive branch before 1966 when, presumably, it was higher.) Although the declines continued between 1972 and 1976 and the drop was especially sharp between 1972 and 1974, the "new mood" was not of as recent origin as Carter implied. Rather, the polls showed that it was just an exacerbation of existing trends.[18]

The polls therefore reinforce what is suggested by popular culture: that by the middle 1970s Americans had reached something of a nadir in their confidence in government and faith in the nation. However, while this national mood was unmistakable and could not have helped but buoy a candidacy that Carter understood to be based in part on faith, it is equally clear that the onset of the mood was earlier. To understand the meaning of Carter's victory in 1976 thus requires more than an understanding of that year's "new mood." It also requires understanding the political circumstances that produced this mood as well as how Carter's preliminary themes of competence and morality attempted to respond to them.

FAITH AS A PROBLEM OF COMPETENCE AND MORALITY

To extract the theme of competence from the more diffuse spiritual malaise and declining trust in government reflected keen insights. For the theme goes well beyond the partisan insights of those who, like Kevin Phillips in his 1970 *The Emerging Republican Majority*,[19] seemed to suggest that the post-1960s era was simply a time of resurgent conservative Republican economic ideology. This resurgence and partisanship was neither so early nor so strong as is sometimes assumed. Even Phillips's predictions were based more on a notion of cultural disaffection among southern and southwestern whites than a more straightforward attraction to Republican economic ideology. Arguably, instead of shifting Republican, the electorate just increasingly desired competence from a government in which they had dwindling confidence — and welcomed that competence regardless of party.

The evidence for a massive turn toward economic conservatism is especially thin. Economic liberalism, in fact, remained strong through most of the 1970s. The earliest plausible dating of the popular discrediting of economic liberalism should probably be 1978, when California succeeded in passing Proposition 13, and talk of a popular tax revolt was in the air. A decade earlier Hubert Humphrey's 1968 presidential candidacy was damaged hardly at all by his forthright economic liberalism. (Most blame his defeat on his association with the Vietnam War while serving as vice president under Lyndon Johnson, together with the attendant fragmentation the war issue caused for the Democratic party in 1968.) Even in 1972 and again in 1976, polls during the primary season often showed his undeclared candidacy stronger than most declared candidacies, including those of eventual nominees George McGovern and Jimmy Carter.[20] Richard Nixon, meanwhile, endorsed many of liberalism's economic policies — including McGovern's so-called ultra-liberal proposal for a guaranteed minimum income. (In another anathema to traditional conservatives, Nixon also extended diplomatic recognition to China.) And in both 1976 and 1980 there was a widespread sense that Senator Edward Kennedy, the Massachusetts liberal, would be a viable and perhaps even victorious presidential candidate. Early in the 1970s Americans who had witnessed only slight increases in inflation and suffered mainly frictional unemployment were simply unpersuaded by conservative criticisms of midcentury liberalism; later in the 1970s, though the tide began to shift, many continued to cling to it.

Americans grew increasingly concerned throughout the 1970s, however, about government efficacy. Indications of this concern were found on both right and left. From the cultural right, George Wallace railed not so much against liberal policies as against the bureaucratic ineptitude and wasteful spending that too often characterized their attempted implementation. Indeed, after the early 1960s Wallace, who persuaded large portions of Alabama's African American voters to support him for reelection to the governorship, discarded his earlier racist rhetoric in favor of promoting populist opposition to unfair taxes and bureaucratic inefficiency. And after bolting from the Democratic party in 1968 to mount an independent candidacy for president, Wallace returned to the party in both 1972 and 1976 to seek its nomination. His return suggested that his differences with the party of historic liberalism were not so deep that he failed to envision a place for himself within it.

From the cultural left, emerging attitudes were strikingly similar despite their superficial differences. Consumer activists inspired in part by Ralph Nader, though generally targeting big business rather than big government, sometimes found themselves uniting with liberal environmentalists to condemn government's regulatory ineptitude. Meanwhile, opponents of the Vietnam War often blamed the "military-industrial complex" for the tragedy. Indeed, whether via the rhetoric of "participatory democracy," the philosophy of "small is beautiful," the decentralized market capitalism of *The Whole Earth Catalog* and even *The Anarchist Cookbook*, or communal experimentation, many on the left expressed a profound mistrust of scale — and particularly of government's scale. In these ways and others, left and right, while emphasizing different government foibles, converged on populist suspicion of big government's efficacy.

In considering George McGovern's 1972 presidential candidacy, one of the most plausible interpretations of his defeat is the one that Jordan offered privately in 1972: that he simply did not "seem competent" to implement liberal government programs effectively.[21] Perhaps the best-remembered example of this perception was his proposal for a guaranteed minimum income. Since Nixon supported a similar initiative, it is difficult to conclude that the liberal objective of the policy was what troubled most voters. More worrisome may have been McGovern's proposal to fund the minimum income solely through hikes in inheritance and gift taxes. When economists doubted that the tax hikes would be sufficient to finance his massive proposal, and voters wondered whether they would be fair, questions were raised about McGovern's fiscal competence — not his liberal intentions.[22]

Similar doubts about executive competence attached themselves to other aspects of McGovern's candidacy. The 1972 Democratic convention, for example, while not degenerating into the riotous schisms of 1968, nevertheless struck many as an amalgamation of special interests over which McGovern exerted little control. When the nominee himself was forced to wait until the wee hours of the morning to deliver his acceptance speech, it was apparent to all that he was not in charge of the proceedings. Worse, McGovern did not even seem to be able to run his own campaign effectively. When he chose, defended, and then abruptly dropped his vice presidential running mate, Senator Thomas Eagleton, after the press reported that Eagleton had undergone treatment for mental illness, McGovern's command over his own campaign was suspect.

Whatever the public's views about McGovern's liberal policy initiatives — and they may have been more favorable than many remember — his candidacy raised doubts about his ability to achieve them. These doubts were exploited by the Republicans, who chose as their 1972 campaign slogan, "Nixon: Now More Than Ever." The slogan juxtaposed Nixon's image of decisive leadership with McGovern's image of well-intentioned but muddling incompetence. The juxtaposition, however, was not so much ideological as pragmatic, and liberalism should no more be blamed for McGovern's defeat than conservatism credited for Nixon's victory.

The underlying explanation of the political mood during the early 1970s may therefore not be ideology but trust. When confidence in government erodes, economic liberalism is vulnerable. Its vulnerability is based not so much on citizen opposition to the principle of an activist government but on citizen mistrust of government's ability to achieve that principle. A national survey conducted after California's 1978 tax revolt illustrates this relationship well. Those who showed the least trust in government were also the most likely to support sharp tax reductions, even when those reductions were said to reduce popular services like health and education. Importantly, the relationship was found across all party and ideological lines. Distrustful Democrats were just as likely as distrustful Republicans to support tax cuts, while distrustful liberals were actually more supportive of tax cuts than trusting conservatives. Trust, rather than party or ideology, was the better predictor of attitudes toward what has since become known as liberalism's "tax-and-spend" agenda.[23]

So, the Carter team's response to mounting distrust with the theme of competence was precisely on target. Not yet willing to relinquish liberalism's values or goals, voters were simply insistent upon government efficacy and executive competence in achieving them. However, it is an open question whether in the long run a mistrustful public will be willing to extend to even a competent Democrat the good will necessary to govern effectively.[24] But if public cynicism prevents a president from being able to exhibit competence, attention must be directed to themes that will counter this cynicism and revive confidence. For Carter, this all-important additional theme was morality, and by seizing it he was not mistaken. However, he was mistaken in his understanding of the moral leadership America really yearned for, which was more subtle and complex than the morality he offered.

While the Carter forces were shrewd to extract a desire for competence from the larger problem of America's declining faith, their grasp of the nation's desire for moral leadership was more problematic. Essentially they assumed that moral *leadership* was best attained by moral *character.* The linkage is common among those who eschew ideology in favor of personality, but its ramifications are disturbing. Whereas moral leadership articulates a vision that others are inspired to realize, moral character merely displays traits that others find laudable. Nations that flounder for lack of faith may find individual moralists appealing — the Carter campaign was right about this — but in the struggle for national faith more may be needed than a moral exemplar. Needed also may be a leadership that propounds a vision of a collective moral future.

The assumption among Carter intimates that moral leadership could be reduced to moral character is evident from the context of Jordan's November 1972 comments about the country's need for moral leadership. This context was his assessment of Senator Edward Kennedy's expected 1976 presidential bid. To Jordan, "the unanswered questions about Chappaquiddick run contrary to this national desire for trust and morality in government." In other words, Kennedy's rumored personal moral failings would be a liability in a country that thirsted for "moral leadership." That, plus his offhand remark that Nixon had not satisfied the desire for moral leadership, either (but McGovern had), was as deeply as Jordan probed the issue.[25] No mention was made of any moral vision that Kennedy or anyone else might articulate. Morality was assumed by Jordan to extend no further than the personal character of the candidate.

Carter thought similarly. Always campaigning tacitly against the legacy of Richard Nixon, Carter once recalled what happened when "Richard Nixon came in the White House in '68." At that moment, Carter asserted, the "people" lost "hope."[26] Listeners to the campaign address were never told why Carter believed the people lost hope in 1968 (and the polls showed that they had begun to lose that hope at least two years earlier, when Nixon had presumably retired from politics). But surely during those post-Watergate days Carter could confidently assume that his listeners would explain the collapse of hope in terms of Nixon's character.

The president who had long before earned the nickname "Tricky Dick," after all, had recently resigned from office amid charges of criminal conspiracy.

But Carter was generally careful during his campaign to avoid singling out Nixon for personal criticism, lest by doing so his accusations backfire and cause him to appear mean-spirited. However, he made his points indirectly. Thus, without directly accusing Nixon of dishonesty, Carter recalled him and then spoke generally about when the people were "excluded" from government and "lied to" by public officials. These failings occurred, Carter went on to say, because of character. "The basic honesty and character of the American people," Carter summarized, were not "exemplified" by elected officials.[27] Likewise, when Carter spoke of recent "scandals" in government he could be sure that most Americans would assume he was speaking about Watergate, if not also the earlier forced resignation of Vice President Spiro Agnew for having accepted bribes while governor of Maryland. However, while Carter generally avoided expressing his personal dislike for Nixon publicly, in private he could be caustic: "I think he's disgraced the Presidency," he said warming to his subject. "I lived in California when he ran against Helen Gahagan Douglas," Carter explained. "I'm a longtime Nixon-hater from way back."[28]

And, against this legacy of Nixon, Carter promoted his own moral character. His famous promise, "I'll never lie to you," is perhaps the clearest instance of this, but there were countless others. And they were effective — sometimes excessively so. Once an Associated Press reporter secretly taped a poster of Carter drawn to resemble Jesus and captioned "J. C. Can Save America" behind him while he gave impromptu interviews.[29] Although Carter was furious when he discovered the reason for the reporters' chortles, the prank could have amused only because it built upon promises already implied by Carter. Indeed, a few citizens apparently took his promises to the extremes that his hyperbole pointed. Some claimed that they really "could see a halo around his head."[30]

Yet in the Carter campaign's understanding of Nixon there was a grave simplification. For they (and many Americans with them) failed to consider that, despite his personal moral failings, Nixon may have exhibited a degree of moral leadership that inspired a measure of national confidence unrecorded since. Suggesting this is naturally contestable to this day. It is even more debatable when attention is directed to the public issue to which Nixon made his strongest moral contribution: the Vietnam War.

But the evidence suggests that Nixon's wartime leadership was both successful and moral.

Received opinion is that McGovern's unequivocal opposition to the war in Vietnam was the morally superior position. This view should be questioned. Lending retrospective credence to the antiwar view is primarily the ignoble conclusion of that war. Had the war ended differently and the U.S. extracted a measure of victory and dignity from its involvement — objectives that Nixon went to his grave believing had been attainable — McGovern's opposition to the war would not today receive the retrospective approval it does. Since in this case as in others ascendant opinions are invariably those of the victorious rather than the vanquished, making popular acceptance of an opinion a poor gauge of its merit, it is worth reconsidering the merits of McGovern's opposition to the war at the time he and others voiced it.

The reconsideration need not entail a review of the entire war effort. That U.S. involvement in Vietnam was a tragic mistake may be granted to McGovern's side. But the question that confronted McGovern in 1972 was not whether U.S. involvement in Vietnam had been mistaken but what he proposed to do about that mistake. By that year everyone knew that the end of U.S. involvement in Vietnam was imminent. The draft had ended, troops were being withdrawn, and Nixon had announced his "secret plan" for ending the war. Although some Americans probably did not believe Nixon and many resented his previous escalation of the war, few could seriously doubt that the war was essentially over. In this context (unlike perhaps in 1968), McGovern's strident opposition to the war was largely irrelevant.

Nor was McGovern's position necessarily the moral one. Since at stake in 1972 was not the withdrawal of U.S. forces from Vietnam but the interpretation and consequences of that withdrawal, McGovern's unequivocal opposition to the war smacked of nihilism. The duty of leadership then — again, as opposed perhaps to 1968 — was not simply to call for an end to a war that was already lost but to extract as much dignity and purpose from the American effort as possible. Yet, having declared that the Senate had "blood on its hands" for its complicity in Vietnam, McGovern proposed no such interpretation of America's misadventure in Vietnam. Instead, to Americans who had lost some 58,000 loved ones in the jungles of Vietnam and who had expended some $1.5 billion in mostly deficit tax dollars on the war effort, McGovern offered only the sting of dishonor and the legacy of guilt.[31]

The legacy of Vietnam in America makes it difficult to conclude that McGovern's position on the war in 1972 was morally complete or nationally palatable. Even granting that he was right in his understanding of the war — indeed, especially if he was right in his understanding — it was incumbent upon him to do more than denounce the effort. Demanded was a denunciation that identified specific errors, called for correspondingly specific corrective reforms, and led the nation in a reflection about their mistakes that simultaneously upheld the dignity, sacrifice, and honorable intentions of those who made or were forced to make them. Without this discussion, opposition to the Vietnam War in 1972 was irrelevant, even nihilistic.

For all the criticism that may be rightly leveled against him, Nixon's conduct of the war in Vietnam should be understood in light of this nihilistic alternative. Campaigning in 1968 on a pledge of "peace with honor," Nixon recognized early that at stake in the war he inherited was not so much victory or withdrawal but, in his 1969 words, the need to avoid a "defeat" that would lead to "inevitable remorse" and "divisive recrimination" and that would "scar our spirit as a people."[32] To forestall this danger, Nixon found himself escalating the war. Yet, while that escalation was and may yet be subject to sharp criticism, it is important to appreciate that Nixon did not authorize it without also envisioning how it would ultimately produce his promised "peace with honor." The escalation in fact was linked to the first cogent policy the U.S. ever had in Vietnam, which Nixon called "Vietnamization."

The plan for "Vietnamization" of the war, which Nixon announced on April 30, 1970, and immediately put into effect, amounted essentially to turning the war over to the South Vietnamese with the aid of U.S. technical and air support. Attending the announcement of this policy therefore was Nixon's simultaneous announcement that he had ordered the bombing of Cambodia. Interpreting this as but another pointless escalation of the war, antiwar protesters launched massive demonstrations, including one that eventuated in the murder of four and wounding of nine students by National Guardsmen at Kent State University on May 4. Despite this vehement opposition, however, the record suggests that Nixon's efforts were supported by the majority of Americans.

The 1970 to 1972 period during which the policy of Vietnamization was pursued stands as the only two-year period in well over a decade when confidence in government did not decline. First detected in 1966, when President Lyndon Johnson's escalation of the Vietnam War was met with rustles of protest, trust in government dropped sharply through 1970. However, after Nixon began pursuing his policy of Vietnamization, confidence held constant (at just over 50 percent) through 1972. Dropping again in 1974, presumably in response to Watergate and the first OPEC oil embargo, confidence continued to plummet through 1980 and has remained well below the 50 percent 1970–72 high ever since. But for two years largely misremembered for the domestic outcry against the Vietnam War — and the last years in which popular music still occasionally expressed hope of finding a national meaning — confidence in government held steady.[33]

Meanwhile, confidence in the presidency actually increased during this period. Climbing from 23 to 29 percent between 1971 and 1973, faith in the executive branch did not exceed this zenith for eleven long years (and then only temporarily).[34] Sadly, perhaps, even polls conducted in Ohio after National Guardsmen opened fire into the crowd of student demonstrators at Kent State University showed the overwhelming majority of respondents siding with the National Guard. Later, a jury found the guardsmen not guilty.[35]

Nixon's own approval ratings testify to the support that the majority of a bitterly divided people lent him during these years. They remained consistently in the 50 to 60 percent range, and a poll conducted simultaneous with his April 30 speech showed his approval rating inching up a point (to 57 percent). Three weeks later — after the shootings at Kent State — his approval ratings were two points higher yet. Two years later, when he ordered the bombing of Haiphong Harbor, Nixon's approval ratings jumped eight percent and his disapproval ratings dropped seven. Enjoying then the approval of 62 percent of the public, Nixon proceeded to defeat McGovern in a landslide of nearly identical proportion. Indeed, Nixon's support among those under 30 was also a solid 60 percent — higher than that of any Republican president since Dwight Eisenhower's war heroism inspired support from a World War II generation twenty years before.[36]

Nixon also wrapped his presidency in a spiritual garb so thick that Charles Henderson, a chaplain at Princeton University, was prompted to write a book on *The Nixon Theology*. Nixon's rhetoric was laced with a pronounced piety, he was not afraid to cast the issues of the day in light of larger spiritual concerns, and the White House held regular quasi-public religious services within its walls. Billy Graham, the famous evangelist, was also a regular participant in executive ceremony and was known to consult privately with the president about matters of religious faith.

Despite this blanketing religiosity of the Nixon presidency, a "longtime Nixon-hater from way back" like Carter managed to overlook it. Indeed, had Carter's aides not persuaded him to substitute a milder biblical text in his inaugural address for his preferred 2 Chron. 7:14, the oversight might have become a public embarrassment. For that precise text was used at Nixon's 1968 inaugural. "If my people who are called by my name shall humble themselves and pray and seek my face and turn from their wicked ways," Billy Graham quoted Carter's preferred text, "then I will hear from heaven and will forgive their sin and will heal their land." The text that was too harsh for Carter was readily appropriated by Nixon.[37]

Some of Nixon's rhetoric even anticipated Carter's own infamous malaise speech. "We're torn by division," Nixon declared at his inaugural, "wanting unity. We see around us empty lives wanting fulfillment. We see tasks that need doing waiting for hands to do them." And finally: "To a crisis of the spirit we need an answer of the spirit."[38]

The similarity of the rhetoric defies easy interpretation. Perhaps, as Henderson implies, Nixon's public morality was simply a duplicitous attempt to cloak more sinister deeds and a darker character. Yet such a conjecture turns on the dubious assumptions that Nixon's public deeds *were* sinister and that they reflected a morally flawed character. Since only the most cynical observer could consider Nixon's presidential policies to have been sinister — one may vehemently dispute his policies in Vietnam, for instance, without resorting to this interpretation — the argument that Nixon's public theology was duplicitous rests solely on a judgment of his character. Although a negative judgment of Nixon's character is itself debatable — surely virtue and vice commingled within him in more equal measure than his detractors allow — the further assumption that morality inheres primarily in character is even more contestable. Indeed, it is no more defensible than the opposite claim: that morality is public and character grows in moral proportion to behavior and rhetoric. Since Nixon both acted and spoke morally, his Vietnam policy and spiritual rhetoric may be understood to have congealed into a degree of moral leadership. The contrary impression arises primarily from those who opposed his policies or so disliked him personally that they found themselves unable to credit him with any moral substance at all. One such "longtime Nixon-hater from way back" even appropriated similar spiritual rhetoric without noting the similarities.

It is understandably difficult for many today to consider Nixon a moral leader. Too much about Nixon, particularly from his anti-Communist days, offended too many. He also fell victim to Watergate. Further, much if not all of his victimization was his own doing. Still, the long shadow cast by the Vietnam War over the early 1970s makes it equally difficult to believe that those were times in which morality was only a matter of personal character. People of superior moral character, most notably Jimmy Carter but also George McGovern, did appear in the country — but the haunting legacy of Vietnam lingered. Indeed, electing the sole Korean War era–veteran to a presidency dominated before and after by the World War II generation may suggest moral escapism rather than moral engagement (just as the setting of three of the top four television shows of 1976–77 in the nostalgic 1950s suggests escapism). The story of America since the 1970s, together with Carter's story, may therefore be one of a nation paralyzed by anguish over Vietnam but hopeful that the lost national purpose might be reclaimed through personal morality.

That story, like most others, may well have been anticipated in the 1972 presidential primaries. Senator Edmund Muskie, an early front-runner for the Democratic nomination who outpolled McGovern until his campaign was derailed by one of Nixon's "dirty tricks," campaigned on a simple anti-Nixon slogan: "Trust Muskie." Except for worrying that Muskie might drink too much, Carter always liked him. He considered him seriously for the vice presidency and appointed him secretary of state in 1980, after Cyrus Vance resigned. Without the rhyme, he also appropriated the gist of his presidential campaign strategy.

Carter was not oblivious to the enormous importance of the Vietnam War in America of the early 1970s. As governor, in fact, he was called upon to make a symbolically potent decision regarding the war. Lieutenant William Calley, a Georgian, was convicted in a Georgia military court for his complicity in the My Lai massacre. Veterans groups and others urged Carter to declare a special state holiday on Calley's behalf following the conviction. Carter, who later claimed to have been repulsed by Calley's murderous acts, nevertheless found a middle ground not unlike the one Nixon grappled for nationally. Refusing to declare a holiday in Calley's honor, Carter instead called a state holiday named "American

Fighting Men's Day." Those who wished to honor William Calley on this day could do so; others could honor more deserving soldiers. Carter also bit his tongue when reporters asked him to comment on the Calley conviction. Sidestepping the question, he cloaked his response in the garb of populism and said that Calley's superiors were "equally" responsible for the atrocity. In this way and others Carter, whose son Jack served in Vietnam while he campaigned successfully for governor and who delivered the nominating speech at the 1972 Democratic convention for avowed Vietnam hawk Scoop Jackson, was generally supportive of the war effort at the same time that he maintained a moral distance from its excesses.[39]

Similarly, during his 1976 campaign Carter courageously tackled the most immediate problem left by the war, when, in a carefully worded address that nevertheless elicited boos from a Seattle American Legion, he proposed to offer a pardon to draft resisters. The pardon, he tried carefully to explain, did not mean amnesty. His offering was of forgiveness for a misdeed, not an admission that no mistake had been made. The distinction may or may not have placated the jeering veterans. (Carter noted that instances of applause outnumbered those of boos during his address; reporters sometimes noted that the applause was scattered and dutiful, while the boos were loud and long.) But in his attempt to make this distinction Carter revealed how deftly he tried to sort out the complex and divisive issue.[40]

Yet, if the truth be told, Carter did not believe that Vietnam was an important issue politically. "You know what McGovern's biggest mistake was?" he asked a reporter early in 1976. "He never should have made the Vietnam War an issue."[41] In Carter's political calculus, Vietnam was an issue that should have been avoided even in 1972. Confirming this calculus, Jordan recalled commenting during their first 1972 discussion of strategy that "with the Vietnam War coming to a close, domestic problems and issues were apt to be a more important consideration."[42] A war that splintered the nation and paralleled the collapse of faith that Carter found so worrisome was dismissed by the Carter campaign as early as 1972, and by Carter himself in 1976, as no longer very important.

☆   ☆   ☆

When Carter spoke about issues of public morality like Vietnam during his presidential campaign, he always anchored those issues in personal character. Then, as he had during his governorship, he tried to show how personal character produces the kinds of government processes in which better or worse policy decisions are made. His argument was populist. In essence, he claimed that when public officials are of high moral character they willingly operate their administrations openly. Since open administrations include input from the people, who by flattering populist definition are always right, high moral character ultimately leads to moral public policy.

Thus, for example, when Carter recalled Nixon in a campaign speech he spoke of how "an isolated person" who "separates himself from you" results in an administration that is poised to do much evil.[43] Often also claiming, as he had in his Law Day speech, that "the overwhelming majority of the American people are touched directly and personally when government is ill-managed or insensitive or callous," he rattled off the consequences of an aloof government for the less privileged. These included inadequate education, health care, and transportation systems together with an unfair tax structure and criminal justice system. The way to avoid these problems, he claimed simply enough, is to take government out of the hands of the "big shots." Yet, while he called for populist correctives to social injustice, Carter also explained that public officials had to be especially moral. "Public servants," he often said, have a "special responsibility" to "run the government in a competent way . . . so that those services which are so badly needed can be delivered."[44]

But where the linkage between moral character and government openness was strongest was in the area of foreign policy. Nixon's secretive conduct of the Vietnam War and other aspects of foreign policy, entrusted mainly to National Security Advisor Henry Kissinger rather than routed through more open State Department channels, prompted many to worry about the dangers of an overly "imperial presidency." In campaign speeches Carter railed against this "Lone Ranger diplomacy" and spelled out the risks of so secretive an approach.[45] "In looking back," he declared, "almost every time we've made a serious mistake as we related to other nations — and we've made a lot of them — it's because the American people have basically been excluded from participation." The mistakes of "Vietnam, Chile, Cambodia, and Pakistan," he named specifically, would not have occurred had "the American people" had "actual involvement" as the "decisions were made."[46] In this way, Carter drew tight the linkage he envisioned between an open administration and the moral caliber of the nation's foreign policy.

So, while Carter was not completely oblivious to the importance of Vietnam but just minimized it, and was also aware that moral leadership was in some ways different from moral character, he ultimately rooted public morality in a process that was in turn anchored in personal character. This view is a cogent and undeniably popular one. It also contains considerable merit. Surely the character of elected officials is not inconsequential in government, and overall an open process of government decision making may well avoid many of the pitfalls that befall those who restrict it only to "big shots" — and especially to "big shots" of questionable character.

Still, the view propounded by Carter has sharp limitations. Among them is that the emphasis on personal morality tends, perhaps unwittingly, to minimize the importance of the institutional structures and evolved patterns of international relationships that influence foreign-policy decisions quite apart from the personal moral views of the individuals involved. Whereas it may be morally comforting to conclude that the mistakes of Vietnam can be blamed on immoral leaders operating in smug secrecy, such a view stretches credulity. The debacle of the war may have been rooted as much in a military-industrial complex and growing tensions of the cold war, which pressured even moral men to promote misguided policies. Carter's moralistic rhetoric, resting much on personal character, suggests little awareness of the ways in which established social structures and historical legacies may imprison even good people in tragic circumstances.

Similarly, Carter's populist faith in the people to make the right moral decisions if only the decision-making process is an open one is hardly acceptable. Indeed, while in some vaguely mystical way Carter seemed to believe his populist rhetoric, his specific actions often belie it. When he identified the ratification of the Panama Canal treaties as his first major foreign-policy initiative, Carter knew that "the people" opposed him in the effort. To credit his consistency, he did proceed in this and other matters with remarkable openness. But his unpopular objectives betrayed the negative verdict that he himself willingly pronounced on his populist rhetoric. For he too was quite willing to defy the people when he believed that he and not they were right. This problem of populism — what to do when the people are wrong — was one that Carter never adequately answered for himself or the nation.

But there is a deeper limitation to Carter's call for leaders of good character to make policy decisions openly. It is that the call is for a process rather than an end. The tacit assumption is that by pursuing this process a moral and democratic end will emerge, but that end is not articulated.

Indeed, faith that the process will generate a vision is substituted for the vision itself. But if a mistrustful people desire moral leadership, that desire can be satisfied only by the articulation of an end. Substituting means for ends, Carter set the stage for failing in his key objective: rekindling a national faith that, by definition, requires an articulation of the final hope.

Carter's December 1974 announcement speech, delivered amid the strains of Billy Swan's "I Can Help" and at a time when he began to link his themes of competence and morality to the larger problem of American faith, aptly summarizes his campaign's thematic thrust. Speaking early in the speech about the "veils of secrecy [that] have seemed to thicken around Washington," the "lost confidence in government," and the "chasm between people and government," Carter further asserted that "the purposes and goals of our country are uncertain and sometimes even suspect." As a corrective he offered his own "competence and integrity" together with a pledge to ask "American citizens" to "join in shaping our nation's future."[47]

The limitations of Carter's promise to America are plain from this announcement speech. For what the nation's future might be once it was shaped by his "competence and integrity" together with "American citizens," he did not say. Instead he listed fourteen "specific steps" that he promised to take to restore "honesty and openness" in government. The promise was of a process, but not of an end.[48]

Then, midway through his speech, Carter admitted this limitation. "As important as honesty and openness are, they are not enough," he said. "There must also be substance and logical direction in government." However, when he proceeded to list the ten substantive issues that would presumably provide "logical direction in government," that direction was elusive. Beginning with reforming the budgeting process and ending with the need for nuclear arms control, Carter's substantive positions were but a plausibly presented litany of discrete issues. They cohered around no central theme and unveiled no vision of what the nation might become.[49]

So, when Carter needed to close his speech on a singular theme, he could only return to the promise of his own character and competence. Pledging "to restore in our country what has been lost," Carter stood proudly and asked, "Why not the best?"[50]

In some ways it was a brilliant speech that launched a brilliant campaign. For the essence of both was to raise profound doubts about the nation's faith without proposing any resolution outside of the person of Jimmy Carter. By implication, voters who wanted their doubts resolved needed only to pull the lever for that candidate. However, even when a bare 50.1 percent majority of them did so it was not clear that Carter's competence and personal morality could be translated into the moral leadership or the revival of America's faith that he promised.

THE MEANING OF VICTORY

The presidential election, like the nation's bicentennial celebration of the year, was by most accounts anticlimactic. Disaffection with politics was at a higher level than ever recorded. Only 54 percent of the voting-age public ultimately cast ballots in the November election, the lowest turnout for a presidential election in twenty-eight years. Of those who were registered but chose not to vote, significant increases were found among those who explained that they either did not like any of the candidates or were simply uninterested in politics.[51] As for the nation's bicentennial celebration, a reporter noted that on July 4 plenty of hotel rooms remained empty in the historic cities of Washington and Philadelphia. "Few felt like celebrating America this year," observed Kandy Stroud, and "there was not that much to celebrate."[52]

Considering only those who chose to vote, the meaning of Carter's victory is ambiguous. His razor-thin 50.1 percent majority, which translated into 297 electoral votes against Ford's 240, was the closest presidential election since 1916. The electoral vote also suggested that the victory should be attributed primarily to regional pride. In temporary defiance of the trend toward southern Republicanism, the promise of electing the first president from the deep South since 1848 enabled Carter to carry eleven of thirteen southern states (losing only Oklahoma and Virginia). However, he lost every western state except Hawaii, lost two out of every three middle western states, and won only seven of a dozen eastern states. The only statistically significant difference between Carter's victory in 1976 and his loss four years later, in fact, was the South. Only in that region did Ronald Reagan elicit significantly more votes in 1980 than Gerald Ford had in 1976.[53]

Exit interviews paint an equally bland portrait of the Carter victory. Eight percent of the Carter voters gave Ford's pardon of Nixon as their reason for supporting Carter, while three percent named Watergate. In contrast, only one percent of Ford's supporters justified their vote on the ground of the Nixon pardon; none mentioned Watergate. The recent Republican scandals tilted the election in favor of the Democrats and would have done so, presumably, regardless of the candidate.[54]

And 1976 was still a good year to run for president as a Democrat. Although doubts about liberal government's efficacy gnawed at voters, fully 78 percent of those who cast ballots in November 1976 claimed that they did so with economic concerns uppermost in mind, and two out of three Americans still believed that Democrats were better able to maintain economic prosperity than were Republicans.[55] October polls showed Carter profiting from this Democratic advantage when he beat Ford among the growing number of independents largely because of his criticism of Ford's handling of the economy. A similar Democratic advantage accrued to Carter through his vice presidential selection, Walter Mondale. Although Carter selected Mondale because he felt most compatible with the Minnesota senator (Mondale's background as a minister's son resonated well with Carter's moral and religious outlook), many in Carter's circle questioned the wisdom of choosing a protegé of Hubert Humphrey and an avowed liberal as a running mate. Yet after the vice presidential debate, which polls revealed was "won" by Mondale against Ford's running mate, Senator Bob Dole, polls showed Mondale adding a solid three percentage points to the Democratic ticket.[56]

The only story that emerges clearly from the 1976 general election is therefore one of region, happenstance, and party. As a southerner Carter was able to woo back into the Democratic fold — perhaps for the last time — a region that had not elected a president in over a century. As the Democratic nominee campaigning in the aftermath of Watergate, Carter was also able to reap the benefit of that scandal. And as the nominee of the party that most Americans still believed better able to maintain economic prosperity — and at a time when the continuation of prosperity was beginning to be in doubt — Carter was positioned for victory, ironically, by the very party and ideology he otherwise eschewed.

Although Carter may be credited with making the best of these advantages, the question that most interpreters asked about his victory was why it was not larger. By late spring, when he was the acknowledged front-runner for the Democratic nomination, polls showed that Carter had an enormous advantage over Ford, sometimes outpolling him by a two-to-one margin. No candidate with so large a lead at that time in the election year had ever gone down in November defeat. But by October, when the race was a dead heat, political commentators prepared their assessments of what many anticipated would be the lead political story of the election: how Carter squandered his lead and lost. Only one voter in a hundred prevented these assessments from being offered.

Yet the assessment of Carter's loss would not have been an easy one, for there is no easy explanation for his plummet. Commenting on Carter's fall as early as September 16, James Reston wrote in the *New York Times* that "something is holding him back" and "hurting his campaign." However, noted Reston after interviewing a number of political strategists, no one knew why. Speculation centered on "something about his personality, his manner of speaking . . . and his switches on major policy issues" — but it was just speculation.[57] The only thing certain was that Carter's candidacy was in a free fall.

It is possible that Carter's declining support during the general election can be explained by party and ideology. After Carter received the nomination, polls did show that he was increasingly likely to be perceived as "liberal" by voters.[58] Since he also believed that the party nomination was a "millstone" on his candidacy,[59] it is possible that some of the erosion in his support came from his increasing identification as a liberal Democrat. Yet, while it is conceivable that Carter's perceived movement to the left during the general election cost him moderate and conservative votes, the evidence from the election itself indicates that this perceived movement may have actually enabled him to win. When the measurable Democratic advantages of Watergate, the economy, and Mondale are tallied up, they show that Carter won because he was perceived to be a liberal Democrat — not in spite of that perception.

A better way to explain Carter's declining popularity during the general election is therefore to question the premise that he enjoyed immense popularity during the spring and summer. Actually, while polls did show tremendous support for Carter during those months, they also revealed that his support was what pollsters and others call "soft." Few of those who supported Carter during those early months did so ardently, making many of them candidates for defection. On July 22, when Carter was near the height of his popularity, Caddell warned Carter of just this problem in a memorandum entitled "The Unenthusiastic Carter vote." A full third of their supporters, noted Caddell, "describe themselves as not very enthusiastic at all about their choice." Further, "there is no state or area" where a "majority of registered voters" is "even somewhat enthusiastic about Jimmy Carter."[60] In other words, summer support for Carter may have been broad but it was not deep. It was therefore predictable that one-fifth of November's voters would cast ballots for a candidate they had not initially supported and an astonishing 12 percent would not even make up their minds until election day (sometimes while in the voting booth).[61] It may also have been predictable that record numbers would not bother to vote. Such are the consequences of "soft" support.

Before then, Carter's victories in the primaries en route to the nomination told a similarly unenthusiastic story. Although he did win a sensational series of primaries and caucuses (which eventually prompted party leaders to abort their brief "anybody but Carter" crusade and credit him with having earned the nomination), his victories were more mixed than is usually recalled. His early "wins" in Iowa, New Hampshire, and Florida, for example, were as much a matter of media interpretation as substantial victories. In Iowa only ten percent of the Democrats voted and fewer than 14,000 of them voted for him ("not enough to elect a city councilman in most average-sized cities," noted Kandy Stroud with only slight exaggeration).[62] Carter's 28 percent plurality in Iowa also fell well below the 37 percent who chose to remain "uncommitted." In New Hampshire, Carter's 30 percent plurality was just six points higher than second-place finisher Morris Udall; interpreted as a victory, it was in fact a lesser percentage than Edmund Muskie had garnered in 1972, which was interpreted as a defeat. In Florida, Carter's 34 to 31 percent win over George Wallace was hardly smashing, especially considering that Carter aggressively solicited "provisional" support solely on the pledge of his ability to "stop Wallace."

Moreover, Carter campaigned harder and longer in each of these early caucus and primary states than any of his opponents. Spending an average of five out of every seven days in 1975 — the year before the primaries and caucuses — campaigning in these and other states, and blanketing most with "Peanut Brigade" volunteers as well as separate campaign appearances by his wife, children, and even an aunt, Carter was as thoroughly poised for victory as any candidate could have been. Characteristically, when it was all over he admitted: "We've possibly had the best-organized campaign the country's ever seen, with the computers, careful budgeting, detailed scheduling, [and] superb organization."[63]

Then, although states that he essentially ignored (like Oklahoma) sometimes gave him pluralities, Carter endured more than a few losses. Mississippi's caucuses went solidly for Wallace, while in Massachusetts

Carter drew a wimpish 14 percent of the primary vote and came in fourth. New York also went decisively against Carter. Later, when Frank Church and Jerry Brown entered the fray, Carter was humbled by unexpected primary losses in Nebraska (to Church) and Maryland (to Brown) in addition to having to forgo wins in their home states of Idaho and California.

Meanwhile, the string of victories that delivered the delegates who ultimately provided the basis for Carter's nomination were rarely substantial. Dogged mostly by Udall (who came in second so often that he quipped, "everyone can't be first; even George Washington married a widow")[64] Carter came within a percentage point of defeat in the crucial Wisconsin and Michigan primaries. Then, with polls showing that many Democrats still preferred undeclared candidate Hubert Humphrey, Carter's defeat of Humphrey's stalking-horse, Henry Jackson, in the Pennsylvania primary was aided by a fluke that enabled him to outspend Jackson three to one and blanket the airwaves with advertisements for ten uncontested days.[65]

When the primaries were over, in fact, Carter's victory had been secured with something less than 40 percent of the Democratic vote. Often, as is the case in such contests, Carter was not even the first choice of those who supported him. Polls generally indicated that, had Hubert Humphrey entered the primaries, he would have defeated Carter. Even without Humphrey, had Udall just increased his vote by as little as one percentage point in two or three primaries — or had Brown and Church entered earlier — Carter would have been denied the nomination. To Carter's credit, his plurality was broadly based. He drew well from most demographic groupings, and, if not the favored candidate of most, he elicited deep opposition from few. But, as the candidate with the least opposition and only a plurality of cobbled-together support, Carter was hardly poised for enthusiastic victory.

The puzzle of Carter's election in 1976 may therefore not be his slim victory following an enormous lead. The puzzle may rather be his short-lived lead. Before and after that time, his support was more fragmentary. The solution suggested by the awareness that even at its height his support was "soft" is, however, straightforward: for a brief few months Americans hoped to find in Jimmy Carter an answer to the nation's problems that, after closer examination, they realized could not be found in any person — no matter how moral or competent. "[A]udiences yearn to believe Jimmy Carter," editorialized the *New Republic* early in the election year,[66] but the yearning was just that. Indeed, when those who bothered to vote did vote, most cast ballots on the time-honored bases of party, ideology, and issues — and faulted Carter especially for his "fuzziness" on the latter.

One of Ford's most successful charges against Carter was that he "wavers, wiggles, wanders, and waffles." The effectiveness of this alliteration rested on its ability to stimulate a concern that sizable chunks of the electorate had long expressed about Carter: that he was fuzzy on the issues. Indeed, Udall registered this concern immediately after the Iowa caucuses. Bothered because Carter took both "the abortion and the antiabortion," "labor and antilabor" vote, Udall complained that "in politics, you can't do that." The complaint did not go completely unheeded, however. By the general election, exit polls revealed that six percent of Ford voters explained their selection by saying that "Carter was too vague/wishywashy on the issues" while less than 1 percent of Carter's supporters said the same about Ford.[67]

There was substantial truth to the charge of fuzziness. Actually, Carter did not even bother to have an issues staff until quite late in his campaign. Then, after he hired an issues coordinator, Stuart Eizenstat, Carter did have a staff disseminate position papers on virtually every issue imaginable. But the *Wall Street Journal* reviewed "a reasonably large number" of Carter's "specific stands" on "specific issues" only to conclude that the "impression left" was of a "shopping list" that permitted "no feel for the instincts of the man," much less "the depth of his conviction on any issue."[68] As he had in his gubernatorial campaign, Carter took so many stands on so many issues that he managed to obscure his position on all of them.

But, on the campaign trail especially, Carter also did what he could to ignore the issues or to manipulate his positions. His usual strategy was to make a general statement of principle and then qualify it with contradictory specifics. For example, he declared that abortion was morally wrong but qualified his view by saying that he could not support a constitutional amendment forbidding it. He further qualified this qualification during a meeting with pro-life Catholics by saying that he simply opposed versions of the amendment he had seen but was willing to consider an as yet unproposed version. Other times, Carter's waffles were more a matter of emphasis than content. Always adept at multiple self-presentations, to some audiences he committed himself to a systematic and phased withdrawal of U.S. forces from Korea; to others he said that the U.S. must honor its military commitment to Korea and consider withdrawing troops only cautiously in a systematic and phased fashion. In still other instances, omissions altered the meanings. To some audiences Carter's roster of great Americans regularly included Martin Luther King Jr.; to others King's name was conveniently excluded.

Even Carter's apparent gaffes permitted strategic interpretations. Once he mentioned his support for the right of neighborhoods to maintain "ethnic purity," a remark that offended many ethnic minorities who had previously supported him ardently. Some noted, however, that the offending remark was made just after Wallace's candidacy fizzled. The inference that Carter made it intentionally in order to move rightward on the race issue was unavoidable. Naturally, Carter denied the charge, but since other instances of his campaign suggested just such duplicity, it was plausible that he had made the "gaffe" on purpose.[69]

The truth is that the Carter campaign had decided as early as 1972 to avoid the issues as much as possible in 1976. Jordan's 1972 memorandum advised: "Most voters would be inclined more favorably toward a candidate stressing personal qualities such as integrity and confidence than those emphasizing ideological stands on the issues."[70] Kirbo likewise remembered saying that "people were not so concerned about issues as they were about finding someone they could have confidence in. . . . I told him not to run his campaign on an intellectual approach to issues, but on a restoration of confidence in government."[71] Carter himself admitted that the only candidates he could recall who had campaigned on issues were Dewey, Goldwater, and McGovern — all losers.[72] And when Carter violated his rule against speaking to the issues and actually took a controversial stand — he proposed removing the federal tax deduction on home mortgage interest during the Massachusetts primary — his defeat was blamed by his aides on his mistake in taking such a stand. "You bastards tell us to get specific," Powell told assembled journalists afterward, "and we burn our ass. . . . Kinda like spitting to a whirlwind."[73]

Moreover, as some of the above remarks attest, among those mistrustful of ideology, avoiding issues can be understood as a necessity if not a virtue. Issues are invariably more complex than they seem, and any nonideological analysis of them is bound to produce idiosyncratic and confusing positions. "I'm not an ideologue," Carter explained, "and my positions are not predictable. . . . I've tried to analyze each question individually; I've taken positions that to me are fair and rational, and sometimes my answers are complicated."[74] In the heat of a campaign, where sound bites are more apt to appear than lengthy explanations, such a candidate is bound to appear fuzzy. Anticipating this perception, it is understandable that Carter would try to avoid speaking to the issues.

Explaining the lackluster enthusiasm exhibited for both major candidates, Kandy Stroud commented that "no strong issue rallied voters to the banner of either candidate. Ford and Carter heatedly trumpeted secondary issues."[75] The assessment, which voters apparently thought more applicable to Carter than Ford, may nevertheless be a given in a general presidential election. As the two major presidential candidates each vie for the undecided-center swing voters, they naturally trumpet secondary issues lest by taking firm stands on controversial issues they give this volatile middle reason to defect to their opponent. This strategic calculation typically produces campaigns that are less substantive than better-informed voters, including political journalists, think desirable.

The same strategic constraints, however, do not hamper second-tier candidates (which may explain why they are second-tier). Among them is therefore where one normally looks to find the issues that really propel an election. Indeed, voters who invariably grow weary of presidential campaigns and exhibit only lackluster support for their preferred candidate by November have often felt quite differently earlier in the election year. Then, rallied behind a second-tier candidate sharply addressing controversial issues, they were genuinely enthusiastic. Only as the candidate pool dwindles and the front-runners look toward the center do the issues grow dim and the election unexciting. And 1976 was no different. Two second-tier candidates sparked more enthusiasm than either of the front-runners. Both Jerry Brown and Ronald Reagan did so, moreover, partly on the basis of the primary issues they trumpeted.

While Carter "wiggled and waffled" his way to victory — and second-tier Democratic candidates Henry Jackson and Morris Udall debated leftish semantics (Udall preferred the term "progressive," Jackson the historic "liberal")[76] — the late entry of California's thirty-eight-year-old governor, Jerry Brown, into the Democratic fray proved to be one of the most exciting episodes of the primary year. After casually announcing a candidacy that appeared almost an afterthought, Brown drew crowds that Carter could only envy, upset the Democratic front-runner in the Maryland primary, robbed him of a California victory, and threatened him elsewhere.[77]

Brown's late entry made it almost impossible for him to win the nomination. As Carter himself reminded a Los Angeles audience: "I would say that someone who has 1,000 delegates is ahead of someone with 25. That is just my twisted logic. Maybe it would not stand up in front of a Zen Buddhist analysis."[78] To judge from Brown's subsequent and unsuccessful presidential bids it is also unlikely that an earlier entry and more systematic effort would have changed his presidential fortunes. In 1976 as afterward, Brown's popularity seemed premised on the awareness that he could not win. Had he been a more viable candidate, certainly he would have been judged harshly by the more sober criteria of presidential stature. But as a dark horse with a touch of the gadfly about him, Brown was greeted with the enthusiasm customarily reserved for exciting second-tier candidates.

The basis of Brown's appeal has never been completely understood. Carter believed, with some justification, that it was similar to his own. Like Carter, Brown exuded populism, and like him he spoke of the spiritual dimensions of public life. But in Brown both themes were more extreme.

While Carter carried his own bags and made his own bed when staying the night with supporters, he had no compunctions against living in Georgia's governor's mansion or traveling by limousine. Brown, as governor of California, chose to rent an apartment in Sacramento instead of living in the opulent governor's mansion (which he sometimes derided as "the house that Ronnie built") and rejected not only limousines but also gas-guzzling cars, choosing to drive a used Plymouth. In speeches and interviews he also challenged government's "pomposity" and made clear his belief that the chief executive was only one person doing one job. He could not and would not promise voters anything more than his best efforts — that he would "try." Indeed, his campaign "promise" was the Zenlike one: "no promises."[79]

Brown's reputed spirituality was also taken to be deep and esoteric. A bachelor who had lived in a Jesuit monastery and studied Zen Buddhism, Brown's gaunt figure and serious, angular face suggested a deeper asceticism than perhaps was warranted. Still, he was a reputed devotee of health foods and sprinkled his rhetoric with quasi-spiritual catchphrases like "appropriate technology," "spaceship earth," "planetary realism," "creative nonaction," and, always, "limits" — limits to the earth, limits to what government can do, personal limits. And, while there was a certain playful half-seriousness to Brown's rhetoric, at some level he appeared genuinely to believe it. Reporters noted that he quickly bored of political discussions only to become animated when the conversation turned to something like appropriate technology. "I've tried to carve out a new path in politics," the candidate many called a "guru" told a university audience in Oregon (where his late entry forced him to run as a write-in candidate). "I'd like to try," he told another audience, "a different ethic, a different approach." To many this "different ethic" suggested a new spirituality.[80]

Yet, while Brown's populist spirituality may be understood to have been but an extreme version of Carter's more modest projection of similar themes, in other ways Brown projected an image different from Carter's. Two differences that stand out are Brown's occasionally ironic view of politics and his adamant refusal to make political promises — or think them possible.

While Carter rested everything on the tragedy of America's collapse of faith and the personal promise of restoring it, Brown seemed to embrace the very faithless cynicism that Carter thought was the problem. A reporter who covered the Brown campaign noted that "he is not entirely serious" but "is mocking political rhetoric" and gets "pleasure and applause out of mocking politics."[81] Although the reporter did not draw this inference, even his last-minute bid for the nomination could be construed as a mild mockery of politics. Had Brown really wanted to be president (or, more important, deemed the office of president worth really wanting), his campaign would not have been so cavalier.

Viewed in light of his ironic political posture, Brown's promise of "no promises" may have carried more than a populist Zen meaning. It may have also suggested the conviction that in its present form the U.S. government was no longer capable of delivering on its promises. So again, while Carter avoided as best he could taking firm positions on controversial issues but promised a vague competence instead, Brown trumped him with the claim that no position was viable and no candidate especially competent. Regularly reminding audiences of his own "limits," the most Brown could conclude about leadership was that it was not by "how much you do" but by "the clarity of mind in laying out alternatives."[82] In Brown's political prognosis, America had reached the point where all assumptions needed to be reconsidered.

Jerry Brown, it should be considered, was probably right in both his diagnosis and prescription. Both the softness of Carter's victory in 1976 and the subsequent failure of his administration to rekindle the nation's faith (it plummeted further during his term) suggest that his more modest approach was not enough. Perhaps, as Pat Caddell concluded when he joined Brown's campaign in 1992, a more thorough reassessment of America's collective values unimpeded by political promises is the only route that the nation can take to moral renewal. Perhaps indeed, the real challenge to leadership today is simply to lay out the alternatives as clearly as possible and to coordinate the discussion that will lead to a "new ethic."

But in 1976 — and subsequently — it was not to be. Brown not only lost to Carter, but even Carter ultimately lost to the other second-tier candidate who sparked enthusiasm in 1976. And on the issue of America's faith, Ronald Reagan advanced a view diametrically opposed to both Brown and Carter. To Reagan the problem of collapsing faith was, like so many other problems, best left unmentioned. Despite three consecutive presidential campaigns and two terms in office, he never once brought up the issue without dismissing it as misguided nay-saying. Instead, he seemed to say, there was no problem too large that it could not be blamed on government and no crisis so profound that it could not be remedied by a frank assertion of America's military power.

Throughout his political career Reagan was an admitted conservative. Although in 1976 this ideological commitment won him solid support from like-minded Republicans, the support remained minority. Even in conservative New Hampshire Reagan lost a close primary race to Ford and proceeded thereafter to lag behind him in the polls. And many believed that Reagan's candidacy was finally derailed when he "pulled a Barry Goldwater" by mentioning that he would consider privatizing the Tennessee Valley Authority. The majority of Americans, even the majority of Republicans, were not yet willing to press their antiliberal views to the point of dismantling this popular New Deal program.[83]

But if conservatism did not enjoy majority support, populist resentment of government did. Indeed, when Reagan cast his conservatism in the less ideological language of antigovernment populism, his popularity soared. In the Texas primary, for instance, it was clear that many former George Wallace supporters crossed over to the Republican primary to support Reagan after Wallace's candidacy fizzled. The same trend was then detected in other open primary states. Since Reagan had no history of Wallacelike racism, and even appeared genuinely to abhor the sentiment, his support among Wallace's constituency had to be explained by the two candidates' similar antigovernment views.[84] The mistake made by previous conservative candidates and even Reagan himself in 1976 was to promote a classical conservative ideology; the genius of the Reagan revolution in 1980, but detectable in selected primaries of 1976, was to repackage conservatism as populism.

Still, enthusiasm for Reagan's candidacy in 1976 was sparked primarily by neither conservatism nor populism. It was ignited by something that startled even him. When during the Florida primary campaign he became aware of recent negotiations between Ford and Panama's General Omar Torrijos concerning the likely transfer of the Panama Canal to that country, he wondered aloud how Ford "would knowingly endorse such action." Then, in his next speech, Reagan found his political voice. To a Sun City retirement community, he asserted: "When it comes to the canal, we built it, we paid for it, it's ours." The applause thundered so loudly that the normally self-assured Reagan lost his place in the speech. What he had not fully anticipated was that, in the words of an aide, "[t]he Panama Canal issue had nothing to do with the canal. It said more about the American people's feelings about where the country was, and what it was powerless to do, and their frustrations about the incomprehensibility of foreign policy over the last couple of decades."[85]

Finding in the Panama Canal issue a means to harness the frustrations that had festered in America since the Vietnam War, Reagan drove the symbolic issue to a sensationally unexpected primary victory over Ford in North Carolina. On the rise, he might have been elected president four years before he was had he not finally faltered on his TVA comments.

Reagan's message, expressed symbolically in comments concerning the Panama Canal, was the opposite of Brown's. While Brown groped meekly for "alternatives" that might illuminate a "different ethic," Reagan simply defied the doomsayers and declared a resurgence of American might. Yet beneath these two extremes lurked a surprisingly similar common ground. Both candidates insisted that the status quo was no place for America to be. Although they disagreed on the direction of needed change, they agreed that fundamental change was sorely needed.

The middle was not therefore a very exciting place to be in 1976. Although it remained — barely — the position of victory, Americans were increasingly convinced that government-as-usual was untenable and that dramatic change was needed. Even a reformist defense of the status quo was scarcely acceptable to the majority of citizens. Defending it while calling for a revival of faith was met with incredulity. Yet this reformist and revivalist position was precisely the one that Carter carved out for himself.

While Carter's hope to win the election coupled with his own nonideological orientation gave him ample reason to avoid taking extreme stands on controversial issues (and the public had ample opportunity to be confused by the stands he did take), he understood something that others normally do not about the role that issues play in a campaign. He recognized that issues do not exist in the abstract, as a kind of grid the electorate places over the candidates, but are in large part created by the candidates themselves in the synergy of the campaign. Pressed by a reporter with the opposite theory — that issues exist and candidates are obliged to respond to them — Carter retorted, "That's not how it works."[86] How it works, Carter implied, was the candidate selects and defines the issues on which he will run and ignores the others.

So Carter felt justified in sidestepping questions about someone else's "issues" — pieces of the grid. However, he also felt called upon to identify and campaign on "his issues." And the issues he did articulate, primarily character and competence, revolved around one central promise of his campaign: that by electing him Americans would enjoy a government "as truthful and honest and decent and fair and compassionate and filled with love as the rest of the American people."[87]

The promise ultimately turned, as Carter observed, on faith. But the faith that Carter hoped would attach itself to his candidacy and catapult him to victory also had an outward object. It was the people themselves. Carter hoped that by convincing voters to trust him he might also persuade them to trust themselves. Indeed, the essence of his political promise was that his election would stimulate a new, more populist American faith.

Soon after the election John H. Patton, a professor of speech communication, accepted the academic task of assessing this promised populist faith. The assessment was favorable. By "upholding an idealized conception of what the people should become," Patton observed, "Carter provides an ultimate, directive goal" for the nation. Indeed, thought Patton, the faith promised nothing less than a "restoration of transcendence to politics" which, in turn, was precisely the sort of symbolic myth that might bind a divided nation into coherence.[88]

But there are problems with this assessment. One is simply that Carter's promised populist transcendence *was* a myth, anchored in symbols rather than experience. Noting that Carter's rhetoric "serves symbolically to reassure the mass public in the deepest sense by affirming their inner nature," Patton nevertheless admitted that the "power" of this symbolic message "vanishes" when taken as either "a logical claim" or one to be "supported by empirical evidence." It was, in short, a myth.[89]

A second problem with the populist myth is that it promised a means but no end. Although Patton supposed that Carter's "idealized conception of the people" provided "an ultimate, directive goal," he proceeded to observe with some inconsistency that "Carter sets forth an ethical method for political action."[90] The latter observation seems more accurate. Little in Carter's campaign rhetoric described what an idealized populist nation, or even the candidate himself, might do. (Such a description would have involved taking stands on more mundane issues and then showing how his solutions to these issues could be achieved by his "ethical method.") Yet, while a myth may not need always to be maintained by immediate experience, it must be sustained by hope in some as yet unrealized future experience. Failing to articulate this future experience, Carter's call for a restoration of populist faith was doubly fragile.

The political term for the vision that Carter failed to articulate is *ideology*. This absence of an articulated set of ideas and issue positions that pointed to a more desirable political community may well have fitted with the preferences of the era. As Daniel Bell commented in a new afterword to his *The End of Ideology*, the "outburst of romantic yearning" of the 1960s and 1970s produced "no ideologies." Nor was Carter alone in his avoidance of ideology. Udall sought to avoid the liberal label by calling himself a progressive; Reagan slowly learned to recast his conservatism as populism; Ford stood in a muddled middle-right; and even Brown called only for laying out alternatives. Still, at least, Bell concluded, the generation was "in search of an ideology."[91] Moral leadership, as opposed to moral character, would have recommended one.

So it was that Carter, whose own distaste for populist politicians like Eugene Talmadge was based on the unrestrained elevation of demagogic personal appeal above all else, found himself campaigning for the presidency in much the same manner. His promise to restore America's faith was premised primarily on his own personal capacities. And the difference between him and Talmadge — or any other anti-ideological populist candidate — was only the caliber of his person.

Having much about his person that was commendable, however, Carter's candidacy was finally successful. Among his aides especially, faith in Jimmy Carter existed in abundance. Even Pat Caddell, who longed for a restoration of American faith perhaps more ardently than anyone besides Carter himself, fell under its sway. Convinced that Carter could "get the country to believe in itself again," Caddell joined Jordan, Powell, Kirbo, and Lance by explaining his conviction in terms of Carter's personal attributes. "I have a sense of his value system and his passion to do what is right," he volunteered anemically.[92]

And as Carter's circle of supporters widened during his four-year presidential campaign, so also did the numbers of Americans who shared this faith in Jimmy Carter. "Most of them didn't give a darn about the issues," explained Carter's old friend, John Pope, about his experiences coordinating the Peanut Brigade and canvassing voters under its auspices. "The personal touch made the difference. It was why he won."[93]

The "personal touch" was in fact the essence of the Carter campaign. Punishing his body to the limit of its endurance, barely a weekday morning went by for two years that Carter was not shaking hands at a factory gate by 6:00 A.M. or so. For those same two years he spent as many evenings as he could giving talks to voters in which he promised — and many say achieved — "intimacy" with them. During the days he met with newspaper editorial boards (a personal campaign strategy upon which many noted he placed great emphasis), gave interviews and, whenever possible, was again at the factory gates when the shifts changed. Meanwhile, his entire family crisscrossed the country independent of him to spread their personal message too, while plane-loads of Peanut Brigadiers did the same. "Hello, I'm Jimmy Carter and I'm running for president" thereby entered the lexicon of America's presidential politics in a way that had never existed before — the quintessential expression of a personal campaign writ enormously large.

Yet, while Carter achieved a near-miracle in politics by winning the presidency on the strength of a personal campaign that even Jordan likened to "running for sheriff in fifty states,"[94] his victory was hardly decisive. Worse, it could not produce the kind of mandate required for governing successfully. Some even suspected that it laid the groundwork for his failure. Writing about "the crisis of mistrust in American politics" years later, for example, Suzanne Garment spoke for many when she observed that the "post-Watergate spirit . . . produced the 1976 election of President Jimmy Carter," but that "Carter was eventually destroyed, in no small part, by the same new standards that elected him."[95] In Garment's opinion Carter simply could not meet the objectives that he set for himself. But even that opinion may be wide of the mark. For Carter could (and did) meet the standards he set for himself; the standards he failed to meet were those of the nation. Promising competence and morality, he delivered both. What he could not deliver was a restoration of faith based upon those personal characteristics.

The price of Carter's victory may therefore be measured not only in the soft support that ultimately elected him, but also in the expectations that were stimulated by his heroic promise of being personally able to rekindle America's faith without recourse to program or ideology. Had he campaigned on selected issues that could be linked to his general promise of renewed faith, then success or failure on those issues would serve as benchmarks for the evaluation of his administration and America's progress. Or, had he articulated a vision, he might have recalled and revived it periodically to reinvigorate a faithless electorate. But Carter campaigned on neither issues nor vision. Offering the nation his own morality and competence was no inconsiderable gift. The question was whether it was enough.

"It's been my theory all along," confided ABC's Sam Donaldson privately when Carter's support began to erode during the general election campaign, "that the simple Carter plan, the magical, mystical, trust-in-me thing wasn't enough."[96] Donaldson missed the forecast of the election by a percentage point. However, he may not have been wrong in his implied prognosis for the ensuing four years. Although Carter held onto a bare majority on election day, the fall 1976 plummet of his support continued through his administration. Indeed, rather than rekindling America's faith, Carter became the president most clearly identified with its collapse.

CHAPTER 8

F CRISIS AND OPPORTUNITY

Recalling a day in 1971 when the White House was besieged by protesters and some two thousand armed soldiers were protectively stationed throughout the executive mansion, an aide to Presidents Nixon and Ford reflected on the comparative tranquillity of the transition period that welcomed Carter to office. "Mr. Carter has a very great opportunity," commented the aide, "one of the greatest in history." With the turmoil and animosities of just a few years before behind him, the new president had every hope of accomplishing things his immediate predecessors could only dream of.[1]

The outgoing president thought similarly. Gerald Ford remarked during the transition that Carter would have "unique opportunities" to achieve "great success." In particular Ford believed that events in both the Middle East and southern Africa were "on the brink of . . . success" while the completion of a second strategic arms limitation agreement with the Soviet Union was imminent. At home, although Ford was mindful of the formidable challenges posed by the restructuring of the economy, he was also persuaded that "great skill and good judgment" could restrain inflation and turn the economy around.[2]

Some leading Democrats were also optimistic. "In the United States," United Auto Workers President Leonard Woodcock reported to his union in early 1977, "we are moving from a period of depression, despair and despondency into a time of renewed hope."[3] Meanwhile, behind-the-scenes party luminary Hubert Humphrey ignored the fever and weakness of his cancer-racked body and met with Carter in Plains during the transition to lend him the advice and goodwill that only a Democrat of his stature could offer. According to Carter's campaign issues director and White House domestic policy chief, Stuart Eizenstat, the once-again junior senator from Minnesota proceeded to extend to the new president the same kind of warm, fatherly support that he had offered for so long to Carter's vice president, Walter Mondale.[4]

The hope greeting Carter's first months as president was even begrudgingly shared by many in the Washington press and policy establishment. Although a few groused about the "Georgia Mafia," as the troupe of Georgians who dominated the White House staff were sometimes called, most were placated when Carter emerged from one of the longest selection processes in history to name a cabinet full of well-known Washington figures. Despite Hamilton Jordan's quip during the campaign that the appointment of people like Cyrus Vance and Zbigniew Brzezinski would signify a sellout of the Carter administration to established Washington powers and prompt his own resignation, Carter's appointment of precisely these men (to secretary of state and national security advisor, respectively) was neither unpopular nor cause for Jordan's resignation.[5] Carter's judicious appointment of experienced and respected Washington figures for his cabinet, coupled with the promise to empower these policy makers in a "cabinet government," reassured an establishment jittery about the Washington outsider.

At the same time, however, Carter gave the public reason to believe that his administration would be democratically different from those of his recent predecessors. Populist flair was added to his inauguration when he defied both tradition and his own Secret Service agents to walk rather than ride the mile and a half during his swearing-in ceremony. Instructing the Marine Corps band to discontinue playing "Hail to the Chief," ordering White House staff to forgo limousines in favor of their own cars, and selling the presidential yacht all suggested real populist commitments. Appearing in an early televised "fireside chat" that one commentator considered "a symbolic tour de force,"[6] the president who insisted upon being known by his familiar nickname "Jimmy" sent strong signals that there would be a sharp reduction of the pomp of the formerly "imperial presidency."

Yet Carter promised that much could be accomplished — and quickly — by a populist president. Tantalizing the public by announcing a series of immediate and usually "comprehensive" legislative initiatives in such intractable areas as welfare reform, tax code revisions, national health care, and energy policy, the new president promised prompt and decisive action on each. The nation's first-ever comprehensive energy policy, for example, was promised in only ninety days. Indeed, the only time Eizenstat ever remembered Carter becoming "really angry" with him was during the transition when he mistakenly informed a *New York Times* reporter that he expected Carter to proceed slowly with moderate legislative initiatives. "You shouldn't have said that," corrected Carter. "I'm going to be an activist president and I'm going to propose a lot of legislation."[7] Ever since Bert Lance gave him a copy of James David Barber's *The Presidential Character* (one of the two or three leading political-science texts on the presidency) in 1972, Carter had determined that he would be, in Barber's typology, an "active-positive" president.[8] And he was. By May 1977, even activist Senator Edward Kennedy remarked that Carter's "reforms are already lined up bumper to bumper."[9]

The public overwhelmingly approved of their new president. February 1977 Gallup polls showed that two-thirds of the American public approved, and only 10 percent disapproved, of Carter's early administration — percentages far higher than the vote count he had just received. But by March, Carter's approval ratings soared to 75 percent, the highest recorded since Lyndon Johnson reached 79 percent after John Kennedy's assassination. For over a quarter of a century (from 1964 to 1991), no other president enjoyed "honeymoon" approval ratings this high.[10]

Confidence in the presidency as an institution was also on the rebound. In the same month that Carter reached historic highs in his approval rating, 28 percent of the public expressed confidence in the executive branch of government. Although still low by absolute standards, the percentage was twice as high as it had been during the preceding two years and remained the highest recorded until 1984.[11]

Perhaps it was this swell of honeymoon euphoria that prompted 57 percent of the voters in 1980 to misremember having voted for Carter in 1976, when in fact only 50 percent of them had.[12] In any case, the euphoria of the winter of 1977 made it difficult to predict anything but the best for the fledgling Carter administration. Truly, Carter enjoyed a great opportunity.

☆   ☆   ☆

But there were signs of impending catastrophe. Perhaps the most substantial of these signs centered around the new president's relationship with Congress. Although Carter enjoyed sizable Democratic majorities in both the House and Senate, some leading congressional Democrats made no secret of their disdain for him — and he for them.

The fissure became apparent when the family of House Speaker Tip O'Neill received "the worst seats in the room" for the inaugural gala. Blaming Hamilton Jordan for the indignity, O'Neill called him a "son of a bitch" to his face and "Hannibal Jerken" from then on behind his back. Determined to be snubbed no more, O'Neill proceeded immediately to object to both the menu and blessings offered at the White House's weekly breakfast with congressional leaders. Served only coffee, juice, and a roll, the burly Speaker complained, "Hell, *Nixon* treated us better than this!" and insisted on a full breakfast of sausage, bacon, eggs, and toast. At the same time, O'Neill and his fellow Catholic representative, Dan Rostenkowski, mocked the president's habit of having grace said before the breakfasts. Privately rating each morning's blessing on a ten-point scale and grousing that Carter appeared only to ask Protestants to offer the morning prayer (while mocking the "eloquence" of Protestant prayer), the Catholic lawmakers' complaint eventually reached a *Newsweek* reporter. When the reporter called the White House for verification, an angry Carter squelched it. But at the next breakfast, which was the requested full meal (complete with grits), a chastened Carter asked Rostenkowski to offer the blessing.[13]

Carter later admitted his personal relationships with selected leading congressional Democrats were "somewhat strained."[14] However, the strain reflected more than personal dislikes and social frictions. It also reflected real differences in the assessment of Congress's importance. After listening to Carter explain how he intended to bypass Congress and take his legislative initiatives directly to the people, O'Neill rebuffed him in their first transition meeting. "Hell, Mr. President, you're making a big mistake." First, the Speaker explained that whatever Carter might think, Congress included "some of the most talented and knowledgeable lawmakers in the world." They did not appreciate Carter's anti-Washington rhetoric or his arrogant assumption that he could ride roughshod over Congress the way he had over Georgia's general assembly. Second, O'Neill continued, most congressional representatives and senators were more popular than Carter in their home districts and states. Three-quarters of the House had run *ahead* of Carter in the November election, the Boston pol reminded him, and many would not hesitate to run *against* him in the future. If Carter really expected to bypass Congress and take his message to the people, the Speaker tried to explain what to him was obvious: Carter would lose while Congress would win.[15]

One of the "great myths about the Carter presidency," according to a senior administration aide, was "that he and Tip O'Neill developed a deep affection for one another." Actually, O'Neill persisted in believing that the Carter administration was "like a bad dream."[16] Still, O'Neill undoubtedly considered himself among the world's most talented and knowledgeable lawmakers, so for the most part he kept his nightmare to himself. He usually worked professionally and successfully on behalf of the president and once, early in the administration, even dazzled onlookers by masterfully pushing Carter's complex energy legislation through Congress to quick passage. Carter also relented somewhat from his arrogance and on occasion worked effectively with Congress.

Even so, O'Neill's transition warnings quickly took on a prophetic aura. For the single most consistent criticism of the Carter presidency, erupting early and never fully squelched, was that he was inept in his dealings with Congress. Although the criticism is arguably overblown, it is difficult to describe relations as good not only when the president vetoes congressional legislation in the area in which he has fought most diligently (energy), but also when a Congress dominated by his own party overrides his veto. By the final year of his administration, however, Carter suffered the humiliation of precisely this sequence of events.[17]

The suffering came, moreover, from a Congress dominated by members of Carter's own party. This intraparty rivalry should not be ignored, for beneath both personal animosities and strategic tensions lurked even more fundamental differences among Democrats. The party of the New Deal coalition that had remained ascendant through the Great Society confronted such ideological disarray that collapse was imminent.

Jordan put the ideological quandary this way: "We . . . had no unifying Democratic consensus, no program, no set of principles on which a majority of Democrats agreed." For some issues "we put together one coalition," for others "an entirely different coalition." Admitting that Carter was able to win his "nonideological" campaign for the presidency in the first place "only because of the fragmentation that's taken place in the Democratic party," Jordan nevertheless quickly recognized that "the same fragmentation that allowed him to be elected president made it more difficult for him to govern." Indeed, added Jordan's assistant, "total paralysis" existed in such staples of the party apparatus as labor, civil rights, women's, and environmental groups. Concurring, Jordan summarized: "the frag-mentation of all these institutions created . . . general chaos in the party.[18]

But the problems were of Carter's making. He lacked an ideological blueprint that would lend order and coherence to his avowed social activ-ism and more conservative commitments to fiscal restraint. He made more campaign promises than any other president of the century (his staff counted more than 200),[19] but he cautioned in his inaugural address "that even our great nation has its recognized limits" and warned again in his 1978 State of the Union speech that "government cannot solve our prob-lems." These views were understandably perceived to be at odds with his plethora of promises and activist orientation, and no coordinating vision was ever offered to reconcile the discrepancies.

As the economy teetered and disagreements about the role government spending should play intensified, the stage was set for more skirmishes between Carter and more liberal Democrats. Edward Kennedy, most no-tably, seized the liberal banner and carried it against Carter throughout his administration. Immediately and then repeatedly resisting Carter's of-fer to phase in a national health insurance plan, Kennedy insisted instead on his own $100 billion-a-year proposal.[20] The Massachusetts senator also regularly and publicly chastised Carter for other presumed failures of lib-eral leadership, and ultimately challenged him for the presidential nomi-nation in 1980.

Others sympathized with Kennedy's charge against Carter, even some within the administration. Carter's insistence upon welfare reform at no additional cost, for instance, baffled Secretary of Health, Education and Welfare Joseph Califano, a veteran of the Johnson administration and a friend of Kennedy's. Califano could scarcely bring himself to devise a pro-posal that did not cost taxpayers at least several billion dollars more annu-ally.[21] Outside the administration opposition was fiercer. Labor unions al-lied with Kennedy and openly defied the president. AFL-CIO President George Meany, for example, met privately with the president only to pub-licly denounce wage hikes for postal workers that were kept within the president's anti-inflationary wage and price guidelines.[22] More generally, a study of evening news broadcasts and front-page newspaper stories dur-ing the first six months of the Carter administration revealed that 85 per-cent of the criticism was instigated by fellow Democrats rather than by Republicans.[23]

In response to these challenges, Carter could and did defeat Kennedy at the polls, dismiss Califano from his cabinet, banish Meany from the White House, and bring Rafshoon into the White House to improve his image. But these steps were reactive rather than proactive, and the costs of the intraparty dissent were real. Neither national health care nor welfare reform passed, and Carter's anti-inflation efforts largely failed. Carter's own popularity plummeted, despite Rafshoon's best efforts, and the fragmented party soon plunged headlong into defeat.

In retrospect, many have concluded that Carter rather than his liberal adversaries had the firmer grasp of the nation's mood. For in 1978 California's Proposition 13 signaled a nationwide tax revolt, and the Supreme Court's *Bakke* decision raised questions about the liberals' social agenda. And whereas Carter called gingerly for government limits, by 1981 Ronald Reagan's inaugural address flatly declared: "Government *is* the problem." Choosing the fight over the Carter administration's efforts to cut CETA (Comprehensive Employment and Training Act) by 15 percent to illustrate the shift in America's mood that caught so many traditional Democrats unprepared, Eizenstat marveled at how shortsighted the liberals had been. "My God," he remembered, "we were lucky not to be lynched" for proposing cuts in CETA, while Reagan just "totally abolished the thing."[24]

Still, while Carter appears in hindsight to have anticipated better than his liberal adversaries the evolving political mood of the country, the appearance may be deceiving. We will never know what might have happened if Carter had emerged a doctrinaire liberal and pressed forward with an ambitious liberal agenda in league with the likes of Kennedy, Califano, and Meany. Perhaps his fall would have been swifter and more decisive. But it is conceivable that the reverse might have occurred: that the majority party would have coalesced around him and persuaded the people to follow.

Nor will we know, more important, what might have happened if Carter had been able to articulate his moderate vision of government in a more positive and compelling way. Of course, it might be maintained that such a vision is impossible. An activist government that promotes social reforms at the same time it reduces or limits spending may be an impotent one. Worse, the government that tries may unwittingly stimulate a deeper problem. Only the insistence that current programs are riddled with fraud and bureaucratic inefficiencies, and that government reorganization can squeeze wasted dollars from bloated bureaucracies, can make such an otherwise inconsistent view plausible. Yet by implying fraud and inefficiency the activist government stimulates precisely the kind of cynicism that prevents the public from adhering to faith in government activism in the first place. How to effect a philosophy of moderate government activism in a time of limits remains elusive, and we will never know how political affairs would have evolved if Carter had successfully articulated such a philosophy.

What is known is that the ideology that ousted Carter was not one of what government can do but one of what it cannot do. Reagan's public philosophy was, after all, unabashedly antigovernment. Unless it is maintained that the victory of this antigovernment creed was inevitable — always a dubious historical proposition — the only certainty is that Carter failed to rally his party and the nation around a positive vision of government. More than anything else, the infighting among the Democrats during Carter's administration attests to both the difficulty and necessity of this frankly ideological task.

But surely few Americans were consciously concerned with the fissures of the Democratic party or contests over ideology. Americans of the middle and late 1970s were increasingly nonideological and nonpartisan in their political orientations. Growing numbers identified themselves as political independents rather than partisans, large chunks of the electorate voted in primaries other than their "own," and record numbers did not even bother to vote. Just as meaninglessness is revealed only from the standpoint of meaning, ideological chaos may be detectable mainly from the standpoint of ideology. An increasingly nonideological populace could not have been perturbed by others' ideological disarray.

Without an ideological connection to Carter, however, the early attraction Americans felt for him may have been tenuous. The majority who approved of him early in his administration may have done so for reasons not unlike those that attracted similar numbers to him a year before — when his high but soft support quickly eroded. Indeed, Pat Caddell found that even after the election fully "fifty percent of the public still does not know where Carter stands on the issues,"[25] a portion that had to include many who approved of his early administration. Perhaps few found reason to worry about the issues. For as Jordan recalled, "When Jimmy Carter took office the country was in trouble but the sense was not acute."[26] Absent a clear sense of Carter's positions as well as a deep commitment to the issues themselves, the public's early massive support for Carter could only have been shallow.

Carter's early support may have also just signified the attraction many felt for the American dream of individual opportunity. The Carter campaign had stimulated this myth of Carter's rise by nominally headquartering the campaign in Plains, by using the peanut as a campaign symbol, and by peppering the public with stories of Carter's rural boyhood and delightfully eccentric family. Carter himself, cloaking his inauguration in populist garb, reinforced this myth.

This more nebulous basis for Carter's popularity is lent credence when it is recalled that a story similar to Carter's riveted the nation at roughly the same time. Sylvester Stallone's Academy Award–winning film *Rocky* opened in late 1976 and continued to attract huge audiences throughout the winter of 1977. (In July the movie's theme song, "Gonna Fly Now," made it to number one.)[27] The fictional story of a boxer from the Philadelphia slums who rises to the championship, the success of *Rocky* was sufficient to merit four sequels and catapult Stallone to stardom. A public so enthusiastic about a film's expression of the American dream may have been poised to approve a similar expression of the dream in their newly elected president. When Plains itself was overrun with tourists, it seemed that some were seeking tangible verification of this dream.

But while *Rocky* contributed little to the popularity and prestige of boxing, so also Carter's inauguration may have contributed little to the popularity and prestige of governing. Polls that showed a fairly significant dozen or so points in increase in the public's confidence in the executive branch of government early in 1977, as noted, still showed that confidence only among about a quarter of the population. Meanwhile, surveys of trust in government generally showed no real improvement, and even a slight one- or two-point drop. Aggregates of confidence in ten major U.S. institutions (including nongovernmental ones) did show minimal improvement in early 1977, but the three-point increase between March 1976 and March 1977 remained within the statistical margin of error. Even that increase left fewer than a third of Americans confident about their major institutions. These numbers suggest that, while Americans were excited by the spectacle of individual opportunity reflected in *Rocky*, their overall attitude toward society may have been better reflected by another top film of 1976, *Network*. Empathizing with the main character, many felt, "I'm mad as hell and I'm not going to take it anymore." The anger and cynicism directed at social institutions contrasted sharply with the spirit of enthusiasm many apparently felt for the heroic individual within those institutions.[28]

And, on closer inspection, the pessimism could be found to pervade government. While Ford and others foresaw "unique opportunities" for Carter, others in the White House were less hopeful. Ford's outgoing budget director, James Lynn, was one of several who expressed this contrary view. Government service is like standing in peat moss, Lynn explained to his incoming counterpart, Bert Lance. When you stand in one place long enough, you leave an impression, but as soon as you leave the impression vanishes. Shifting his metaphors to reinforce his point, Lynn likened government service to building a road in the jungle. Very soon after it is built, it is engulfed once again by the jungle.[29]

At government levels lower and closer to the people, the pessimism was more palpable. Watching a televised session of Carter during the transition, a White House secretary found herself sighing, "the same old garbage," just "more names to learn to spell." A nearby security guard yawned as he thumbed through a magazine, too bored to care what the president-elect would or would not do.[30]

These and other signs of diffuse anger and festering pessimism, perhaps as much as the tensions and conflicts within the Democratic party, suggested the challenge that lurked beneath the euphoria of Carter's early months as president. For if the party required a unifying ideology, so also did the people. The difference was that many party activists recognized the problem and fought over it, while a more disinterested public only dimly perceived it. Surely, if Carter needed to supply Democrats with a new ideology for governing, he needed even more to supply the people with a fresh vision of what their nation might become.

NO NEW DREAM

Inside the Carter team, the task of culling a governing strategy from victory fell to Pat Caddell. Still only in his mid-twenties, Caddell admitted that "the clear formulation" of the kind of "ideology" Carter required to govern was "beyond" his "intellectual grasp."[31] But he was as close as the administration had to an intellectual point man. The others — Jordan, Powell, Kirbo, and Lance — had long before eschewed philosophical reflection in favor of busy loyalty to Carter. The cabinet that so pleased the Washington establishment was also drawn from existing constituencies with well-established agendas. Men like Joseph Califano and Cyrus Vance were among the most able of their breeds, but so entrenched were they and their colleagues in old ideas that none of them could be counted on to develop truly new ones. Vice President Walter Mondale was a second-generation liberal who gave little evidence of ever fashioning for himself a creed that could coordinate his genuine compassion and policy acumen into a larger philosophical fabric; he mainly endorsed the liberalism created by his predecessors. Gerald Rafshoon, at times insightful, nevertheless maintained a devotion to his craft and business that prevented him from interceding often on matters other than "image." Even Stuart Eizenstat, whose full and final membership on the team filled the crucial domestic-policy vacancy, failed to display talents that countered James Fallows's impression of him as "a skilled version of an unimaginative breed. He would give you a lucid diagnosis of the four options placed before him, but would be the last man to suggest that some unlisted fifth option might be the necessary answer."[32] For Jimmy and Rosalynn Carter, who despite a life spent jointly stretching the boundaries of their limited rural worldview remained bereft of a governing philosophy that extended beyond their personalistic Christian faith, ideological advice was sorely needed. The task of dispensing it was left to their pollster.

At Carter's behest, Caddell delivered the president-elect a fifty-seven-page "Initial Paper on Political Strategy" on December 10, 1976. In it he offered his "analysis of the current political situation" together with "a series of suggestions on specific political strategies." Admiring in Caddell then as later the kind of comprehensive grasp of ideas that he himself struggled to attain, Carter relaxed his rule against offering praise and pronounced the memorandum "excellent." He also saw to it that Caddell's missive was routed through his staff and especially to Mondale, with whom he met to discuss it.[33]

Beyond his enthusiastic approval, what Carter made of Caddell's memorandum is lost to history. But the memorandum itself remains, and the main lines of Caddell's arguments are clear. Of particular concern to Caddell were the "long-term forces that are at work in this country," the "most striking" of which was "the decline of partisanship" and fact that the voters were "less ideological" than they had ever been. These changes could be detected in a number of trends in the 1976 election, including Carter's lower-than-customary vote among traditional Democrats, the volatility of blue-collar ethnics, and the threat Jerry Brown had posed by advancing "a new definition of American politics" that "fitted no tradition" and "was refreshing to voters." Although Caddell culled from these trends the especially insightful early prediction that "more of the opposition to Carter programs will come from Democrats than from Republicans" and, further, that "the mid-term convention could be the scene of a massive attack on the Administration," the pollster saw a larger opportunity to be grasped amid the changes. Chiefly, "the time is ripe," argued Caddell, "for a political realignment in America."[34]

So Caddell narrowed his focus to what needed to be done for the Carter administration to succeed. Since Carter was "neither a traditional liberal nor a conservative" and, Caddell even believed, was perceived as "fuzzy" mainly because he emitted "contradictory cues" that failed to conform to existing political stereotypes, Carter was "uniquely positioned" to fashion a new "philosophy" that would cut "across traditional ideology" and shape a new Democratic "coalition." However, Caddell warned that the creation of this new ideology would not be easy. "What we require" is not "stew," not a "patch-up job," not "bits and pieces of old policies." Any attempt by Carter "to try to be liberal on some issues and conservative on others is not likely to result in a new coalition, but will appear as an attempt to play both sides" and "run the risk of alienating the ideologues on both sides." Required, rather, was a "fundamentally new ideology" or a new "ideological paradigm." Waxing Hegelian, Caddell insisted upon neither "thesis" nor "antithesis" but a real "synthesis of ideas." Still, he promised: "Leadership that offers fresh ideas has the opportunity to reshape the basic structure of this society." And practically, a "conscious framing" of a new "philosophy" would "attract large numbers of voters."[35]

On the cusp of a presidency that began with euphoria but ended in humiliation, Caddell may have sighted the challenges that lay ahead better than anyone else. The problem was that the pollster could only identify the need for a new Democratic ideology, not develop one himself. Nor, it soon became apparent, could anyone else.

☆   ☆   ☆

Caddell's belief that the nation needed a new philosophy was so strong that he urged Carter "to lay down a new ideology of progress for America" as early as his inaugural address. Although he also suggested that Carter use the inaugural to make "symbolic gestures" through the "ostentatious use of guests," such as Martin Luther King Sr., and use it as well to "set some kind of foreign policy tone," he listed the need for a new ideology first. The new ideology was paramount.[36]

Despite this "excellent" advice, Carter allowed his inaugural to pass without articulating a new domestic ideology. His "symbolic gestures" were thick. Martin Luther King Sr. did join him on the podium. He also set a clear foreign-policy tone. A full and somewhat unusual third of his address was devoted to describing his commitment to global human rights. But about a domestic ideology or any need for one he remained silent. Instead he celebrated a nebulous "new spirit" of "unity and trust," repeated his general campaign conviction that government could be "both competent and compassionate," and mentioned values like "liberty," "work," and "family" while promising to continue to tear "down the barriers that separated those of different race and region and religion." But if a domestic theme could be discerned, it was negative. "More is not necessarily better," he declared just before reminding Americans of the nation's "limits." And he called for "individual sacrifice" for a "common good" that he neglected to describe. Carter even declared: "I have no new dream to set forth today."

Why Carter heeded Caddell's advice in two out of three areas but ignored it in a crucial third is not easily explained. Perhaps he simply possessed no "new ideology of progress," so was incapable of articulating one. But this interpretation is only partially satisfying; Carter's nonideological inclinations had not prevented him in the past from using ideology for political advantage. Since the thesis of Caddell's memorandum was that "governing with public approval requires a continuing political campaign," Carter clearly understood that his inaugural address was a premier political occasion. Aloof indifference to ideology may explain why Carter was a poor ideologue and weak visionary, but it cannot account for his apparent failure to try to articulate a "new ideology of progress."

A second possible explanation is that Carter believed he did articulate a "new ideology of progress for America." Although even the most charitable interpretation of his address can find little to support this conjecture, Carter's previous experience delivering an inaugural address suggests its possibility. Once this possibility is detected, hints from the address itself can be discerned to support it.

When Carter was sworn in as governor of Georgia and dramatically called for an end to discrimination in his state, he enjoyed considerable notoriety for his moral proclamation. Arguably, it substituted for something like a new ideology for Georgia. It follows that Carter may have hoped to achieve a similar result in his 1977 presidential inaugural address, which he personally wrote and rewrote even into the morning of its delivery. Yet, understanding that America was not the South and that the South had made great strides in racial progress since his 1971 remarks, Carter knew that it would not suffice to simply repeat his support for racial equality in his presidential inaugural. What he could do, he may have reasoned, was extend the domestic principle of racial equality to a national mandate for global human rights. By doing this, Carter may have hoped to revive and expand America's moral values by linking them not to domestic initiatives but to foreign policy instead.

The address itself offers support for this interpretation. Carter's unusually strong focus on foreign policy at a time when the country was at peace, for example, may be explained by his hope to substitute the mandate for global human rights for his more limited moral domestic vision. Conversely, Carter's insistence on domestic "limits" and even "individual sacrifice" makes sense if his framework is global rather than national. Finally, whereas Carter promised "no new dream" domestically, he concluded his address with the promise of an "ever expanding American dream." The difference was context: the promise of "no new dream" was made in a domestic context, the "ever expanding" dream referred to foreign affairs. For Carter, the "moral strength" of "our own most precious values" could offer an "ever expanding American dream" if applied to "international policies."

The possibility that Carter proposed to substitute a global vision for a domestic ideology is numbing. On one hand it heaps praise on a president who in retrospect has rightly become known as one of the most distinguished global humanitarians ever to have occupied the Oval Office. But on the other hand it suggests that even at the moment of his inauguration Carter was strangely oblivious to the ideological requirements of governing successfully. Even if Americans could be persuaded to endorse his enlightened moral vision of global affairs, it is difficult to conceive of such a vision substituting for domestic ideology. Other than in times of war, U.S. presidents are not normally elected on the basis of their foreign policies; domestic policy is always paramount. Yet Carter, whose own mother had effectively abandoned her family only to command praise for serving others less fortunate, may have reasoned otherwise. He may have hoped that a moral foreign policy could substitute for domestic cohesion. If so, he was sadly mistaken. Lacking the anchor of a compelling domestic vision, Carter's foreign policy was also tossed in a sea of dissent and indifference.

Before Carter's presidential administration began, Georgia's director of the Office of Energy Resources noted that during Carter's last years as governor he became "extremely interested in energy and deeply concerned about the energy shortage's impact on humans, the environment and the economy."[37] The blend of scientific, social, and environmental problems made energy precisely the kind of complex issue that engaged Carter's intellect and fed his desire to develop "comprehensive" solutions. It comes as no surprise, then, to learn that Carter hinged the domestic agenda of his presidency's first year on the successful passage of a comprehensive energy policy. Rather, surprise arises when it is recalled that "energy was an extremely minor issue in the campaign," and it is discovered that Carter's dogged fight for a national energy policy dominated his domestic agenda not only during his first year but also during his entire administration — and eclipsed almost everything else in the process.[38]

By May 1977, as Kennedy observed, Carter's domestic reforms were already "lined up bumper to bumper." But *Congressional Quarterly* summarized the singular role that energy policy played that year when it noted that "the first session of the 95th Congress could be said to have had two agendas: energy and everything else."[39] Carter chose energy as the topic of his first February 2 "fireside chat" (where he appeared wearing a cardigan sweater and sitting next to a burning fireplace) and delivered a televised April 18 speech on the energy legislation that he would submit to Congress two days later. Seizing the strongest metaphor he could to rally public support for his energy proposals, Carter borrowed William James's phrase, "the moral equivalent of war." Then, when six months passed only to find Carter's energy policy floundering in a recalcitrant Senate, Carter still willingly staked the evaluation of his domestic achievements on energy policy. "I have equated energy policy legislation with either success or failure of my first year in office as a leader of our country in domestic affairs," *Time* magazine quoted him saying on October 31, 1977.[40] As a result, for the third time in less than a year, on November 8 Carter found himself on television pleading with Americans to support his energy initiatives. There was little doubt but that establishing an energy policy would be the measure of Carter's success — or failure — in domestic policy.

The obstacles were steep. When Tip O'Neill received Carter's five phone-book-sized volumes of energy legislation, he admitted that he "took one look at it and groaned." Leafing through the enormous policy labyrinth, the Speaker realized that it would have to be routed through seventeen different committees and subcommittees, none of which would completely support its provisions. Carter's main proposals included new gasoline taxes, new taxes on domestically produced crude oils, ascending penalties for cars that consumed more gasoline than the average, price increases for newly discovered natural gas, and increased reliance on nuclear energy. States, industries, and interest groups would all find something even in these main goals of the legislative package that they opposed, and this opposition would be reflected on the several committees and subcommittees. Worse, there was no constituency solidly in favor of the policy. O'Neill therefore feared that Carter's energy legislation would be gutted, and he forecast that, at minimum, its passage would pose "the toughest fight this Congress ever had."[41]

Nor was congressional will to support any painful initiative by the president strong. Having vetoed a bill for federal funding of nineteen water projects in seventeen states on February 22 because they were "pork-barrel" excesses, Carter alienated many of the representatives and senators who had already promised the federal plums to their constituents. Later Carter recognized that the fight over the water projects "caused the deepest breach between me and the Democratic leadership."[42] Bert Lance went even further, calling the veto "absolutely the worst political mistake he made."[43] However severe the error, the veto made it difficult for Carter to extract accommodations from an already embarrassed and angry Congress. Yet Carter's energy proposal essentially asked an even larger number of representatives and senators to support legislation that would negatively impact their districts and largest financial contributors.

It was at this juncture that O'Neill came to Carter's temporary rescue. Displaying the political finesse that had earned him his elevated position in his party, the Speaker alighted upon the unorthodox strategy of creating an ad hoc committee solely for the purpose of considering Carter's energy bill. The strategy worked. On August 5, 1977, O'Neill succeeded in ramrodding Carter's energy legislation through the House to a favorable vote.

But the fight was far from over. Although energy policy passed the House and Carter was able to take the symbolic step of establishing a separate cabinet Department of Energy, the legislation itself still had to pass the Senate and then a House and Senate conference committee. The Senate proved to be its undoing. In that more deliberative body Carter's energy legislation was not routed through an ad hoc committee but divided among five different ones, each of which took its ax to the legislation while angry fights ensued.

The administration offered little help. Once, liberal senators staged the first filibuster in thirteen years to stave off a vote that they assumed the president also opposed. The administration, however, quickly capitulated and ordered Vice President Mondale to end the filibuster without even notifying the supportive senators. Incensed by the administration's indifference to their efforts, Carter's Senate supporters soured on active support for his energy program. Indeed, Senator Abraham Ribicoff summarized the status of the bill in late 1977 by saying that, frankly, it was "a shambles."[44]

As bad, Carter's hyperbolic rhetoric on behalf of energy policy failed to inspire public support. Whether the issue was just too technical to interest most Americans, whether the temporary reprieve in rising energy prices convinced many that energy was not a serious problem after all, or whether a culture of apathy invigorated by no compelling presidential vision just found Americans slipping perilously deeper into malaise is unknown. But a summer 1977 *New York Times*/CBS poll found that "too few people believe the nation's energy problems are serious enough — and even fewer understand them well enough — to provide broad support for the Administration's energy program."[45] The interpretation may have been too charitable. Three separate *New York Times*/CBS polls conducted between July 1977 and January 1978 found that fully half of Americans believed that the energy shortage was simply a ploy used by oil and gas companies to allow them to "charge higher prices," while only 38 to 43 percent believed the shortages were "real."[46] Caddell's late summer polls even showed a "decline" in the public's belief that energy was "a major issue" and found Americans more likely to mention the economy, government waste, and welfare reform as the nation's leading problems.[47] Meanwhile, Ralph Nader dismissed Carter's saber-rattling about energy by calling him "a sheep in wolf's clothing."[48] About energy being the moral equivalent of war, laughs were elicited by reducing it to its acronym "MEOW" while reporters joked among themselves, "yeah, the *Vietnam* War."[49]

Dispirited but tenacious, Carter thus found himself pressing onward with energy policy during his second year. He also continued to advance a wildly ambitious agenda of domestic reforms. Declaring in his 1978 State of the Union address that "we now have a priceless opportunity to address persistent problems," he appended to his declared text an unusual separate "message to Congress" that listed more than a hundred domestic policy initiatives under some two dozen separate headings. But even more than in 1977, Carter's 1978 reforms were subordinated to energy policy. As it languished, so also did the others.

Joseph Califano, Carter's cabinet secretary for HEW, sensed as early as December 1977 that Carter's devotion to energy policy was preventing him from attending to other domestic initiatives. Califano noted, for example, that Carter seemed already "unwilling to devote much of his time or dwindling political capital" to welfare reform. Six months later the secretary reached the same conclusion about health care. "For the first time," Califano recalled thinking on June 1, 1978, "I felt that Carter might abandon his commitment . . . to achieve significant reform of the health system." Indeed, after having called the U.S. tax code "a disgrace to the human race" during his campaign and promising its "comprehensive reform," Carter also drastically reduced his goals for reform in this area. He insisted in 1978 on submitting an anemic tax reform proposal to Congress that had as its mostly laughable linchpin the elimination of tax deductions for "three-martini lunches." In these and other ways Carter signaled throughout 1978 that, despite his hope of becoming an "active-positive" president, his almost singular focus on energy was thwarting his goal.[50]

The president's failures were not missed by many Americans. The *New Republic* editorialized on August 5, 1978, that "the administration has a remarkable record. Almost everything it proposes turns to ashes." Mentioning that the "list of wrecks is impressive," the left-leaning magazine singled out energy for special mockery: "The energy program has spent 15 months being launched and is still in danger of going under."[51] At the same time, less sophisticated Americans may have found that another event dramatized the domestic failures of their new president more sharply than energy policy — though it was ironically related.

On December 6, 1977, some 165,000 United Mine Workers walked off the job after failing to reach a satisfactory labor agreement with the Coal Operators Association. Older Americans could recall four similar strikes during the Truman administration, each met by decisive presidential action. But when Carter confronted the 1977–78 coal strike, he vacillated. The strike continued for a record 109 days, prompted real fears about dwindling coal stocks, and caused sporadic school and factory closings. The boy who had once stood motionless, unable to decide between cookies and rocks, may have learned early to empathize with different viewpoints and various values. But when the president seemed paralyzed in a labor/management dispute, many Americans saw the inaction as symbolic of an administration with no clear idea of where it wanted to lead the country.

Although a scholar considering the coal strike afterward concluded that "there was probably little more Carter could have done to shorten the strike or mitigate its impact,"[52] press and public opinion at the time differed. Three winter and spring editions of *Newsweek* progressively berated the president for alternating "between repeated threats of Federal action and repeated pleas to negotiators," for setting deadlines for "decisive action" only to "let all of them pass," and finally for "weak and indecisive leadership in the crisis."[53] Whether the criticisms were fair or not, two-thirds of the public surveyed believed that Carter performed poorly during the strike.[54]

Received opinion is that Carter's honeymoon with the public ended with the "Bert Lance affair" during August and September 1977, when Lance was accused of having engaged in illegal banking practices (charges for which he was later acquitted) and forced to resign. Lance's alleged misdeeds are thought to have tarnished Carter's own image of personal morality and hence diminished his popularity. The polls, however, tell a different story. Gallup's tracking of Carter's approval ratings, which hovered between 60 and 67 percent throughout the summer of 1977, shows that they held at 66 percent in middle and late August when the affair unfolded, dropped to 54 percent in early September at the time of Lance's resignation, but then bounced back up to 59 percent in early October. These numbers make it difficult to attribute much sustained downward movement to "the Lance affair."[55] Caddell reached a similar conclusion on the basis of his polls. "Confidence in Carter shows little sign of erosion over the affair," he wrote the president on November 2, 1977. "While Americans thought Lance should resign, 65 percent approved of the way Carter handled the affair" and, on the whole, it was simply not "a political issue."[56]

The steep and politically disastrous drop in Carter's public approval actually occurred during the coal strike. After bobbing between the middle and low fifties from October through January, Carter's approval ratings first dipped below 50 percent in the February 1978 polls. By April, just after the coal strike finally ended, they dropped to a dismal 40 percent.[57]

Although there is no proof that the coal strike caused these declining ratings, at least one news magazine assumed it did. *U.S. News & World Report* detected "a significant change of mood" regarding the president in late February, and by March put the best spin on a situation it assumed to be awful. The headline then blared: "How Carter's Staff Plans to Avoid Another Round of Blunders." The explanation for voters' "second thoughts" about the president, the editors were also certain, was Carter's "failure to end the coal walkout in a brisk fashion."[58] And with but two brief and easily explained exceptions (when Carter announced the consummation of Middle East peace negotiations, and immediately after the U.S. Embassy in Tehran was overrun by terrorists), Carter's approval ratings never again exceeded 50 percent. Often as not they dipped to nearly half that.[59]

Ultimately, Carter's tenacious pursuit of an energy policy did partially pay off. On October 15, 1978, Congress finally passed an energy bill that Carter was able to sign into law. Yet, coming a year after his self-imposed deadline and reflecting deep compromises from his initial proposal, the victory was only a partial one, by Carter's own admission. It also came at the expense of other initiatives and followed a protracted coal strike that dramatized his failures.

Meanwhile, in the vacuum created by Carter's absorption in energy policy and absent overall vision, full-scale ideological warfare erupted. On one side, as forecast by Caddell, the Democrats' midterm convention turned into an assault on the administration, led in part by Edward Kennedy, who delivered an "electric" speech to the disproportionately liberal delegates. It was fast becoming clear that Kennedy was positioning himself to challenge the president for reelection and that many liberals were eager to support him. When a number of Democratic representatives and senators also went down in defeat in the midterm elections, always a referendum on the president, Carter's inability to bolster the party was even more apparent.

On the other side a New Right began to crystallize around a host of not always consistent domestic and foreign policy issues. But the passage of California's Proposition 13 in June 1978 enabled the conservative coalition to appropriate a potent domestic issue. Rallying around the cry for tax relief, old-style economic conservatives joined newer populist conservatives to launch a movement that would grip the nation for a decade or more.

Ironically, Carter's own limited domestic vision fueled this conservative rallying cry even as it stimulated liberal opposition. If government really proposed no new popular domestic initiatives, conservatives had every reason to call for scaling back taxes. The same limited domestic ideology, however, also goaded liberals into proposing a resurrection of ambitious government activism.

Striving to carve out for himself a middle position of a limited government committed to competence and compassion, Carter found his centrist position squeezed by resurgent ideologues on both sides. Remaining in an ever-eroding and increasingly compromised middle, Carter also had little of substance to show for his middling position. Nor had he alighted upon a centrist ideological synthesis that might make his position compelling despite its immediate failures. As Caddell had warned, Carter's attempt to be "liberal on some issues and conservative on others" had not resulted in "a new coalition" but had simply "alienated the ideologues on both sides." Instead of "a fundamentally new ideology," Carter had offered "stew" made of "bits and pieces of old policies." And he suffered for it. Although his successful negotiation of the Camp David Accords during the fall of 1978 boosted his approval ratings back up over 50 percent, by the new year they were back down and falling fast.[60]

Carter's 1979 State of the Union address seemed to reflect his awareness of domestic failure. Absent from the address were the spate of ambitious proposals offered the year before, and no separate "message to Congress" was appended. Speechwriters did for the first time strike a potentially effective theme — a call for a "new foundation" for America. But of what that foundation consisted the president did not really say. Indeed, his words were more negative than before. Complaining that America's problems "are more subtle, more complex, and more interrelated" than ever, Carter reminded listeners that "government alone cannot solve these problems." And he only bothered to mention two domestic problems, along with the economy, that he intended to tackle that year — campaign finance reform and hospital cost containment (the remainder of his previously promised comprehensive national health-care reform as well as an anti-inflation tactic). As the year progressed, both initiatives failed and the economy worsened.

So, when the winter of 1979 saw the fall of Iran's shah and oil prices once again spiraling upward, Carter seized the opportunity to return to his energy crusade. But even the renewed crisis atmosphere did little to stimulate public support for the energy initiatives he had harped on for more than two years. Indeed, despite its being delivered amid sporadic gasoline shortages, Carter's fourth televised speech on energy policy on

April 5, 1979, left both Congress and the public unmoved. Popular opinion, in fact, was even more cynical than before. In late April and early May the Gallup poll found that only 14 percent of the public believed there was a "real" energy shortage while an astonishing 77 percent believed the crisis had been "deliberately brought about by oil companies."[61] In the minds of the public and inaction in the Congress, Carter's primary domestic initiative was once again failing miserably.

Frustrated by his failing efforts to overcome the lethargy and disbelief of seemingly the entire country on energy, Carter found himself attracted to the memorandum submitted to him by Caddell on April 23 which outlined the more general "crisis of confidence" in America. Although the memorandum was the one unofficially tagged the "Apocalypse Now" by cynics inside the White House, Caddell's approach was actually more upbeat. His title was "Of Crisis and Opportunity."[62] Sensing its accuracy, Carter took the unprecedented step of canceling his fifth scheduled speech on energy and, two months later when he did speak to the nation on July 15, 1979, focused first on the problem of national "malaise" and only secondly on energy policy. The indictment, however, had been evolving. In his abbreviated State of the Union speech that year, which Caddell had also influenced, Carter had declared: "The duty of our generation of Americans is to renew our Nation's faith."

Carter was not mistaken about the nation's malaise. Nor was he mistaken in thinking that the inability of the nation to come together on an energy policy was symptomatic of it. Even so, he was mistaken in another way, and the crisis persisted while the opportunity was squandered. His mistake was to believe that faith could be revived on the basis of a complex and technical policy emboldened by "no new dream" and driven by no new "ideology of progress."

That at least was the conclusion reached by the nation's chief theorist of American civil religion, Robert Bellah, after watching Carter's infamous "malaise speech" from his home in the Berkeley hills. Having been summoned to Camp David by Carter, via Caddell, to advise the president about the nation's faith, Bellah had used his presidential audience to urge Carter to become "almost a Jeremiah." Much that was uncomfortable needed to be said to the American people, and Bellah (together with Rabbi Marc Tanenbaum of the American Jewish Committee) urged Carter to say it. But once the speech was delivered, Bellah was incensed. He found his proposed prophetic speech "pathetic," as Carter substituted "morale boosting" for a "serious consideration of what the options are as we move into a different world." Worse, Bellah finally realized, Carter simply had "no social vision."[63]

The polls showed the majority of Americans agreeing. Although they temporarily approved of the speech, much as they had the campaign promise of renewed faith, when asked in May whether "Jimmy Carter has the vision to provide solutions to the country's problems," only 39 percent of the public agreed; 40 percent did not. (During 1977 between 54 and 69 percent of the public had agreed.) Asked also whether "Carter is providing strong and inspired leadership for the country," an overwhelming 59 percent disagreed while only a paltry 28 percent agreed.[64] Inside the government the negative verdict was even more pronounced. A postadministration survey of department and agency heads found that 55 percent thought Carter lacked "vision" while only 17 percent thought he possessed it.[65]

Despite his ambitious reform agenda and forward-looking attention to energy policy, the beleaguered president's message, and legacy, was reduced to its barest essentials: the need for faith. But in what domestic "ideology of progress" Americans might place their faith Carter did not say. Indeed, he did not know.

A CONTESTED GLOBAL VISION

In the area of foreign policy both the challenges and the opportunities were different. There Carter not only called for "an ever expanding American dream" but did so on the basis of a coherent philosophy. Even, and perhaps especially, his critics recognized this philosophical coherence. "Understanding . . . the recent failures of American policy," wrote Jeane Kirkpatrick toward the end of Carter's term, requires "that we disregard the notion that the failure of the Carter policy was the personal failure of a man unskilled in the ways of diplomacy." However "unskilled" Carter may have appeared to be in domestic affairs, Kirkpatrick assured us that his foreign policy rested upon a "philosophy of foreign affairs that inspired and informed that policy." The philosophy was not, of course, original with Carter or limited to him. But its "whole cluster of ideas . . . was enormously attractive to Jimmy Carter. No sooner was he elected than he set out to translate them into a new policy."[66]

Kirkpatrick called the cluster of foreign-policy ideas that attracted Carter "the globalist approach." George Moffett, a foreign-policy expert who served in the Carter administration, called the same views "liberal internationalism."[67] By whatever name, however, opponents and proponents agreed on their gist. The philosophy rejected America's cold war view of an essentially bipolar world in which U.S. foreign policy was driven primarily by the objective of "containing" Soviet expansionism and replaced it with a multipolar view in which U.S. foreign policy would be propelled by more abstract moral principles applied more or less uniformly everywhere on the globe. To detractors like Kirkpatrick, this "vague, abstract universalism" ignored "the realities of culture, character, geography, economics, and history," even as it led to the U.S. being "threatened" by "a ring of Soviet bases on and around our southern and eastern borders."[68] To Carter, reaffirming "America's commitment to human rights as a fundamental tenet of our foreign policy" would "create a wider framework of international cooperation suited to the new and rapidly changing historical circumstances" in which the U.S. might even move "to engage the Soviet Union in a joint effort to halt the strategic arms race."[69] Both sides agreed on the essence of the philosophy, and both understood that the new philosophy, arose in large part as a reaction to U.S. military involvement in Vietnam (which prompted the intellectual departure from the consensus on the need for Soviet "containment"). What the two sides disagreed sharply about were the merits of the new philosophy.

It is easy to understand Carter's attraction to this new foreign-policy philosophy. Most proximally, his main foreign-policy instruction had come through his membership in the Trilateral Commission, an association established by "liberal internationalists" in order to promote their views. The leading proponent of these views, moreover, was thought even by Kirkpatrick to be Zbigniew Brzezinski. Serving first as chief foreign policy advisor to Carter's presidential campaign and then as his National Security Advisor, Brzezinski had ample opportunity to press his views on the president. Indeed, as the formal relationship developed, Carter and Brzezinski met daily for foreign-policy briefings which sometimes led to "wide-ranging discussions." Always an eager student, Carter availed himself of Brzezinski's willingness to tutor well into his presidency.[70] It was easy therefore to understand how another Trilateral Commission member could consider Carter the "prophet" of the commission.[71]

Yet more than accidental association explains the coherence of Carter's foreign-policy views. For the one moral commitment he made early in life and never wavered from was his belief in racial equality. From this commitment Carter readily extracted the more general commitment to the moral universalism from which it arose. To racial equality Carter then added commitments to gender equality, as well as opposition to barriers of opportunity based upon region, class, and physical or mental handicap. It followed that when Carter grasped that the same principle of universalism was at stake in the contest between the new and old foreign-policy creeds, he instinctively gravitated toward the new, more universalistic philosophy.

This biographical basis for Carter's foreign-policy views was made clear in his first major foreign-policy address. At the University of Notre Dame on May 22, 1977, Carter explicitly connected his foreign policy to the history of African Americans' struggle for equality. Mentioning Martin Luther King Jr.'s "I Have a Dream" speech as an example of the power words have to promote human rights, Carter proceeded to extrapolate from Abraham Lincoln's belief that the "Nation could not exist half slave and half free" the foreign-policy corollary that "a peaceful world cannot long exist one-third rich and two-thirds hungry." For Carter, "the strands that connect our actions overseas with our essential character as a nation" were linkages rooted in America's universalistic commitment to civil rights.

Yet, perhaps because the civil rights movement had moved from the universal principle of equality to the more contestable particularist terrain of school busing and affirmative action, Carter had difficulty persuading Americans to embrace the same moral connection. Little evidence exists that editorial writers or news commentators noted the connection, much less commented favorably upon it. At a time when the civil rights crusade did not seem as morally pristine as it had just a few years earlier — and when domestic values more generally were in flux — Carter's attempt to link foreign policy to racial equality seemed lost on the public. The churning waters of domestic values even seemed to muddy rather than clarify Carter's philosophy of foreign policy.

But this did not mean that Americans were indifferent to foreign policy during Carter's presidency. One foreign-policy issue alone, the 1977–78 debate over ratification of the Panama Canal treaties, absorbed some forty days of congressional hearings, produced the longest floor debate in the Senate since the Versailles Treaty of 1919–20, and galvanized the nation as no foreign-policy issue since the Vietnam War had. Combined with it were debates over the production of the B-1 bomber and neutron bomb, negotiations of a second Strategic Arms Limitation Treaty (SALT II) with the Soviets, instability in the Middle East and Central America, the United States' relationship with China, and, ultimately, a fourteen-month hostage crisis in Iran simultaneous with a hostile Soviet invasion of Afghanistan. For a period of peace, there was much on America's foreign-policy plate that, to a surprising degree, ordinary Americans attended to.

However, the popular foreign-policy debate that arose during Carter's presidency had little to do with the competing philosophies debated by the experts. The popular debate focused on something more visceral: American might in the aftermath of Vietnam. Of concern to the public, noted countless editorials and news analyses at the time, was not so much which foreign-policy view was right or even which was most pragmatic; of concern was whether, after its defeat in Vietnam, America was still strong. So, while Carter was arguably correct to maintain, as he did in his inaugural address, that "strength [is] based not merely on the size of an arsenal but on the nobility of ideas," popular opinion tended to discount ideas in favor of things like arsenal size.

The ratification of the Panama Canal treaties therefore became the main foreign-policy issue of the first years of the Carter administration not because of the merits of the treaties but because they served as a symbol for harnessing public fears of declining U.S. strength. Expert opinion (including two-thirds of the nation's newspapers, every living ex-president, and even leading conservatives like George Will and William Buckley) generally favored proceeding with the treaties, which had been negotiated by two Democratic and two Republican presidents over thirteen years. The consensus was that they were as much in the United States' interest as Panama's. Valid counterarguments were few. The chief one was that the economic consequences of the treaties for the United States were based on guesswork that might easily prove mistaken and hence make the treaties extremely costly. Amazingly, however, this argument was rarely made.[72] Besides this practical argument, perhaps the most persuasive argument against the treaties was that, in the face of the popular opposition, a further delay would not materially affect the United States. Writing in the *New Republic*, for instance, Ken Bode argued that "the canal issue was . . . the sort of job you take on when you're coming off a big victory or else save for the first year of the second term." Still, Bode's charge that "Carter's timing couldn't be worse" was based not on any assessment of real difficulties with the treaties but on the recognition that they had obviously become a "flash point with the public."[73] Why they became such a "flash point" was the larger question.

The pragmatically minded editorial page of the *Wall Street Journal* pretended not to understand the issue's importance. "We don't much care whether the canal treaties are accepted or rejected," it blared in feigned evenness. "Our biggest problem with the Panama Canal issue," it earlier insisted, "has always been figuring out what the fuss is all about." Even six months later, when the debate over the treaties had nearly paralyzed Congress and dominated the news, the *Journal* continued to insist that "the Panama Canal is a strategic sideshow."[74]

Despite its persistent pragmatism, even the *Journal* recognized what was really at stake in the Panama Canal treaties. Although it disapproved, it admitted that the issue had become "the occasion for an epic debate on the grand directions of U.S. foreign policy." At stake, it recognized, were not "practical matters" but "an emotional tone." This emotion, which editorial writer Vermont Royster admitted was "understandable," drew from a feeling that the United States had been "pushed back from its once preeminent role in world affairs, the culmination of which was our defeat in Vietnam." Since the treaties would "withdraw us from another outpost, one which was once the very symbol of American world power," many Americans found themselves thinking "enough is enough." Moreover, the *Journal* editors believed Carter's "publicity blitz" in support of the treaties stimulated just such misplaced emotion. Carter "seemed to say the U.S. should abnegate the canal to atone for past sins" even as others went so far as to say that the canal is "an ugly imperialist symbol" rather than "the realization of a historic dream." So, while a guest editorial concluded that "there are good reasons to ratify the Panama Canal treaties, but shame for our behavior in Panama is not one of them," another admitted: "The American people still think Yankee-style imperialism is not a bad thing, all things considered."[75]

But the *Wall Street Journal* lagged behind other media in probing the symbolic importance of the canal. Writing in the *New York Times* in August 1977, Tom Wicker forecast that the "powerful challenge" of the canal treaties would "test whether the American people . . . can adapt themselves sensibly to a changing international order" even more than did the Vietnam War. A few days later the *Times* observed that "Panama arouses emotion out of all proportion to its size" and in January 1978 editorialized that "there have always been two battles between proponents and opponents of the Panama Canal treaties" — one "rational" and the other "deeply subjective." By April, the editors found it useful to remind readers that "recent newspaper and television coverage notwithstanding, [the debate] is not about Jimmy Carter's manhood." The same theme had already been addressed by William Buckley in *U.S. News & World Report*, in which he warned against making opposition to the treaties a "prideful" assertion of "our national masculinity." Meanwhile, the *Progressive* declared that "logic is not involved" in a debate of "a potent symbol — perhaps the last unambiguous one — of American imperial power"; *America* warned that "what is really at stake in this debate is the symbolic expression of our national purpose"; and the *Nation* chastised that the "image" of "strength and steadiness of purpose" symbolized by the canal "is evaporating in the hot air generated in the Senate chamber."[76]

However indifferent Americans may have been to the merits or demerits of the treaties, many found the emotions symbolized by the debates riveting. Most who did so, further, sided with opponents of the treaties. Moreover, public opinion did not budge. Based upon polls that showed those opposed to the treaties were also the least knowledgeable about them, Carter tried to turn public opinion around through a massive public education campaign. His efforts, however, failed. A careful examination of numerous polls shows that the 26 to 29 percent of the public who supported the treaties in the late summer and early fall of 1977 inched up to only 29 to 30 percent by April of 1978. More important, opposition to the treaties either remained stable or actually increased, going from a 49 to 61 percent range to a 53 to 60 percent range over the same period. Whereas, as often happens in polling, different question-wording produced different results that in some polls suggested a groundswell of support for the treaties, the truth was there was no such groundswell and, by almost a two-to-one ratio, public opinion remained opposed to the treaties even on the dates of their ratification.[77] A majority of Americans, it appeared, agreed with Senator Strom Thurmond when he declared in a paid television program on October 30, 1977, that "we are still a proud people, and we have every right to be proud about our canal."[78] A minority only half as large agreed with Carter when he declared in a free television speech (that one major network refused to broadcast and another delayed until late in the evening) on February 1, 1978, that "we believe in good will and fairness, as well as strength."

The debate over the canal was therefore widely recognized as a symbolic one that turned as much on a visceral sense of "pride" in the nation's "strength" as on substantive concerns. Yet beneath this symbolic contest lurked a more substantial political battle of a different kind. The New Right, a fledgling coalition of cultural and usually religious conservatives responding to the moral fragmentation of the late 1970s by calling for a reassertion of "traditional" and typically authoritarian Judeo-Christian values, alighted upon the canal issue as a pretext to build their movement. Why they chose this issue is not altogether clear. Others more reflective of their agenda might more logically have been chosen. However, since the New Right's chief organizer, Richard Viguerie, was mainly experienced in advertising, especially in direct mail, and was also keenly aware of the poll results concerning the canal, the inference might be that Viguerie simply believed the canal issue was the one likely to reap the most benefits for the movement. In any event, Viguerie pressed ultraconservative Illinois congressman Phillip Crane into writing an antitreaty diatribe, *Surrender in Panama*, which Viguerie published. The New Right then mailed 100,000 paperback copies of the book to opinion leaders and supporters. Meanwhile, and never shy about promoting what they believed was their privileged access to absolute values, the New Right organized a "truth squad" to travel the country promoting its positions. Viguerie estimated that the combined efforts of their antitreaty crusade resulted in adding 400,000 names to his mailing list and in defeating twenty "liberal" senators and representatives. Their crusade also — both supporters and opponents agreed — catapulted the New Right to national prominence.[79]

Only the motives of the principal actors in the next presidential drama, Ronald Reagan and Jimmy Carter, remain mysteries. Why Reagan vehemently opposed, while Carter dramatically supported, the Panama Canal treaties is ultimately a puzzle that goes to the heart of the two men's differing political and moral viewpoints.

Reagan had to know that on the issue that he very nearly rode to victory in the 1976 Republican primaries he was terribly mistaken. Whereas he might have discounted a *New York Times* editorial that accused him of perpetuating "a dangerous myth" and of "demagoguery" on the canal issue[80] on the grounds that the piece simply represented the liberal media establishment, surely it was more difficult for him to dismiss the criticism the *Wall Street Journal* was forced to level against him. Its editorial-page editor, Robert Bartlett, was, after all, one of those present in the Manhattan restaurant when the "Laffer curve" justification for Reagan's "supply side" economic agenda of the 1980s was scribbled on a napkin over a steak dinner in the late 1970s. Yet even the *Journal* felt compelled to point out that "Mr. Reagan's insistence on U.S. sovereignty in the Canal Zone rests on a thicket of confused, doubtful legal assumptions," and again that "Mr. Reagan's position . . . combines factual error with poor judgment."[81] With leading conservatives (including fellow actor John Wayne) openly sup-

porting the treaties, how could Reagan maintain his vehement opposition?

The easy answer is the most cynical one. As Tom Wicker noted in the
New York Times (using polling data lower than most), 46 percent of Americans opposed ratification of the Panama Canal treaties, while only 20 percent called themselves Republicans. Since "two plus two equals four,"
Wicker predicted that the Republican party would "rebuild its long-
declining fortunes by appealing to those who oppose the canal treaties."[82]
George Bush, himself angling for the nomination in 1980, seized the issue
to boost his chances. To the Republican faithful in Idaho Falls early in
1978 Bush declared that the canal treaties convey "a perception of United
States impotence."[83] If even Bush was willing to use "Reagan's issue," it
followed that Reagan might well use it again himself. Moreover, Reagan
admitted that Carter was "the enigma to me that he is to a great many
people." Drawing little of the "political fire" from him that a more liberal
Democratic presidency would, the Carter presidency left Reagan without
the kind of strong issues that he might use to bolster his own candidacy.
So, as he continued to field some 200 speaking invitations a week, Reagan
increasingly returned to the canal issue to catapult his candidacy.[84]

None of which is to deny that at some level and despite all evidence,
Reagan was a true believer. In the strange way that Reagan chose to play
only roles in which he could believe, but then believed in those roles more
intently for playing them, the divorced candidate of estranged children,
whose schedule was determined in part by astrologers, believed deeply
that the treaties were wrong and the Christian Coalition right.[85]

For Jimmy Carter, the question of motives is even more troublesome.
The easy answer is that Carter simply underestimated the degree of opposition the treaties would elicit. Granted that he was committed to a
foreign-policy philosophy that deemphasized East–West tensions and
sought to promote fairness and equity globally, including in Central
America, Carter was far from alone in subscribing to this philosophy or
in promoting consummation of the Panama Canal treaties as an instance
of it. Even before he was inaugurated, for example, the *New York Times*
called for Carter to "reject outmoded policies based on domination and
paternalism" and to recognize that a new Panama Canal treaty was "one
of the most important of all foreign policy issues confronting the United
States in 1977."[86] The majority of informed citizens, the vast majority of
newspaper editors, and ultimately the requisite two-thirds of the Senate

shared this or a similarly supportive view of the treaties. Surely no one — the president included — could have forecast the degree of opposition to the canal treaties that eventually erupted during 1977–78. Indeed, since some portion of that opposition was manufactured by a New Right advertising guru who seized the canal issue in order to promote his own more general political agenda, and other portions were orchestrated by Republican presidential hopefuls seeking leverage against a Democratic president whose moderate policies elsewhere offered few openings for sharp criticisms, some of the opposition to the canal treaties probably was unforeseeable. Given the widespread support for the treaties and impossibility of predicting the vigor of the opposition, there is every reason to suppose that Carter did not anticipate the difficulties he would confront with the initiative.

A postadministration interview with Hamilton Jordan suggests that the administration did simply underestimate the degree of opposition the canal treaties would generate. According to Jordan, the administration considered the issue "as being important in itself but also as a dry run for SALT ratification."[87] The expectation, in short, was that the canal issue would produce a quick foreign-policy victory which in turn would provide the momentum for subsequent victories. Insofar as the administration calculated this way, the worst that can be concluded is that they miscalculated.

Still, there is evidence that more than miscalculation was at stake in Carter's decision to proceed with the Panama Canal treaties early in his administration. Mainly, Carter's campaign for the presidency showed that he fully understood the explosive nature of the canal issue and even took pains to mislead the voters about his position on it. In a campaign statement the *Washington Post* took to mean that he would "renege on the Ford administration's promise" to Panama, he said, "I would never give up full control of the Panama Canal." Again, in his televised debate with Ford, Carter took the harder line: "I would not relinquish practical control of the Panama Canal Zone any time in the foreseeable future." Publicly stating the more politically palatable position, Carter left it to Cyrus Vance to reassure a jittery foreign-policy establishment. "Campaign talk is sometimes imprecise," confided Vance diplomatically in private about Carter's strident antitreaty campaign statements.[88]

Perhaps, just as Carter misled Georgia voters about his racial views only to make a startling speech in favor of racial equality, he also misled

American voters about his foreign-policy views with the intention of shocking them with his commitment to global human rights and liberal internationalism. Also plausible is that Carter's private way of atoning for misleading campaign statements was to fight even harder for the opposites once he was elected. Whatever the explanation, it is certain that Carter had a firm grasp of the politics of canal ratification prior to pressing forward with it his first year. Although he may also have underestimated the opposition that would erupt, he could not have been completely surprised that it did.

Moreover, it was true that, as the *Wall Street Journal* chided, Carter did seem to gravitate toward a moral rhetoric of guilt and atonement in his defense of the treaties when a rhetoric of national self-interest would have been more compelling. After undertaking a scholarly analysis of Carter's rhetorical strategy in support of the treaties, for example, Ronald A. Sudol concluded that "the whole purpose of the speech seems to be to minimize the appearance of advantage to the United States and instead to emphasize the desire to compensate Panama for the disadvantages it has suffered in the past." Worse, continued the speech communications expert, "by adopting a rhetoric of fairness, Carter precludes the use of most tactical arguments — the very ones most likely to persuade those who remain unpersuaded." Sudol also noted that Carter's "rhetoric of strategic retreat" with respect to the canal echoed both the U.S. withdrawal from Vietnam and the problems of energy. In all instances "a consciousness of less rather than more" was promoted. By contrast, the opposition to the canal treaties couched their arguments in a language of "strength" — a rhetorical strategy bound to be more successful.[89]

Finally, evidence suggests that to at least some extent Carter purposely picked the fight over the canal in order to dramatize his new philosophy of foreign policy. Dispatching Rosalynn on a "good will" tour of Latin America early in 1977, Carter signaled his intentions early of using Latin American relationships as a proving ground for his liberal internationalism. By August, U.N. ambassador Andrew Young told reporters that the treaties were the first test of the Carter administration's "new approach to Latin America."[90] Although Carter later admitted that had he foreseen the "terrible battle" over the canal "it would have been a great temptation for me to avoid the issue — at least during my first term," he followed the admission by claiming that the treaties were "worth the price." The reason was moral: "We are a nation that believes in equality, justice, honesty, and truth," he wrote.[91] To some extent, the promise of this moral engagement attracted Carter to the canal issue, even as the same promise attracted his opponents.

Although Carter finally won the ratification battle that Latin Americans heralded as "a triumph for the hemisphere," the April 1978 victory was a hollow one for Carter at home. Amazingly, *U.S. News & World Report* was able to report that some senators considered that Carter's victory over such tremendous opposition "disclosed once again his ineptness in dealing with Congress." More practically, the news magazine reported the views of Georgia senator Sam Nunn and others to the effect that "Carter may have expended too much political capital in winning approval," leaving little left over for other initiatives. "A lot of Senators feel that Carter had made them walk the plank for him on Panama," explained Senator Paul Laxalt. "It is going to get very tough up here for Carter." Writing in the *New York Times*, Hedrick Smith agreed: "[H]e has still not achieved the kind of breakthrough that will stimulate political support for his other major initiatives." Perhaps, noted Smith in a subsequent news analysis, the reason was not so much his "ineptness" with Congress as the kind of victory Carter achieved coupled with his faltering domestic agenda. Noting that in the aftermath of the coal strike and foundering energy legislation Carter "desperately needed . . . to prove his leadership at home," Smith believed that the canal victory "was yet another sign of the retrenchment of American power in the post-Vietnam era." Such a sign was not the stuff of political momentum.[92]

Nor did Carter's other foreign-policy initiatives alter the impression that his was a policy of weakness rather than strength. He canceled the production of the B-1 bomber, for instance, and demurred on deployment of the neutron bomb. There were solid strategic reasons for both decisions. The still-top-secret stealth bomber (used successfully in the Gulf War) was a superior replacement for the B-1 bomber, so Carter approved it while canceling production of the outmoded bomber. With regard to the morally contentious neutron bomb (which kills people while leaving buildings intact), Chancellor Helmut Schmidt of Germany ultimately decided that he would not deploy it. Since the weapon was intended to bolster NATO defenses, German rejection left little justification for the United States to proceed. Still, to a nation thirsting for militaristic symbols of strength, Carter's decisions appeared weak.

The perception may well have been similar when Carter was able to announce the normalization of the relationship with China on December 15, 1978, and then welcome Deng Xiaoping to Washington in late January 1979. Unquestionably a foreign relations success achieved more quickly than many expected, and perhaps also a testimony to the merits of the liberal internationalist's creed, the move did little to bolster perceptions of U.S. power in world affairs. Likewise, when three months earlier Carter emerged from intense negotiations with Anwar Sadat and Menachem Begin at Camp David to announce that a historic peace agreement had been reached between Egypt and Israel, richly deserved credit was bestowed upon the otherwise beleaguered president. (To this day many believe that Carter should have also been honored by the subsequent Nobel Peace Prize that was shared equally by Sadat and Begin.) Yet, while Carter's approval ratings shot back up to the halfway mark, some grumbled that his abilities were better suited to the position of secretary of state than president. An excellent mediator and dedicated peacemaker, Carter's success with the Camp David Accords did little to augment Americans' national self-image of strength.

But nothing did more to solidify the perception of Carter's foreign policy weakness, created in large part by the Panama Canal debates, than his apparent bungling with the Soviet Union. Still a grave military threat, in the second week of his administration Carter seemed already to squander what good will there was between the two superpowers. Allowing his State Department to accuse Czechoslovakia, then a Soviet satellite, of violating the standards for human rights established by 1975 Helsinki agreements, Carter ignored superpower etiquette forbidding either from criticizing the other's internal affairs. But the Soviets were more furious when Carter followed the insult by publicly proclaiming Soviet dissident Andrei Sakharov a "champion of human rights" and sending him a personal note of support. By the time Carter sent Vance to Moscow in March 1977 to propose additional cuts in the SALT II agreement already negotiated by the Ford administration, Soviet leader Leonid Brezhnev suspected a trick and simply canceled negotiations without so much as offering a counterproposal. (Since Vance had made the Carter administration's proposals publicly, the Soviets suspected that Carter's real aim was to embarrass them further rather than to reach a real agreement.) When tempers cooled and Carter was able to sign an only marginally improved SALT II with Brezhnev in June 1979, however, the Soviets subsequently invaded Afghanistan. The invasion, coupled with his depleted political capital, forced Carter to withdraw the treaty from Senate consideration lest it fail — which it most assuredly would have.[93]

It is impossible to know what would have happened if Carter had followed his strident early accusations of Soviet human rights violations with a convincing threat of force. Ronald Reagan, who coupled even more strident anti-Soviet rhetoric with a massive military buildup — complete with the promise of a "star wars" defense system — is perhaps rightly credited with hastening the end of the cold war and the collapse of the Soviet empire. Surely if Carter had proceeded similarly he would have spoken from a text that the Soviets understood as well as one that instilled the pride of strength in the American people. Yet, it must not be forgotten that such a strategy entailed no small risk. Even in the 1980s it was not certain that the strategy would produce the desired U.S. victory; it might have foreseeably resulted in a war of horrible destruction. Jimmy Carter had no intention of taking this risk. Indeed, he neither believed nor wanted to believe that he lived in a world so awful.

So it was not until the Soviet Union invaded Afghanistan in December 1979 that Carter adopted a rhetoric of military resolve. "Let our position be absolutely clear," he finally declared in his 1980 State of the Union address. "An attempt by any outside force to gain control of the Persian Gulf region [a plausible Soviet objective for invading Afghanistan] will be regarded as an assault on the vital interests of the United States of America, and such an assault will be repelled by any means necessary, including military force." This enunciation of the "Carter doctrine" was welcomed by masses of American people. Even so, February polls showed that by a 60 to 33 percent margin the public still felt that Carter was not "tough enough" in his dealing with the Soviet Union.[94] Nor did his subsequently announced U.S. boycott of the Moscow Olympics and Soviet grain embargo strike a majority of Americans as appropriate retaliation.[95] Later, when in the summer of 1980 the press discovered that Billy Carter had hired out as a well-paid lobbyist for Libya without even bothering to file the required authorizing documents, familial embarrassment was added to the perception of Carter's vacillating foreign-policy weaknesses.

And in the way that people often prefer stories that symbolize complex issues to discussion of the issues themselves, a story that went around the nation in 1979 and 1980 seemed to symbolize public attitudes toward Jimmy Carter's foreign policy. The story, based on fact, was of a "killer rabbit."

While fishing in a pond on his farm, Carter was confronted by a swamp rabbit that struggled to climb into his boat. Rather than allow the apparently berserk rabbit into his boat, the president used his paddle to splash and otherwise dissuade the animal from entering. It was the kind of unusual fishing story that is often passed on among friends, and Carter related it to Jody Powell and a few other aides one afternoon at the White House over lemonade. Failing to anticipate the metaphorical significance of the story, Powell passed it on to an Associated Press reporter, Brooks Jackson. The reporter waited a day and then filed the human interest story for use by any newspaper needing to fill a news hole.

By the time the *Washington Post* got hold of the story, however, the news hole was apparently a gaping abyss. For they placed the story on the front page under a headline that blared: "President Attacked by Rabbit." The more reserved *New York Times* buried their "killer rabbit" story on page A-12, but that did not prevent all three major television networks from broadcasting the "story" on the evening news.

The story's symbolic significance was dutifully plumbed. Three prime ministers, a king, and heads of large U.S. corporations were all allegedly queried about their perceptions of the U.S. president's apparently timid response to the attack. The consensus of opinion was, as conservative columnist George Will reportedly told associates, that Carter's weak response to the attacking rabbit created the climate that allowed Iranian dissidents to believe they could attack the U.S. embassy with impunity. Columnist Robert Novak later added that the Soviets' invasion of Afghanistan was likewise attributable to the same rabbit-induced climate of U.S. weakness. Closer to home, Jerry Falwell noted that in the Book of Revelation swamp rabbits are associated with Satan and Carter should have summarily killed it. And on Capitol Hill, congressional leaders chortled that Carter had only himself to blame. If he had not sold the presidential yacht in a fit of populist excess, he would not have been in that godforsaken south Georgia swamp in the first place.[96]

While apparently innocuous, the "killer rabbit" story of 1979 and 1980 seemed to harness many of the more formless feelings that Americans harbored toward their president as he entered the final year of his administration. Perhaps more important, it expressed these feelings in an acceptable allegorical way. While Mark Rozell convincingly demonstrates that press coverage of Carter was by this time biased against him,[97] most journalists strove to avoid outright displays of bias in a valiant effort to remain "objective." What the real opinion of many in the media may have been, however, leaked through at least once. As a kind of in-house joke

Kirk Scharfenberg, an editorial writer on the *Boston Globe*, headlined a March 1980 editorial on a Carter economic address as "Mush from the Wimp." Striking is not merely that Scharfenberg would joke in this manner but also that the headline passed editorial censor and that 161,000 copies of the *Globe* were distributed before the error was caught and the headline changed to "All Must Share the Burden."[98] Journalistic embarrassment of this sort could be avoided by publishing stories like the "killer rabbit" — which conveyed a similar meaning allegorically.

None of which is to conclude that Americans wanted war. Surely few did. But many wanted reassurances that their nation was strong and their values certain. The last president to offer those reassurances, Richard Nixon, had failed to deliver on them largely because he was thought to possess a detestable personal character. Carter, who was always perceived to have sterling personal character, was nonetheless tardy in his enunciation of military resolve, had weak follow-through, and was bereft of domestic vision. As such and despite the defensible merits of liberal internationalism, he proved incapable of providing the nation with the deeper reassurances it craved.

"I'M AFRAID IT'S GONE"

"Fuck the Shah," retorted Carter in an unusual public use of profanity that reflected the mounting tensions in the White House. "He's just as well off playing tennis in Acapulco as he is in California."[99] The occasion of the remark is unclear but its circumstances are not. After having been supported by the United States for decades according to the logic of the very containment policy Carter rejected, the Iranian dictator was overthrown by Islamic radicals in January 1979. In exile, however, the Shah was in failing health and desperate to obtain lifesaving medical treatment in the United States. Aware that allowing the Shah to enter the United States would inflame anti-American sentiment in Iran, Carter repeatedly resisted the Shah's pleadings. The tensions mounted, however, and his resistance was worn thin by appeal to his conscience.

When Carter finally relented and allowed the Shah to enter the United States, his fears were realized. On Sunday, November 4, 1979, the U.S. Embassy in Iran was overrun by terrorists. Taking some sixty-two Americans hostage, most of whom remained in captivity for the duration of Carter's presidency, the Islamic revolutionaries paraded burning effigies of Carter and flaming American flags in front of waiting television cameras. At home the crisis produced a new television news show, *Nightline*, which every evening brought the anti-American images into the nation's living rooms.

Carter was powerless to end the crisis. A military strike, which Carter agreed would have felt good, would nevertheless almost certainly have resulted in the murder of the hostages. Even a tactical rescue attempt, plans for which had been prepared from the beginning, was thought not feasible. When in April Carter finally approved a refined plan for a rescue mission, over the objections of many, including Secretary of State Vance (who resigned over the decision), it indeed failed miserably. Blinded by swirling desert sands, first one helicopter crashed, then another. Death and embarrassment were thus added to an already desperate situation.

Nor was there a viable alternative. While Vance had insisted on steady pursuit of evenhanded negotiations rather than military engagement, the truth was that for most of the period there was no one with whom the United States could negotiate. Iran's revolutionary regime was in such diplomatic disarray that at one point Carter resorted to outfitting Hamilton Jordan with a disguise and dispatching him to secret negotiations with shadowy Frenchmen who purported to have access to the revolutionary regime's decision makers.[100] But the international espionage succeeded no better than the rescue mission. Shifting Iranian leaders, each with dubious authority over the terrorists, repeatedly proved to be unreliable negotiators. Meanwhile, Carter, whose empathic disposition inclined him to befriend the families of the hostages and share their personal anguish, was forced along with the rest of the nation to watch helplessly as Iranian protesters set his own likeness as well as the flag aflame for the reeling videotape.

Ironically, the hostage crisis helped Carter retain the nomination of his party for a second term. Had it not been for the crisis, Edward Kennedy may well have defeated him. On the day the hostages were taken, Carter's approval rating languished at 32 percent and previous polls had shown that Democrats preferred Kennedy to Carter as their nominee by a stunning 52 to 17 percent margin. By chance, however, the Sunday evening in November when the Massachusetts senator announced his challenge in a one-hour television interview with Roger Mudd proved to be an inopportune moment for the challenger. Not only was the interview aired opposite the popular movie *Jaws*, but Kennedy also amazed pundits by seeming to fumble for any real reason beyond personal ambition to justify his race against the sitting president. Worse, that very day the hostages were taken. Although the effect was not immediate, in the way that Americans rally behind their president in times of international crisis Carter soon saw his approval ratings rising. By the end of November they once again crossed the 50 percent mark; by January they approached 60 percent. Only slowly did a public that registered 61 percent approval for the way Carter was handling the Iranian crisis in January dwindle to 40 percent by late March, when Carter's approval ratings also dropped back down to the low forties and high thirties. But the public's rallying behind Carter during the crisis in Iran had lasted just long enough for him to defeat Kennedy in the early primaries using nothing more than a "rose garden strategy."[101]

Still, the Kennedy challenge did not recede. After allowing anger to get the better of him when he dismissed Kennedy's challenge by saying "I'll whip his ass," Carter did in fact win seven of the first eight primaries (losing only Kennedy's home state of Massachusetts). But by late March, as his approval ratings dipped, Carter lost decisive simultaneous primaries in Connecticut and New York. He then went on to win three more, only to lose Pennsylvania narrowly on April 22 and the District of Columbia on May 6. A string of unbroken victories was then shattered by simultaneous June 3 upsets in California, New Jersey, and New Mexico.[102] Carter was the clear winner in the primary contests and polls showed since March that Democrats nationwide favored him over Kennedy 59 to 31 percent, but both he and others suspected that every time his renomination looked certain the voters used Kennedy's candidacy as a vehicle to register "protest" votes against him.[103]

If many of the primary votes for Kennedy were actually protest votes against Carter, Kennedy chose not to interpret them this way. The refusal had some justification. Not only was Kennedy heir to his brothers' legacies but also he was a nationally prominent liberal with a well-defined domestic agenda that contrasted favorably with Carter's. Even in February, when still buoyed by the hostage crisis Carter enjoyed a 55 percent approval rating and 53 percent approval of his foreign policy, only 40 percent approved of "the way Carter is handling our domestic problems" while 52 percent disapproved.[104] In addition, until early April Jerry Brown was also in the race. Had Democrats wished only to register protest votes against Carter they might have voted for the candidate who declared in his announcement speech to the National Press Club, "My principles are simple: Protect the earth, serve the people, and explore the universe."[105] But in 1980, unlike 1976, even the Democrats seemed resigned to give up hope for a new ideology in favor of a return to the old one. Only once, when he received 11.8 percent of the vote in Wisconsin's primary, did Brown's share of the vote break into double digits in a contested primary. Presumably, the 2.9 percent of the Democrats nationwide who voted for him were true believers; a similar presumption may be extended to many of the 37.6 percent who voted for Kennedy.[106]

Whatever the rationale of voters or candidates, Kennedy took his fight all the way to the convention. The Carter forces were incensed. But Kennedy and his supporters insisted upon challenging the party's rule that bound delegates to support the candidate to whom they were pledged on the first ballot. Hoping to release delegates from this obligation, Kennedy also hoped to steal the nomination from Carter on the convention floor. The challenge was eventually turned back, but amid the wrangling and then the spectacle of a disgruntled Kennedy refusing to do more than pretend to support his party's nominee, many thought they smelled the distinct odor of Democratic defeat. Realistically, the pungent odor had been in the air for quite some time.

☆   ☆   ☆

Even before the simultaneous Kennedy challenge and hostage crisis, however, the Carter administration was reeling from a more insipid calamity that was exacerbated by both. The economy seemed to be in a tailspin as 1979 registered sharp spikes in the inflation rate coupled with unacceptably high levels of unemployment. Although an annual 1977 inflation rate below 7 percent and a 1978 rate still under 9 percent were defensible by the standards of the immediately preceding administrations (inflation in the Ford and Nixon administrations averaged 8.1 and 6.2 percent, respectively), the climb above 13 percent in 1979 was not. Indeed, in perhaps the surest sign of dour economic conditions, the measures of consumer confidence that had moved upward through 1977 and remained comfortably above the customary threshold of 100 throughout most of 1978 dropped over twenty points in 1979. The next year, as inflation remained above 12 percent, consumer confidence plummeted almost thirty more points.[107]

The causes were manifold. Among them, however, were the revolution in Iran as well as the same forces that produced the Kennedy challenge. Early in 1979 the Iranian revolution once again caused oil prices to rise, which alone accounted for 10 percent or more of that year's inflation rate.

(The core rate of inflation in 1979, meaning the cost of all items except food and energy, was approximately two percentage points lower than the overall rate.)[108] Meanwhile, on such initiatives as hospital cost containment, which Carter proposed as much for its anti-inflationary impact as for its being the first step toward a national health care policy, Kennedy and other congressional liberals balked. Aided by powerful hospital lobbies who were hedging their bets in the hopes of forestalling any reform, liberals decided to resist the president in order to wait for the more comprehensive Kennedy reform (that never came). Similarly, the unions who were solidly behind Kennedy's candidacy felt free to ignore Carter's recommended voluntary wage and price controls, while other liberal interests chaffed at any presidential urging that largesse be limited. Fighting for fiscal responsibility in such an atmosphere — and pummeled by yet another oil crisis — made Carter's economic battles tough and, for the most part, futile.

It followed that Carter's association with "an economy blighted by ballooning inflation" in response to which he proposed mere "economic doodling" was a perception not completely deserved.[109] Other evidence also suggests that both accusations were at least partially mistaken, even though the popular perception is undeniable.

In addition to keeping early inflation rates down to levels similar to those during the administrations of both Nixon and Ford, Carter also enjoyed an average annual inflation rate of only 8 percent across the whole of his term. Not only was this inflation rate similar to that under both Nixon and Ford, but it was also only 1 percent higher than the 7 percent average annual inflation rate during Reagan's first term. Moreover, given the customary assumption of a trade-off between inflation and unemployment, it merits notice that the 1 percent drop in inflation during Reagan's first term was offset by an identical increase in the average unemployment rate. Whereas unemployment during the Carter administration averaged 6.5 percent, during Reagan's it averaged 7.5 percent. (The average unemployment rate during Ford's administration was an even higher 8.1 percent.) To use the phrase then popular in political rhetoric, the "misery index" (a sum of inflation and unemployment rates) was 16.2 percent during Ford's administration and an identical 14.5 percent during both Carter's administration and Reagan's first term.[110]

Yet the trend in the inflation rate during Carter's administration was dramatically upward, doubling in only three years. Lagging slightly behind the inflation rate, interest rates also more than doubled during the Carter years. These upward trends may have concerned voters more than the administration averages did. Even so, it is not clear that voters are especially attuned to trends. The trends in both inflation and interest rates were dramatically down during Ford's administration, yet Carter still managed to reap the benefits of the economic issue in his challenge to Ford. Moreover, although slight, the rate of inflation in 1980, Carter's last year, was lower than it had been in 1979. Although interest rates, which tend to follow rather than precede evidence of inflation, continued to rise through 1980, the case could have been made by Carter in 1980 that inflation was beginning to be brought under control. Indeed, he made just this case.

Looking at economic indicators other than inflation, however, an ample number show Carter managed the economy surprisingly well. Growth in real GNP during the Carter years, for example, stood at an average 3.1 percent per year, stronger than Nixon (2.4 percent), Ford (1.8 percent), and Reagan (3 percent). The rate at which jobs were created during the Carter years was also higher than during the Nixon, Ford, or Reagan years. Corporate profits, the average value of business formations, and capital investments were also stronger during the Carter administration than during the three presidential terms surrounding his. Although real wages were slightly lower during Carter's term than Nixon's, they were higher than those under either Ford or Reagan. Similarly, while the Carter years tied the Nixon years for the lowest average poverty rate (11.9 percent), this rate was lower than Ford's (12.1 percent) and sharply lower than Reagan's (14.1 percent). The Carter administration also enjoyed the lowest business failure rate ever recorded. Meanwhile, Carter's average annual budget deficit was 10 percent lower than Ford's and only a third as large as Reagan's — and Carter was the only president ever to make a payment of principal on the national debt.[111]

The accusation that Carter was an "economic doodler" is also dubious. Although Carter may have lacked a "definite economic attitude," a deficiency that prompted Tom Wicker to conclude that his simultaneous attention to unemployment and inflation created "vacillation and reversal,"[112] Carter's chief economic advisor, Charles Schultze, was more sympathetic. "If I scratch Ronald Reagan," he said by way of illustration, "I know which way his knees are going to jerk." Such "an ideologically-oriented president doesn't have a lot of difficulty" making tough economic decisions. "The problem" that ran "right through the Carter presidency," however, was that Carter was "quite good" at understanding economic "complexity" and recognized that most economic decisions were "very close calls" that required delicate "balancing of complex issues." Admitting that a more certain ideological thrust would have likely benefited the Carter administration politically, the academic economist nevertheless clearly admired Carter's more thoughtful approach.[113]

Indeed, Schultze and other informed observers easily lay to rest any notion that Carter's economic acumen was below par. Just as his background in mathematics made it "relatively easy" for Carter's chief economic advisor in Georgia, Henry Thomassen, to convey "quantitative formulations to him [that involved] the interaction of two or three forces simultaneously," so also Schultze marveled as Carter just "snapped up, gobbled up" complex economics. "It was natural to him," concluded Schultze, illustrating his point by remembering "once watching him invent for himself the concept of marginal opportunity cost, you know, no small thing." A note from Carter to Eizenstat likewise confirms this impression of a president comfortable with technical economic issues. "Find out for me how many different econometric models we are using for international analysis and whether the CIA needs one," he wrote early in his administration. Compared to a president like John Kennedy, who is remembered to have plaintively asked his chief economic advisor, "Tell me again, how do I distinguish between monetary and fiscal policy?" Carter comes across as an economic whiz.[114]

Still, the economic trends moved against Carter's reelection. But why they did so may have had more to do with absent ideology than with limited knowledge. Indeed, in one of the most disturbing features of economic performance under Carter, it appears that the president not only failed to persuade Congress to support his economic initiatives but also was unable to inspire the public in his — or their — ability to maintain prosperity.

The disturbing economic data concern worker productivity during the Carter years. It was dramatically and inexplicably down. Despite four to ten times the average annual growth in real spending on new plants and equipment during Carter's as opposed to Ford's and Reagan's administrations, and despite higher real wages, growth in worker productivity was a whopping eighty-five times greater during the Ford years and fifty times greater during the Reagan years than during Carter's tenure. Mysteriously, American workers increased their productivity at an anemic annual rate of only .03 percent during Carter's presidency despite a strong 6.56 percent annual investment by their employers in new plants and equipment.[115]

What explains this sluggish growth in worker productivity? The harsh Hoover-like answer, which in the absence of other plausible ones might be entertained, is that workers were simply lazier during the Carter years than before or after them. But why might this have occurred? A people suffering double-digit inflation and slipping ever more perilously into malaise and selfishness may well have simply demanded more for producing less. And by the late 1970s others besides Hoover-like conservatives were proposing just such an explanation of the culture. Christopher Lasch's Marxist-Freudian critique of American society, *The Culture of Narcissism*, sounded essentially this conservative theme. And in a separate critique of the culture written solely for the administration, Lasch warned Carter of a "decline of the work ethic" and "desire to enjoy life in the present," both premised upon a "lack of faith in the future." Carter underlined the phrases.[116]

If attitudes and habits like these did arise during the late 1970s, they may have contributed to the very inflation that helped create them in the first place. An inestimable portion of inflation, after all, is created by inflationary expectations. Workers who fear inflation bid up wages even as manufacturers, gripped by the same fears, raise prices. With little or no real additional value being added to the economy, a wage-price spiral spins ever higher. Trapped inside it, workers especially but also managers are sapped of the incentives that both once thought were offered for hard work.

Stuart Eizenstat was incredulous when, worried that he "couldn't get any damn gas" for his car and "couldn't get to work to chair [his] five o'clock energy meetings," he discovered that Carter was crediting Caddell's more spiritual interpretation of the nation's woes.[117] He and Vice President Mondale insisted that the country's economic problems were rooted in real economic conditions, especially the energy crisis, and that Carter should respond in kind. Yet, while the policy-oriented liberals were right in arguing that the problems extended beyond a vague cultural malaise and had much instead to do with Carter's apparent inability to lead the country substantively, by 1979 and 1980 Carter was right to credit the cultural interpretation. Inflation, no less than the Panama Canal and the killer-rabbit story, had become symbolic of Carter's failure and the nation's decline. What was worse, the symbol was by then a self-fulfilling prophecy — creating the very reality it feared.

"You suffer because you are held to have no vision," wrote Caddell to Carter in August's preparation for the campaign against Ronald Reagan, pausing just long enough to underline the crucial sentence in his memorandum. If Carter hoped to win, Caddell insisted, he needed to set out "an idea of where you would take the country" and seek a "general mandate." Doing so would enable Carter to win in a "landslide." However, Caddell warned, "the greatest argument against you is the idea that the next four years will be like the last four."[118] For four years Carter had attempted to govern without vision and so without a mandate. Any hope he had of governing for four more, Caddell urged one last time, depended upon his remedying this deficiency.

But no evidence exists that Reagan enjoyed a mandate, either, despite the success conservatives later had in imposing one upon his victory. On such Christian Coalition issues as women's rights (support for the Equal Rights Amendment), for instance, the electorate split 45 to 35 percent in favor of Carter. Yet more pro-ERA voters supported Reagan than anti-ERA voters supported Carter, as only 15 percent of the women and 7 percent of the men named this as a deciding issue in the campaign.[119] Indeed, while a huge 87 percent of the public still judged Carter to be "a religious person" in mid-September and only 40 percent held the same view of Reagan, a sizable chunk of the evangelical Christians who had supported Carter in 1976 swung back into the Republican fold in 1980.[120] Similarly, on less overtly moral issues like the choice between cutting taxes and balancing the federal budget, by a 53 to 30 percent margin voters supported Carter's more restrained balanced-budget position over Reagan's tax-cutting proposals. Despite his favored position on the issue, however, Carter lost to Reagan among both groups by almost identical percentages. It was not until Reagan was elected that Colorado congresswoman Patricia Schroeder popularly nicknamed him the "Teflon President" for his uncanny ability to keep controversial issues from "sticking" to him. But his issue-deflecting ability was already apparent in the 1980 election. Whether people agreed or disagreed with Reagan on the issues, the swing to the Republican candidate in 1980 was measurable and unmistakable. And the Gallup poll concluded that "the vote for President-elect

Ronald Reagan was more a vote against President Carter than for Reagan" even as it was "less enthusiastic than in earlier presidential elections."[121]

The evidence suggests that the voters made up their minds in 1980 largely on the bases of three broader thematic issues. The evidence further suggests that while Carter was favored on one of these thematic issues, Reagan was favored on the other two — a two-to-one advantage that only slightly overpredicts the eventual 51 to 41 percent vote.[122]

One of the broader issues was the economy. Although there is little evidence that the majority of the electorate was persuaded by the theory of "supply-side" economics, polls clearly showed that the economy was an overriding voter concern in 1980. Preelection polls indicate that by a 44 to 28 percent margin voters expected Reagan to be more successful than Carter in reducing inflation. They were less convinced that Reagan would do a better job than Carter at reducing unemployment, but still gave the Republican candidate the edge 41 to 32 percent. Perhaps, just as voters elected Franklin Roosevelt in 1932 hoping that he would at least "try something," the majority cast their lots for Reagan. Worse for the Democrats, the year became the first one in which the public's long-standing perception of the Democrats' superior ability to manage prosperity was replaced with a more prevalent popular faith in Republicans. From the first Democratic president since Grover Cleveland to preside over a recession, the voters seemed to be extracting a due not unlike they had when they ousted Cleveland and ushered in three decades of Republican presidential rule.[123]

The other two most important themes of the campaign reflected a division in the usually united foreign-policy views. Reagan was perceived to be the candidate of foreign-policy strength — and this portion of the issue benefited him. However, when the question was which candidate would be more likely to preserve peace, the solid edge went to Carter. Americans, who still approved of Carter personally, were enthusiastically supportive of his peacemaking skills. By a two-to-one margin (49 to 25 percent for women, 50 to 26 percent for men), the public believed that Carter was more likely than Reagan to keep the country out of war. Moreover, a midcampaign survey showed Carter favored over Reagan 43 to 37 percent on the general issue of "foreign relations." However, by the sole late-campaign debate when Carter referred to his daughter Amy's fears of nuclear war while Reagan managed to reassure voters that he was not unduly militaristic, many experts concluded that even the general "foreign relations" issue tilted to Reagan's advantage. Carter seemed silly; Reagan confident and restrained. Had Reagan not benefited from a stolen copy of Carter's briefing book, most believed that the debate still would have gone to him on the themes. Carter was granted the peace issue, but the strength issue combined with the economic issue gave Reagan the overall edge.[124]

Even so, the voters waffled. Preelection polls taken by both Gallup and ABC News/Harris in the days immediately preceding the election showed Reagan ahead by only three and five percentage points, respectively, while a *Newsweek* poll showed Carter ahead by a percentage point. The week before, Gallup showed Carter defeating Reagan by six points among "likely voters." And exit polls later revealed that by the same record percentage discovered in 1976 fully 17 percent of the voters waited until the final two weeks of the campaign to make up their minds, while a higher percentage than ever (9 percent) waited until the day of the election. Carter had severe disadvantages. Independent candidate John Anderson was taking more votes from him than from Reagan, and the election was ominously scheduled on the very date that marked the anniversary of the hostage taking in Tehran. Still, through the weekend preceding the vote it was anybody's race.[125]

"Kaboom," said Caddell to the assembled Carter aides at the White House when he arrived at 2:00 on the morning of the election with the results of his election-eve poll. It was the first anyone knew of the outcome. Looking devastated in his rumpled jeans, Caddell explained that the undecideds were bolting for Reagan. "A lot of working Democrats are going to wake up tomorrow and for the first time in their lives vote Republican," he added. To illustrate the magnitude of the defeat, Caddell pointed to the globe. Carter, who was then in Seattle for an election-eve rally, would fly back to Georgia without passing over a single state he would win.[126]

Someone had to tell Carter. The call went out to Powell, who was with him in Seattle. But Powell could not bring himself to break the news. A second call went out. Carter snatched the phone, "What's happening, Patrick?"

"Mr. President, I'm afraid it's gone."

Emotionless, Carter instructed the team "to draft something I can say in Plains that might help" and then asked them not to say anything to Rosalynn. He wanted to tell her himself.[127]

That morning, Caddell believed that the loss was attributable mostly to undecided Democrats who were frustrated with both the economy and the hostage crisis. But that was just the proximal explanation. The larger one, which Caddell had insisted upon both at the outset of the administration and again just before the 1980 general election campaign, was that Americans were desperate for "a new ideology or progress" and "vision" to direct them. Without that, the people suffered from malaise, Carter was unable to govern effectively, and he lost his bid for reelection.

Polls confirm this interpretation. Whereas a preelection survey showed that a staggering 83 percent of the public continued to believe that Carter was "a man of high moral principles," less than a third of the public believed he was able to translate these principles into a governing vision. The same survey showed that only 27 percent thought Carter had "a well-defined program for moving the country ahead." Suggestive of the importance the public placed on a program of progress as opposed to personal morality, only 31 percent agreed that Carter possessed "strong leadership qualities."[128]

Worse, by the same percentage he lost to Reagan, Carter's supporters simply stayed home from the polls in 1980. Had those who voted for Carter in 1976 and who still supported him four years later bothered to vote, Carter might have won. But in an election with a voter turnout even lower than in 1976, Carter simply failed to inspire his supporters to make the minimal November trip to the polls.[129]

☆   ☆   ☆

In a foretaste of what was to come, as well as a reflection of his character, Carter achieved perhaps his most significant victories during his remaining presidential months. He continued to work tirelessly for the release of the hostages, who ultimately left captivity during the very hour his term ended. He also pressed the lame-duck Congress, which partly because of his defeat was losing many of its Democratic members (the Senate would enjoy a Republican majority for the first time in a generation), hard on environmental legislation. Working in relative harmony for almost the first time since he was elected, the president and Congress succeeded in passing both a bill to protect vast areas of Alaska from environmental destruction and the Superfund legislation, which forced polluters to pay for cleanup. The two bills may, ironically, be his most enduring domestic achievements.

Then, following a final weekend at Camp David, the Carters stopped at the fishing camp where Jimmy and his father used to take their summer trips. Involuntarily leaving elective office, and embarrassed by it, he was also, Kirbo apprised him about the finances he had placed in a blind trust during his presidency, almost broke. Young enough to do something else and poor enough to need to, Carter began considering his options. As a going-away present his staff had given him a complete set of woodworking tools. But while Carter turned with therapeutic relish to the furniture-making projects that had long attracted him, he knew he had to do more to make his life meaningful.

CHAPTER 9

JIMMY CARTER AT SEVENTY

On a steamy June Tuesday in 1994, his seventieth year, Jimmy Carter joined a small ceremony on the grounds of the state capitol in Atlanta to observe the unveiling of a bronze commemorative sculpture of himself. Positioned on a small granite plaza, the sculpture depicts the former governor and president as a populist "working man" dressed in khaki pants and a work shirt with sleeves rolled up. The statue's arms reach out in a gesture of humanitarian openness while the face is purposely indistinct, lacking most noticeably the characteristic Carter grin. Believing that Carter's smile had become so overused as to suggest caricature, sculptor Frederick Hart chose to omit it. His intent, he explained, was to portray Jimmy Carter as something of an "everyman": one who represents the humanitarian potential in all of us.

The crowd was small but adoring. Present were several dozen dignitaries and former Carter associates, many of whom had contributed to the $400,000 memorial. Also present were perhaps a hundred or two more average citizens. To the assembled well-wishers, Carter confessed to understandably "mixed emotions" about being honored in life by the kind of tribute usually paid only posthumously. He said he was "grateful and proud" but "at the same time ... embarrassed." Then, searching for words to please his largely Georgian audience, the former president repeated a view he had often stated over the preceding decade. The significance of his presidency, he said, had receded in his memory over the years in favor of memories of the "full life" he had led before and after it as a "Georgian" and a "southerner."[1]

To many at the ceremony, the tribute the commemorative statue paid to Jimmy Carter was long overdue. While some reservations had surfaced during the planning stages about the ability of the crowded capitol grounds to absorb another monument (its eighth), no one went on record opposing the addition. Many remarked instead that the statue was only slightly larger than life-size, that it blended tastefully with the surrounding landscape, and that it was an appropriate "final" addition to the pantheon of Georgia leaders that graced the capitol grounds.[2] And at least one onlooker's spontaneous outburst of emotion seemed to reflect the dominant spirit of those assembled for the unveiling. Cecil Randolph reached out to touch the outstretched hands of the sculpture and explained, "There are so many people he's helped. I had to touch him."[3]

It had not always been so good for Jimmy Carter. Just ten years before, a tribute of the sort he enjoyed in Atlanta would have been unimaginable. Then, Meg Greenfield of the *Washington Post* found that Carter was suffering an "unfair fate" as a "shunned figure." Observing that "no one seems willing or able, in or out of Georgia, to give him a break or bit of dignity on anything," Greenfield thought that public attitudes toward Carter were actually "getting more hostile" than they had been when he lost his reelection bid.[4]

Stimulating the growing hostility toward Carter in 1984 was that year's presidential election, the first since Carter's ignoble defeat in 1980. Reagan aides were quoted in late 1983 saying that "whoever" the Democratic nominee might be he would "be much harder to beat in 1984 than Jimmy Carter was in 1980."[5] Explaining the Republican attitude the next week, syndicated columnist James Kilpatrick concluded that "Carter was to Reagan what Hoover was to Roosevelt." With "soaring inflation, the hostages, the malaise, the tree house he built for his nuclear expert [Amy], the whole maliciously wicked business of Dogpatch on the Avenue," Kilpatrick admitted that Republicans found Carter to be "a lovely lump to kick around." Never mind that even in 1980 the attacks were "brutally unfair"; Carter was such a "beautiful target to assail" that the GOP could not resist doing it again in 1984.[6]

The Democrats were no more approving. Trying to wrest the Democratic nomination from front-runner Walter Mondale, Ohio senator John Glenn attacked the former vice president for the "failed, disastrous policies" of the Carter administration "that gave us 21 percent interest rates and 17 percent inflation rates."[7] For his part, Mondale avoided appearing in public with Carter and took pains to dissociate himself from unpopular Carter policies, like the Soviet grain embargo, which he really had opposed.

Dissenting opinions were few. Syndicated columnists Jack Germond and Jules Witcover, virtually alone, judged the Carter connection a small plus for Mondale. However, the minuscule benefits that accrued to Mondale as a result of his association with Carter rested upon little more than Carter's continuing popularity among African Americans and Mondale's ability to tout his experience as a vice president. But few doubted that African Americans would flock to the Democratic party anyway, and even Germond and Witcover noted that Mondale was "sounding for all the world that he was really vice president in the administration of President Hubert Humphrey."[8] Most Democrats therefore concurred with their party leaders who, uncomfortable with the idea of excluding their only living ex-president from their summer convention altogether, split the difference by stipulating in their invitation to him that he could not speak at prime time or on a subject other than foreign policy.

Nor was the larger political culture of the early and middle 1980s conducive to admiration of the president Ronald Reagan had defeated. After hovering around the low forties and even dipping occasionally into the thirties during 1982 and most of 1983, Reagan's approval ratings rebounded to over 50 percent in November 1983 and remained comfortably above the halfway mark throughout 1984. Indeed, although it may have only reflected the success of Reagan's reelection campaign, confidence in the presidency as an institution rose to 42 percent in November 1984, higher than it had been since the mid-1960s. (Since March 1984 polls showed this confidence at only 19 percent, and November 1985 and March 1986 polls showed it at 30 and 21 percent, respectively, however, the 42 percent confidence rating proved to be a temporary aberration.) At 44 percent in 1984, trust in government in general also stood at the highest level since 1972 (though it too was lower both before and after this temporary high).[9]

Even Reagan's critics found themselves forced to admit the renewed American confidence. *Washington Post* syndicated columnist Mary McGrory, for example, flailed Reagan for instituting "policies that are hard on people, even mean" and for "shamelessly choos[ing] guns over butter." Yet even she recognized that Americans were "less cynical and pessimistic" in 1984 than they had been in 1980, a turnaround she attributed to Reagan's "image."[10] But the image *was* culturally important. For a majority of voters Reagan's sensationally effective 1984 "morning in

America" commercial spoke to their genuine feelings of renewed pride and resurgent patriotism, regardless of their awareness or approval of his policies.[11]

The pride and patriotism sparked by Reagan were not limited to him; rather, America in the early 1980s was a nation brimming with renewed confidence. *Dallas* and its imitator *Dynasty* riveted television viewers with the guts and glamour of the self-made superrich. In film, the *Rambo* (1982, 1985, 1988), *Indiana Jones* (1984, 1989), and *Star Wars* (1977, 1980, 1983) series showed strong and successful American heroes pitted against unambiguous evils — and in the case of Rambo that strength was consciously juxtaposed with the preceding weakness of U.S. policy in Vietnam. Meanwhile, films like *An Officer and a Gentleman* (1982) and *Flashdance* (1983) perpetuated the myth of individual opportunity in America. In books, the top-selling nonfiction title of 1983 was *In Search of Excellence*, a book about corporate management, by Thomas J. Peters and Robert H. Waterman Jr., while trailing the top-seller in the number-four position was one by California's minister of the giant Crystal Cathedral, Robert H. Schuller's *Tough Times Don't Last but Tough People Do*. In popular music, which may have enjoyed waning influence during the 1980s, owing to proliferation of markets and splintering of the medium, the "Reagan revolution" was nevertheless able to appropriate Lee Greenwood's "I'm Proud to Be an American" even as the theme songs of both *An Officer and a Gentleman* and *Flashdance* became number one hits in late 1982 and mid-1983, respectively.

Perhaps nothing illustrated America's culture of resurgent nationalism, or its power to co-opt contrary sentiments, than the fate of Bruce Springsteen's 1984 "Born in the USA" tour. Although the New Jersey rock star openly opposed Reagan, refused to appear in public with him, and wrote songs (including "Born in the USA") that were bitterly critical of the country, both the president and conservative columnist George Will heralded Springsteen as a champion of their cause. Like the effort to attract blue-collar voters, the effort to enlist the working-class "Boss" into the conservative cause worked. During his 1984 concert tour Springsteen was often as not greeted by fans who waved American flags.[12]

If even a popular working-class troubadour could find his message so mangled, how much more likely was it that growing hostility would attach itself to Ronald Reagan's predecessor — who was popularly remembered for having harped on the nation's limits, complained about collective malaise, presided over an inflationary economy, and endured a year-long hostage crisis after having "given away" the Panama Canal?

Nor, as Greenfield also noted, were Carter's fellow Georgians willing to "give him a break." A 1983 column by a person of no less stature than the political-page editor of the *Atlanta Journal*, Frederick Allen, castigated him viciously. "An awful lot of folks in Georgia are growing deathly tired of Jimmy Carter," wrote Allen. They were tired of Carter's "self-importance," of his "acting like a stuffed shirt" and "puffing up like a blowfish." So Allen decided to tell Carter in print what he assumed his fellow Georgians wanted to say to his face: "Oh, shut up." Explaining the collective Georgian attitude, Allen said: "We've always felt a little guilty about palming Carter off on the other 49 states," and "we don't appreciate having him around as a constant reminder."[13]

Although Allen had no way of knowing that within two weeks of his column Lillian Carter would die, he was obviously oblivious to Carter's feelings. For he did choose to publish his column only three weeks after Ruth Carter Stapleton passed away, prematurely, at fifty-four. The sister to whom Jimmy had often turned for comfort in times of distress, and Rosalynn's best childhood friend, Ruth had been expecting a miracle, only to succumb to the same cancer of the pancreas that killed her father at almost the same age. Her passing, however, exerted few restraints on the venomous expression of hostility toward Carter.

The public hostility exacerbated the Carters' other problems. Although contracts for their memoirs (*Keeping Faith* and *First Lady from Plains*) together with the sale of their heavily mortgaged peanut warehouse relieved them of the debt they confronted when leaving the White House, progress was slow on their hope of eventually building a library, museum, and policy center in Atlanta. At home, neighborhood residents protested the highway (renamed the "presidential parkway") slated to connect the Carter Center with Atlanta's other major arteries, and a prolonged policy skirmish erupted between Carter and Atlanta's in-town neighborhood groups. Away from home, things were not much better. Although Carter had some luck soliciting much needed donations from foreign businessmen, his fund-raising abilities in his own country were sometimes embarrassing. At a 1983 New York fund-raising auction fewer than 100 people bothered to attend (including aides and reporters), and many items donated by celebrities were sold at half their value.[14]

The plaintive tone of Carter's opening remarks to scholars interviewing him in late 1982 is therefore understandable. "It's very encouraging to me to know that there will be an objective and fairly definitive analysis of what did occur," he remarked about an administration many believed had failed. Indeed, he added, "I'm eager to cooperate as much as possible." And if anyone from his administration resisted participating, Carter promised, he still had "some influence" over them and would use it to persuade them to comply. He also volunteered his willingness to return for "follow-up" questions, should any be desired. He was, in short, eager to please and had ample time on his hands to do so.[15]

More privately, John and Betty Pope, the Carters' old friends from Sumter County, also recall the plaintive tone of Jimmy and Rosalynn's early requests to get together. It seemed to the Popes that the Carters were unbearably lonely. So, after the Carters spent their first Fourth of July out of office at the Popes' mountain cabin near Ellijay, Georgia, their hosts offered to carve twenty acres out of their tract for the Carters. Jimmy and Rosalynn bought the property, and for the next two years spent most of their free time building their mountain cabin. Every piece of furniture in it was handmade by the former president — who had little else to do.

Yet, barely a decade later Carter found himself neither shunned by the public nor relegated to his mountain cabin on the periphery of events. As spring turned to summer in 1994 Carter was once again at Georgia's state capitol enjoying a tribute in bronze that only seven of his predecessors had received. Moreover, he was very much a player in world events.

That very summer — scheduled around a July week building houses for the poor on a South Dakota Sioux reservation, an August trip to Africa to work toward eradicating Guinea worm disease and river blindness, and September visits to both the world population conference in Cairo and a conference on media in Moscow — Carter was once again catapulted to the national and international limelight. The notoriety followed two dramatic achievements. In late June he successfully diffused tensions between North and South Korea, bringing both to the negotiating table and averting a dangerous confrontation with the United States over North Korea's nuclear weapons buildup. Then, in September — while invading planes were in the air — he headed the negotiating team that won a peaceful transfer of power in Haiti and halted the hostile U.S. invasion there.

The accolades that followed were swift and broad. The public at large was mostly approving. Although when president Carter had endured the lowest approval ratings ever recorded and a 1992 poll found his national approval rating still only a modest 41 percent, by late September 1994 a *Wall Street Journal*/NBC News poll discovered that 60 percent of Americans held a positive view of him. Carter's negative ratings also dropped to 15 percent, less than half of what they had been two years previously and about a quarter of what they had been during much of 1979 and 1980.[16] Moreover, these national ratings trailed those in his home state, where by 1990 he was already approved of by 74 percent of his fellow Georgians.[17]

Capitalizing on this rising popularity, the October 3, 1994, issue of *Time* magazine once again featured Carter on its cover, while other news magazines and newspapers covered his achievements with only slightly less fanfare. At home, the Sunday *Atlanta Journal/Constitution* had little use for the criticisms of a decade earlier and ran a front-page feature followed by two full pages of text and photographs in celebration of his seventieth birthday.[18] There was even speculation that the Nobel Peace Prize, which many thought he deserved in 1978 for the Camp David Accords (and for which he was rumored to be nominated on five separate occasions), would be awarded to him later on October 14.[19] When it was bestowed on others, Carter's 1994 accolades were diminished only marginally.

Critics, of course, continued to fault Carter — or at least to urge restraint of praise until the final consequences of his actions became known. Twice during the summer, for example, *New York Times* columnist William Safire linked Carter to President Bill Clinton — and criticized both together under editorials entitled "Jimmy Clinton" and "Jimmy Clinton II."[20] Writing in *Newsday*, Murray Kempton saw his editorial critical of Carter published again in the *New York Review of Books*. According to Kempton, Carter's "lust to be a public man once more" prompted him to engage in activities, some of them dubious, that were orchestrated "to persuade voters that they were wrong not to reelect a saint."[21] Others, boasting but clear heads and hard noses, simply tried to do their journalistic job. Thus, the *San Francisco Examiner* headlined an Associated Press story about Carter's Korean negotiations, "Carter: 'Dupe' or Statesman?" while Richard Matthews asked on the editorial page of the *Atlanta Journal*, after the Haitian negotiations, "Will Carter's Kind of Peace Really Save Lives?"[22] These latter kinds of pieces, however, merely urged that praise for Carter be tempered by caution. And on the whole Carter's critics were outnumbered by his supporters by a more pronounced ratio than ever before in his career.

This, the final phase of Carter's tumultuous public career, may hence be among the most revealing of this still enigmatic American moralist.

THE REHABILITATION OF JIMMY CARTER

Before his 1980 defeat, but as the campaign seemed to falter, Betty Pope told Carter, "You don't need this trash." She felt that the Lord meant for him to get out of politics and predicted that he had "something more to give."[23] Although it was not until 1987 that readers were able to glimpse the Carters' postpresidential vision through their jointly authored book, *Everything to Gain: Making the Most of the Rest of Your Life,* the first public recognition that Carter had something more to give may have occurred earlier, even in his darkest hour.

The week after Mondale kicked off his 1984 presidential campaign by marching down Fifth Avenue in New York's annual Labor Day parade, reporters could not fail to notice that Jimmy Carter was also in town. Unlike Mondale, however, Carter was not on Fifth Avenue; he was at a burned-out apartment building on the Lower East Side. Also unlike Mondale, Carter had not arrived by plane only to be whisked about town in a limousine to visit and dine with the powerful; he had arrived on a Trailways bus that stopped at a Burger King. He was — the journalists were incredulous — a volunteer for Habit for Humanity, devoting a week to rehabilitating the devastated apartment building. Not only was he suitably attired for the endeavor, wearing work clothes and a hard hat, but he also seemed genuinely intent upon working. He expressed annoyance only when a reporter tripped over the cord to his electric saw, causing it to come unplugged and interrupting his carpentry.[24]

The jokes quickly followed. One comedian suggested that Carter might consider becoming a guest host of PBS's home repair show. Yet, as poverty rates rose to their highest level in decades and federal funds for low- and moderate-income housing were slashed by eighty-five percent, Americans were increasingly confronted by the specter of homelessness.[25] The thoughtful may well have doubted whether a small volunteer program like Habitat for Humanity would have a substantial impact on the nation's housing crisis, but it was difficult to fault the charity for trying. Even more, it was difficult to fault Carter for expressing the spirit of voluntarism and pitching in where the need was so great.

Later Carter marveled over the power his week-long volunteer work with Habitat for Humanity had in reshaping his reputation. Actually, the charitable program was neither his brainchild nor one formally associated with his presidential center. Habitat for Humanity was an outgrowth of Koinonia Farm, the racially integrated Christian community that had long struggled for survival in the hinterland of his boyhood. Virtually defunct after the 1969 death of its founder, Clarence Jordan, an Alabama lawyer in search of deeper spiritual fulfillment, Millard Fuller, sought to rejuvenate it in 1976. While serving as a missionary in Zaire, Fuller originated the concept of using volunteers to build homes for the poor, who would pay for the houses both with their own labor and through interest-free mortgages. Approaching Carter with his plan for Habitat early in the 1980s, the ex-president at first agreed only to serve on the board of directors. But, when his mountain cabin was finished and Carter too found himself desiring deeper spiritual fulfillment, he finally relented in 1984 to volunteer a week of his time to the actual construction and rehabilitation of dwellings. A decade later, when Carter joined the other volunteers on the Sioux reservation, it was his eleventh consecutive year as a Habitat volunteer.

While Habitat snatched the headlines, Carter's broader vision rested with the as yet uncompleted Carter Center. The vision was twofold. First, instead of simply building a library that would stand as a monument to his presidency, Carter hoped to create an interactive museum that would offer "one helluva civics lesson."[26] Second, Carter hoped to establish a policy center that would take an active and ongoing role in solving world problems. In particular, Carter recognized that most of the world's conflicts are civil wars in which the United Nations is forbidden by its charter to intervene and in which many countries are also reluctant to intervene. A policy center allied with both the Centers for Disease Control and Emory University that was further bolstered by his prestige as a former U.S. president and architect of a Middle East peace might therefore successfully intervene in global crises where others could not.

Even before the Carter Center officially opened in 1986 the dual vision began to take shape. Contracting architect Henri Jova V and his Honolulu firm with Lawton, Umemura & Tamaoto for the $25 million complex, Carter oversaw designs for a generally understated cluster of small, cylindrical buildings partially submerged beneath hills from which General Sherman once viewed the burning of Atlanta. Resulting in part by donations from wealthy Japanese philanthropists, Japanese gardens were then added to the cluster. As for the museum itself, it was outfitted with an interactive video system that allows visitors to receive answers from Carter to some 200 commonly asked questions.

The policy center also took early shape. Two programs established during his presidency but abandoned by Reagan, Friendship Force and Global 2000, were quietly resurrected as private charities by Carter during the early 1980s. An international program of person-to-person exchange, Friendship Force places residents of the United States in foreign homes and foreign residents here, with the goal of fostering enhanced cross-national understanding. Global 2000, essentially a world health task force, quickly allied itself with the Centers for Disease Control and by the middle 1980s already identified the eradication of Guinea worm disease as its chief objective. Unknown in the industrial world but affecting some ten million people throughout Africa as well as in India and Pakistan, the Guinea worm grows inside the body after its larva is ingested through contaminated drinking water. When after about a year it reaches its mature length of nearly three feet, it erupts through a painful, fist-sized sore that leaves the victim incapacitated for weeks. If Guinea worm disease is eradicated (as of this writing it persists), it will be the first time in history that the West has eliminated a disease that it does not itself suffer and only the second time a disease will have been fully eradicated on earth (the first was smallpox).

While these programs were taking shape, Carter spent the early and middle 1980s preparing for even more intractable human struggles. Invited to deliver an inaugural lecture in Macon under the auspices of the 1983 Carl Vinson Memorial Lecture Series, Carter used the opportunity to hone his views on negotiating strategies. The effort resulted in a slim book, *Negotiation: The Alternative to Hostility.* Simultaneously, he undertook a careful study of the Middle East. Although lacking source citations and other staples of scholarship, Carter's 1985 *The Blood of Abraham: Inside the Middle East* was generally heralded as a thoughtful and responsible assessment of the region's historic tensions. Carter hoped, moreover, that the effort would reap immediate dividends: the first major conference scheduled for the freshly opened Carter Center was one with Middle East leaders. Indeed, through frequent foreign trips that doubled as both fundraising and learning ventures, Carter continued to immerse himself in world problems in preparation for addressing them as head of his policy center.

Still, the unfolding vision of the Carter Center did not meet instant or automatic approval. Learning about it in 1984, Frederick Allen, for one, was not enthused. To Allen, Carter's museum amounted to little more than a "'Jimmyland' attraction for the city's school kids, tourists and conventioneers," while his policy center was just "Camp David South."[27] Such opinions of Jimmy Carter were still very much in evidence.

But a year later, Bill Shipp was less caustic. Noting in November 1985 that Carter aides admitted that the center was confronting "cash-flow problems," Shipp followed Carter to Atlanta's Rotary Club. Recalling that "in the 1980 presidential election, Carter undoubtedly lost the Atlanta Rotary Club vote by a sizable margin," Shipp wondered aloud whether "this upscale crowd of mostly white businessmen" could be persuaded to "see Carter as an asset to the community" and support his center. But the longtime Carter-watcher concluded his column by reporting that Carter had recently trudged through four feet of snow to reach an altitude of 18,500 feet on Mt. Everest and claimed that he could have gone farther had he not run out of time. The implication was clear: such a man was in the habit of reaching his goals, even when others considered them ludicrous.[28]

Ironically, it may have been Ronald Reagan who ultimately nudged Carter to the summit. Invited along with other dignitaries to the formal opening of the Jimmy Carter Presidential Center on October 1, 1986, Carter's sixty-second birthday, Reagan stunned the assembled crowd with a warm and enthusiastic speech.

"Your countrymen have vivid memories of your time in the White House still," said the president about his former opponent. "They see you working in the Oval Office at your desk with an air of intense concentration; repairing to a quiet place to receive the latest word on the hostages you did so much to free; or studying in your hideaway office for the meeting at Camp David that would mark such a breakthrough for peace in the Middle East." Such memories prompted Reagan to offer with apparent genuineness: "You gave yourself to your country, gracing the White House with your passion and intellect and commitment."

Reagan did admit to political differences — but he celebrated them. "We can be proud of our differences," Reagan insisted, "because they arise from goodwill — from love of country, from concern for the challenges of our times, from respect for . . . the democratic processes."

He also touched on Carter's regional greatness. "The story of President

Carter is a story of the South," he said. "For when Jimmy Carter was born on this date in 1924, many southerners knew only poverty and millions lived lives that were separate and unequal because of the color of their skin." Noting that "the world has changed now . . . because men and women like Jimmy Carter stood up in church to protest the exclusion of black people from worship," Reagan proceeded to quote the famous lines from Carter's inaugural address to the hushed audience: "'I say to you quite frankly that the time for racial discrimination is over. No poor, rural, weak or black person should ever again have to bear the additional burden of being deprived of the opportunity of an education, a job or simple justice.'" The South changed, Reagan also volunteered, because "Jimmy Carter spoke those words in his inaugural address as governor of Georgia."

Then the sitting president credited his political opponent with "perhaps the most basic value of all, the value of faith." Indeed, said Reagan, "Yours is a story of dedication to so many of the fundamental values that made our nation flourish and grow great."

The *Atlanta Journal* was ecstatic, covering the speech in a long article beginning on page one, and conspicuously absent were the nay-sayers of just a year before. Indeed, the next morning the *Atlanta Constitution* editorialized: "[T]hanks for everything, Mr. President" (referring to Carter). Meanwhile, Carter himself was pleased but humbled. All he could say when the Reagan oration concluded was, "As I listened to you speak a few minutes ago, I understood more clearly than I ever have before in my life why you won in November 1980 and I lost." Even so, by 1986 most of the old political wounds had healed. Carter was no longer interested in a political career, having succeeded in establishing what Bill Shipp considered "maybe Carter's grandest achievement" in the Carter Center.[29]

A fledgling "draft Carter" movement did arise during the 1988 presidential campaign, but its efforts were limited to New Jersey, where candidates can be placed on the primary ballot without their consent. (Organizers never succeeded in getting the required thousand signatures, however, and Carter's name did not appear on the ballot.) More revealing of Carter's rising political capital was Delaware senator Joseph Biden's willingness to break Democratic ranks and openly solicit his endorsement for his bid for the 1988 presidential nomination. Although the hoped-for endorsement was not forthcoming (Carter has generally expressed continuing Democratic loyalty while refusing to endorse primary candidates), Biden did opt to meet publicly with Carter at his presidential center rather than privately as the press reported the other candidates did.[30] Later, another unsuccessful primary contender, Bruce Babbitt, volunteered a guest editorial praising the former president.[31]

Meanwhile, the *Los Angeles Times* editorialized approvingly that in addition to the book writing and "sulking" that dominate the activities of most ex-presidents, Carter "is still working hard on achieving what eluded him in office." Indeed, concluded the *Times*, "Our 39th president is a prophet without honor in his own land, and that is a shame."[32] Noting that revisionist accounts of the Carter presidency were also beginning to appear in such disparate places as the *New Republic* and the *Wall Street Journal*, Democratic organizers not only decided to invite Carter to address their 1988 convention during prime time and with no restrictions, but also chose Atlanta as the site for their convention. The "Carter factor," concluded leading Democrats, was still not a "positive," but it was "neutralized as a negative."[33] A summer 1988 poll found that Americans approved of the Carter presidency by a 47 to 43 percent margin.[34]

But the less-than-majority support for the remembered Carter presidency still prompted many Republicans to target the Carter administration for criticism. Early in his campaign George Bush reminded voters who had to choose between him and Michael Dukakis, the former Massachusetts governor, about the last time they "gambled back in the '70s on an unknown governor." (Presumably Reagan was a *known* governor, so no "gamble.") But some Republican strategists urged Bush to curtail his criticism of Carter, thinking it might backfire. Carter also counterattacked. "My name is Jimmy Carter and I'm not running for president," he told delegates to the Democratic convention in a paraphrase of his famous introduction. But then he added: "Did you hear that, George?" With experts and advisors debating the political merits of yet another Republican presidential campaign mounted against the memory of Carter, Bush decided to delegate most of the Carter-bashing to his running mate, Dan Quayle. Thus the denigration of Carter continued even into the Bush administration as something of a sideshow, delighting those who agreed but minimized before more mainstream audiences.[35]

Carter's rising esteem enabled him to challenge publicly conservative policies he believed mistaken. In 1987, after Reagan nominated Robert Bork for a seat on the Supreme Court, Carter sent a letter to the Senate

Judiciary Committee considering the nomination deriding Bork's views, especially on civil rights, as "particularly obnoxious." Seizing upon the Iran-Contra scandal in a speech the same year at Princeton University, Carter declared that "the morality issue is becoming a matter of transcendental importance." In published remarks made at the Carter Center a few weeks later, he criticized the United States for contributing to human-rights violations around the world by being in default on its payment of dues to both the United Nations and the Organization of American States. Earlier in the year he publicly sided with his daughter Amy, who was arrested along with Abbie Hoffman for protesting covert CIA activities in Central America. The CIA's activities, Carter said, were "improper and illegal." The next year he participated just long enough in a conference on "Theology, Politics and Peace," cosponsored by Emory University and the Carter Center, to deliver a speech that castigated the pope, academic theologians, and especially fundamentalists within his own southern Baptist denomination for failing to deal adequately with world problems.[36]

Even so, Carter reserved most of his energies for his international work. Forming an International Negotiating Network (INN) supported in part by the United Nations and a host of other private and public sponsors, Carter did convene a conference that searched for a Middle East peace. Although there was no "breakthrough," most believed that the talks fostered an improved climate for future negotiations. A similar verdict was pronounced after the Carter Center coordinated talks between the Ethiopian government and the Eritrean Liberation front, who had been at war since 1961. A resolution was not reached, but additional dialogues were scheduled.

Carter also helped to establish the Council of Freely Elected Heads of Government, an international consortium headquartered at the Carter Center and devoted to promoting democracy in the Americas. Under its auspices, Carter led the team that monitored Panama's 1989 elections — and which declared General Manuel Noriega's victory a fraud. Invited then to monitor elections in Nicaragua, Carter quietly persuaded the Bush administration to cancel its plans to funnel $3 million in aid to candidate Violeta Barrios de Chamorro, so that the election could be held without undue foreign influence; Chamorro won, anyway. A subsequent invitation to monitor elections in Haiti then prepared the way for Carter's successful aversion of the 1994 U.S. invasion there and the restoration of Jean-Bertrand Aristide to power without bloodshed.

Meanwhile, Carter enlisted the support of Houston philanthropist

Dominique de Menil to establish a $100,000 Carter-Menil Human Rights Prize, awarded annually (beginning in 1985) in recognition of a person's or group's contribution to global human rights. (The award is similar to the Nobel Peace Prize.) Simultaneously, the former president continued to travel the globe in his own quest for human rights and launched an increasingly voluminous barrage of articles and editorials to the nation's leading newspapers and magazines to support his objectives.

Global 2000 expanded its work. In China, for instance, Carter helped initiate a program to provide artificial limbs for amputees. Even so, the primary focus remained Africa, where as a former farmer Carter was especially excited about introducing new seeds and fertilizers while overseeing work on disease eradication. Indeed, in Africa as among African Americans, esteem for Carter may have risen the highest. He was named an honorary "chief" in the village of Ojobi in Ghana, and residents of nearby villages wrote songs in honor of the former American president.[37]

The tributes must have been welcome as Carter began to face the specter of his own mortality. In the autumn of 1988, five years after Ruth succumbed to pancreatic cancer, Billy Carter also died of the fatal disease. He was only fifty-one. The next year Gloria Carter Spann was also diagnosed with the same rare form of cancer that had killed her father, sister, and brother. It was clear that something in the Carter family encouraged the disease. Carter therefore agreed to regular screenings lest he too develop the disease. If he did, though, there was little that he or anyone else might do about it, for the cancer is almost always fatal within a year. And perhaps he wondered why his life alone was spared.

As the last surviving member of his family, it was fitting that Carter added an additional volunteer stint with Habitat for Humanity to his crammed summer 1994 schedule. For it enabled him to help build a new home for the seventy-seven-year-old Annie Mae Rhodes, whose house was among those destroyed by the floods that ravaged the low-income neighborhood in Albany, Georgia, that summer. For twenty-two years Rhodes had been employed by the Carters as a nanny and housekeeper. Both she and Carter recalled that she had been the one who held Earl Carter when he died, more than forty years before.[38]

Carter also turned increasingly to poetry to express the lifetime of accumulated feelings and experiences that would be gone when he was. Although the resulting 1995 collection, *Always a Reckoning, and Other Poems*, cannot be considered excellent by the literary standards established by the great poets he admired, it did reveal the former president's craftsmanlike effort to grapple with his past. The majority of selections attended to the people, places, and events that shaped his life in childhood.[39]

It could not have been the baby the Grady Memorial Hospital staff called "Pumpkin" who provided Carter with the inspiration for his 1991 effort to combat urban poverty in the United States, the Atlanta Project. Carter did not even see the one-pound baby, abandoned by her cocaine-addicted mother, in the hospital's incubator until the week he launched the project. Yet when he saw her he cried. "I never knew about it," he said. "God knows I should have. I've been governor of this state. I've been president of the United States. I didn't even know about things like this."[40] With these remarks one of the nation's most ambitious private urban-improvement projects was inaugurated.

It remains too early to tell whether the Atlanta Project — or Carter's national spin-off, the America Project — will have a substantial impact on the lives of the urban poor. Many policy analysts and veteran social workers have their doubts. Carter's idea of empowering urban neighborhood clusters by linking them with committed churches and private businesses cannot be faulted for its intent. Nevertheless, the plight of the urban poor can arguably be alleviated only by significant policy changes that extend beyond well-intentioned and amply financed charitable activities. In Atlanta, moreover, the project quickly degenerated into schisms as minorities protested underinclusion (in response to which Carter simply expanded the board to include more minorities) and then lost media momentum as the city turned its attention to hosting the summer 1996 Olympics. Whether momentum will be regained and genuine achievements realized remains to be seen.

Yet by at least one measure the Atlanta Project proved to be a tremendous success. With the goal of raising $25 million in private donations, by 1993 the project raised $32 million. Carter, whose fund-raising abilities only a few years earlier had sometimes proved embarrassing, extracted donations of more than a million dollars each from nearly a dozen corporations and foundations, together with scores of smaller donations.[41] So impeccable was his integrity, in fact, that his reputation was scarcely tarnished by his association with Agha Hasan Abedi, the Pakistani businessman who founded the infamous Bank of Commerce and Credit International that collapsed in 1991 after years of fraudulent loans and other dubious international financial dealings. Rather than impugn Carter, whose presidential center benefited from huge donations from Abedi and who personally helped arrange for Abedi's 1988 heart transplant, investigators pounced upon Bert Lance (whose innocence was so obvious that he was never even indicted).

So, it was hardly surprising that the *New York Times* reported, "History Looking Kindly on Carter Presidency," or that the *Washington Post* declared, "Jimmy — Come Back! All Is Forgiven!", both in 1990. Nor was it completely far-fetched for the *Economist* to ask, "Jimmy Carter in '92?" later the same year. By early 1991, Carter was even deemed worthy of his own prime-time television profile on the Discovery Channel special "Citizen Carter." And the next year, instead of dodging the legacy of the ex-president, Nebraska senator Robert Kerrey freely referred to him as the "finest living ex-president" during the New Hampshire primary that he hoped would establish his own bid to be the first Democratic executive to follow Carter. Then, when the Bush-Quayle campaign veered once again into the territory of Carter-bashing by trying to link Clinton to Carter, real protests were heard. Indeed, the Republican ticket lost.[42]

After the election bookstores were jammed when Carter appeared to autograph copies (sometimes as many as 1,500 during a single session) of his then most recent literary effort, *Turning Point*. The next year the National Park Service reported that visitors to Plains were triple what they had been in 1987 and were projected to reach 100,000 annually. Meanwhile, the Maranatha Baptist Church, where Carter continued to teach Sunday school, had long been accustomed to several hundred visitors for each of the ex-president's lessons. And, after Johnny Carson retired from the *Tonight Show*, his replacement, Jay Leno, invited Carter to appear as a guest on the show at every opportunity he could, even as Carter also agreed to appear as a guest on the competing show *Late Night with David Letterman*. By then it seemed that the rehabilitation of Jimmy Carter was complete.[43]

THE BRIGHTEST STAR IN THE GALAXY

President Bush never enjoyed Ronald Reagan's reputation as a "great communicator." But he did occasionally have help from the same speechwriter, Peggy Noonan. And perhaps the most distinctive imprint Noonan placed on the Bush presidency came in the acceptance speech she wrote for him to deliver to the 1988 Republican convention. The speech was a crucial one. It needed to close a fourteen-point gap that had arisen after the Democratic convention, by articulating a vision of America that was even more powerful and compelling than the Democrats'. It also needed to weave two somewhat disparate themes together. First, traditional Republican values of restricted government social-welfare spending, particularly as they had been promoted by Ronald Reagan, had to be upheld. But second, the speech had to establish the vice president as a man capable of presidential leadership on his own, independent of Reagan. A speech that described an America superior to the Democrats', promised to continue the Reagan revolution, and yet revealed George Bush as his own man was no small challenge.

After weeks of work and plenty of drafts, Noonan finally alighted upon her master metaphor. It was, ironically, the same stellar one that Reagan used to promote his massive defense buildup. But in Bush's hands, the stars became "kinder and gentler." Noonan wrote:

> For we are a nation of communities, of thousands and tens of thousands of ethnic, religious, social, business, labor union, neighborhood, regional and other organizations, all of them varied, voluntary, and unique.
>
> This is America: the Knights of Columbus, the Grange, Hadassah, the Disabled American Veterans, the Order of Ahepa, the Business and Professional Women of America, the union hall, the Bible study group, LULAC, Holy Name — a brilliant diversity spread like stars, like a thousand points of light in a broad and peaceful sky.

And "at the bright center" of the galaxy, Noonan had Bush say in affirmation of the quintessential American tradition of moral individualism, "is the individual."[44]

Not long after Bush's speech Jimmy Carter was singled out by some as among the brightest of these thousand lights.[45] His reputation revived on the basis of his postpresidential career, Carter epitomized the ethic of voluntarism that Bush chose to celebrate. And, just as George Bush saw the light of the individual "radiating" out into communities, so also Carter chose to stress one "special message" to the Democrats in his 1988 convention speech. That message, Carter said, was unity. Lest its importance be overlooked, the exemplary moral individualist said, "One more time: unity."[46] For both the Republican and the Democrat, the challenge and genius of America was to create unity out of moral individualism.

Yet the ability of both presidents' vision to create a united America ultimately proved limited. George Bush no less than Jimmy Carter presided over a nation that slipped more perilously into cynicism and fragmentation. For Bush as for Carter, already weak inherited measures of confidence in government and major social institutions evaporated further, and each experienced a crushing decline in his own approval ratings. Each also ultimately received only about 40 percent of the vote in his reelection bid and was soundly defeated.

Importantly, however, no evidence exists that during either's administration moral individualism itself declined; both four-year epochs reveal at least the usual, if not a heightened, search for moral certainty and spiritual fulfillment among Americans. Instead, during each administration Americans simply found it more difficult to link their individual moral aspirations to the wider society and body politic. The individual that Bush so hoped would "radiate" outward to community and nation simply did not do so with sufficient brilliance to illuminate the darkening national sky, just as a decade earlier Carter's pleadings for renewed faith failed to bring the nation together into the critical mass that might pass a comprehensive energy policy and restore American confidence.

About his failure Bush was more forthright than Carter. He admitted "the vision thing" eluded him. But it also eluded Carter. Both presidents championed individual morality and hoped that it would provide the basis for national unity; but both stumbled at the impasse that separated the moral individual from a united and invigorated republic.

None of which is to say that Reagan offered the vision that Carter and Bush lacked. Reagan's domestic cultural offering was in fact essentially the identical one. Like them, Reagan heralded the moral individual as the basis for a strong and united nation. His relative success (and his success was relative, remaining by historic standards both partial and erratic) may be attributable as much to his superior rhetorical gifts and personal image as to his distinctive vision. For in Reagan, as Carter discovered after listening to his 1986 speech at the opening of the Carter Center, moral individualism could be celebrated in a truly compelling, if somewhat sentimental, way.

In addition to Reagan's superior rhetorical gifts, however, it must not be forgotten that he coupled his sentimental view of the moral individual with a massive military buildup and rhetorical assault on the Soviet Union. Surely aggressive militarism is no final substitute for a compelling domestic vision, particularly in the nuclear and post-cold-war era. Still, in times past, American confidence has been sustained in part by militarism, even by the quest for empire. Indeed, when George Bush displayed military prowess during the Persian Gulf War he also succeeded in rallying the nation behind the effort. It must therefore be concluded that, while militaristic rhetoric bolstered Reagan's domestic vision, in the last analysis his vision was not much different from Carter's or Bush's. Without the militarism, moreover, Reagan's domestic vision would not have stood as sturdily.

Overall, then, the evidence suggests that the similar vision of a nation united in moral individualism, expressed by three successive presidents of both parties, failed by itself to inspire the American people. Not since Lyndon Johnson's dream of a "Great Society" was shattered by the nightmare of Vietnam, in fact — and then after Richard Nixon ultimately failed to produce his promised "peace with honor" — has America enjoyed the hope of a common faith and vision that would unite disparate individuals into a moral community. And evidence further indicates that under President Clinton the prospects for an America united by an ethic of moral individualism has grown even dimmer. Indeed, while Carter celebrated his seventieth birthday amid rising enthusiasm for his humanitarian achievements and revisionist interpretations of his presidency, America's malaise returned with a vengeance.

In the midst of the 1994 summer in which pollsters found Jimmy Carter's personal reputation "skyrocketing," other pollsters found more disturbing trends. Polls for the Times Mirror Center for the People and the Press discerned "no clear direction in the public's political thinking" beyond "frustration with the current system." As a result, "responsiveness to alternative political solutions and appeals" was widespread. In fact, 20 percent of the population said they were "fed up" with both political parties and ready to support a third party, while more than half thought that the emergence of a third party would be a good idea even if they might not personally support it. The pollsters interpreted these results to show that the public as a whole was too "embittered" and "cynical" to believe in any political party or veteran politician. Indeed, the polls forecast that Americans were on the brink of massive political revolt over a system of government they distrusted.[47]

At first the political malaise that swept the country seemed to attach itself primarily to the Democrats, and in particular to the Democratic president. Bill Clinton was elected with only 43 percent of the popular vote (independent candidate Ross Perot took 19 percent away from both parties) and entered office with neither a mandate nor, it soon became apparent, the goodwill of Congress and the electorate. His campaign's economic promises resulted in a budget bill so gutted by opponents that even he was displeased with it, while that very budget became fodder for opponents to deride him as a "liberal." Clinton's other main policy initiative, universal health insurance, emerged stillborn in the summer of 1994 after dominating the news for nearly a year.

Meanwhile, seemingly unaware that their real concerns centered on public rather than personal morality, Clinton's opponents chose to savage his character. He was accused of draft dodging, illegal stock trading, adultery, sexual harassment, and a host of other major and minor offenses. Embittered and mistrustful of government, Americans couched their complaints in the only language they knew: individual morality. Indeed, they seemed unaware that they had recently rejected a Republican president of respectable personal character (Bush) and not too long ago had rejected a Democratic president of exceptional personal character (Carter).

As the party out of power as well as the one that generally envisions a more limited role for government, the Republicans were the immediate beneficiaries of the hostile mood. The midterm elections swept Republican majorities into both houses of Congress for the first time in four decades. Nevertheless, only a slim slice of Republican ideologues seemed convinced (perhaps in the hopes of convincing others) that the massive midterm Republican victory was a sign of resurgent Republican strength.

"While Republicans touted their electoral surge on Tuesday as a repudiation of President Clinton and an endorsement of conservative Republican policies," noted Richard Berke in a *New York Times* post mortem on the election, "there was little evidence that these motivations moved most voters." On the op-ed page John B. Judis registered the same doubt: "In all likelihood, this election does not augur a new Republican realignment, but rather more instability." Predictably, perhaps, Clinton's chief pollster, Stanley Greenberg, also thought the partisan interpretation of the elections mistaken. "People feel betrayed by both parties," he observed. "The public has lost faith in America's institutions and its own capacity to rebuild a sense of community." Also agreeing, however, was the main architect of Nixon's 1968 victory, Kevin Phillips. "The public has lost faith in seven straight Presidencies of both parties," he noted. "And 1994 is only a beginning; more upheaval is coming."[48]

Even before the election, there were indications that neither political party would really emerge victorious and that the casualty would be the political system itself. Polls conducted for California's gubernatorial race, for instance, showed that by September both major candidates were already perceived unfavorably by a majority of the electorate.[49] Confronted by such perceptions, California campaigners seeking victory had little choice but to cater to the disaffection and run negative, oppositional advertising. Ironically, having felt forced as a political advisor to California's Senator Alan Cranston in 1988 to recommend a similarly negative campaign strategy based upon polls that showed voter alienation, Pat Caddell helped inaugurate the trend. Afterward, he abandoned polling in shame and disgust.[50] In any event, by October 1994 California's statewide candidates were predicted to spend upwards of $40 million on television commercials that all hammered home the same theme: "Nothing is right with the world in California. Every candidate is a sleaze, every proposal a trick, every utterance a lie."[51]

But California races were only larger and more expensive than most others. Oppositional campaigning prompted by voter alienation was widespread across the nation. Kathleen Hall Jamieson, an expert on campaign advertising, commented that there was "more rapid and rabid advertising" generally in 1994 than previously.[52] Worse, for the most part the negative strategy proved to be successful. The victorious candidates in 1994 generally resembled those they replaced in terms of demographic characteristics and personal backgrounds; besides their more conservative leanings their one distinguishing characteristic was that they had raised and spent more money than their opponents.[53] Indeed, the advertisements that attacked their opponents were successful for largely the same reasons that Caddell had urged Senator Cranston to wage a negative campaign in 1988: they so alienated voters that most of them stayed home. The Republican tide was not so high, noted Jesse Jackson about the midterm elections that produced an abysmal turnout especially among the poor and minorities, but the Democratic walls were too low.

Even in Georgia, which saw its onetime gadfly Republican Newt Gingrich catapulted to the Speaker of the House after the 1994 election, Bill Shipp noted that the atmosphere had changed so drastically that senior senator Sam Nunn was seriously considering retiring from public life. With "rancor replacing civility," noted the dean of political reporting in Georgia, "there may be no place left in Washington for a reticent, thoughtful and moderate Democrat."[54] Before long the prophecy was fulfilled. Sam Nunn did announce his retirement. But he was not alone.

More than two dozen mostly moderate incumbents of both parties used the rancor of 1994 as a prod to leave elective office for good.

Still other signs indicated that the 1994 election was more of an assault on the political system than an affirmation of the Republicans. Pollsters still found billionaire independent presidential candidate Ross Perot enjoying a double-digit following despite considerable infighting in his organization, United We Stand — a testimony to the disaffection many Americans felt toward both major political parties. Voters in seven states registered their discontent with all politicians by approving referenda limiting the length of terms members of Congress from either party can serve, bringing the number of states with such laws up to twenty-two. Also in 1994, fifteen state legislatures passed resolutions declaring their sovereignty and admitting only the narrowest of federal government roles. Early the next year the National Governor's Association was forced to cancel a conference after a barrage of objections were raised by citizens who feared the conference would become a constitutional convention and embolden the federal government.[55]

Meanwhile, the idiosyncratic acts of solitary individuals and isolated groups suggested the extremes to which fear and hatred of the federal government had driven some. In January, a man armed with a .45 staked out President Clinton's jogging route; in September, a pilot purposely crashed a stolen airplane into the White House; in October, twenty-seven rounds from a semiautomatic weapon were fired at the executive mansion; in December, more shots by someone else were fired on the White House. The next April, paramilitary domestic terrorists bombed the federal building in Oklahoma City and murdered 168 men, women, and children — apparently for no other reason than because it was a federal building. Even before then, a municipal court judge in western Montana was terrorized by a paramilitary group that protested her authority to enforce routine traffic laws and threatened to try her in their own common-law "court."[56]

Social values were equally strained. On the same day that Jimmy Carter graced the cover of *Time*, a *New York Times* piece quoted a professor of American Studies announcing "a revival of '80s' selfishness." But, the professor continued, "it's a selfishness that doesn't have confidence in itself" but was rather "more meanspirited and individualistic." Another expert, a cultural historian, commented on the "return to triumphalism and economic aggression." The author of the piece simply noted that "the greedy and arrogant 1980s" had returned — minus even the thin film of moral justification 1980s' ideology had pasted over it. Writing in the December issue of *Esquire*, Pete Hamill put the situation this way: "American civil society, long founded on the notion of 'from many, one,' *e pluribus unum*, is being swept away by a poisonous flood tide of negation, sectarianism, self-pity, confrontation, vulgarity, and flat-out, old-fashioned hatred."[57]

Polls seeking to understand Americans' attitudes toward racial equality also revealed telling changes. At two-thirds of the public, the percentage of Americans who supported a person's right to date someone of another race in 1994 had increased a substantial 22 percent just since 1987. However, popular support for the social equality of the races did not extend to support for government policies that fostered that equality. A majority of whites — 9 percent more than just two years earlier — also said that they thought equal rights had been pushed too far.[58] "No subject," said another survey using in-depth interviews, "expressed hostility toward minorities per se, but many felt alienated from a society that refused to acknowledge whites' victimization." Indeed, an estimated "1-in-10 white men has been injured by affirmative action."[59] In tandem with these findings, 1994 poll results showed a 14 percent decline in support for government social welfare programs over just the previous seven years.[60]

What was true for race seemed also to hold for sexual orientation. The 1994 elections saw twenty-four openly homosexual candidates elected and two major antihomosexual referenda defeated. Yet there was little evidence of support for legislation protecting homosexuals as a social category. With sexual preference as with race, Americans seemed willing to extend rights to individuals but deny those same individuals protectionist policies earmarked for them as members of groups.[61]

Collective outrage was also directed at lawbreakers. Despite a tripling of the prison population between 1980 and 1994, voters in 1994 continued to express a majority willingness to pump even more collective dollars into prisons by approving tough mandatory sentencing laws in several states. Again thinking in terms of individual morality rather than group plights, voters seemed unconcerned that over half the prison population nationwide was African American, more than four times their representation in the population, or that even four decades after the onset of the civil rights movement black families still earned household incomes that averaged just over half of that earned by white families. Rather, for those seeking a larger pattern in the race, poverty, and crime statistics, Richard Herrnstein and Charles Murray offered a resurrection of the old social

Darwinist argument. In the sensation created by their book, *The Bell Curve* (if not in the book itself), many found evidence for the genetic inferiority of African Americans that explained their higher-than-average rates of poverty and crime. But genetic inferiority is not amenable to social engineering; indeed, during his book tour Charles Murray courteously but decisively lashed out against government welfare programs that, in his view, encouraged the reproduction of the genetically inferior.[62]

The turn away from collective social values in favor of individualism was once again anchored in economic reality. Census Bureau figures released in October of 1994 showed that economic inequality was again on the rise. The number of Americans living below the poverty line was inexplicably up, the income of the poorest fifth of Americans was at its lowest level in decades, and the income of the richest Americans was growing disproportionately. Median family income remained flat and was, in fact, lower than it had been even in 1987 (which, in turn, represented little improvement from ten years earlier).[63] Although inflation and interest rates remained comparatively low, the pattern of economic stagnation and growing inequality first detected in the 1970s continued twenty years later. Indeed, whereas only 6 percent of full-time workers with some college education in 1979 earned low wages, by 1990 the percentage had almost doubled to 11 percent.[64] When the 1994 Census Bureau report failed to show a reversal of this trend, Department of Labor Secretary Robert Reich did not disguise his alarm. "America is in danger of splitting into a two-tiered society," he said. "This is not anyone's idea of progress."[65]

But the split was more than one separating the haves from the have-nots. The census data also revealed that the median income of men had actually declined between 1979 and 1993, although it rose during the same period for women. Indeed, white men experienced the largest average drop in income, 10 percent. No wonder that "angry white men" were the vanguard of the 1994 electoral assault.[66]

Explaining the meaning of the events of 1994, pundits and pollsters agreed. "If you are looking for a basic meaning in the last election," wrote A. A. Rosenthal in the *New York Times*, "it is that Americans are beginning to understand that the unwritten contract between them and their society is being torn up." Reflecting that "we've been led to such depths of cynicism that only the perverse sounds credible to us," Cox Newspapers columnist Tom Teepen reported the judgment of pollster Daniel Yankelovich, according to whom the American mood was "foul." Yankelovich further predicted that the mood "will harden into class warfare, generational warfare, exacerbated racial tensions, polarization and political extremism, demagoguery and instability as we careen from one overly simplistic solution to another." Less sensationally, a *New York Times*/CBS News poll found that Americans were "profoundly alienated" as they were mired in "deepening powerlessness and pessimism." Indeed, discovered the pollsters, "the public has not appeared so disconsolate since 1979." The discontent extended to the supernatural. A late 1994 poll by *U.S. News & World Report* discovered that nearly 60 percent of the public believed that the world will come to an end or be destroyed, and fully a third thought the end would come within the next few years. While only 44 percent believed in a final battle of Armageddon, 49 percent predicted the rise of a personal embodiment of evil — the Antichrist.[67]

It was natural for attention during the early 1990s to drift back to the malaise of the Carter years. On the cusp of the decade, the *Boston Globe* surveyed a number of intellectuals and social critics only to report that, "More than a decade after President Jimmy Carter warned of a crisis of the spirit in America . . . a broad spectrum of the nation's social and intellectual leadership is coming to the conclusion that Mr. Carter was right." Yet, the article continued, "Now, they say, the crisis has deepened." The spectrum was even broader when disgust for popular culture's revival of 1970s "camp and tackiness" was added to the mix. Moreover, lest there have been any doubt about where one freshman Republican congressman from Georgia formed his political sensibilities, Charlie Norwood found himself sputtering about "votes to give the Panama Canal away" as late as 1995.[68]

But Americans did not have to read newspapers or even vote to know that the anger that erupted in the 1990s recalled the malaise of the 1970s. In 1994 the film that riveted moviegoers more than any other — and then proceeded to sell more than seven million copies the first week it was available on videocassette (more than any other non-Disney production) — *Forrest Gump*, presented a simpleton's review of America since the onset of the crisis of confidence. "*Gump* hit the whole spectrum of demographics," noted Bruce Pfander, senior vice president of Fox Home Video. So desperate were Americans for a solution to their malaise that they turned to the cinematic equivalent of the village idiot.[69]

☆   ☆   ☆

The response to the return of an even angrier malaise was predictable: American moralists sought to rejuvenate individual virtue. Leading this effort for moral renewal was undoubtedly William Bennett's *The Book of Virtues*, which clung high on the rungs of the best-seller list throughout 1994.[70] Along with it, however, were many similar efforts. Gertrude Himmelfarb's *The De-Moralization of Society*, for instance, attracted more than passing interest in intellectual circles.[71] Yet both of these efforts and the many like them rest their hopes on a doubtful foundation: that social renewal will arise through a revival of individual virtue, whether of the more classical (Bennett) or Victorian (Himmelfarb) type.

What neither these nor the spate of other clarions of virtue admit is that the evidence for a decline in morality is thin or nonexistent. Indeed, if anything, individual morality has been on the *rise* since the onset of malaise. Workers who used to wing it morally are now sent to mandatory ethics seminars; campuses that used to wink at sexual peccadilloes have established explicit policies governing relationships (between students and students as well as between faculty and students); criminals who used to get by with light sentences or even probation are increasingly incarcerated and for longer durations, or even put to death; language that used to insult unintentionally is now deemed offensive and banned; racism and bigotry have declined, while the racially "insensitive" are sent to "diversity awareness" seminars; smoking and drunk driving are increasingly opposed; mild offenses by public officials that used to be routine are increasingly subject to thorough public scrutiny and likely prosecution; animals are now deemed to have "rights," principled vegetarianism is reasonably widespread, and fast-food restaurants tout their use of recycled paper. Even the much decried proliferation of lawyers and lawsuits may reflect not the relaxing of morals but a keener interest in them. Where if not the courtroom — or its television surrogate — are finer moral distinctions applied with more gripping drama? And where, overall, is there evidence for declining personal morality?

The case for a decline in spiritual values is also difficult to make. Whereas the Christian Coalition that crystallized so effectively during the debates over the ratification of the Panama Canal treaties unquestionably declined in influence, the reason for that decline may ironically be the perceived immoral excesses of many of its supposed leaders. Besides this, there is no evidence of declining enthusiasm for spirituality, and there is even evidence of its upswing. "In the last few years readers have begun gobbling up an even broader range of books on religious and spiritual topics," noted the *New York Times* on a business page in 1995, adding that publishers were "scrambling" for even more religious books.[72] Indeed, while *The Book of Virtues* spent the whole of 1994 on the nonfiction best-seller list, for the last eight weeks of the year it was outsold by Pope Paul II's more recently published *Crossing the Threshold of Hope*. Meanwhile, on the better-selling fiction list, James Redfield's offering of spiritual insights, *The Celestine Prophecy*, ended the year with a consistent forty-three weeks near the top of the list.[73]

Important anecdotal evidence also casts doubt on the view that the nation's collective malaise is rooted in a decline of individual morality and religious faith. Paul Hill, a forty-year-old Presbyterian minister, was surely not lacking in either when he shot and killed Dr. John Britton and James Barrett in Pensacola, Florida, on July 29, 1994. As he explained in court, his premeditated murders were justified because they prevented the greater harm of the physician's performance of abortions. So adamant was Hill in his moral belief that he refused to defend himself when the judge disallowed his using them for his defense.[74]

Although only the fringe few would agree with Hill's moral justification for murder, even fewer can deny that he was motivated by genuine moral conviction. Perhaps more telling is that for two decades the nation engaged in a bitter debate over legalized abortion before opponents resorted to such extreme acts. By 1993, however, when the first murder was committed, the long-frayed bonds of civility had apparently unraveled — not because individuals were less moral, but because their individual morality was no longer constrained by an encompassing collective moral creed. Lacking was not personal moral conviction, but common moral vision.

The real crisis confronting America is thus not one of diminishing morality; the real crisis is an excessively individualistic morality that has mushroomed into moral solipsism. Americans are not less moral than they used to be; they are more so and perhaps even more willing to act on their moral convictions. But equally refined moral individualists do not agree in their moral judgments — and no common moral vision exists to bind them together despite their disagreements.

The crisis was long in the making and is rooted deeply in the culture. "To believe that what is true for you in your private heart is true for all men," wrote Ralph Waldo Emerson, is the "genius" of America.[75] Before long the political consequences of this moral self-reliance were spelled out by Henry David Thoreau. "Resistance to civil government," proclaimed Thoreau in the original title of *Civil Disobedience*, is not merely allowable but also actually required when individual conscience dictates. Yet neither of these seminal American thinkers nor their followers seriously address the question of what would occur when masses of self-reliant moral individualists actually do place the dictates of conscience above the common creed.

So, Rheta Grimsley Johnson, the syndicated columnist who judged Carter to be among Bush's most brilliant points of light, was only half right when she explained the failure of Bush's "thousand points of light" credo this way:

> If all of us were like Mr. Carter, the Thousand Points of Light idea just might work. Unfortunately, a lot of us are like Mr. Bush. We bass fish on Saturdays and fudge on our taxes. We are selfish and uncreative about off time. If we do something good for somebody, we want tax credits and our picture in the newspaper. That's why the poor will always be with us, as the Bible declares, and why cutting too many government social services is tantamount to genocide.[76]

The starker reality was overlooked by Johnson, who assumed that we would all agree on moral truths. That reality is, rather, that even when moral individualism radiates brilliantly, celestial collisions are as likely as beautiful constellations.

No less an influence on Carter than Admiral Hyman Rickover understood this eventual American dilemma well:

> In our system of society, no authority exists to tell us what is good and desirable. We are each free to seek what we think is good in our own way. . . . Perhaps the liberal tradition never really could believe that vice, when unconstrained by religion, morality and law, might lead to viciousness. It never really could believe that self-destructive nihilism was an authentic and permanent possibility that any society had to guard against. It could refute Marx effectively, but it never thought it would be called upon to refute Marquis de Sade. . . .[77]

Little could Rickover have anticipated when he offered this observation that by the 1980s the Marquis de Sade would indeed replace Karl Marx as the cult hero of the intellectual classes, largely through the influence of philosopher Michel Foucault and the attendant desconstructionist movement.[78] Whereas the movement has much to recommend it, more middlebrow cultural gatekeepers see it for what to them it is. "Its completely subjectivist and relativistic view of the world," noted a *New York Times* book reviewer about a deconstructionist's interpretive effort, "make[s] anything . . . signify everything, and in doing so signify nothing."[79] Focusing more on the political "culture of liberal individualism," another reviewer observed that it "treats communal attachments and civic engagement as optional extras on a fixed menu of individual choice and market exchange." The result, predicted John Gray, is likely a "Columbianization of the United States, in which failing political institutions become increasingly marginal in an ungovernable, criminalized and endemically violent society."[80] Indeed, for Foucault as for de Sade, sex, violence, and even death are the "limit experience" the enlightened ultimately seek.

Among those whose enlightenment takes a more pedestrian form, a review of a book on America's spiritual searchings during the 1980s and 1990s in the *Washington Post* unsurprisingly noted that "utter solipsism" reigns. The same book revealed the results of a survey of American gurus and other spiritual teachers, which showed that 90 percent of those who had not taken a vow of celibacy at least occasionally augmented their quests for enlightenment by having sex with one or more of their disciples.[81] Such is, of course, morally permissible where solipsism reigns.

And whether the "morale boosting" of Jimmy Carter on July 15, 1979, his subsequent humanitarian achievements, or the barrage of moralists who hope to reinvigorate individual virtue, the quest to renew common life on the basis of moral individualism seems a futile and misguided one. Indeed, its prospects for success are dim.

Emerson and Thoreau, together with a century of their followers, unwittingly discovered a pathway out of the moral nihilism to which their ideas ultimately led. It was, ironically, to promote their ideas. For all their individual self-reliance, after all, Emerson and Thoreau both chose to disseminate their ideas in the common forum. Both were also committed to the abolitionist movement, opposing slavery as they did all other social encumbrances of the individual. The nation's leading promoters of individualism were, in short, engaged in a *social* crusade to promote the very individualism they otherwise celebrated.

It has been likewise throughout U.S. history. The ethos of moral individualism sustained a common life, ironically, because its goals were not achieved. Seeking to promote moral individualism, Americans have historically gravitated to collective causes to foster the creed. Whether in the founding of the republic, the abolitionist movement, the struggle for women's rights, the fight to make the world safe for democracy, the war against Nazi tyranny and Japanese imperialism, the civil rights movement, or the cold war against Soviet totalitarianism, Americans have always found moral cohesion not in individualism but in common efforts to promote it.

The irony may therefore be that the very triumph of moral individualism has produced the disintegration of the American nation. For once it is victorious, moral individualism provides no guidelines for creating or sustaining a nation.

Carter's postpresidential career — indeed, his earlier attempt to substitute the liberal internationalist's creed for a domestic vision during his presidency — can thus be explained by the need of the moral individualist to remain invigorated by fighting against instances of its denial. For unless moral individualism expands, it loses its power to bind. Seeking the community he was denied in childhood and was incapable of promoting when president, Carter therefore turned his attention to the struggle to promote moral individualism globally — never realizing that his very malaise was a product of the success of that same creed.

So, despite the consensus that has emerged that praises Carter for bringing the issue of America's malaise to public attention, Jimmy Carter remained silent on the subject. Indeed, except for the Atlanta Project and occasional injections of opinion into national debates, Carter has ignored domestic issues altogether since his presidency.

Ample indicators suggest that many Americans would welcome Carter's involvement in domestic entanglements and, particularly, the malaise issue. When the editors of two major newspapers published excerpts from his 1992 book, *Turning Point*, for instance, both wrote headlines that implied a greater connection to then present problems than was the case. Although *Turning Point* had little to say about contemporary affairs (it was a universalist's rehash of the election fraud and racial oppression during Carter's 1962 campaign for Georgia's state senate), the *Los Angeles Times* headlined its excerpt, "A New Turning Point: America's Economically Fueled Segregation," while the *Atlanta Journal/Constitution* chose "Society's at 'Turning Point' to Heal Itself" for its headline.[82] Wishing Carter would speak on pressing domestic issues — or feeling that their readers wished him to — these editors chose headlines that suggested such a focus, even if that focus was lacking.

But the headline writers had little choice. When Carter chose to write under his own byline, he ignored most pressing domestic issues. Two-thirds of the more than fifty articles he wrote for U.S. newspapers and magazines during the early 1990s took foreign affairs as their subject. The remaining third included four articles on the Atlanta Project, four on health care, two on tobacco policy, two on regional environmental issues, one on congressional ethics reform, one on voter registration, one on libraries, and one on fishing. Although Carter even found the time to write a letter to the editor of the Atlanta papers defending an appointment to the Georgia State Patrol, he never found time to write about race relations, economic disparities in the United States, trust in government, American morality, or malaise. Undoubtedly it was because he had little to say on the subject.

Carter's humanitarian achievements should in no way be diminished. Neither should a political career that on the balance proved more competent than not be disparaged. Even so, an aura of tragedy clings to the legacy of a president who is best-remembered for alerting Americans to their festering malaise, only to prove incapable of addressing it. More important, a real moral challenge lurks beneath this aura. Can America sustain itself on the basis of a creed that, once victorious, encourages the moral fragmentation and social atomization of the very society that propounded it?

The tragic aura also clings to Carter personally. That which he most thirsted after in life was a community to which he could belong. Although the community was denied to him by the very injustices that he spent his life struggling to eradicate, the moral individualism and attendant philosophy of universalism never offered him the community he wanted. Indeed, the only community he ever discovered was in the crusade for an ethic that, in the end, makes community unachievable.

Perhaps this was what puzzled visual-arts critic Catherine Fox about Frederick Hart's sculpture of Carter when it was unveiled on Georgia's capitol grounds in 1994. The face did not quite look like him, the pose was wooden, and the meaning of the gesturing hands struck her as confusing. To Fox, the entire sculpture suggested a concept rather than a person. For, as a sculpture of a person, the monument suggested "no inner life."[83]

The puzzlement is understandable even if the judgment is mistaken. For Fox mistook an absent outer life for an absent inner life. The two are easily confused. Whereas some individuals seem so much a product of their societies that no distinctive "inner life" can be detected, others may be so removed from the molding and sustaining influence of a community that even a rich and diverse inner life seems to flail incoherently — appearing little more than an arbitrary point in a meaningless universe. Two poems in Carter's 1995 collection suggest just such metaphorical worries. One considers the "void" of the universe and admits, "it troubles me." The other contemplates "nature's laws" and the various theories of same, only to wonder whether the universe will "cataclysmically blow apart."[84]

What Fox may have observed and Hart may have intended, then, was simply a life propelled by the abstract principle of universal individualism rather than one anchored in a particular community. Such a life is naturally more concept than person. Suggesting it, the Atlanta sculpture aptly depicts not only Carter but also the end to which the concept inevitably leads.

NOTES

1. Estimates of viewership are reported in Robert A. Strong, "Recapturing Leadership: The Carter Administration and the Crisis of Confidence," *Presidential Studies Quarterly* 16 (Fall 1986), p. 647.

2. According to Carter's pollster, Patrick Caddell, only 8 percent of Americans named energy as the number one problem facing the country in the spring of 1979, and only 29 percent agreed that it was among the nation's top five problems. See Memorandum, Cambridge Survey Research to the Democratic Committee, 5/24/79, "Caddell [Patrick] [2]," Box 33, Hamilton Jordan's Files, Jimmy Carter Library.

3. George C. Edwards, *Presidential Approval: A Sourcebook* (Baltimore: Johns Hopkins University Press, 1990). For the four weeks preceding the speech, Carter's approval ratings hovered in the 28–29 percent range, exactly half his disapproval ratings. These numbers followed six months of steadily declining ratings and represented among the lowest ever recorded for any president. Indeed, Carter was in striking distance of Nixon's all-time low of 24 percent during the week of his resignation.

4. Steven M. Gillon, *The Democrats' Dilemma: Walter F. Mondale and the Liberal Legacy* (New York: Columbia University Press, 1992), pp. 261–65; interview with Stuart Eizenstat, Miller Center Interviews, Carter Presidency Project, vol. 13, January 29–30, 1982, pp. 79–85, Jimmy Carter Library.

5. Carter to Caddell, July 16, 1979, Box 139, President's Handwriting File, Jimmy Carter Library.

6. The remark was made in a speech to the California State Senate on May 20, 1976. It is reprinted in Jimmy Carter, *A Government as Good as Its People* (New York: Simon and Schuster, 1977), p. 102.

7. No one who reads Carter's campaign autobiography, *Why Not the Best?* (Nashville: Broadman Press, 1975) or his other books, or who otherwise attends to his career, can fail to detect the deep moral imprint of both populism and the civil rights movement on him. Yet Robert N. Bellah, the chief theorist of America's "civil religion" and the intellectual force behind Caddell's understanding of America's spiritual challenges, reportedly was disturbed by Carter's apparent failure to grasp his ideas. See John Raeside's interview with Bellah, "A Night at Camp David," *East Bay Express*, July 27, 1979. The two, however, were enough in sync later to share appearances on a Bill Moyers's television special, "The Good Society." For a discussion of the linkages between at least populism and civil religion, see Rhys H. Williams and Susan M. Alexander, "Religious Rhetoric in American Populism: Civil Religion as Movement Ideology," *Journal for the Scientific Study of Religion* 33 (1994): 1–15. For a discussion of Georgia's populist tradition, see C. Vann Woodward, *Tom Watson: Agrarian Rebel*, 2d ed. (Savannah, Ga.: Beehive Press, 1973). The linkages between civil religion and the civil rights movement are, I hope, obvious.

8. Carter's July 15, 1979, speech carries the official but little-known title, "Energy and the Crisis of Confidence." Though the phrase "crisis of confidence" might have been drawn from a number of sources, it is likely that it was drawn — consciously or subconsciously — from Christopher Lasch's *The Culture of Narcissism: American Life in an Age of Diminishing Expectations* (New York: Norton, 1979), where it appears in the first paragraph of the preface. Carter read this book early in 1979 upon the recommendation of Caddell, while rethinking his presidency, and Lasch had been invited to the White House to discuss his ideas more fully with the president. Of course, another possible source of the phrase, perhaps the text from which Lasch drew it, would be Arthur M. Schlesinger Jr.'s *The Crisis of Confidence: Ideas, Power, and Violence in America* (Boston: Houghton Mifflin, 1969).

9. See, e.g., Robert C. Fuller, *Americans and the Unconscious* (New York: Oxford University Press, 1986); and Donald Meyer, *The Positive Thinkers: Popular Religious Psychology from Mary Baker Eddy to Norman Vincent Peale and Ronald Reagan*, rev. ed. (Middletown, Conn.: Wesleyan University Press, 1988).

10. Media coverage of Carter's 1976 campaign, and later his administration, often emphasized his religious faith. Mainstream journalists, however, rarely probed beyond the superficial to understand this faith well. An interesting study of the popular presentation of Carter's religiosity is Alette Hill's "The Carter Campaign in Retrospect: Decoding the Cartoons," *Semiotica* 23 (1978): 307–32. Hill shows that political cartoons featuring Carter regularly recalled his religiosity, but often in a superficial and condescending way.

11. Jimmy Carter, *Keeping Faith: Memoirs of a President* (New York: Bantam, 1982), p. 19.

12. Theodore H. White, *America in Search of Itself: The Making of the President, 1956–1980* (New York: Harper & Row, 1982), p. 268.

13. Carter used the word *malaise* on several occasions during his presidential campaign, and the word may even have been in an earlier draft of the speech. But Carter specifically resisted using French words in his prepared speeches because he believed that they were often pretentious and difficult to understand. His goal, he often told his speechwriters, was to be understood by a person he knew (not his brother) who worked at a service station near Plains.

14. Author interview with Patrick H. Caddell, Santa Monica, Calif., March 1991.

15. In addition to Strong's "Recapturing Leadership" and several examinations of the speech in the context of larger books and essays, two other papers have been published solely on this speech. They are Dan F. Hahn's "Flailing the Profligate: Carter's Energy Sermon of 1979," *Presidential Studies Quarterly* 10 (1980): 583–87; and J. William Holland's "The Great Gamble: Jimmy Carter and the 1979 Energy Crisis," *Prologue: Quarterly Journal of the National Archives* 22 (Spring 1990): 63–79. If this scholarly attention to Carter's "Energy and the Crisis of Confidence" is accepted as a benchmark criterion of the speech's perceived importance, it is not only Carter's most memorable speech but also one of the more memorable speeches delivered by any president. Very few presidential addresses, after all, have merited even one separate after-the-fact academic paper.

16. Author interview with Bert Lance, Calhoun, Ga., March 1992.

17. Data on the speech's reception are reported in Holland, "The Great Gamble" and Strong, "Recapturing Leadership," as well as elsewhere.

18. Two books have made an especially strong contribution to understanding Carter's religious faith. They are Niels C. Nielsen Jr., *The Religion of President Carter* (Nashville: T. Nelson, 1977); and *The Spiritual Journey of Jimmy Carter: In His Own Words*, compiled by Wesley G. Pippert (New York: Macmillan, 1978). Neither these nor the plethora of popular media accounts of Carter's faith, however, have adequately grappled with Carter's public morality, or the distinction between it and his private faith. A number of scholars have, however, probed this distinction and striven to explicate Carter's public morality as a separate dimension of his thought and rhetoric. See, e.g., Keith V. Erickson, "Jimmy Carter: The Rhetoric of Private and Civic Piety," *Western Journal of Speech Communication* 44 (Summer 1980): 221–35; Ronald B. Flowers, "President Jimmy Carter, Evangelicalism, Church-State Relations, and Civil Religion," *Journal of Church and State* 25 (1983): 113–32; Christopher Lyle Johnstone, "Electing Ourselves in 1976: Jimmy Carter and the American Faith," *Western Journal of Speech Communication* 42 (1978): 241–49; Richard V. Pierard and Robert D. Linder, "Jimmy Carter and That Old-Time (Civil) Religion," in Pierard and Linder, *Civil Religion and the Presidency* (Grand Rapids, Mich.: Zondervan, 1988); Leo P. Ribuffo, "God and Jimmy Carter," in M. L. Bradbury and James B. Gilbert (eds.), *Transforming Faith: The Sacred and Secular in Modern American History* (Westport, Conn.: Greenwood, 1989); and James S. Wolfe, "Exclusion, Fusion, or Dialogue: How Should Religion and Politics Relate?" *Journal of Church and State* 22 (1980): 89–105.

To provide additional leverage for an understanding of Carter's role as a public moralist, it might even be suggested that his posture be considered more "prophetic" than "priestly." Whereas presidents are often thought to conform primarily to the priestly mode of civil religious leadership, defined essentially as a role that upholds and celebrates a collective national faith, on more than a few occasions Carter appeared to depart from this expected role and lash out prophetlike against a wayward public. This metaphor should probably not be pressed to extremes, but the juxtaposition of the two possible rhetorical roles does help to underscore the comparatively unique position of Jimmy Carter in the pantheon of U.S. presidents.

The theoretical distinction between prophet and priest (along with mystic) as ideal types of religious leadership is derived from Max Weber, *The Sociology of Religion*, trans. Ephraim Fischoff (Boston: Beacon Press, 1964). The notion that the president's religious role is essentially priestly is widespread in the literature. For a review and assessment, see James David Fairbanks, "The Priestly Functions of the Presidency: A Discussion of the Literature on Civil Religion and Its Implications for the Study of Presidential Leadership," *Presidential Studies Quarterly* 11 (Spring 1981): 214–32. Not incidentally, it has also been suggested that the United States embraces two separate civil religions, one priestly and the other prophetic. See, e.g., Martin E. Marty, "Civil Religion: Two Kinds of Two Kinds," in his *Religion and Republic: The American Circumstance* (Boston: Beacon, 1987).

19. Bruce Mazlish and Edwin Diamond, *Jimmy Carter: A Character Portrait* (New York: Simon and Schuster, 1979); Betty Glad, *Jimmy Carter: In Search of the Great White House* (New York: Norton, 1980).

20. The argument here is also that, as a leader, Carter's morality reflects and personifies more general cultural values. Although there are other theories of leadership that argue that leaders direct and define followers' values rather than reflect them, these other theories have rarely been found applicable to American circumstances. Most interpreters of leadership in America find it to be more a matter of personifying than of directing values. See, e.g., Ralph Waldo Emerson, *Representative Men* (New York: Collier, 1900) for the classic statement of this view or, more recently, Daniel J. Boorstin, *The Image* (New York: Atheneum, 1962).

21. Many understandings (including Patrick Caddell's) of the spiritual or cultural crisis of recent years are rooted in Robert N. Bellah's notion of an American Civil Religion threatened with collapse during the 1970s. See his *The Broken Covenant: American Civil Religion in a Time of Trial* (New York: Seabury, 1975). The idea that America has entered an era of "culture wars" is thoughtfully probed by James Davison Hunter in *Culture Wars: The Struggle to Define America* (New York: Basic Books, 1991). Importantly, Hunter detects the onset of the modern culture wars in events of the 1970s, even though the phrase itself did not come into being until later.

22. Tom Wolfe, "The Me Decade and the Third Great Awakening," in his *The Purple Decades: A Reader* (New York: Berkley Books, 1983); Nicholas Lemann, "How the Seventies Changed America," *American Heritage* 42 (July/Aug. 1991): 39–49; Tad Friend, "Rhinophilia," *New Republic*, Aug. 17 & 24, 1992, p. 9; Jonathan Alter, "All Grown Up and Nowhere to Go," *Esquire*, May 1991, pp. 96–104.

23. For a thoughtful interpretation of the film western's social values, see Will Wright, *Six Guns and Society: A Structural Study of the Western* (Berkeley: University of California Press, 1975). John Wayne's *True Grit* (1969) and *Rio Lobo* (1970) were the last popular westerns to offer a hopeful view of society. Beginning in 1969 with such westerns as *Butch Cassidy and the Sundance Kid* and *The Wild Bunch*, the western hero was depicted as less supportive of society and more self-interested.

24. Data on television viewership are found in Cobbett S. Steinberg, *TV Facts* (New York: Facts on File, Inc., 1980); and Karen Heller, "It's No Dream: 'Dallas' Is Dead," *Atlanta Journal/Constitution*, Apr. 28, 1991, "TV Week," p. 3.

25. Associated Press, "Great Memories of a Great Blackout," *Atlanta Constitution*, Nov. 8, 1990, p. A9.

26. Fear of crime, which peaked in 1975, is discussed by pollster Louis Harris in *Inside America* (New York: Vintage, 1987), pp. 183–87. Concerns about declining civility were central themes in both Lasch's *The Culture of Narcissism* and Robert N. Bellah's "Religion and Legitimation in the American Republic" (*Society* 15 [May/June 1978]: 6–23) — both sources that influenced Carter. For another celebrated meditation on the subject at the time, see Richard Sennett, *The Fall of Public Man: On the Social Psychology of Capitalism* (New York: Knopf, 1977).

27. Joel Garreau's *Edge City: Life on the New Frontier* (New York: Doubleday, 1991) provides a competent if somewhat uncritical review of these trends.

28. Robert J. Ringer's *Winning through Intimidation* (New York: Fawcett Crest, 1974) and *Looking Out for #1* (New York: Fawcett Crest, 1991) each placed second on the annual best-seller lists in the year following their initial publication, 1975 and 1977, respectively. Other best-selling titles of the decade, like Harry Browne's

You Can Profit from a Monetary Crisis (1973) and Paul E. Erdman's *The Crash of '79* (1976), suggest that this fascination with profiting from economic catastrophe was not limited to a single author.

29. Data reported in Kenneth C. W. Kammeyer, George Ritzer, and Norman R. Yetman, *Sociology: Experiencing Changing Societies*, 4th ed. (Boston: Allyn & Bacon, 1990), p. 259.

30. For a review of this survey data, see Harris, *Inside America*; and Seymour Martin Lipset and William Schneider, *The Confidence Gap: Business, Labor, and Government in the Public Mind*, rev. ed. (Baltimore: Johns Hopkins University Press, 1987). For Caddell's assessment of these trends, see his article "Trapped in a Downward Spiral," *Public Opinion* 2 (Oct./Nov. 1979): pp. 2–7, 52–55, 58–60. Comments describing Caddell are from Richard L. Berke, "Brown or Perot? Former 'Boy Wonder' of Politics Isn't Sure Whom to Help," *New York Times*, April 16, 1992, p. A10; and Paul A. Gigot, "Democratic Guru: Fear, Loathing, and Party Suicide," *Wall Street Journal*, April 3, 1992.

31. Not considered here are the number of cyclical and linear theories of history which might help account for the culture of the 1970s. Among the cyclical theories that might be entertained are Fred Davis's notion of the alternating cultural significance of decades ("Decade Labeling: The Play of Collective Memory and Narrative Plot," *Symbolic Interaction* 7 [1984]: 15–24); Arthur M. Schlesinger Jr.'s theory of America's cyclical history (*The Cycles of American History* [Boston: Houghton Mifflin, 1986]); and William Strauss and Neil Howe's notion of generational change (*Generations* [New York: Morrow, 1991]). Among the linear theories of history that might be considered are Ronald Inglehart's thesis of broad-based cultural realignments in all Western societies (*Cultural Shift in Advanced Industrial Society* [Princeton: Princeton University Press, 1990]); Daniel Bell's conjectures about the cultural challenges attending postindustrial society (*The Cultural Contradictions of Capitalism* [New York: Basic Books, 1976]); and the variety of ideas associated with postmodernist critiques. Whereas these several theories add much to an understanding of the 1970s in general, all by their very nature fail to account for the decade's cultural distinctiveness. To each, of course, the 1970s are but part of a larger cultural sweep, whether a cyclical or a linear one.

32. Pollsters, perhaps because of the atheoretical tradition of their craft, tend to subscribe to these explanations. This is essentially the "theory" proposed by Lipset and Schneider's *The Confidence Gap*, as well as by Caddell's "Trapped in a Downward Spiral," for example. Caddell, however, grappled for a broader cultural explanation in person and in memoranda, even if in his article he stuck to the pollster's piecemeal explanation.

33. Robert Wuthnow's *The Restructuring of American Religion: Society and Faith since World War II* (Princeton: Princeton University Press, 1988) provides a useful overview of these trends.

34. See Jeffrey K. Hadden and Anson Shupe, *Televangelism, Power, and Politics on God's Frontier* (New York: Henry Holt, 1988) for a discussion of these developments.

35. The movement is described in ethnographic context by Alan Peshkin, *God's Choice: The Total World of a Fundamentalist Christian School* (Chicago: University of Chicago Press, 1986).

36. See, e.g., Robert M. Pirsig, *Zen and the Art of Motorcycle Maintenance: An Inquiry into Values* (New York: Morrow, 1974); Carlos Castaneda, *Journey to Ixtlan: The Lessons of Don Juan* (New York: Simon and Schuster, 1972) and *The Teachings of Don Juan: A Yaqui Way of Knowledge* (New York: Simon and Schuster, 1974); Fritjof Capra, *The Tao of Physics: An Exploration of the Parallels between Modern Physics and Eastern Mysticism* (New York: Bantam Books, 1977); Tom Robbins, *Another Roadside Attraction* (Garden City, N.Y.: Doubleday, 1971) and *Even Cowgirls Get the Blues* (Boston: Houghton Mifflin, 1976); Annie Dillard, *Pilgrim at Tinker Creek* (New York: Harper's Magazine Press, 1974); Gabriel Garcia Marquez, *One Hundred Years of Solitude* (New York: Harper & Row, 1970); Raymond A. Moody Jr., *Life after Life: The Investigation of a Phenomenon — Survival of Bodily Death* (New York: Bantam, 1975).

37. The popularity of "Stairway to Heaven" is not easily measured by customary indicators of song popularity, such as chart position. Most critics point out, however, that the eight-minute song, though never released as a single, became the most requested rock song in history and that Led Zeppelin's 1973 American tour broke box office records, many previously held by the Beatles. See Nick Logan and Bob Woffinden (comp.), *The Illustrated Encyclopedia of Rock* (New York: Harmony Books, 1977), p. 138; and Ed Ward, Geoffrey Stokes, and Ken Tucker, *Rock of Ages: The Rolling Stone History of Rock & Roll* (New York: Rolling Stone Press, 1986), pp. 484–85.

38. See, e.g., Carl R. Rogers, *On Becoming a Person* (Boston: Houghton Mifflin, 1961); and R. D. Laing, *The Divided Self: An Existential Study in Sanity and Madness* (New York: Penguin, 1969).

39. The phrase derives from Martin L. Gross, *The Psychological Society: A Critical Analysis of Psychiatry, Psychotherapy, Psychoanalysis, and the Psychological Revolution* (New York: Random House, 1978).

40. Hunter, *Culture Wars*, p. 378.

41. Ibid., p. 244.

42. Alan Patureau ("Ciao, Yuppies!" *Atlanta Constitution*, July 3, 1991, p. B1) credits Bob Greene with coining the term "yuppie." Along with it, the acronyms "buppies" (black urban professionals) and "dinks" (dual income no kids) also arose.

43. See, e.g., Harris, *Inside America*; Lipset and Schneider, *The Confidence Gap*; and Edwards, *Presidential Approval*.

44. Mona Charen, "In Our Land of Plenty, a Moral Crisis Deepens," *Atlanta Constitution*, Oct. 6, 1992, p. A19. See also *Forbes*, Sept. 14, 1992, 47–195.

45. White, *America in Search of Itself*, pp. 268–69; Raeside, "A Night at Camp David."

CHAPTER 2: FAMILY AND PLACE

1. Jimmy Carter, *Why Not the Best?* (Nashville: Broadman, 1975), p. 13.

2. Jimmy Carter, *An Outdoor Journal: Adventures and Reflections* (New York: Bantam, 1988).

3. Carter's ancestry is reported in a number of places, including Kenneth H. Thomas Jr., "Georgia Families — Carter-Gordy," *Georgia Life* 3 (Winter 1976):

40. Hugh Carter's *Cousin Beedie and Cousin Hot: My Life with the Carter Family of Plains, Georgia* (Englewood Cliffs, N.J.: Prentice-Hall, 1978) and Ruth Carter Stapleton's *Brother Billy* (New York: Harper & Row, 1978), pp. 12–18, repeat some of the same facts but sometimes suggest different ones.

4. Robert Humphrey, *The Carters of Kings Langley: The President's Roots* (Kings Langley: John Bourne, 1978) relates this ancestry in what is essentially a lengthy travel brochure for a British village.

5. This story of Littlebury Walker Carter's demise is disputed by Hugh Carter in *Cousin Beedie and Cousin Hot*, p. 168. Basing his version on his father's recollection, Hugh Carter relates that Littlebury Walker Carter was not mortally wounded in the fight, and neither did his wife die the day of his funeral. Rather, he died the day after his wife from the same unmentioned disease. If true, the faulty reconstruction of the story in Carter family lore may be explained by a family desire to remember their ancestry in more crisp moral terms than was actually the case. The moral lessons seem to be two: a cautionary tale of business dealings gone awry and, second, a romantic tale of a loyal wife.

6. Interview with Jeanette Lowery, Carter/Smith Oral History Interviews, November 11, 1978, p. 33, Jimmy Carter Library.

7. Interview with Betty Jennings Carter, Carter/Smith Oral History Interviews, November 11, 1978, p. 54, Jimmy Carter Library.

8. Interview with David Wise, National Park Service Oral History Interviews, December 17, 1985, pp. 3, 10, Jimmy Carter Library.

9. Interview with a neighbor who asked to remain anonymous, May 29, 1977, Betty Glad's files.

10. Hugh Carter, *Cousin Beedie and Cousin Hot*, p. 21.

11. Interview with Don Carter, Carter/Smith Oral History Interviews, November 3, 1979, p. 15, Jimmy Carter Library.

12. Interview with Jeanette Lowery, Carter/Smith Oral History Interviews, November 11, 1978, p. 11, Jimmy Carter Library.

13. Interview with a neighbor who asked to remain anonymous, 1977, Betty Glad's files.

14. Interview with Betty Jennings Carter, Carter/Smith Oral History Interviews, November 11, 1978, p. 58, Jimmy Carter Library.

15. Georgia's economic climate at this time is described in Charles B. Floyd and Lawrence R. Hepburn, "Economic Growth and Change," in Hepburn (ed.), *Contemporary Georgia* (Athens, Ga.: Carl Vinson Institute of Government, The University of Georgia, 1987); Hepburn, "Historical Setting," ibid., pp. 1–36; and William F. Holmes, "Part Five: 1890–1940," in Kenneth Coleman (ed.), *A History of Georgia* (Athens: The University of Georgia Press, 1977).

16. Rosalynn Carter, *First Lady from Plains* (Boston: Houghton Mifflin, 1984), p. 11 mentions the bank failure.

17. Interview with Jimmy Carter, National Park Service Interviews, May 11, 1988, p. 168, Jimmy Carter Library.

18. Interview with David Wise, National Park Service Interviews, December 17, 1985, p. 19, Jimmy Carter Library.

19. Interview with Gloria Carter Spann, National Park Service Interviews, December 7, 1988, p. 69, Jimmy Carter Library.

20. Interview with Jimmy Carter, National Park Service Interviews, May 11, 1988, p. 223, Jimmy Carter Library.

21. It follows that acreage estimates of the Carter land holdings are all misleading, and an accurate figure is unimportant since Carter bought and sold land throughout his adulthood. Ruth Carter Stapleton, in *Brother Billy* (p. 17), however, does state that her father's initial farm was 700 acres (though she wrote from recollections and was not always accurate with her facts). In *An Outdoor Journal* (p. 20), Jimmy Carter writes that his family farm was only 350 acres. Referring to her husband's farm at the time of their marriage, Lillian Carter said, "I think it was about 400 acres in those days" (interview with Lillian Carter, Carter/Smith Oral History Interviews, September 26, 1978, p. 14, Jimmy Carter Library). Bruce Mazlish and Edwin Diamond in *Jimmy Carter: A Character Portrait* (New York: Simon and Schuster, 1979) (p. 30) by contrast report that Earl Carter's land holdings exceeded 4,000 acres. The conflicts are resolved by assuming that the land the Carters considered their family farm was likely fairly small (perhaps 350 acres) and at one time included an adjacent farm of roughly equivalent acreage. But at his economic prime Earl Carter probably owned ten or twelve times that acreage dispersed throughout the region and leased to tenants. For comparison purposes, the average farm size in Georgia in 1945 was 105 acres (see Douglas C. Bachtel, "Georgia's Changing Agricultural Environment: An Industry in Transition," *Issues Facing Georgia* 2 [Athens, Ga.: The University of Georgia College of Agriculture, Cooperative Extension Service, 1990]), which reflected increases over previous decades. Hugh Carter, similarly, remembered that when "Jimmy and I both was boys . . . a farm of say 100 to 200 acres was considered a pretty good little farm" (interview with Hugh Carter, National Park Service Interviews, December 17, 1985, p. 6, Jimmy Carter Library).

22. Interview with Willard Slappey, Carter/Smith Oral History Interviews, June 18, 1979, p. 13, Jimmy Carter Library. Slappey does use the more polite term "defecate," though it is unlikely that this was the word the tenants used.

23. Interview with Ruby Lamb, May 1977, Betty Glad's files.

24. Interview with Lillian Carter, Carter/Smith Oral History Interviews, September 26, 1978, p. 25, Jimmy Carter Library. See also Ruth Carter Stapleton, *Brother Billy*, p. 7, who relates the same story but adds the year and make of her father's car.

25. Hugh Carter, *Cousin Beedie and Cousin Hot*, p. 91.

26. The description of Earl Carter as possessing a "Midas touch," originated by his older brother, was subsequently repeated by others. See, e.g., Ruth Carter Stapleton, *Brother Billy*, p. 14.

27. Hugh Carter, *Cousin Beedie and Cousin Hot*, p. 6.

28. The notion of the Carters as "rural royalty" crops up from time to time in family recollections. One such place it appears is in Ruth Carter Stapleton, *Brother Billy*, p. 25.

29. Interview with Lillian Carter, Carter/Smith Oral History Interviews, September 26, 1978, pp. 22–23, Jimmy Carter Library.

30. Betty Glad heard gossip about black prostitutes at the pond house and mentions it in notes identified as "5/24/77 — prior to Tom Peterson Interview" in her files.

31. Interview with Eleanor Forrest, National Park Service Interviews, December 18, 1985, p. 27, Jimmy Carter Library.

32. Interview with Miriam Timmerman Saylor, December 9, 1976, Betty Glad's files.

33. Interview with Willard Slappey, Carter/Smith Oral History Interviews, June 18, 1979, p. 13, Jimmy Carter Library; Interview with Lillian Carter, Carter/Smith Oral History Interviews, September 26, 1978, p. 20, Jimmy Carter Library.

34. Interview with Miriam Timmerman Saylor, December 9, 1976, Betty Glad's files.

35. Interview with Lillian Carter, Carter/Smith Oral History Interviews, September 26, 1978, p. 20, Jimmy Carter Library.

36. Interview with Willard Slappey, Carter/Smith Oral History Interviews, June 18, 1979, pp. 13–15, Jimmy Carter Library.

37. Interview with Ruth Jackson, National Park Service Interviews, December 20, 1985, p. 8, Jimmy Carter Library.

38. Interview with Gloria Carter Spann, National Park Service Interviews, December 7, 1988, p. 72, Jimmy Carter Library.

39. Ibid., p. 70.

40. Interview with a Plains resident who asked to remain anonymous, 1977, Betty Glad's files.

41. Interview with Miriam Timmerman Saylor, December 9, 1976, Betty Glad's files.

42. In *Dasher: The Roots and the Rising of Jimmy Carter* (New York: Summit Books, 1978), p. 81, James Wooten writes, "'There were only two kinds of white people,' Earl would often say, 'those who will "abuse a nigger" and those who won't.'" Although the assertion is consistent with other reports of Earl Carter's racial attitudes (firm in his belief in white superiority, but fair-minded and kind-hearted toward the blacks he deemed inferior), Wooten provides no citation for this or other of his assertions. Presumably the attributions are based upon his first-hand reporting — but one cannot know for sure.

43. Interview with Lillian Carter, Carter/Smith Oral History Interviews, September 26, 1978, p. 32, Jimmy Carter Library.

44. Interview with Joseph Bacon, May 25, 1977, Betty Glad's files.

45. Interview with J. Frank Myers, September 16, 1977, Betty Glad's files.

46. On the basis of interviews with Gloria Carter Spann, Mazlish and Diamond (*Jimmy Carter*, pp. 38–40) conclude that Earl Carter was himself "a very timid man." His daughter even claimed that the secrecy of his good deeds was a result of the embarrassment he would have felt had they been found out. If true, Earl Carter likely went to great lengths to mask his shyness, for no one else reported it.

47. Jimmy Carter, *Turning Point: A Candidate, a State, and a Nation Come of Age* (New York: Times Books, 1992), pp. 6–9; interview with J. Frank Myers, September 16, 1977, Betty Glad's files.

48. The remnants of Georgia's planter elite and their business-minded urban counterparts following the Civil War are generally referred to as "Bourbons." They described themselves, however, as "New Departure Democrats," a label that suggests both their traditional party allegiance and their eagerness to move beyond the previous Southern economic and social system. They were therefore

the ones to call, via the rhetoric of Henry Grady during the 1880s, for a new, industrialized South. The epithet "Bourbon," however, underscores their failure to bring widespread industrial prosperity to the South at the same time they managed to maintain their wealth and power in a land of want. See Coleman, *A History of Georgia.*

49. Interview with Mary Anne Thomas, May 31, 1977, Betty Glad's files.

50. William Anderson's *The Wild Man from Sugar Creek: The Political Career of Eugene Talmadge* (Baton Rouge: Louisiana State University Press, 1975) tells the story of Talmadge well. For background on Tom Watson's Populism, see C. Vann Woodward's *Tom Watson: Agrarian Rebel* (Savannah, Ga.: Beehive, 1973).

51. Interview with a neighbor who asked to remain anonymous, May 29, 1977, Betty Glad's files.

52. Ibid.

53. Wooten, *Dasher,* pp. 96, 134.

54. Carter (*Turning Point,* p. 7) writes of rejecting Talmadge demagoguery despite being taken to the rallies. A close friend of Carter during the 1950s and 1960s who asked to remain anonymous spoke of Carter's expecting to see his father in heaven (June 20, 1977, Betty Glad's files).

55. Interview with Lillian Carter, Carter/Smith Oral History Interviews, September 26, 1978, p. 8, Jimmy Carter Library.

56. See Carter, *Turning Point,* pp. 3–4.

57. Interview with Lillian Carter, Carter/Smith Oral History Interviews, September 26, 1978, p. 7, Jimmy Carter Library.

58. Jimmy Carter (*Turning Point,* pp. 3–4) repeated this conviction that his grandfather was close to Watson as well as the originator of rural free delivery (RFD) as late as 1992. Ironically, Woodward, in *Tom Watson,* suggests that Watson himself may not even have originated the idea of RFD. Woodward also discusses the prevalence of Georgians naming children after Watson.

59. Interview with Lillian Carter, Carter/Smith Oral History Interviews, September 26, 1978, p. 6, Jimmy Carter Library.

60. Betty Glad (*Jimmy Carter: In Search of the Great White House* [New York: Norton, 1980], p. 27) called Gordy a "bodyguard." See also Herman Talmadge, *Talmadge: A Political Legacy, a Politician's Life* (Atlanta: Peachtree, 1987); and Coleman, *A History of Georgia.*

61. Interview with Lillian Carter, Carter/Smith Oral History Interviews, September 26, 1978, p. 6, Jimmy Carter Library.

62. Interview with Willard Slappey, Carter/Smith Oral History Interviews, June 18, 1979, p. 16, Jimmy Carter Library.

63. Interview with Lillian Carter, Carter/Smith Oral History Interviews, September 26, 1978, p. 8, Jimmy Carter Library.

64. The history of Georgia progressivism is traced most ably by Numan V. Bartley in *The Creation of Modern Georgia* (Athens: The University of Georgia Press, 1983).

65. Interview with Lillian Carter, Carter/Smith Oral History Interviews, September 26, 1978, p. 12, Jimmy Carter Library.

66. Interview with a neighbor who asked to remain anonymous, 1977, Betty Glad's files.

67. Interview with Janet S. Merritt, May 3, 1978, Betty Glad's files.

68. Interview with Lillian Carter, Carter/Smith Oral History Interviews, September 26, 1978, p. 13, Jimmy Carter Library.

69. Glad, *Jimmy Carter*, p. 25.

70. Interview with Lillian Carter, Carter/Smith Oral History Interviews, September 26, 1978, p. 17, Jimmy Carter Library.

71. Ibid., pp. 15–16.

72. Interview with Jeanette Lowery, Carter/Smith Oral History Interviews, November 11, 1978, p. 10, Jimmy Carter Library.

73. Interview with Lillian Carter, Carter/Smith Oral History Interviews, September 26, 1978, p. 16, Jimmy Carter Library.

74. Ibid., p. 23.

75. Interview with Gloria Carter Spann, National Park Service Interviews, December 6, 1989, pp. 10–11, Jimmy Carter Library.

76. Jimmy Carter, *An Outdoor Journal*, p. 20; Mazlish and Diamond, *Jimmy Carter*, p. 83.

77. Ruth Carter Stapleton, *Brother Billy*, pp. 17–18.

78. Interview with Lillian Carter, Carter/Smith Oral History Interviews, September 26, 1978, p. 9, Jimmy Carter Library.

79. Interview with a neighbor who asked to remain anonymous, May 29, 1977, Betty Glad's files.

80. Interview with David Wise, National Park Service Interviews, December 17, 1985, p. 23, Jimmy Carter Library.

81. Quoted in Mazlish and Diamond, *Jimmy Carter*, p. 46.

82. Interview with Gloria Carter Spann, National Park Service Interviews, December 6, 1989, p. 7, Jimmy Carter Library.

83. Interview with Willard Slappey, Carter/Smith Oral History Interviews, June 18, 1979, p. 26, Jimmy Carter Library.

84. Interview with Gloria Carter Spann, National Park Service Interviews, December 7, 1988, pp. 26–27, Jimmy Carter Library.

85. "Lillian Carter Talks about Racism, the Kennedys, and 'Jimmy's Reign,'" *Ms.*, Oct. 1976, p. 52.

86. "'My Son the President': Interview with Lillian Carter," *U.S. News & World Report*, Mar. 7, 1977, p. 53.

87. Interview with Gloria Carter Spann, National Park Service Interviews, December 7, 1988, p. 45, Jimmy Carter Library.

88. Hugh Carter, *Cousin Beedie and Cousin Hot*, p. 43.

89. Interview with Gloria Carter Spann, National Park Service Interviews, December 7, 1988, p. 30, Jimmy Carter Library.

90. Interview with Jimmy Carter, National Park Service Interviews, May 11, 1988, p. 4, Jimmy Carter Library.

91. Interview with Willard Slappey, Carter/Smith Oral History Interviews, June 18, 1979, p. 16, Jimmy Carter Library.

92. Interview with Jimmy Carter, National Park Service Interviews, May 11, 1988, p. 200, Jimmy Carter Library.

93. Interview with Lillian Carter, Carter/Smith Oral History Interviews, September 26, 1978, p. 26, Jimmy Carter Library.

94. Mazlish and Diamond, *Jimmy Carter*, p. 49.

95. Interview with a neighbor who asked to remain anonymous, May 29, 1977, Betty Glad's files.

96. Quoted in Paul H. Elovitz, "Three Days in Plains," *Journal of Psychohistory* 5 (1977): 177.

97. Interview with Lillian Carter, Carter/Smith Oral History Interviews, September 26, 1978, p. 25, Jimmy Carter Library.

98. Interview with Ruby Lamb, May 1977, Betty Glad's files.

99. Interview with Lillian Carter, Carter/Smith Oral History Interviews, September 26, 1978, p. 21, Jimmy Carter Library.

100. See, e.g., J. Renvoize, *Incest: A Family Pattern* (London: Routledge & Kegan Paul, 1982).

101. Interview with Lillian Carter by Gloria Carter Spann, *Ladies' Home Journal*, August 1977, p. 120.

102. Ruth Carter Stapleton, *The Gift of Inner Healing* (Waco, Tex.: Word Books, 1976), p. 16.

103. Interview with Don Carter, Carter/Smith Oral History Interviews, November 3, 1979, p. 17, Jimmy Carter Library.

104. "'My Son, The President,'" p. 54.

105. As late as 1992 Jimmy Carter still described his mother as encouraging her "black friends" to "enter through the front door and, as much as their discomfiture would permit, she treated them as equals." See *Turning Point*, p. 17. Others doubt both the frequency and the boldness of these acts of Jim Crow defiance. Glad (*Jimmy Carter*, p. 41), for example, narrows the occasions of a black approaching the front door of the Carter house to one. Since in *Why Not the Best?* (p. 33) Jimmy Carter also wrote that only one black "habitually" came to the front door, and it is the same individual identified by Glad (Alvan Johnson), it may be presumed that only Johnson, once or a few times, approached the Carters' front door. So far as her "black friends" are concerned, a colleague who served with Lillian Carter in the Peace Corps, Larry Brown, concluded that she was "deluding" herself about the extent of their friendships. See Mazlish and Diamond, *Jimmy Carter*, pp. 50–51. But based on a September 26, 1978, interview with her (Carter/Smith Oral History Interviews, p. 28, Jimmy Carter Library), it appears that it was Jimmy, not Lillian, who was "deluded." There she said, "I have never had a black person to come to my front door to visit me. They respect me too much. They'll come to my kitchen door." Carter's 1992 remarks may have been a bit overstated. The truth seems to be that Lillian Carter did befriend blacks, was more willing than most whites to tolerate infractions to the Jim Crow customs, and may even have quietly encouraged defiance of them, but for the most part she was not close friends with blacks and abided by the customs of the time.

106. Ruth Carter Stapleton, *Brother Billy*, p. 56.

107. Interview with Gloria Carter Spann, National Park Service Interviews, December 7, 1988, Jimmy Carter Library.

108. "Lillian Carter Talks about Racism," p. 51.

109. Interview with Jimmy Carter, National Park Service Interviews, May 11, 1988, p. 213, Jimmy Carter Library.

110. Bill Schemmel, "My Son Jimmy," *Ladies' Home Journal*, August 1976, p. 142.

111. Interview with Jimmy Carter, National Park Service Interviews, May 11, 1988, p. 303, Jimmy Carter Library.

112. Jimmy Carter, *An Outdoor Journal*.

113. Hamilton Jordan, *Crisis: The Last Year of the Carter Presidency* (New York: Berkley Books, 1982), p. 61.

114. E-mail from Jimmy Carter to Jennifer Maschiano, January 4, 1994, Prodigy Computer Service.

115. Jimmy Carter, *Why Not the Best?*, p. 32.

CHAPTER 3: AN IMPERILED SELF AND SEARCH FOR COMMUNITY

1. Jimmy Carter, *Why Not the Best?* (Nashville: Broadman, 1975), dust jacket.

2. See, e.g., "Why Carter Is Still a Mystery," *U.S. News & World Report*, Oct. 17, 1977, pp. 26–28. For many more examples, see Mark J. Rozell, *The Press and the Carter Presidency* (Boulder, Colo.: Westview, 1989), especially pp. 13–15.

3. Norman Mailer, "The Search for Carter," *New York Times Magazine*, Sept. 26, 1976, pp. 69, 74, 78.

4. William Lee Miller's interpretations were published both in the article "The Yankee from Georgia," *New York Times Magazine*, July 3, 1977, pp. 16–35; and in his book *Yankee from Georgia: The Emergence of Jimmy Carter* (New York: Harper & Row, 1978).

5. "The 'Real' Jimmy Carter: Interview with Charles Kirbo," *U.S. News & World Report*, Dec. 20, 1976, p. 15.

6. Interview with Joe Andrews, July 9, 1977, Betty Glad's files.

7. Peter G. Bourne, "Jimmy Carter: A Profile," *Yale Review* 72 (Oct. 1982): 131.

8. Mailer, "The Search for Carter," p. 88.

9. Bourne, "Jimmy Carter: A Profile," p. 134.

10. See Rozell, *The Press and the Carter Presidency*.

11. Louis Harris survey release 7/6/78, "PR 15 6/1/78–12/31/78," Box PR 75, WHCF — Subject File — Executive, Jimmy Carter Library.

12. Memo to the Democratic National Committee from Cambridge Survey Research, May 25, 1979, "Caddell [Patrick] [3]," Box 33, Hamilton Jordan's Files, Jimmy Carter Library.

13. Interview with Jimmy Carter, Miscellaneous Interviews (Vision Associates), November 1, 1984, p. 5A–15, Jimmy Carter Library.

14. Memo from Patrick H. Caddell to the president, 8/18/80, [Campaign Strategy] Caddell [Patrick], Box 77, Chief of Staff (Jordan), Jimmy Carter Library.

15. Rozell, *The Press and the Carter Presidency*, p. 174.

16. The notion of "instrumental" or "technical" reasoning, understood as a reductionistic manipulation of means with no apparent end, has a long literature in numerous fields. Theorists associated with the Frankfurt school, most recently

Jürgen Habermas, have perhaps made the most of the practice. See his *Knowledge and Human Interests*, trans. Jeremy J. Shapiro (Boston: Beacon, 1971). Paul Tillich, a theologian Carter claimed to have read and who was himself briefly associated with the Frankfurt school, also offered a critique of this type of reasoning in his *Systematic Theology*, vol. 1, *Reason and Revelation, Being and God* (Chicago: University of Chicago Press, 1951), pp. 71–81. But it is also important to understand that Max Weber's life-long lament over the "rationalization" of the West was itself based upon a historical critique of instrumental or technical reason, not of all rational thought. According to Weber, the rational calculation demanded by capitalism was originally pressed into the end of otherworldly salvation. But, with the decline of the spiritual dimension of capitalism, the rational pursuit of profit for its own sake became the irrational end of capitalism. Hence, reason became oriented toward means only while ends were left irrational. See his *The Protestant Ethic and the Spirit of Capitalism*, trans. Talcott Parsons (New York: Scribner's, 1958). Importantly, if Weber's thesis is accurate, Carter but exhibited the intellectual orientation that was characteristic of his age. Also, Carter's search for an alternate intellectual orientation (see below) is characteristic of the spiritual longings Weber thought central to this age's unhappiness.

17. Louis Harris Survey release 7/6/78, "PR 15 6/1/78–12/31/78," Box PR 75, WHCF — Subject File — Executive, Jimmy Carter Library.

18. James Fallows, "The Passionless Presidency: The Trouble with Jimmy Carter's Administration," *Atlantic*, May 1979, pp. 34, 40, 42.

19. Bourne followed his training in psychiatry with antiwar activities and a master's degree in anthropology. He met Carter in 1971 when he accepted a job coordinating state-level drug treatment programs in Carter's gubernatorial administration. For the next several years Bourne turned most of his attention to political activities on behalf of Carter and served in the White House until, ironically, he was forced to resign for allegedly prescribing recreational drugs for another staff member.

20. The main psychobiographies of Jimmy Carter, most of them advancing a diagnosis of narcissism, include Lloyd deMause and Henry Ebel, *Jimmy Carter and American Fantasy: Psychohistorical Explorations* (New York: Two Continents/ Psychohistory Press, 1977); Paul H. Elovitz, "Three Days in Plains," *Journal of Psychohistory* 5 (Fall 1977): 175–99; Betty Glad, *Jimmy Carter: In Search of the Great White House* (New York: Norton, 1980); and Bruce Mazlish and Edwin Diamond, *Jimmy Carter: A Character Portrait* (New York: Simon & Schuster, 1979).

21. Otto F. Kernberg (*Borderline Conditions and Pathological Narcissism* [New York: J. Aronson, 1985]) describes the narcissistic personality this way: They "present an unusual degree of self-reference in their interactions with other people, a great need to be loved and admired by others, and a curious apparent contradiction between a very inflated concept of themselves and an inordinate need for tribute from others. Their emotional life is shallow. . . . They envy others. . . . [T]heir relationships with other people are clearly exploitative and sometimes parasitic. . . . [B]ehind a surface which is very often charming and engaging, one senses coldness and ruthlessness. . . . [T]hey are completely unable really to depend on anybody because of their deep distrust and depreciation of others" (p.

17). Glad's interpretation of Carter is in part based upon this definition of narcissism.

22. Bourne, "Jimmy Carter: A Profile," pp. 127, 134.

23. Mailer, "The Search for Carter," p. 92; Fallows, "The Passionless Presidency," p. 34.

24. Memo to the Democratic National Committee from Cambridge Survey Research, May 25, 1979, "Caddell [Patrick] [3]," Box 33, Hamilton Jordan's Files, Jimmy Carter Library.

25. George Herbert Mead's theoretical orientation is perhaps most thoroughly presented in his *Mind, Self & Society: From the Standpoint of a Social Behaviorist*, vol. 1, ed. Charles W. Morris (Chicago: University of Chicago Press, 1934). The classic statement of Erving Goffman's perspective is *The Presentation of Self in Everyday Life* (Garden City, N.Y.: Doubleday, 1959). A number of other theorists from this tradition might also be cited. However, since my aim here is not to establish and defend the theory according to which I believe Carter is best interpreted but just to suggest the general outlines of the theoretical orientation I adopt as an alternative to psychoanalysis, I cite only these main orienting sources.

26. Mead, *Mind, Self & Society*, pp. 164, 140, 144.

27. Ibid., p. 142.

28. Ibid., p. 168.

29. Jeremy Rifkin and Ted Howard, eds. and comps., *Redneck Power: The Wit and Wisdom of Billy Carter* (New York: Bantam, 1977).

30. Bill Schemmel, "My Son Jimmy," *Ladies' Home Journal*, August 1976, p. 145.

31. Willie Carter Spann, "The Other Carter," *Hustler*, May 1977, p. 52.

32. David R. Beisel, "A Psychohistory of Jimmy Carter," *Journal of Psychohistory* 5 (1977): 212.

33. Interview with Gloria Carter Spann, National Park Service Interviews, December 7, 1988, p. 60, Jimmy Carter Library.

34. Ibid., p. 44.

35. Interview with Jimmy Carter, National Park Service Interviews, May 11, 1988, p. 27, Jimmy Carter Library.

36. Interview with Gloria Carter Spann, National Park Service Interviews, December 7, 1988, p. 31, Jimmy Carter Library.

37. Interview with Ruby Lamb, May 1977, Betty Glad's files.

38. Ruth Carter Stapleton, *Brother Billy* (New York: Harper & Row, 1978); and "Christmas with the Carters," *Ladies' Home Journal*, Oct. 1977, pp. 74+.

39. Interview with Jeanette Lowery, Carter/Smith Oral History Interviews, November 11, 1978, p. 41, Jimmy Carter Library.

40. Interview with Gloria Carter Spann, National Park Service Interviews, December 7, 1978, p. 57, Jimmy Carter Library.

41. Interview with Willard Slappey, Carter/Smith Oral History Interviews, June 18, 1979, p. 30, Jimmy Carter Library.

42. Interview with Joe Andrews, July 9, 1977, Betty Glad's files.

43. Gloria Carter Spann, "Miss Lillian," *Ladies' Home Journal*, August 1977, p. 34.

44. Interview with Gloria Carter Spann, National Park Service Interviews, December 6, 1989, p. 20, Jimmy Carter Library.

45. Interview with Jimmy Carter, National Park Service Interviews, December 8, 1988, p. 47, Jimmy Carter Library.

46. Ruth Carter Stapleton, *Brother Billy*, p. 10.

47. Jimmy Carter, *An Outdoor Journal: Adventures and Reflections* (New York: Bantam, 1988), pp. 19, 34.

48. Interview with a classmate who asked to remain anonymous, June 1977, Betty Glad's files.

49. Interview with Lillian Carter, Carter/Smith Oral History Interviews, September 26, 1978, p. 23, Jimmy Carter Library.

50. Interview with Gloria Carter Spann, National Park Service Interviews, December 7, 1988, p. 44, Jimmy Carter Library.

51. Interview with Gloria Carter Spann, National Park Service Interviews, December 6, 1989, pp. 28–29, Jimmy Carter Library.

52. Interview with Jimmy Carter, National Park Service Interviews, May 11, 1988, pp. 6, 27, 213, Jimmy Carter Library.

53. Interview with Allie Smith, National Park Service Interviews, December 19, 1985, p. 8, Jimmy Carter Library.

54. Interview with Bobby Logan, October 11, 1976, Betty Glad's files.

55. Interview with Willard Slappey, Carter/Smith Oral History Interviews, June 18, 1979, pp. 8, 15, Jimmy Carter Library.

56. The story of Jimmy Carter's youthful entrepreneurship under his father's tutelage, including his moral assessment of the people who purchased his wares as "good" and those who did not as "bad," is repeated many places, including in his *Why Not the Best?*, pp. 23–25. Revealing of his disrespect for the less ambitious is his description of other townspeople as "checker players and other loafers" (p. 25). Years later, in *Turning Point: A Candidate, a State, and a Nation Come of Age* (New York: Times Books, 1992), he revealed the same contempt for townspeople who, "with not much else to do," were successful at "embroiling" him in "long discussions on the more controversial issues of the day" during his first (1962) campaign by calling them, again, "loafers" (p. 64). Though he learned not to show it directly, Jimmy Carter grew up not only ambitious but also contemptuous of those with less ambition than he.

57. Ruth Carter Stapleton, *The Gift of Inner Healing* (Waco, Tex.: Word Books, 1976), p. 17.

58. Quoted in Elovitz, "Three Days in Plains," p. 193.

59. Jimmy Carter, *An Outdoor Journal*, p. 43.

60. Ibid., pp. 12–15.

61. Interview with Willard Slappey, Carter/Smith Oral History Interviews, June 18, 1979, pp. 8–9, Jimmy Carter Library.

62. Interview with Jimmy Carter, National Park Service Interviews, May 11, 1988, p. 28, Jimmy Carter Library.

63. Ibid., pp. 6, 213.

64. Jimmy Carter, *Turning Point*, p. 7.

65. Jimmy Carter, *An Outdoor Journal*, p. 20.

66. Jimmy Carter, *An Outdoor Journal*, p. 38.

67. Jimmy Carter, *Always a Reckoning, and Other Poems* (New York: Times Books, 1995), pp. 99–100.

68. Jordan wrote Carter a 1977 memorandum urging him to restrain his hyperbolic excesses, and together with Rafshoon and others fought the tendency throughout their years in Carter's service. See his *Crisis: The Last Year of the Carter Presidency* (New York: G. P. Putnam's Sons, 1982), p. 324.

69. Interview with a classmate who asked to remain anonymous, June 1977, Betty Glad's files.

70. Zbigniew Brzezinski, *Power and Principle: Memoirs of the National Security Advisor 1977–1981* (New York: Farrar, Straus, Giroux, 1983), pp. 21–22.

71. Carter's diary is found in the Vertical File, Jimmy Carter Library.

72. See, e.g., Alette Hill, "The Carter Campaign in Retrospect: Decoding the Cartoons," *Semiotica* 23 (1978): 307–32.

73. Lloyd deMause ("Jimmy Carter and American Fantasy," *Journal of Psychohistory* 5 [1977]: 151–73) predicted that Carter would lead the nation into war in 1979, probably in the Middle East.

74. Wesley G. Pippert ("Jimmy Carter: My Personal Faith in God," *Christianity Today*, Mar. 4, 1983, pp. 14–21) was among many who expressed this assessment. Not incidentally, Carter himself believed that restraint of aggression was among his main presidential accomplishments. See his *Keeping Faith: Memoirs of a President* (New York: Bantam, 1982), p. 596. He also genuinely feared that Ronald Reagan would lead the country into war. See chapter 8.

75. Earl Carter's different parenting styles with his two sons and his feelings of failure over raising Jimmy are discussed in Ruth Carter Stapleton, *Brother Billy*; and Hugh Carter, *Cousin Beedie and Cousin Hot*.

76. Interview with Bobby Logan, October 11, 1976, Betty Glad's files.

77. Ruth Carter Stapleton, *Brother Billy*, p. 55.

78. Interview with Jimmy Carter, National Park Service Interviews, May 11, 1988, pp. 195–96, Jimmy Carter Library.

79. My speculation is that, before Carter had fully learned to control his rage and mask it with a smile, he committed one or more acts of arson of which his father was aware but kept quiet. The evidence for this speculation is, however, weak and circumstantial. Hugh Carter (*Cousin Beedie and Cousin Hot*) wrote, "Looking back, I realize that there were a lot of fires at Plains — too many to be justified by the law of averages" (p. 14). More narrowly, a never-explained fire was the burning of the high-school gymnasium in 1940, when Carter was a junior. Carter mentioned in his oral history interview with the National Park Service (May 11, 1988, p. 93, Jimmy Carter Library) that some had accused him of setting the gymnasium fire, since he and a classmate had been the last ones in the adjacent shop before the fire. With surprising equivocation, he added, "But I never did admit that was true." Although his denial perhaps just reflected a poor word choice, it is interesting that he did not deny setting the fire but only claimed never to have admitted setting the fire. For a former politician experienced in disguising unpleasant truths with manipulative phrasing, this phrasing may be salient. Also, one of Jimmy Carter's six remembered and reported whippings came in consequence of his apparent attempt to set fire to his father's barn. In short, it is plausible to ask whether Carter vented his rage in arson.

80. See Hugh Carter, *Cousin Beedie and Cousin Hot*, pp. 40–41.

81. Anne Lawson-Beerman, "Survey Shows Avian Decline by Numbers," *Atlanta Constitution*, June 18, 1993, p. P4.

82. Jimmy Carter, *Turning Point*, pp. 17–18.

83. Interview with Rosalynn Carter, National Park Service Interviews, May 11, 1988, p. 148, Jimmy Carter Library.

84. Jimmy Carter, *Why Not the Best?*, p. 60.

85. See Reinhold Niebuhr's *Moral Man and Immoral Society* (New York: Scribner's, 1932).

86. Ruth Carter Stapleton, *Brother Billy*, pp. 8–9.

87. Interview with Gloria Carter Spann, National Park Service Interviews, December 7, 1988, pp. 35, 38, 45, Jimmy Carter Library.

88. Interview with Willard Slappey, Carter/Smith Oral History Interviews, June 18, 1979, p. 26, Jimmy Carter Library.

89. Interview with Bobby Logan, October 11, 1976, Betty Glad's files.

90. Interview with Rachel Clark, Carter/Smith Oral History Interviews, November 9, 1978, p. 3, Jimmy Carter Library.

91. Ruth Carter Stapleton (*The Gift of Inner Healing*) wrote that her mother's behavior toward her "registered on my emotions as rejection" (p. 17).

92. Interview with Gloria Carter Spann, National Park Service Interviews, December 7, 1988, p. 29, Jimmy Carter Library.

93. Interview with Willard Slappey, Carter/Smith Oral History Interviews, June 18, 1979, p. 5, Jimmy Carter Library.

94. Interview with Ruby Lamb, May 1977, Betty Glad's files.

95. See, e.g., Beisel, "A Psychohistory of Jimmy Carter"; and Elovitz, "Three Days in Plains."

96. Interview with Jimmy Carter, National Park Service Interviews, May 11, 1988, p. 6, Jimmy Carter Library.

97. Schemmel, "My Son Jimmy," p. 73.

98. "'My Son, The President,'" p. 52; Spann, "Miss Lillian," p. 34.

99. When interviewing Lillian Carter, Elovitz ("Three Days in Plains") wrote, "When I declared my interest in Jimmy's childhood . . . [s]he seemed much more interested in talking about her daughter Gloria" (p. 177). In the "'My Son, the President'" interview, Lillian Carter said, "Jimmy was just an ordinary little boy. . . . Actually, his sister Gloria is the most intelligent one in the family" (p. 52).

100. Dr. Richard Morley, an Atlanta family therapist, explained that in many families fathers and mothers tend to favor alternate children according to birth order, the father's preference beginning with the firstborn. Although no one would expect this pattern to apply without frequent exception, it is interesting that Lillian Carter seemed to be the parent most devoted to her second-born, Gloria, while Earl Carter was the dominant influence in Jimmy's life and favored Ruth, the first- and third-born children. Later, however, when Billy was born Earl Carter also favored him. But birth-order conjectures usually assume that when the age gap is great between children, as it was between Billy Carter and his siblings, the original alternating pattern dissolves.

101. Glad, *Jimmy Carter*, p. 503.

102. Jimmy Carter, *An Outdoor Journal*, p. 21.

103. Interview with Eleanor Forrest, National Park Service Interviews, December 18, 1985, p. 18, Jimmy Carter Library. Hugh Carter (*Cousin Beedie and Cousin Hot*, p. 51) repeats the story. Jimmy Carter, unsurprisingly, claims not to remember it.

104. Don Carter, who alternated nights staying with his grandmother with his brother Hugh and cousins Jimmy and Willard, mentions sleeping in the same bed. Interview with Don Carter, Carter/Smith Oral History Interviews, November 3, 1979, p. 41, Jimmy Carter Library.

105. It might be objected that Carter also had an abundance of alternate male role models to draw upon, including the many who worked for his father, school teachers, townsmen, etc. But if it is assumed that the male role at the time was defined primarily in terms of achievement — while the female role, in terms of nurturance — the reason that Carter could easily find mother surrogates but not father surrogates is obvious. No man in Carter's immediate milieu and few elsewhere equaled his father's achievement; none could therefore stand in as a father surrogate. By contrast, since women's provision of nurturance was more or less independent of their or their husbands' worldly achievement, several mother surrogates were available.

106. Interview with a girlfriend who asked to remain anonymous, no date, Betty Glad's files; interview with a girlfriend who asked to remain anonymous, August 25, 1978, Betty Glad's files.

107. Interview with Lottie Tanner, October 15, 1977, Betty Glad's files. Other classmates made similar comments. For example, interview with Grace Wiggins McCoy, October 18, 1977, Betty Glad's files.

108. Hugh Carter, *Cousin Beedie and Cousin Hot*, p. 68.

109. Interview with John and Betty Pope, National Park Service Interviews, June 28, 1989, p. 17, Jimmy Carter Library; interview with Ruby Lamb, May 1977, Betty Glad's files.

110. Wesley G. Pippert ("Viewing the Family from the Oval Office," *Christianity Today*, Sept. 9, 1977, pp. 60–61) provided a brief synopsis of Carter's early publicly expressed attitudes toward his own and others' family lives.

111. Carter's remark about "lust in his heart" was quoted in Robert Scheer, "Jimmy, We Hardly Know Y'All," *Playboy*, Nov. 1976. In *Power and Principle*, Brzezinski spiced up his dry memoir by revealing that he and Carter often caught each other gawking at attractive women (p. 29).

112. The story appeared in Jimmy Carter, *Why Not the Best?*, p. 38. But it was also captured by journalist Hunter S. Thompson at an extemporaneous speech Carter delivered at the University of Georgia in 1974 and subsequently published in both *Rolling Stone* and his own "Jimmy Carter and the Great Leap of Faith," in his *The Great Shark Hunt* (New York: Summit Books, 1979), p. 490. Chances are that Carter repeated the story on other, unrecorded occasions.

113. It is also likely that Carter was writing his campaign autobiography during the spring of 1974, so the story was fresh in his mind on the occasion of the extemporaneous 1974 speech.

114. Jimmy Carter, *An Outdoor Journal*, p. 12.

115. Interview with Eleanor Forrest, National Park Service Interviews, December 18, 1985, p. 28, Jimmy Carter Library.

116. Hugh Carter, *Cousin Beedie and Cousin Hot*, p. 50.

117. In his address to the 1992 Democratic convention, Carter opened with the same line — but added, "I'm *not* running for President."

118. Jimmy Carter, *Why Not the Best?*, p. 19.

119. Ruth Carter Stapleton, *Brother Billy*, p. 28.

120. Interview with Ruby Lamb, May 1977, Betty Glad's files.

121. Interview with Rachel Clark, Carter/Smith Oral History Interviews, November 9, 1978, p. 5, Jimmy Carter Library.

122. Interview with a classmate who asked to remain anonymous, June 1977, Betty Glad's files.

123. Interview with a classmate who asked to remain anonymous, October 15, 1977, Betty Glad's files; interview with a classmate who asked to remain anonymous, no date, Betty Glad's files; interview with Thomas Lowery, October 15, 1977, Betty Glad's files.

124. Interview with Bobby Logan, October 11, 1976, Betty Glad's files.

125. Interview with Rosalynn Carter, National Park Service Interviews, May 11, 1988, p. 11, Jimmy Carter Library.

126. Interview with a neighbor who asked to remain anonymous, May 29, 1977, Betty Glad's files.

127. Interview with Rosalynn Carter, National Park Service Interviews, December 8, 1988, p. 22, Jimmy Carter Library.

128. Interview with Lang Sheffield, National Park Service Interviews, June 27, 1989, p. 43, Jimmy Carter Library.

129. Interview with Jimmy Carter, National Park Service Interviews, May 11, 1988, p. 111, Jimmy Carter Library.

130. Interview with Jan Williams, National Park Service Interviews, December 20, 1985, p. 46, Jimmy Carter Library.

131. Leo Sandon Jr., "Pilgrimage to Plains," *Christian Century*, Feb. 16, 1977, p. 145.

132. Of course, other presidents have been associated with the same sort of small-town myth that Carter was. Next to Abraham Lincoln, perhaps this myth was most prominent for Dwight Eisenhower. Although Eisenhower's home was repeatedly said to be in small-town Kansas, he himself never chose to live there even in retirement. There is little doubt, however, but that the small-town symbolism aided his campaign and his reputation. Interestingly, however, the myth of Eisenhower's small-town roots seems to have been imposed on his reputation by journalists and the public more than cultivated by him as a campaign tactic. See Kenneth E. Morris and Barry Schwartz, "Why They Liked Ike: Tradition, Crisis, and Heroic Leadership," *Sociological Quarterly* 34 (1993): 133–51.

133. Interview with Rachel Clark, May 27, 1977, Betty Glad's files.

134. Interview with Jimmy Carter, National Park Service Interviews, May 11, 1988, p. 259, Jimmy Carter Library.

135. "'My Son, The President,'" p. 52.

136. Elovitz, "Three Days in Plains," p. 194.

137. Interview with Rachel Clark, Carter/Smith Oral History Interviews, November 9, 1978, p. 17, Jimmy Carter Library.

138. Jimmy Carter, *Why Not the Best?*, pp. 35–36; Hugh Carter, *Cousin Beedie and Cousin Hot*, pp. 31–32.

139. Interview with Ruby Lamb, May 1977, Betty Glad's files.

140. Interview with Gloria Carter Spann, National Park Service Interviews, December 7, 1988, pp. 20–21, Jimmy Carter Library.

141. Jimmy Carter, *An Outdoor Journal*, pp. 21–22, 45–47.

142. Jimmy Carter, *Why Not the Best?*, p. 35.

143. Ibid., pp. 36–37. For a more general account of the significance of this fight for African American pride, see Lawrence W. Levine, *Black Culture and Black Consciousness: Afro-American Folk Thought from Slavery to Freedom* (New York: Oxford University Press, 1977), pp. 429–38.

144. Glad, *Jimmy Carter*, p. 44.

145. Interview with Ruth Jackson, National Park Service Interviews, December 20, 1985, p. 12, Jimmy Carter Library.

146. Interview with William Wise, September 29, 1976, Betty Glad's files.

147. See, e.g., Jimmy Carter, *Turning Point*, pp. 42–44.

148. Interview with Willard Slappey, Carter/Smith Oral History Interviews, June 18, 1979, p. 12, Jimmy Carter Library.

149. Interviews with William Wise, September 29, 1976; Lottie Wise Tanner, October 15, 1977; and Grace Wiggins McCoy, October 18, 1977, Betty Glad's files.

150. Interview with Jimmy Carter, Miscellaneous Interviews (Vision Associates), November 1, 1984, p. 2A–9, Jimmy Carter Library.

CHAPTER 4: THE QUEST FOR LEADERSHIP

1. Interview with Lillian Carter, Carter/Smith Oral History Interviews, September 26, 1978, pp. 32–33, Jimmy Carter Library.

2. Jimmy Carter, *Why Not the Best?* (Nashville: Broadman Press, 1975), pp. 41–42; James Wooten, *Dasher: The Roots and the Rising of Jimmy Carter* (New York: Summit Books, 1978), pp. 152–54; interview with Jimmy Carter, National Park Service Interviews, May 11, 1988, pp. 10–11, Jimmy Carter Library.

3. Interview with Laurence Gellerstedt (classmate), April 29, 1977, Betty Glad's files.

4. Jimmy Carter's diary entry, June 26 and 27, 1943, vertical file, Jimmy Carter Library.

5. Ibid.

6. Interview with Laurence Gellerstedt, April 29, 1977, Betty Glad's files.

7. Jimmy Carter, *Turning Point: A Candidate, a State, and a Nation Come of Age* (New York: Times Books, 1992), p. 170.

8. Jimmy Carter, *Keeping Faith: Memoirs of a President* (New York: Bantam, 1982), p. 364.

9. Telephone interview with Leo Ribuffo, September 23, 1994.

10. Hugh Carter, *Cousin Beedie and Cousin Hot: My Life with the Carter Family of Plains, Georgia* (Englewood Cliffs, N.J.: Prentice-Hall, 1978), p. 61.

11. Interview with Doris Cosby Osborne; letter from James E. Hendrix to Betty Glad, June 21, 1977; questionnaire completed by Edward Brooks, Betty Glad's files.

12. Interview with Laurence Gellerstedt, April 29, 1977, Betty Glad's files.

13. Letter from James H. Forbes to Betty Glad, November 25, 1977, Betty Glad's files.

14. Interview with Albert Rusher, October 5, 1976, Betty Glad's files.

15. Questionnaire completed by Carter's Spanish instructor, Betty Glad's files.

16. See, e.g., Bruce Mazlish and Edwin Diamond, *Jimmy Carter: A Character Portrait* (New York: Simon & Schuster, 1979), p. 102; and Betty Glad, *Jimmy Carter: In Search of the Great White House* (New York: Norton, 1980), p. 59.

17. Letter from J. H. Lucas (a former Tech professor) to Betty Glad, May 19, 1977, Betty Glad's files.

18. Interview with Albert Rusher, October 5, 1976, Betty Glad's files.

19. Letter from James H. Forbes to Betty Glad, November 25, 1977, Betty Glad's files.

20. Ibid.

21. Interview with Bryan Brown, December 3, 1977, Betty Glad's files; questionnaire completed by Wayne R. Lippert, February 3, 1978, Betty Glad's files.

22. Questionnaire completed by a classmate who asked to remain anonymous, Betty Glad's files.

23. Interview with Bobby Logan, October 11, 1976, Betty Glad's files.

24. Interview with Albert Rusher, October 5, 1976, Betty Glad's files.

25. Interview with Jimmy Carter, National Park Service Interviews, May 11, 1988, p. 234, Jimmy Carter Library.

26. Questionnaire completed by Chester H. Shaddeau, November 29, 1979, Betty Glad's files.

27. Reported in Glad, *Jimmy Carter*, p. 52.

28. Carter (*Why Not the Best?*) lists his weight upon entry into the academy at 121 pounds; at 135 pounds upon graduation (p. 44). Others remember that he grew taller during these years too.

29. Interview with Grace Wiggins McCoy, October 18, 1977, Betty Glad's files.

30. Interview with Bryan Brown, December 3, 1977, Betty Glad's files.

31. Clark's remarks are found in a series of letters and interviews, April and May 1977, Betty Glad's files.

32. Interview with Joseph Flanagan, November 13, 1977, Betty Glad's files.

33. Questionnaire completed by William Strickler, November 26, 1977, Betty Glad's files.

34. Interview with a classmate who preferred to remain anonymous, December 2, 1977, Betty Glad's files.

35. Interview with Albert Rusher, October 5, 1976, Betty Glad's files.

36. Letter from Ellery Clark to Betty Glad, May 7, 1977, Betty Glad's files.

37. Questionnaire completed by a classmate who preferred to remain anonymous, December 10, 1977, Betty Glad's files.

38. Peter G. Bourne, "Jimmy Carter: A Profile," *Yale Review* 72 (October 1982): 126–40.

39. Ibid.

40. Rosalynn Carter, *First Lady from Plains* (Boston: Houghton Mifflin, 1984), pp. 28–30.

41. Ibid.

42. Mazlish and Diamond, *Jimmy Carter*, p. 102.

43. Kandy Stroud, *How Jimmy Won: The Victory Campaign from Plains to the White House* (New York: Morrow, 1977), p. 284.

44. Jimmy Carter, *Why Not the Best?*, p. 49.

45. "'My Son, The President': Interview with Lillian Carter," *U.S. News & World Report*, Mar. 7, 1977, p. 53.

46. Rosalynn Carter, *First Lady from Plains*, pp. 29–30.

47. Jimmy Carter, *Why Not the Best?*, p. 52.

48. Ibid., p. 49.

49. Quoted in Glad, *Jimmy Carter*, p. 60.

50. Interview with Warren Colegrove, December 4, 1977, Betty Glad's files.

51. Interview with Roy Smallwood, November 12, 1977, Betty Glad's files.

52. Jimmy Carter, *Why Not the Best?*, p. 49.

53. Interview with Lowell Fitch, November 19, 1977, Betty Glad's files.

54. Roth S. Leddick, "Submarine School Recollections," June 8, 1977, Betty Glad's files.

55. Interview with Warren Colegrove, December 4, 1977, Betty Glad's files.

56. Interview with Roy Cowdrey, November 19, 1977; letter from Francis Joe Callahan to Betty Glad, no date, Betty Glad's files.

57. Letter from Francis Joe Callahan to Betty Glad, no date, Betty Glad's files.

58. Elmo R. Zumwalt Jr., *On Watch: A Memoir* (New York: Quadrangle/New York Times Book Co., 1976), pp. 85–122.

59. Norman Polmar and Thomas B. Allen, *Rickover* (New York: Simon and Schuster, 1982), p. 344.

60. Theodore Rockwell, *The Rickover Effect: How One Man Made a Difference* (Annapolis: Naval Institute Press, 1992), pp. 238–39, 323; Jimmy Carter, *Why Not the Best?*, p. 57.

61. Rockwell, *The Rickover Effect*, p. 361.

62. Ibid., p. 3.

63. Zumwalt, *On Watch*, pp. 86–95.

64. Rockwell, *The Rickover Effect*, p. 237.

65. Ibid., p. 4.

66. Zumwalt, *On Watch*, pp. 86–95.

67. Rockwell, *The Rickover Effect*, p. 240.

68. Letter from Francis Joe Callahan to Betty Glad, no date, Betty Glad's files.

69. Jimmy Carter, *Why Not the Best?*, p. 57.

70. Interview with an associate who preferred to remain anonymous, October 5, 1976, Betty Glad's files.

71. Letter from Francis Joe Callahan to Betty Glad, no date, Betty Glad's files.

72. Rockwell, *The Rickover Effect*, p. xiii.

73. Polmar and Allen, *Rickover*, pp. 341–42.

74. Interview with William Lalor, October 15, 1976, Betty Glad's files.

75. Carter, *Why Not the Best?*, p. 60.

76. Interview with Albert and Ruby Trottier, September 23, 1977, Betty Glad's files.

77. Quoted in Paul Elovitz, "Three Days in Plains," *Journal of Psychohistory* (Fall 1977): 188.

78. Jimmy Carter, *Why Not the Best?*, p. 65.

79. Jimmy Carter, *Turning Point*, p. 49.

80. Interview with Mary Anne Thomas, May 31, 1977, Betty Glad's files.

81. Carter, *Turning Point*, pp. 20–21.

82. Interview with Jimmy and Rosalynn Carter, May 11, 1988, National Park Service Interviews, pp. 271–99, Jimmy Carter Library.

83. "Mr. and Mrs. Carter Are Hosts at Dance," *Americus Times-Recorder*, November 29, 1955.

84. Interview with John Pope, June 20, 1977, Betty Glad's files.

85. Interview with Jimmy Carter, May 11, 1988, National Park Service Interviews, pp. 130–31, Jimmy Carter Library.

86. Interview with John Pope, June 20, 1977, Betty Glad's files.

87. Jimmy Carter, *Turning Point*, pp. 22–23. Interestingly, Carter's remembered remarks to the assembled council members were not in defense of civil rights but, rather, an attempt to stimulate rural populist resentment against the power structure of the Citizens' Councils. He remembered saying, "[B]esides, there are a few politicians in Atlanta who are taking the dues from all over the state and putting the money in their pockets, just because folks are worried about the race issue."

88. Interview with Mary Anne Thomas, May 31, 1977, Betty Glad's files.

89. Jimmy Carter, *Turning Point*, p. 59.

90. Interview with a tenant who preferred to remain anonymous, October 29, 1976, Betty Glad's files.

91. Willie Carter Spann, "The Other Carter," *Hustler*, May 1977, pp. 53, 92.

92. Interview with a resident who preferred to remain anonymous, October 12, 1977, Betty Glad's files.

93. Jimmy Carter, *Turning Point*, p. 21.

94. Ibid., 43–44; Jimmy Carter, *Why Not the Best?*, p. 66.

95. Rudy Hayes and Clarence Graddick, "Merger Beaten, Boards to Proceed with Plan," *Americus Times-Recorder*, July 19, 1961, p. A1.

96. Interview with Miriam Timmerman Saylor, May 26, 1978, Betty Glad's files.

97. Willie Carter Spann, "The Other Carter," pp. 50, 52–53, 92.

98. Ibid., p. 50.

99. Letter from Lottie Wise Tanner to Dennis Rendleman, October 21, 1977, Betty Glad's files.

100. Willie Carter Spann, "The Other Carter," p. 53.

101. Interview with a friend who preferred to remain anonymous, June 2, 1977, Betty Glad's files.

102. Interview with an acquaintance who preferred to remain anonymous, December 13, 1978, Betty Glad's files.

103. Interview with a friend who preferred to remain anonymous, June 20, 1977, Betty Glad's files.

104. Interview with John Pope, June 20, 1977, Betty Glad's files. In fairness, Carter had announced his candidacy after Pope had already committed to the Republican candidate, and Pope did actively support Carter in 1970.

105. Jimmy Carter, *Turning Point*, p. 56.

CHAPTER 5: THE SPIRITUAL PASSION OF POLITICS

1. Quoted in Robert W. Dubay, "Marvin Griffin and the Politics of the Stump," in Harold P. Henderson and Gary L. Roberts (eds.), *Georgia Governors in an Age of Change* (Athens: University of Georgia Press, 1988), p. 101.

2. Jimmy Carter, *Turning Point: A Candidate, a State, and a Nation Come of Age* (New York: Times Books, 1992), p. 35.

3. Dubay, "Marvin Griffin and the Politics of the Stump," p. 101.

4. See, e.g., Taylor Branch, *Parting the Waters: America in the King Years 1954–63* (New York: Simon & Schuster, 1988).

5. Jerome L. Rodnitzky, *Minstrels of the Dawn: The Folk-Protest Singer as Cultural Hero* (Chicago: Nelson-Hall, 1976), pp. 107–8.

6. Numan V. Bartley, "1940 to the Present," in Kenneth Coleman (ed.), *A History of Georgia* (Athens: University of Georgia Press, 1977), p. 370.

7. Brooks Pennington, a state senate colleague of Carter's, wrote that "Carter, with his Kennedy image, did attract press attention. In Carter's early years in the Senate, Kennedy was very popular" (questionnaire completed by Brooks Pennington, May 20, 1977, Betty Glad's files).

8. John A. T. Robinson, *Honest to God* (Philadelphia: Westminster Press, 1963). Quotation from Lonnie D. Kliever, *The Shattered Spectrum: A Survey of Contemporary Theology* (Atlanta: John Knox Press, 1981), p. 27.

9. Thomas S. Kuhn, *The Structure of Scientific Revolutions* (Chicago: University of Chicago Press, 1962); Rachel Carson, *Silent Spring* (Boston: Houghton Mifflin, 1962).

10. Marshall McLuhan, *The Gutenberg Galaxy: The Making of Typographic Man* (New York: New American Library, 1962).

11. Cobbett S. Steinberg, *TV Facts* (New York: Facts on File, 1980), pp. 58, 167–68, 170.

12. Charles Kaiser, *1968 in America: Music, Politics, Chaos, Counterculture, and the Shaping of a Generation* (New York: Weidenfeld & Nicolson, 1988), p. 154.

13. Fred Bronson, *The Billboard Book of Number One Hits* (New York: Billboard Publications, 1985), pp. 103–21.

14. Peter Guralnick, *Sweet Soul Music: Rhythm and Blues and the Southern Dream of Freedom* (New York: Harper & Row, 1986), p. 27.

15. Little Richard had already enjoyed considerable influence on popular music by 1962. However, his influence was largely unmatched by popular celebrity. In the fall of 1962, for instance, Richard's concert in Liverpool, England, was arranged by Brian Epstein, manager of the Beatles. The Beatles had long been admirers of Little Richard, covered several of his songs, and tried to imitate his style. With the release of their first single in the fall of 1962, "Love Me Do/P.S. I Love You," the acclaim that awaited the Beatles would stimulate Little Richard's

as well. See, e.g., Philip Norman, *Shout: The Beatles in Their Generation* (New York: Simon & Schuster, 1981), pp. 208–11; and Charles White, *The Life and Times of Little Richard* (New York: Simon & Schuster, 1984).

16. Bronson, *The Billboard Book of Number One Hits*, pp. 103–21.

17. Guralnick, *Sweet Soul Music*, p. 46.

18. Bronson, *The Billboard Book of Number One Hits*, p. 118.

19. Dubay, "Marvin Griffin and the Politics of the Stump"; Bartley, "1940 to the Present," pp. 365–66.

20. A table reflecting the discrepancies of political power between heavily populated and sparsely populated Georgia counties in 1962 is published in Charles Pyles, "S. Ernest Vandiver and the Politics of Change," in Henderson and Roberts (eds.), *Georgia Governors in an Age of Change*, p. 151.

21. Dubay, "Marvin Griffin and the Politics of the Stump."

22. Jimmy Carter, *Turning Point*, pp. xix–xxiii.

23. Eugene D. Genovese has been in the forefront of historians who describe antebellum southern society as essentially particularist in contrast to the more universalistic North. For him as for others, the War Between the States dealt the decisive blow to southern particularism, although later southern particularist voices could also be heard. See his (with Elizabeth Fox-Genovese) "The Religious Ideals of Southern Slave Society," in Numan V. Bartley (ed.), *The Evolution of Southern Culture* (Athens: University of Georgia Press, 1988); and *The Southern Tradition: The Achievement and Limitations of an American Conservatism* (Cambridge: Harvard University Press, 1994). It is also worthwhile in this connection to consider Garry Wills's explication of Abraham Lincoln's Gettysburg Address (*Lincoln at Gettysburg: The Words That Remade America* [New York: Simon & Schuster, 1992]). Wills argues that in this address Lincoln lifted the universalistic principle of equality from minor to major significance in the American creed. If Wills is correct, the entire nation may have moved further along the universalistic path as a consequence of the Civil War. Finally, it merits mention that Martin Luther King Jr. often rooted the moral claims of the civil rights movement in values stimulated by Lincoln. The march on Washington, for instance, was rhetorically justified in part as a centennial celebration of the Emancipation Proclamation.

24. Herman E. Talmadge, *Talmadge: A Political Legacy, A Politician's Life* (Atlanta: Peachtree, 1987), p. 105.

25. Ibid., p. 106.

26. Peter's vision and its universalistic consequences are found in Acts 10. Although it has become commonplace to trace universalism to Christianity, it is also important to point out that Christian universalism can easily be interpreted as implying only a vague spiritual equality, and even that not completely. In 1 Cor. 12, for instance, Paul asserts that even the gifts of the spirit are distributed unequally. It has therefore always been dubious to extrapolate from Christian universalism the principle of social equality, and Christian societies have not always done so. Thinkers on the left, including Eugene Genovese, have therefore long followed Karl Marx in arguing that market forces have played a larger role in establishing universalism as a social principle than has Christianity. Although thinkers on the right are naturally reluctant to employ Marx's ideas, I cannot think

of a reason they would object to this added interpretation. Nevertheless, whatever role the market economy has played in fostering universalism's sweep, it bears emphasis that universalism remains a spiritual principle. Individuals are obviously unequal in modern market societies, leaving the belief in their equality an article of faith, not fact.

27. Interview with Janet S. Merritt, May 3, 1978, Betty Glad's files; Jimmy Carter, *Turning Point*, p. 62.

28. Interview with an area state legislator who preferred to remain anonymous, October 29, 1976, Betty Glad's files.

29. Interview with Mary Anne Thomas, May 31, 1977, Betty Glad's files.

30. Jimmy Carter, *Turning Point*, p. 20.

31. Interview with Mary Anne Thomas, May 31, 1977, Betty Glad's files.

32. Jimmy Carter, *Turning Point*, p. 83.

33. Ibid., p. 20.

34. Carter's account in *Turning Point* about his early political ambitions, or lack thereof, is a bit disingenuous. Portraying Jones as an arch segregationist, for instance, Carter implies that he could not have beaten him because of his own less popular liberal racial views. That may or may not have been an accurate assessment. However, what Carter fails to mention is that Sumter County had two House seats. He never explains why he rejected the idea to run for the other seat or accused its occupant of segregationist views. The inescapable inference is that Carter calculated his political viability in general and usually found it wanting, but then later chose to present his liabilities only in terms of his civil rights stand.

35. Interview with an area state legislator who preferred to remain anonymous, October 29, 1976, Betty Glad's files.

36. Jimmy Carter, *Turning Point*, pp. 65–69.

37. Ibid., p. 72.

38. Interview with John Pope, June 1, 1977, Betty Glad's files.

39. Although there are doubts about precisely what Hurst did (and why he did it), the general facts about the fraudulent balloting in Georgetown were substantiated in court and have never been seriously challenged. Carter's *Turning Point* relates these facts as well as any other source.

40. Interview with John Pope, June 1, 1977, Betty Glad's files.

41. William Anderson, *Wild Man from Sugar Creek: The Political Career of Eugene Talmadge* (Baton Rouge: Louisiana State University Press, 1975).

42. "Georgia Association of Historians Survey of Georgia Governors, May 1985," in Henderson and Roberts (eds.), *Georgia Governors in an Age of Change*.

43. Interview with a neighbor who preferred to remain anonymous, June 14, 1977, Betty Glad's files.

44. Interview with Janet S. Merritt, May 3, 1978, Betty Glad's files.

45. Lawrence R. Hepburn (ed.), *Contemporary Georgia*, 2d ed. (Athens: Carl Vinson Institute of Government, The University of Georgia, 1992), pp. 81, 113, 118, 206; Ann V. Peisher and Douglas C. Bachtel, "Poverty in Georgia," *Issues Facing Georgia* 1 (March 1984).

46. Jimmy Carter, *Turning Point*, p. 187.

47. Quoted in Betty Glad, *Jimmy Carter: In Search of the Great White House* (New York: Norton, 1980), p. 99.

48. Interview with Bill Shipp, August 21, 1978, Betty Glad's files.

49. Interview with Mary Beazley, September 1, 1978, Betty Glad's files.

50. Interview with an area state legislator who preferred to remain anonymous, October 29, 1976, Betty Glad's files.

51. Letter from Sam Caldwell to Betty Glad, June 23, 1977, Betty Glad's files.

52. Questionnaire completed by Brooks Pennington, May 20, 1977, Betty Glad's files.

53. Interview with a state senator who preferred to remain anonymous, October 28, 1976, Betty Glad's files.

54. Interview with Al Holloway, October 19, 1978, Betty Glad's files.

55. Jimmy Carter, *Turning Point*, pp. 185–86.

56. Interview with Gerald Rafshoon, Miller Center Interviews, Carter Presidency Project, vol. 21, April 8, 1983, p. 1, Jimmy Carter Library.

57. Interview with an area state legislator who preferred to remain anonymous, October 29, 1976, Betty Glad's files.

58. Questionnaire completed by Brooks Pennington, May 20, 1977, Betty Glad's files.

59. Interview with Bill Shipp, August 21, 1978, Betty Glad's files.

60. Questionnaire completed by Brooks Pennington, May 20, 1977, Betty Glad's files.

61. Interview with Charles Kirbo, September 30, 1976, Betty Glad's files.

62. Questionnaire completed by Brooks Pennington, May 20, 1977, Betty Glad's files.

63. Jimmy Carter, *Why Not the Best?* (Nashville: Broadman, 1975), p. 97; letter from Bo Calloway to Betty Glad, May 31, 1977, Betty Glad's files.

64. Jimmy Carter, *Why Not the Best?*, p. 97.

65. The following résumé of Maddox's career is based largely on Bruce Galphin's *The Riddle of Lester Maddox* (Atlanta: Camelot, 1968). Galphin was a reporter who covered Maddox during the period.

66. Bronson, *The Billboard Book of Number One Hits*, p. 195.

67. Hamilton Jordan, *Crisis: The Last Year of the Carter Presidency* (New York: Berkley Books, 1982), pp. 16, 351.

68. Ibid., p. 16.

69. Letter from a reporter who preferred to remain anonymous to Betty Glad, no date, Betty Glad's files.

70. Jimmy Carter, *Why Not the Best?*, pp. 98, 100.

71. Descriptions of Carter's warehouse office are found in Steve Ball Jr., "Carter Again Underdog, Looks to Maddox Country," *Atlanta Constitution*, Apr. 7, 1970.

72. Jimmy Carter, *A Government as Good as Its People*, p. 14.

73. "The Guard Changes" (editorial) and Reg Murphy, "Carter's Inaugural Speech Like 1966," *Atlanta Constitution*, Jan. 13, 1971, p. A4.

74. Bill Shipp, "Carter's Pledge to End Bias Shows Times Have Changed," *Atlanta Constitution*, Jan. 13, 1971, p. A3.

75. Jimmy Carter, *A Government as Good as Its People*, p. 17.

76. Ibid.

77. James Agee and Walker Evans, *Let Us Now Praise Famous Men* (Boston:

Houghton Mifflin, 1941). Carter's mention of this as his favorite book appears, among other places, in an Associated Press article, "Reading by Starlight: Famous Bookworms," *Atlanta Constitution*, May 29, 1991, p. B10.

78. Jimmy Carter, *"I'll Never Lie to You: Jimmy Carter in His Own Words*, ed. Robert W. Turner (New York: Ballantine, 1976), p. 20.

79. Jimmy Carter, "Priorities of Some Mexican Children" and "Miss Lillian Sees Leprosy for the First Time," *Georgia Journal* (Fall 1992): 20.

80. Both Glad's *Jimmy Carter* and Bruce Mazlish and Edwin Diamond's *Jimmy Carter: A Character Portrait* (New York: Simon & Schuster, 1979) trace Carter's sympathy for the less privileged to his analogous childhood experiences of emotional deprivation. The interpretations are persuasive but, like most psychobiography, suffer from a tendency to minimize later experiences in order to accentuate formative childhood experiences. My contention is not so much that these authors are mistaken in what they assert about Carter's personality as it is that their psychobiographical assumptions led them to stress unduly the importance of childhood experiences and minimize those in later life.

81. Norman Mailer, "The Search for Carter," *New York Times Magazine*, Sept. 26, 1976, p. 76.

82. "Bill Moyers Interview with Jimmy Carter," *USA: People and Politics*, PBS, WETA and WNET, Washington and New York, May 6, 1976.

83. Interview with Mary Anne Thomas, May 31, 1977, Betty Glad's files. Important for the chronological record is that Thomas remembered trying to discuss Altizer with Carter. Since Altizer's *The Gospel of Christian Atheism* (Philadelphia: Westminster Press, 1966) was the book that brought his ideas about "the death of God" to popular attention, she and Carter would have had to have read the book no earlier than 1966. The point helps to substantiate Carter's reading of theology during the late 1960s, rather than earlier.

84. Jimmy Carter, *I'll Never Lie to You*, p. 70.

85. James Fallows, "The Passionless Presidency: The Trouble with Jimmy Carter's Administration," *Atlantic*, May 1979, p. 42.

86. Ibid. See also Jimmy Carter, *The Spiritual Journey of Jimmy Carter: In His Own Words*, comp. Wesley G. Pippert (New York: Macmillan, 1978), p. 99.

87. Fallows, "The Passionless Presidency," p. 42.

88. Jimmy Carter, *The Spiritual Journey of Jimmy Carter*, p. 98.

89. Jimmy Carter, *A Government as Good as Its People*, p. 17.

90. Quotations describing Carter's conversion experience are drawn from a number of sources, including Mazlish and Diamond, *Jimmy Carter*, pp. 151–54; "Bill Moyers Interview with Jimmy Carter," *USA: People and Politics*, PBS, WETA and WNET, Washington and New York, May 6, 1976; Jimmy Carter, *The Spiritual Journey of Jimmy Carter*, p. 59.

91. "Bill Moyers Interview with Jimmy Carter," *USA: People and Politics*, PBS, WETA, and WNET, Washington and New York, May 6, 1976.

92. Interview with Hoyt Robinson, Sept. 28, 1977, Betty Glad's files.

93. Jimmy Carter, *The Spiritual Journey of Jimmy Carter*, p. 14.

94. Interview with Hoyt Robinson, Sept. 28, 1977, Betty Glad's files.

95. Ernst Troeltsch, *The Social Teaching of the Christian Churches*, vol. 2, trans. Olive Wyon (Chicago: University of Chicago Press, 1976), p. 1013.

96. H. Richard Niebuhr, *Christ and Culture* (New York: Harper & Row, 1951).

97. James M. Powell, "A Medieval View of Jimmy Carter," *America*, Oct. 23, 1976, p. 249.

98. Jimmy Carter, *Why Not the Best?*, p. 79.

99. See, e.g., David O. Moberg, *The Great Reversal: Evangelism versus Social Concern* (Philadelphia: Lippincott, 1972).

100. Jimmy Carter, *The Spiritual Journey of Jimmy Carter*, p. 93.

101. "Bill Moyers Interview with Jimmy Carter," *USA: People and Politics*, PBS, WETA and WNET, Washington and New York, May 6, 1976.

102. Ibid.

103. In an op-ed piece published in the *Wall Street Journal* (April 28, 1976, p. 18) entitled "God and the 1976 Election," Arthur Schlesinger Jr. led the critics who charged that Carter misunderstood Niebuhr. My agreement with the essentials of this charge is explained below. This agreement, however, should not be confused with an assent to the gist of the arguments advanced by Schlesinger in this piece about the desirability of a complete separation of religion from politics. I think Schlesinger is mistaken in this insistence and grossly overargues his case.

104. A good overview of Niebuhr's thought in context is Richard Fox's *Reinhold Niebuhr: A Biography* (San Francisco: Harper & Row, 1985).

105. Jimmy Carter, *A Government as Good as Its People*, pp. 77, 93; Jimmy Carter, *The Spiritual Journey of Jimmy Carter*, pp. 79, 91, 93, 168, 233, 256.

106. Jimmy Carter, *The Spiritual Journey of Jimmy Carter*, pp. 14, 176, 244.

107. Jimmy Carter, *I'll Never Lie to You*, p. 70.

108. The criticism is Robert Bellah's. See John Raeside, "A Night at Camp David," *East Bay Express*, July 27, 1979.

109. Alexis de Tocqueville, *Democracy in America*, trans. George Lawrence, ed. J. P. Mayer (Garden City, N.Y.: Doubleday, 1969), p. 508.

110. Nixon, it is sometimes forgotten, essentially endorsed the liberals' "war on poverty." He was even a supporter of a guaranteed minimum income for all Americans, a policy that is normally construed as wildly liberal (even though it also has the backing of such conservative economists as Milton Friedman). See, e.g., Tom Wicker, *One of Us: Richard Nixon and the American Dream* (New York: Random House, 1991).

111. Jerry Rubin was perhaps the most flamboyant of the late 1960s countercultural leaders. In a later book, *Growing (up) at Thirty-Seven* (New York: M. Evans, 1976), he admitted that his countercultural excesses had been essentially oriented toward nihilistic destruction of the existing social order rather than toward the establishment of a more just society. He explained, for example, that the term "yippie" stood for no more than the liberated yell, and even admitted that at the same time he threw cash away on Wall Street he was secretly a stockholder. More telling about Rubin's underlying philosophy, however, is the conclusion of his 1976 confessional book. He wrote: "I am now working on myself to become a spiritually high, nonattached human being" (p. 208). Spirituality coupled with nonattachment may well have been his chief cultural contribution even earlier. In 1994 he was killed when hit by a car crossing a street in Los Angeles. News accounts indicated that at the time of his death he was a businessman promoting a

line of New Age health-food products that promised increased health and longevity.

112. Sex and violence were also beginning to be linked culturally. Perhaps the best-known linkage was found in the then-popular book, based in part on Freud's metapsychology, by Herbert Marcuse, *Eros and Civilization: A Philosophical Inquiry into Freud* (Boston: Beacon, 1956). Although published much earlier, Marcuse's work enjoyed a renaissance during the late 1960s when, as a professor at the University of California at San Diego, he influenced a number of counterculture intellectuals. His thinking, however, was not so much about sex and violence as it was about sex and death. During the 1970s, Woody Allen's movies often dabbled with these themes too, and perhaps pushed them to a more popular cultural forefront. Not until the 1980s, however, when Michel Foucault became a widely influential intellectual in the United States, were sex and violence positively linked. An admitted participant in sadomasochistic sexual practices, Foucault celebrated the "limit experiences" of both sex and death. Violent sex, Foucault borrowed from the Marquis de Sade, was the best sex. See, e.g., Jim Miller, *The Passion of Michel Foucault* (New York: Simon & Schuster, 1993).

113. John Flinn, "North Beach: Still Can't Stop It," *San Francisco Examiner*, June 19, 1994, p. B1.

114. Interestingly, and unlike many other social changes of the era, the relaxation of standards regarding the display of nudity and sex during the late 1960s is traceable to no single legal or legislative catalyst. The chief Supreme Court ruling allowing such displays was *U.S. v. Roth*, decided in 1957. Later rulings as well as much legislative action were the main oriented toward curbing rather than enhancing the liberties permitted by the 1957 ruling. It follows that the shifting standards for sexual display and nudity reflect a real change in both the culture and many people's values rather than a simple relaxation of legal prohibitions against them.

115. At 2.4 divorces per 1,000, the 1964 divorce rate had already climbed from a postwar low of 2.1 in 1958. By 1969, the rate was 3.2 (or a 30 percent increase over the rate in 1964). The rate continued to rise during the 1970s, peaking at 5.4 in 1979. This was the point at which demographers could predict that roughly half of all marriages would end in divorce. The 1969 prediction was the more modest but still sensational one that a third of marriages would conclude with divorce. Data are from the Department of Health and Human Services, National Center for Health Statistics, and published annually in the *Information Please Almanac* (Boston: Houghton Mifflin).

116. James Alan Fox, quoted in "Mass Murderer Speck Dies of Heart Attack," *Atlanta Constitution*, Dec. 6, 1991, p. A6.

117. Truman Capote, *In Cold Blood* (New York: Random House, 1965).

118. For a general discussion of this tendency, see Marshall Berman, *The Politics of Authenticity: Radical Individualism and the Emergence of Modern Society* (New York: Atheneum, 1970). Jon Wiener's *Come Together: John Lennon in His Time* (New York: Random House, 1984) shows how the tendency to replace authority with authenticity characterized the influence of one of the era's chief cultural leaders.

119. Quoted in Kaiser, *1968 in America*, p. 154.

120. Todd Gitlin, *The Sixties: Years of Hope, Days of Rage* (New York: Bantam, 1987), p. 437.

121. Ibid., p. 428.

122. Quoted in Rodnitzky, *Minstrels of the Dawn*, p. 71.

123. "Carter Checks Family Landmark," *Atlanta Constitution*, Dec. 30, 1969.

124. "Bill Moyers Interview with Jimmy Carter," *USA: People and Politics*, PBS, WETA and WNET, New York and Washington, May 6, 1976.

125. Jimmy Carter, *I'll Never Lie to You*, p. 70.

126. Peter G. Bourne, "Jimmy Carter: A Profile," *Yale Review* 72 (Oct. 1982): 137.

127. Jimmy Carter, "*I'll Never Lie to You*," p. 91.

128. Jimmy Carter, *The Spiritual Journey of Jimmy Carter*, p. 62.

129. The phrase is the one Wade Clark Roof uses in his book *A Generation of Seekers: The Spiritual Journeys of the Baby Boom Generation* (San Francisco: HarperSanFrancisco, 1993).

130. Jimmy Carter, "*I'll Never Lie to You*," p. 79.

131. Rosalynn Carter, *First Lady from Plains* (Boston: Houghton Mifflin, 1984), p. 63.

CHAPTER 6: GOVERNOR — AND BEYOND

1. "Bill Moyers Interview with Jimmy Carter," *USA: People and Politics*, PBS, WETA and WNET, Washington and New York, May 6, 1976.

2. Peter G. Bourne, "Jimmy Carter: A Profile," *Yale Review* 72 (Oct. 1982), p. 127.

3. Quoted in Kandy Stroud, *How Jimmy Won: The Victory Campaign from Plains to the White House* (New York: Morrow, 1977), p. 191.

4. Quoted in Jules Witcover, *Marathon: The Pursuit of the Presidency 1972–1976* (New York: Viking, 1977), p. 107.

5. Interview with Jimmy Carter, Miller Center Interviews, Carter Presidency Project, vol. 19, November 29, 1982, p. 2, Jimmy Carter Library.

6. James T. Wooten, "Carter's Georgia Guru," *New York Times Magazine*, March 20, 1977, pp. 14–18.

7. James Fallows, "The Passionless Presidency," *Atlantic*, May 1979, p. 45.

8. Bourne, "Jimmy Carter," p. 134.

9. Jody Powell, *The Other Side of the Story* (New York: Morrow, 1984), p. 14.

10. "The President's Boys," *Time*, June 6, 1977, p. 17.

11. Ibid.

12. Fallows, "The Passionless Presidency," p. 42.

13. Interview with Hamilton Jordan (including Landon Butler), Miller Center Interviews, Carter Presidency Project, vol. 6, November 6, 1981, p. 32, Jimmy Carter Library.

14. Quoted in Wooten, "Carter's Georgia Guru," p. 16.

15. "The 'Real' Jimmy Carter: Interview with Charles Kirbo," *U.S. News & World Report*, Dec. 20, 1976, p. 16.

16. Interview with Charles Kirbo, September 30, 1976, Betty Glad's files.

17. Bert Lance, *The Truth of the Matter: My Life in and out of Politics* (New York: Summit Books, 1991), p. 31.

18. Quoted in "The President's Boys," p. 20.

19. Carter did often flatter others hyperbolically. When he did so, however, one can be certain that the person to whom he referred was not an inside member of his working group but an outsider whose approval he hoped to win. Insiders eschewed flattery.

20. Powell, *The Other Side of the Story*, p. 8. Interestingly, Powell's remark did not mention Carter by name but referred to him indirectly as "the man from Plains." The indirect reference may indicate that Powell understood this written praise to be a violation of the unwritten code of conduct forbidding open praise and so sought to soften his violation.

21. Quoted in James Fallows, "The Passionless Presidency II," *Atlantic*, June 1979, p. 77. Neither the speaker nor the listener is identified by Fallows as other than a "Georgian," so it is not clear who they were.

22. Lance, *The Truth of the Matter*, p. 30.

23. Interview with Charles Kirbo, September 30, 1976, Betty Glad's files.

24. Harry Murphy, "Carter Wooing Rednecks, Whitenecks, Blacknecks," *Atlanta Constitution*, July 28, 1970.

25. Gary L. Roberts, "Jimmy Carter: Years of Challenge, Years of Change, An Interview," in Harold P. Henderson and Gary L. Roberts (eds.), *Georgia Governors in an Age of Change* (Athens: University of Georgia Press, 1988), p. 253.

26. Ibid.

27. Hamilton Jordan, *Crisis: The Last Year of the Carter Presidency* (New York: Berkley Books, 1982), p. 17.

28. Jimmy Carter, *Why Not the Best?* (Nashville: Broadman, 1975), p. 100.

29. Murphy, "Carter Wooing Rednecks, Whitenecks, Blacknecks."

30. Jimmy Carter, *Why Not the Best?*, p. 100.

31. Murphy, "Carter Wooing Rednecks, Whitenecks, Blacknecks."

32. Ibid.

33. Bill Shipp, "Exploding the Myths of the '90 Campaign," *Athens Daily News and Banner Herald*, Oct. 28, 1990.

34. Interview with a state senator who preferred to remain anonymous, October 4, 1977, Betty Glad's files.

35. Interview with Bill Pope, September 6, 1978, Betty Glad's files.

36. Letter from a reporter who preferred to remain anonymous to Betty Glad, no date, Betty Glad's files.

37. Jimmy Carter, *Why Not the Best?*, p. 101.

38. Address to laymen of the Disciples of Christ, Lafayette, Indiana, June 18, 1976. Published in Jimmy Carter, *The Spiritual Journey of Jimmy Carter: In His Own Words*, Wesley G. Pippert (comp.) (New York: Macmillan, 1978), p. 233.

39. Steve Ball Jr. ("Carter Again Underdog, Looks to Maddox Country," *Atlanta Constitution*, Apr. 4, 1970) reported that, according to Carter, a February 1970 poll pitting him against Sanders showed Sanders ahead 60 percent to 40 percent. In her *Jimmy Carter: In Search of the Great White House* (New York: Norton, 1980), Betty Glad reprinted a note Carter had allegedly written on a yellow

legal pad in 1968 listing some of his "rough ideas" for "driving a wedge" between Sanders and himself (p. 127).

40. Interview with a state senator who preferred to remain anonymous, October 4, 1977, Betty Glad's files.

41. Interview with Bill Shipp, August 21, 1978, Betty Glad's files.

42. See, e.g., "Carter Specifies Sanders 'Abuses,'" *Atlanta Journal*, May 8, 1970; Steve Ball Jr., "Charges Exchanged by Sanders, Carter," *Atlanta Constitution*, Aug. 27, 1970, and "Office Misused by Sanders, Carter Claims," *Atlanta Journal and Constitution*, Aug. 30, 1970.

43. Joe Brown, "Sen. Carter Qualifies and Reveals Aims," *Atlanta Constitution*, June 14, 1966.

44. Gene Stephens, "Carter Announces, Raps Carl Sanders," *Atlanta Constitution*, Apr. 4, 1970, pp. A1, A20.

45. Ball, "Carter Again Underdog, Looks to Maddox Country."

46. Murphy, "Carter Wooing Rednecks, Whitenecks, and Blacknecks."

47. "Georgia Association of Historians Survey of Georgia Governors, May 1985," in Henderson and Roberts (eds.), *Georgia Governors in an Age of Change*.

48. Stephens, "Carter Announces, Raps Sanders."

49. Bill Shipp, "HHH Backs Sanders (Buttons, That Is)," *Atlanta Constitution*, Apr. 6, 1970.

50. Harry Murphy, "Carter Sniffs, Says Sanders Seeks to Fly to Senate," *Atlanta Constitution*, June 28, 1970.

51. Hubert Humphrey, it is probably fair to say, was an across-the-board liberal in the way that term was usually defined at the time. The ideological allegiances of Richard Russell were more complex. Russell actually entered the Senate as a New Deal liberal, sponsored such liberal policies as the school lunch program, and maintained a conception of himself as a historic liberal throughout his career. His identification as a conservative emerged primarily through his support for the Vietnam War and his opposition to civil rights legislation.

52. "Carter Would Invite Wallace to Georgia," *Atlanta Constitution*, Aug. 26, 1970.

53. Interview with Charles Kirbo, September 30, 1976, Betty Glad's files.

54. "Carter Specifies Sanders' Abuses," *Atlanta Journal*, May 8, 1970; Duane Riner, "Democrats Pledging," *Atlanta Constitution*, Sept. 3, 1970.

55. "'Did Carter Con Griffin?' Stoner Asks," *Atlanta Constitution*, Sept. 5, 1970.

56. Interview with Bill Shipp, August 21, 1978, Betty Glad's files.

57. I discovered an example of this advertising in the Gerald M. Rafshoon Collection, 1976 Campaign, Subject File, Box 7 (File Clippings, 1970), Jimmy Carter Library. The advertisement pictured both Carter and Williams and, in the text, explicitly charged that Carter met with Williams in order to make a "deal" for black votes. The advertisement further claimed that "Sanders wouldn't even let him [Williams] in the Governor's Office." Where this advertisement was published or distributed, however, is unclear. But the advertisement is clearly dated after the primary election and during the run-off campaign. This timing fits with Glad's interpretation of the election in *Jimmy Carter*, pp. 123–40. She observed that only during the run-off did the Sanders campaign finally retaliate with the same sort of "dirty tricks" that the Carter campaign had used all along.

58. Interview with Nancy Carter Dunn, October 19, 1978, Betty Glad's files.

59. Interview with a top-level person in the Sanders campaign who preferred to remain anonymous, October 30, 1976, Betty Glad's files.

60. "Georgia Association of Historians Survey of Georgia Governors."

61. Ball, "Carter Again Underdog, Looks to Maddox Country."

62. "It's a funny thing," remarked Carter's campaign press secretary, Bill Pope. "During the campaign I never heard him mention reorganization. I understand later that when he talked to a small private business group he talked about it but never publicly. I never heard the word 'reorganization.'" But, continued Pope, "it's not a very good campaign theme anyway because to be perfectly frank most people aren't interested." (Interview with Bill Pope, September 6, 1978, Betty Glad's files.)

63. Quoted in Steve Ball Jr., "Maddox Warns Carter at Meet," *Atlanta Constitution*, Oct. 7, 1970.

64. Reg Murphy, "Carter's Inaugural Speech: Like 1966," *Atlanta Constitution*, Jan. 13, 1971.

65. Interview with Nancy Carter Dunn, October 19, 1978, Betty Glad's files.

66. Bobby Hill, quoted in Jeff Nesmith, "Maddox-Carter Conflict Seen in Speeches," *Atlanta Constitution*, Jan. 13, 1971, p. A3.

67. Quoted in Murphy, "Carter Wooing Rednecks, Whitenecks, Blacknecks."

68. Quoted in Bill Collins, "Maddox Rails at Carter over No. 2 Job," *Atlanta Constitution*, Apr. 4, 1971.

69. Gary M. Fink, "Jimmy Carter and the Politics of Transition," in Henderson and Roberts (eds.), *Georgia Governors in an Age of Change*, pp. 247, 248.

70. Ibid., p. 248.

71. In a May 25, 1977, letter from Robert J. Shaw, chairman of the Republican party of Georgia between 1971 and 1975, to Betty Glad (her files), Shaw reported that Carter's own polls showed him receiving only 19 percent of the vote against Herman Talmadge and only 26 percent against the state school superintendent, Jack Nix. Whereas Shaw's partisanship is obvious, the general consensus was that Carter could not win another election in the state.

72. Lance, *The Truth of the Matter*, p. 59.

73. Interview with Charles Kirbo, September 30, 1976, Betty Glad's files.

74. A portion of this letter was read into the transcript of an interview with Janet S. Merritt, May 3, 1978, Betty Glad's files.

75. Witcover, *Marathon*, p. 107.

76. The memorandum is published in Stroud, *How Jimmy Won*, pp. 23–27.

77. Witcover, *Marathon*, pp. 106–7; Stroud, *How Jimmy Won*, p. 19.

78. Jimmy Carter, *Why Not the Best?*, p. 137.

79. Interview with Hamilton Jordan (including Landon Butler), Miller Center Interviews, Carter Presidency Project, vol. 6, November 6, 1981, p. 3, Jimmy Carter Library.

80. Witcover, *Marathon*, p. 110.

81. Jimmy Carter, *Why Not the Best?*, p. 140.

82. Quoted in Stroud, *How Jimmy Won*, p. 426.

83. Quoted in Witcover, *Marathon*, pp. 109–10.

84. Ibid.

85. Ibid., p. 111.

86. Quoted in Martin Schram, *Running for President 1976: The Carter Campaign* (New York: Stein and Day, 1977), pp. 52–58.

87. Gary M. Fink, *Prelude to the Presidency: The Political Character and Legislative Leadership Style of Governor Jimmy Carter* (Westport, Conn.: Greenwood, 1980).

88. Letter from Robert J. Shaw to Betty Glad, May 25, 1977, Betty Glad's files.

89. Quoted in Stroud, *How Jimmy Won*, p. 292.

90. Jimmy Carter, *Why Not the Best?*, p. 112.

91. Interview with Robert Lipshutz, September 30, 1976, Betty Glad's files.

92. Interview with Bill Pope, September 6, 1978, Betty Glad's files.

93. Author interview with Bert Lance, Calhoun, Ga., March 17, 1992.

94. Interviews with Bill Shipp (August 21, 1978) and a state senator who preferred to remain anonymous (October 4, 1977); and questionnaires completed by state senator Battle Hall and a state official who preferred to remain anonymous, Betty Glad's files.

95. Interview with Bill Roper, August 18, 1978, Betty Glad's files.

96. Quoted in Fink, "Jimmy Carter and the Politics of Transition," p. 245.

97. Quoted in Fink, *Prelude to the Presidency*, pp. 117, 108, 164. Ben Fortson, Georgia's secretary of state, was the one who compared Carter to a south Georgia turtle.

98. Interview with Duane Riner, September 1, 1978, Betty Glad's files.

99. Interview with a state senator who preferred to remain anonymous, October 4, 1977, Betty Glad's files.

100. Arthur K. Bolton, "A Lawyer's View of Jimmy Carter," *Georgia State Bar Journal* 13 (Feb. 1977): 108–9.

101. Interview with Gerald Rafshoon, Miller Center Interviews, Carter Presidency Project, vol. 21, April 8, 1983, p. 29, Jimmy Carter Library.

102. Furman Smith Jr., "Environmental Law — The Carter Years," *Georgia State Bar Journal* 13 (Feb. 1977): 110–11.

103. Ken Foskett, "'Working Man' Likeness Pleases Former President," *Atlanta Constitution*, June 8, 1994, p. D3.

104. Interview with Duane Riner, September 1, 1978, Betty Glad's files.

105. Interview with Bill Roper, August 18, 1978, Betty Glad's files.

106. Interview with Gerald Rafshoon, Miller Center Interviews, Carter Presidency Project, vol. 21, April 8, 1983, p. 11, Jimmy Carter Library.

107. Aristotle, *Poetics*, 1450a 19-19.

108. Interview with Bill Shipp, August 21, 1978; and letter from a reporter who preferred to remain anonymous, no date, Betty Glad's files.

109. Gallup polls conducted September 24 to September 27, 1976, reported on October 26 and 27, 1976.

CHAPTER 7: 1976 IN AMERICA

1. Jimmy Carter, *A Government as Good as Its People*, (New York: Simon and Schuster, 1977), pp. 54, 60.

2. Jimmy Carter, *A Government as Good as Its People*, p. 102. He offered the

same assessment of his campaign operating on two different levels other times and to other audiences. See, e.g., Kandy Stroud, *How Jimmy Won: The Victory Campaign from Plains to the White House* (New York: Morrow, 1977), p. 342.

3. Jimmy Carter, *A Government as Good as Its People*, p. 106.

4. Ibid., p. 125.

5. Elizabeth Drew, *American Journal: The Events of 1976* (New York: Random House, 1977), pp. 218–19.

6. Fred Bronson, *The Billboard Book of Number One Hits* (New York: Billboard Publications, 1985), p. 300; Joel Whitburn, *The Billboard Book of Top 40 Albums*, rev. and enl. (New York: Billboard Books, 1991), pp. 54, 337.

7. Bronson, *The Billboard Book of Number One Hits*, p. 305.

8. Ibid., p. 309.

9. The rise of country music during the 1970s was phenomenal. Whereas it is commonly remembered as part of the CB (citizens band radio) craze, there was much more to it. Not only did numerous country artists "cross over" to the popular music charts, but some, like Dolly Parton and Willie Nelson, became every bit as popular as mainstream singers. There was also a sensational growth in radio stations with country music formats during this decade. (In New York City alone the number of country music radio stations went from zero to ten.) This was also the period when the Grand Ole Opry's Ryman Auditorium in Nashville was replaced by the much larger Opryland theme park and when the television show *Hee Haw* succeeded in introducing country music into prime time. See, e.g., Patrick Carr (ed.), *The Illustrated History of Country Music* (Garden City, N.Y.: Doubleday, 1979).

10. Betty Glad (*Jimmy Carter: In Search of the Great White House* [New York: Norton, 1980], pp. 234, 262) describes these efforts of Capricorn's founder and president, Phil Walden, on Carter's behalf.

11. Bronson, *The Billboard Book of Number One Hits*, pp. 270, 296, 326, 338, 360, 375, 383, 384, 385, 393, 406.

12. Ibid., pp. 426, 431, 434, 436, 438, 443, 445.

13. Ibid., p. 384.

14. Tim Brooks and Earle Marsh, *The Complete Directory to Prime Time Network TV Shows, 1946–Present*, 5th rev. ed. (New York: Ballantine, 1992), pp. 1101–3.

15. Robin Wood, *Hollywood from Vietnam to Reagan* (New York: Columbia University Press, 1986), pp. 46–69.

16. Stroud, *How Jimmy Won*, p. 422.

17. See Stanley B. Greenberg's *Middle Class Dreams: The Politics and Power of the New American Majority* (New York: Times Books, 1995), pp. 286–87; and Seymour Martin Lipset and William Schneider, *The Confidence Gap: Business, Labor, and Government in the Public Mind*, rev. ed. (Baltimore: Johns Hopkins University Press, 1987), pp. 17, 48–49. Although the data are drawn from numerous polls, the most frequently cited source is American National Election Studies, available through the Center for Political Studies, Inter-University Consortium for Political and Social Research, University of Michigan. I have analyzed these data myself and found the reported patterns.

18. Ibid.

19. Kevin Phillips, *The Emerging Republican Majority* (Garden City, N.Y.: Dou-

bleday, 1970) is of course the now classic prediction of the Republican resurgence that characterized the 1980s. Lending further credibility to Phillips's views is that in manuscript form the book is thought to have strongly influenced Richard Nixon's 1968 campaign, especially his southern strategy.

20. Data are reported in Michael Barone, *Our Country: The Shaping of America from Roosevelt to Reagan* (New York: Free Press, 1990), p. 501, and Glad, *Jimmy Carter*, p. 260.

21. Quoted in Jules Witcover, *Marathon: The Pursuit of the Presidency 1972–1976* (New York: Viking, 1977), p. 110.

22. Barone (*Our Country*, p. 502) discusses this reaction to McGovern's proposal during California's primary.

23. Reported in Lipset and Schneider, *The Confidence Gap*, p. 344.

24. Landon Butler, for instance, observed that mistrust of the Democratic agenda proved to be Carter's undoing. "We all avoided the obvious conclusion that the Democratic agenda was unpopular. . . . We hoped that this man that was doing all these unpopular things would be seen as courageous; instead he simply became unpopular." (Interview with Hamilton Jordan [including Landon Butler], Miller Center Interviews, Carter Presidency Project, vol. 6, November 6, 1981, p. 7, Jimmy Carter Library.) In this connection, the temptation to draw parallels between Carter's and Clinton's administrations is strong. The only Democrat to be elected president after Carter, Bill Clinton campaigned under the aegis of the "New Democrats," which largely emphasized a competent approach to economic policy. Yet, perhaps also like Carter, Clinton's attempts to demonstrate his competence were thwarted at almost every turn. His attempt to reform health care, for example, may have failed in large part because Americans distrusted government's ability to manage so massive a program effectively. Carter's earlier and admittedly less ambitious effort to reform the nation's health care was similarly stillborn. Taken together, it would seem that even a Democrat convincing enough to win election to president faces an almost impossible challenge persuading Americans that liberal government programs can be effectively implemented.

25. Quoted in Witcover, *Marathon*, p. 111.

26. Jimmy Carter, *A Government as Good as Its People*, p. 77.

27. Ibid., p. 69.

28. Quoted in Stroud, *How Jimmy Won*, p. 16. Carter's personal antipathy toward Nixon helps account for an anomaly in his 1976 campaign. Whereas in his three previous campaigns Carter seemed to need to identify opponents to castigate personally in order to propel his competitiveness — Joe Hurst in 1962, Bo Calloway in 1966, and Carl Sanders in 1970 — and in the 1980 campaign his strident anti-Reagan rhetoric seemed to reflect personal animosity, in 1976 Carter was for the most part an affable opponent. The explanation for this affability may be that his emotional opponent in 1976 was really Richard Nixon, not Gerald Ford or any of his primary opponents, and that the few anti-Nixon comments he made went unnoticed because his opinions were shared by the majority of Americans.

29. Ibid., p. 329.

30. Ibid., p. 421.

31. See, e.g., Barone's discussion in *Our Country*, pp. 507–8.

32. Quoted in Charles P. Henderson Jr., *The Nixon Theology* (New York: Harper & Row, 1972), p. 163.

33. See, e.g., data reported in Greenberg's *Middle Class Dreams*, pp. 286–87; and Lipset and Schneider's *The Confidence Gap*, p. 17. Although each reports a 1 percent drop in confidence over these two years, that drop is well within the expected range of measurement error. (Since both draw from the same data, the error would also be repeated by both.) Striking, therefore, is the apparent stability in confidence between 1970 and 1972 amid the much longer 1964 to 1980 pattern of decline. Whether this stability can be attributed to Nixon's conduct of the war is, of course, unprovable. There may also be an inherent weakness in any event-oriented explanation of the decline of America's confidence in government and other large institutions. Dwindling confidence in institutions is arguably simply a consequence of the society's progressive embrace of individualistic universalism. The hallmark of this philosophy, after all, is to deny the relevance and even the existence of collectivities of all sorts. Yet, insofar as specific events are credited with helping to trigger or further the decline, all but the Vietnam War fail to persuade. The assassination of President John Kennedy could not be responsible, because confidence remained high in 1964; the assassinations of Robert Kennedy and Martin Luther King Jr. in 1968, together with the attendant turmoil of that year, cannot explain a decline that was already in full swing two years earlier. Watergate, the simultaneous energy crisis, and the later economic woes of the 1970s and 1980s may explain periodic dips in confidence, but they cannot explain why confidence failed to rebound after the crises passed. In short, little beyond the war can account convincingly for an event-oriented explanation of America's decline in confidence. And insofar as the war accounts for the decline, it may also account for the temporary halt of that decline between about 1970 and 1972.

34. Lipset and Schneider report this data, based on Harris and NORC surveys, in *The Confidence Gap*, pp. 48–49. Predictably, however, they label this period only "Early Seventies" while choosing more explanatory labels (like "Watergate," "Carter Malaise," "Reagan Recession," etc.) for most other periods. This subtle unwillingness — or even inability — to credit Nixon with moral achievements or to interpret his conduct of the war differently than Johnson's even when presenting tabular data may reflect the very "liberal bias" that Nixon always thought went against him.

35. Reported by Joseph Kelner, chief counsel to the victims and their families, in "Kent State at 25," *New York Times*, May 4, 1995, p. A17.

36. George C. Edwards III, *Presidential Approval: A Sourcebook* (Baltimore: Johns Hopkins University Press, 1990), pp. 57, 61, 62.

37. It was also appropriated by Ronald Reagan, though not in official ceremony. See Paul D. Erickson, *Reagan Speaks: The Making of an American Myth* (New York: New York University Press, 1985), pp. 74–75.

38. Quoted in Henderson, *The Nixon Theology*, p. 6.

39. Duane Riner, "Carter Decrees Day of Tribute," *Atlanta Constitution*, April 2, 1971.

40. Jimmy Carter, *A Government as Good as Its People*, pp. 147–52.

41. Steven Brill, "Jimmy Carter's Pathetic Lies," *Harper's*, March 1976, p. 77.

42. Witcover, *Marathon*, p. 109.

43. Jimmy Carter, *A Government as Good as Its People*, p. 77.

44. Ibid., pp. 135, 137.

45. Ibid., p. 115.

46. Ibid., p. 69.

47. Ibid., pp. 43–50.

48. Ibid.

49. Ibid.

50. Ibid.

51. "The Presidential Election — A Gallup Poll Analysis," *Gallup Poll*, November 7, 1976.

52. Stroud, *How Jimmy Won*, p. 422.

53. Joseph A. Melusky, "A Comparative Analysis of the Regional Strength of Major Party Presidential Candidates in 1976 and 1980: Some Tactical Prescriptions for 1984 in View of Electoral Vote Shifts," *Presidential Studies Quarterly* 13 (1983): 482–89.

54. "The Presidential Election — A Gallup Poll Analysis."

55. Ibid.

56. *New York Times*–CBS and Harris surveys, discussed in Stroud, *How Jimmy Won*, pp. 376–77.

57. Quoted in Stroud, *How Jimmy Won*, p. 347.

58. "Political Positions," *Gallup Poll*, October 24, 1976.

59. Interview with Jimmy Carter, Miscellaneous Interviews, November 1984, (Vision Associates), Jimmy Carter Library.

60. Quoted in Martin Schram, *Running for President 1976: The Carter Campaign* (New York: Stein & Day, 1977), pp. 219–20.

61. "The Presidential Election — A Gallup Poll Analysis."

62. Stroud, *How Jimmy Won*, p. 237.

63. Ibid., p. 433.

64. Morris K. Udall, *Too Funny to Be President* (New York: Holt, 1988), p. 30.

65. William F. Levantrosser, "Financing Presidential Campaigns: The Impact of Reform Campaign Finance Laws on the Democratic Presidential Nomination of 1976," *Presidential Studies Quarterly* 11 (1981): 280–88.

66. TRB, *New Republic*, February 7, 1976.

67. Udall is quoted in Stroud, *How Jimmy Won*, p. 258. Exit interviews are from "The Presidential Election — A Gallup Poll Analysis."

68. Quoted in Glad, *Jimmy Carter*, p. 313.

69. See ibid., pp. 306–11 for a description of these techniques and numerous examples.

70. Quoted in David L. Rarick et al., "The Carter Persona: An Empirical Analysis of the Rhetorical Visions of Campaign '76," *Quarterly Journal of Speech* 63 (Oct. 1977), p. 258.

71. Quoted in Stroud, *How Jimmy Won*, p. 202.

72. Glad, *Jimmy Carter*, p. 304.

73. Quoted in ibid., p. 243 (from Timothy Carlson, *Harvard Crimson*, February 28, 1976).

74. Robert Scheer, "Interview," *Playboy*, Nov. 1976.

75. Stroud, *How Jimmy Won*, pp. 372, 422.

76. Udall (*Too Funny to Be President*, pp. 36–38) discusses his preference for the term *progressive* as well as the flap that arose as a result of his stated preference. (The press, in particular, considered it to be disingenuous.) More than Udall, however, I suspect that the flap was more than a debate over semantics. Although it was not until the 1988 elections that "the 'l' word" became an epithet (hurled against Michael Dukakis), Udall's switch to the subsequently more palatable term *progressive* anticipates the fissures that were beginning to be detected in liberalism as early as 1976. Additionally, the preference for the label *progressive* among former liberals like Udall and subsequent ones reveals the gropings of many for a neoliberalism that has yet to emerge fully.

77. Brown, who announced his candidacy to a couple of reporters in Sacramento without previously informing his staff, explained his rationale this way: "Well, I looked at the thing and didn't think any of the candidates were catching on. I knew I was popular in California. I figured, 'Well, why not?'" (Quoted in Drew, *American Journal*, p. 204.)

78. Quoted in Glad, *Jimmy Carter*, p. 256.

79. Drew, *American Journal*, p. 199; Witcover, *Marathon*, p. 331.

80. Drew, *American Journal*, pp. 194–209.

81. Ibid., p. 198.

82. Ibid., p. 206.

83. Witcover, *Marathon*, p. 427.

84. Ibid., pp. 419–20.

85. Quoted in ibid., pp. 402–3. The aide was David Keene.

86. Brill, "Jimmy Carter's Pathetic Lies," p. 77.

87. Quoted in Stroud, *How Jimmy Won*, p. 425.

88. John H. Patton, "A Government as Good as Its People: Jimmy Carter and the Restoration of Transcendence to Politics," *Quarterly Journal of Speech* 63 (Oct. 1977): 255.

89. Ibid., p. 251.

90. Ibid., p. 256.

91. Daniel Bell, *The End of Ideology: On the Exhaustion of Political Ideas in the Fifties* (Cambridge: Harvard University Press, 1988), pp. 432–33.

92. Quoted in Stroud, *How Jimmy Won*, p. 191.

93. Quoted in Stroud, *How Jimmy Won*, p. 428.

94. Hamilton Jordan, *Crisis: The Last Year of the Carter Presidency* (New York: Berkley Books, 1982), p. 318.

95. Suzanne Garment, *Scandal: The Crisis of Mistrust in American Politics* (New York: Times Books, 1991), p. 36.

96. Quoted in Stroud, *How Jimmy Won*, p. 304.

CHAPTER 8: OF CRISIS AND OPPORTUNITY

1. Haynes Johnson, *In the Absence of Power: Governing America* (New York: Viking, 1980), p. 32.

2. Ibid.

3. Carter quoted Woodcock's remark in his May 17, 1977, speech to the con-

vention, *Public Papers of the Presidents of the United States: Jimmy Carter (1977–1981)*, vol. 1 (Washington, D.C.: GPO, 1977), p. 894.

4. Humphrey's visit is described in Johnson, *In the Absence of Power*, pp. 19–20. Remarks about the Humphrey–Carter relationship were made by Stuart Eizenstat in his interview, Miller Center Interviews, Carter Presidency Project, vol. 13, January 29–30, 1982, p. 106, Jimmy Carter Library.

5. Calvin G. Mackenzie, *The Politics of Presidential Appointments* (New York: Free Press, 1981), p. 64.

6. Robert Locander, "Carter and the Press: The First Two Years," *Presidential Studies Quarterly* 10 (1980): 115.

7. Interview with Stuart Eizenstat, Miller Center Interviews, Carter Presidency Project, vol. 13, January 29–30, 1982, p. 27, Jimmy Carter Library.

8. Bert Lance (*The Truth of the Matter: My Life in and out of Politics* [New York: Summit, 1991], p. 59) describes the gift of James David Barber's *The Presidential Character: Predicting Performance in the White House* (Englewood Cliffs, N.J.: Prentice-Hall, 1972).

9. Quoted from a speech Kennedy delivered to the UAW, in Joseph A. Califano Jr., *Governing America: An Insider's Report from the White House and the Cabinet* (New York: Simon and Schuster, 1981), p. 98.

10. George C. Edwards III and Alec M. Gallup (*Presidential Approval: A Sourcebook* [Baltimore: Johns Hopkins University Press, 1990]) provide data on approval ratings. For comparison purposes, Richard Nixon's highest approval rating was 67 percent; Gerald Ford's, 71 percent; and Ronald Reagan's, 68 percent. Both John Kennedy and Dwight Eisenhower, however, reached occasional highs that matched Lyndon Johnson's 79 percent in 1964. George Bush also enjoyed higher approval ratings during the Persian Gulf War. Except for Bush's wartime highs (which quickly fell after the war), all approval ratings higher than Carter's were recorded prior to the decline of American confidence, first noted in 1966.

11. Increased confidence in the executive branch is shown by Seymour Martin Lipset and William Schneider, *The Confidence Gap: Business, Labor, and Government in the Public Mind*, rev. ed. (Baltimore: Johns Hopkins University Press, 1987), pp. 48–49.

12. Mention of the misremembered Carter vote in 1976 is made in William Schneider, "The November 4 Vote for President: What Did It Mean?" pp. 212–62 in Austin Ranney (ed.), *The American Elections of 1980* (Washington: American Enterprise Institute, 1981), p. 238.

13. Tip O'Neill, *Man of the House: The Life and Political Memoirs of Speaker Tip O'Neill* (New York: Random House, 1987), pp. 310–11, 315–16.

14. Jimmy Carter, *Keeping Faith: Memoirs of a President* (New York: Bantam, 1982), p. 73.

15. Johnson (*In the Absence of Power*, pp. 21–22) reports this exchange and claims that it took place in Plains. O'Neill (*Man of the House*, pp. 302–3) recalls essentially the same exchange occurring in his office.

16. These remarks were made "off the record" by a senior Carter aide in the course of a Miller Center Interview, available at the Jimmy Carter Library.

17. The most complete study of Carter's relationship with Congress, which partially confirms but also modifies this long-standing criticism of the Carter ad-

ministration, is Charles O. Jones's *The Trusteeship Presidency. Jimmy Carter and the United States Congress* (Baton Rouge: Louisiana State University Press, 1988). In his presidential memoir, *Keeping Faith*, Carter repeats *Congressional Quarterly's* finding that, in roll call votes, his four-year victory percentage of 75 percent was just a little lower than Johnson's 82 percent (p. 88). This percentage record is misleading, however, since it fails to differentiate between more and less important bills, does not count bills which were not introduced or were withdrawn prior to vote because of expected failure, and ignores compromises on legislation prior to voting. Taking these and other factors into account, an independent academic assessment of Carter's record of legislative success shows that it was only marginally poorer than might otherwise have been predicted. See Jon R. Bond and Richard Fleisher, *The President in the Legislative Arena* (Chicago: University of Chicago Press, 1990). Still, it was poorer. And Congress's June 1980 override of Carter's veto of an oil import fee was the kind of election-year loss for Carter that can be taken as confirmation of this poor relationship.

18. Interview with Hamilton Jordan (including Landon Butler), Miller Center Interviews, Carter Presidency Project, vol. 6, November 6, 1981, pp. 3–16, Jimmy Carter Library.

19. Michael G. Krukones, "The Campaign Promises of Jimmy Carter: Accomplishments and Failures," *Presidential Studies Quarterly* 15 (1985): 143.

20. See, e.g., Califano, *Governing America*, pp. 88–135.

21. Ibid., pp. 320–67.

22. Burton I. Kaufman, *The Presidency of James Earl Carter, Jr.* (Lawrence: University Press of Kansas, 1993), p. 101.

23. Interview with Hamilton Jordan (including Landon Butler), Miller Center Interviews, Carter Presidency Project, vol. 6, November 6, 1981, p. 34, Jimmy Carter Library. According to Jordan, the study was undertaken by Tom Donilon.

24. Interview with Stuart Eizenstat, Miller Center Interviews, Carter Presidency Project, vol. 13, January 29–30, 1982, p. 64, Jimmy Carter Library.

25. Patrick H. Caddell, "Initial Working Paper on Political Strategy," December 10, 1976, Jody Powell's files, Box 4, Jimmy Carter Library.

26. Interview with Hamilton Jordan (including Landon Butler), Miller Center Interviews, Carter Presidency Project, vol. 6, November 6, 1981, p. 13, Jimmy Carter Library.

27. Fred Bronson, *The Billboard Book of Number One Hits* (New York: Billboard Publications, 1985), p. 468.

28. The object of anger in *Network* was, of course, primarily the press rather than government. At confidence ratings ranging from 18 to 28 percent during 1976 and 1977 (and with no discernible trend), however, the press's ratings were only a little lower than those for most other institutions. The data are found in Lipset and Schneider, *The Confidence Gap*, pp. 17, 48–49.

29. Johnson, *In the Absence of Power*, p. 34.

30. Ibid., p. 31.

31. Caddell, "Initial Working Paper on Political Strategy."

32. James Fallows, "The Passionless Presidency II," *Atlantic*, June 1979, p. 76.

33. Caddell, "Initial Working Paper on Political Strategy." Carter's handwritten note to Mondale, proclaiming it "excellent," remains on the document.

34. Ibid.

35. Ibid.

36. Ibid.

37. Omi Walden, quoted in Furman Smith Jr., "Environmental Law — The Carter Years," *Georgia State Bar Journal* 13 (Feb. 1977): 111.

38. Interview with Stuart Eizenstat, Miller Center Interviews, Carter Presidency Project, vol. 13, January 29–30, 1982, p. 28, Jimmy Carter Library.

39. Quoted in Jimmy Carter, *Keeping Faith*, p. 105.

40. Quoted in Barbara Kellerman, *The Political Presidency: Practice of Leadership* (New York: Oxford University Press, 1984), p. 200.

41. Ibid., p. 191; O'Neill, *Man of the House*, pp. 320–21.

42. Jimmy Carter, *Keeping Faith*, p. 78.

43. Lance, *The Truth of the Matter*, p. 114.

44. Kellerman, *The Political Presidency*, pp. 198–99.

45. Quoted in ibid., p. 197.

46. "On Energy and Canal, Opinions Are Nearly Unchanged," *New York Times*, Jan. 18, 1978.

47. "Summary of Issue Concerns of the American People (DNC Field Survey, 1500 Interviews), August 31–September 12, 1977," Hamilton Jordan's Files, Box 33, Jimmy Carter Library.

48. Quoted in Kellerman, *The Political Presidency*, p. 190.

49. Ibid.; Leo P. Ribuffo, "'Malaise' Revisited: Jimmy Carter and the Crisis of Confidence," paper delivered at the American Historical Association Convention, 1992.

50. Califano, *Governing America*, pp. 352, 111, 362, 358. A fuller account of the failed attempts of the Carter administration to pass welfare reform legislation is found in Laurence E. Lynn Jr. and David deF. Whitman, *The President as Policymaker: Jimmy Carter and Welfare Reform* (Philadelphia: Temple University Press, 1981).

51. Quoted in Kellerman, *The Political Presidency*, p. 206.

52. Kaufman, *The Presidency of James Earl Carter, Jr.*, p. 78.

53. Cited in Casper Schmidt, "Two Specific Forms of Trial Action," *Journal of Psychohistory* 11 (Fall 1983): 217.

54. Kaufman, *The Presidency of James Earl Carter, Jr.*, p. 78.

55. Edwards, *Presidential Approval*, p. 77.

56. Memo to the president from Pat Caddell, November 2, 1977, "Caddell [Patrick] [1]," Box 33, Hamilton Jordan's Files, Jimmy Carter Library.

57. Edwards, *Presidential Approval*, pp. 78–80.

58. John W. Mashek, "When You Revisit 3 States Where Carter Boom Began," *U.S. News & World Report*, Feb. 27, 1978, pp. 28–30; and "How Carter's Staff Plans to Avoid Another Round of Blunders," *U.S. News & World Report*, Mar. 20, 1978, pp. 21–22.

59. Edwards, *Presidential Approval*, pp. 78–90.

60. Ibid., pp. 82–83.

61. "Energy Situation," *Gallup Poll*, May 20, 1979, p. 167.

62. Patrick Caddell, "Of Crisis and Opportunity," April 23, 1979, "Memo-

randa: President Carter 1/10/79–4/23/79 [CF, O/A 519]," Box 40, Jody Powell's Files, Jimmy Carter Library.

63. John Raeside, "A Night at Camp David" (interview with Robert Bellah), *East Bay Express*, July 27, 1979.

64. Memorandum to the Democratic National Committee from Cambridge Survey Research, May 25, 1979, Box 33, Hamilton Jordan's Files, Jimmy Carter Library.

65. James G. Benze Jr., "Presidential Management: The Importance of Presidential Skills," *Presidential Studies Quarterly* 11 (1981): 470–78.

66. Jeane Kirkpatrick, "U.S. Security and Latin America," *Commentary* 71 (January 1981): 30. Some foreign-policy experts dispute this contention. In *The Carter Administration's Quest for Global Community* (Columbia: University of South Carolina Press, 1987), for instance, Jerel A. Rosati identifies four different expert assessments of Carter's philosophy of foreign policy, one of which is "lack of a worldview" (pp. 7–12). Others, like Gaddis Smith in *Morality, Reason, and Power: American Diplomacy in the Carter Years* (New York: Hill & Wang, 1986), suggest that Carter was often torn between two different foreign-policy outlooks, one represented by Secretary of State Cyrus Vance and the other by national security advisor Zbigniew Brzezinski. Whereas there were undoubtedly inconsistencies in Carter's philosophy and he frequently agonized over specific foreign policy decisions (on which he did receive conflicting advice), it seems to me that Kirkpatrick and others are generally right in pointing to the essential coherence of Carter's views. Indeed, since Brzezinski is thought to have pressed Carter to take a firmer stand against the Soviets in world affairs than Vance yet is also the one Kirkpatrick and others credit with promoting the new, weaker foreign policy philosophy, it is difficult to understand how disagreements between Vance and Brzezinski would have created serious conflicts in Carter's broader foreign-policy perspective.

67. George D. Moffett III, *The Limits of Victory: The Ratification of the Panama Canal Treaties* (Ithaca: Cornell University Press, 1985), pp. 48–70.

68. Kirkpatrick, "U.S. Security and Latin America." Her earlier piece, "Dictatorships and Double Standards" (*Commentary* 68 [Nov. 1979], pp. 34–45), was even more critical of Carter's approach.

69. Carter's remarks are drawn from his May 22, 1977, speech at the University of Notre Dame.

70. Zbigniew Brzezinski, *Power and Principle: Memoirs of the National Security Advisor 1977–1981* (New York: Farrar, Straus, Giroux, 1983), p. 18.

71. C. Fred Bergsten, quoted in Moffett, *The Limits of Victory*, p. 52.

72. Moffett (*The Limits of Victory*, pp. 181–202) surveys these problems and marvels over the failure of treaty opponents to emphasize them.

73. Ken Bode, "Carter and the Canal," *New Republic*, Jan. 14, 1978, p. 9.

74. "Aw, Comeawn," *Wall Street Journal*, Apr. 14, 1978; "Panama Palaver," *Wall Street Journal*, Sept. 12, 1977; and "The Panama Compromise," *Wall Street Journal*, Feb. 3, 1978.

75. "The Panama Compromise"; Vermont Royster, "Touchstone for Political Orthodoxy," *Wall Street Journal*, Feb. 8, 1978; Kenneth H. Bacon, "The Panama Canal Debate," *Wall Street Journal*, Sept. 7, 1977; Herbert and Mary Knapp, "A

View from the Canal Zone," *Wall Street Journal*, Feb. 1, 1978; and Jude Wanniski, "Panama and Pax Americana," *Wall Street Journal*, Apr. 7, 1978.

76. Tom Wicker, "The Real Canal 'Giveaway,'" *New York Times*, Aug. 30, 1977; Warren Weaver Jr., "Panama Arouses Emotion out of All Proportion to Its Size," *New York Times*, Sept. 4, 1977; "Beyond the Panama Canal Treaties," *New York Times*, Jan. 28, 1978; "Panama: The Senate's Final Test," *New York Times*, Apr. 18, 1978; William F. Buckley, "Heart of Panama Debate," *U.S. News & World Report*, Feb. 6, 1978, p. 36; "The Canal as Symbol," *Progressive*, Oct. 1977, p. 11; "New Treaties and New Symbols," *America* 138 (Feb. 18, 1978), p. 112; and "The Panama Embarrassment," *Nation*, Mar. 11, 1978, p. 260.

77. Moffett (*The Limits of Victory*, pp. 112–37) describes this stability in public opinion.

78. Quoted in Adam Clymer, "TV Campaign Begun against Canal Treaty," *New York Times*, Oct. 31, 1977.

79. Craig Allen Smith ably summarizes the rise of this opposition in "Leadership, Orientation, and Rhetorical Vision: Jimmy Carter, the 'New Right,' and the Panama Canal," *Presidential Studies Quarterly* 16 (Spring 1986): 317–28. News accounts consulted include Adam Clymer, "Conservatives Map Drive against the Canal Treaty," *New York Times*, Aug. 16, 1977; Clymer, "TV Campaign Begun against Panama Canal Treaty"; and Graham Hovey, "Canal 'Truth Squad' Plans a 5-Day Blitz," *New York Times*, Jan. 10, 1978. See also Philip M. Crane, with an introduction by Ronald Reagan, *Surrender in Panama: The Case against the Treaty* (Ottawa, Ill.: Dale Books, 1978); and Richard A. Viguerie, *The New Right: We're Ready to Lead* (Falls Church, Va.: The Viguerie Company, 1981).

80. "The Panama Issue," *New York Times*, Apr. 17, 1976.

81. "Politics, Passions and the Panama Canal," *Wall Street Journal*, Apr. 23, 1976; and Robert Keatley, "The Big Flap over the Canal," *Wall Street Journal*, Apr. 29, 1976.

82. Tom Wicker, "Last Ditch for the G.O.P.?" *New York Times*, Oct. 4, 1977.

83. Adam Clymer, "Bush a Hot Property on G.O.P. Dinner Circuit," *New York Times*, Feb. 19, 1978.

84. Albert R. Hunt, "Reagan: 'A Man, a Plan, a Canal . . . ,'" *Wall Street Journal*, Aug. 26, 1977.

85. At least two books about Reagan emphasize the relationship between his actor's role-playing orientation and his genuine convictions. They are Paul D. Erickson, *Reagan Speaks: The Making of an American Myth* (New York: New York University Press, 1985); and Lou Cannon, *President Reagan: The Role of a Lifetime* (New York: Simon & Schuster, 1991).

86. "Policy for the Americas," *New York Times*, Dec. 21, 1976.

87. Interview with Hamilton Jordan (including Landon Butler), Miller Center Interviews, Carter Presidency Project, vol. 6, November 6, 1981, p. 20, Jimmy Carter Library.

88. Quoted in Moffett, *The Limits of Victory*, pp. 49, 50, 51.

89. Ronald A. Sudol, "The Rhetoric of Strategic Retreat: Carter and the Panama Canal Debate," *Quarterly Journal of Speech* 65 (1979): 379–91.

90. "Young Says Policy Change Should Precede Cuba Ties," *New York Times*, Aug. 14, 1977.

91. Jimmy Carter, *Keeping Faith*, p. 184.

92. Juan deOnis, "Latins Are Relieved at Canal Treaties," *New York Times*, Apr. 20, 1978; "After Carter's Panama Victory," *U.S. News & World Report*, May 1, 1978, pp. 25–27; Hedrick Smith, "After Panama, More Battles," *New York Times*, Apr. 20, 1978; and Hedrick Smith, "For President, A Vital Victory," *New York Times*, Mar. 17, 1978.

93. Kaufman (*The Presidency of James Earl Carter, Jr.*, pp. 39–42) summarizes this early breech in U.S.–Soviet relations.

94. "President Carter," *Gallup Poll*, Feb. 24, 1980, pp. 52–53.

95. The public also opposed the Olympic boycott 61 to 30 percent ("The Olympics," *Gallup Poll*, March 12, 1980, pp. 62–63). I have not found comparable survey data regarding the grain embargo, but my impression is that public opinion was similar.

96. Jody Powell (*The Other Side of the Story* [New York: Morrow, 1984], pp. 104–7) summarizes this "killer rabbit" story and reactions to it.

97. Mark J. Rozell, *The Press and the Carter Presidency* (Boulder: Westview, 1989).

98. "Kirk Scharfenberg, 48; Shared a Pulitzer Prize," *New York Times*, July 29, 1992.

99. Interview with Jimmy Carter, Miller Center Interviews, Carter Presidency Project, vol. 19, November 29, 1982, p. 37, Jimmy Carter Library. In the interview, Carter chose to omit the "expletive" he says he used by recalling his words as "'blank' the Shah."

100. Hamilton Jordan's *Crisis: The Last Year of the Carter Presidency* (New York: Berkley Books, 1982) interweaves this story of the hostage negotiations with his other recollections of association with Carter.

101. "Democratic Presidential Candidates," *Gallup Poll*, June 24, 1979, p. 187; "Iranian Situation," *Gallup Poll*, Jan. 9, 1980, p. 11; "Iranian Situation," *Gallup Poll*, Apr. 8, 1980, p. 83; Edwards, *Presidential Approval*, pp. 86–88.

102. Ranney's *The American Elections of 1980* lists primary election results, pp. 361–64.

103. "Democratic Presidential Candidates," *Gallup Poll*, March 31, 1980, p. 79 reports this Carter advantage. Jimmy Carter (*Keeping Faith*, p. 530) offers the interpretation of late Kennedy victories as protest votes.

104. "President Carter," *Gallup Poll*, Feb. 24, 1980, pp. 49–51.

105. Quoted in Elizabeth Drew, *Portrait of an Election: The 1980 Presidential Campaign* (New York: Simon & Schuster, 1981), p. 35.

106. Ranney, *The American Elections of 1980*, pp. 361–64.

107. A graph depicting Bureau of Labor Statistics on inflation rates from 1965 through 1994 was published as "A Year of Gentle Price Rises" (*New York Times*, Jan 12, 1995). A similar graph of consumer confidence from 1976 through 1992, based upon Congressional Budget Office data, was published as "The Cycles of Consumer Confidence" (*Wall Street Journal*, Nov. 11, 1992).

108. "A Year of Gentle Price Rises."

109. Kim Ezra Shienbaum and Ervin Shienbaum, "Public Perceptions of Presidential Economic Performances: From Johnson to Carter," *Presidential Studies Quarterly* 12 (1982): 421; Sidney Weintraub, "Carter's Economic Doodling," *New Leader*, Sept. 22, 1980, pp. 3–5.

110. Data are derived from *Economic Report of the President* (Washington: United States Printing Office, 1990), pp. 299, 333, 339, and 376. The data and many of the economic comparisons based upon them were brought to my attention in a paper delivered by Ann Mari May, "Economic Myth and Economic Reality: A Reexamination of the Carter Years," at Hofstra University's Eighth Presidential Conference on the Carter Presidency, November 1990. Professor May, of the Department of Economics, University of Nebraska-Lincoln, provided me with a copy of her paper, and much of my understanding of economic performance during the Carter years is informed by her analysis.

111. May, "Economic Myth and Economic Reality."

112. Tom Wicker, "A Failure of Politics," *New York Times*, Jan. 16, 1981, p. A23.

113. Interview with Charles Schultze, Miller Center Interviews, Carter Presidency Project, January 8–9, 1982, pp. 3–4, Jimmy Carter Library.

114. These comments are all reported in Biven, "Economic Advice in the Carter Administration." Since my copy of Biven's paper is unpublished, I list his sources for the quotations: Erwin C. Hargrove and Samuel A. Morley, *The President and the Council of Economic Advisors: Interviews with the CEA Chairmen* (Boulder: Westview, 1984), pp. 465–67; Memorandum, President to Eizenstat, March 2, 1977, White House Central File, Subject File, CM 9, Box CM-6, Jimmy Carter Library; "Oral History with Walter Heller, Kermit Gordon, James Tobin, Gardner Ackley, Paul Samuelson," by Joseph Pechman, August 1, 1964, John F. Kennedy Library, pp. 196–97.

115. May, "Economic Myth and Economic Reality."

116. Christopher Lasch, *The Culture of Narcissism: American Life in an Age of Diminishing Expectations* (New York: Norton, 1979); Letter from Christopher Lasch to Jody Powell, June 10, 1979, Box 140, President's Handwriting File, Jimmy Carter Library.

117. Interview with Stuart Eizenstat, Miller Center Interviews, Carter Presidency Project, vol. 13, January 29–30, 1982, p. 85, Jimmy Carter Library.

118. Memorandum from Patrick H. Caddell to the president, August 18, 1980, [Campaign Strategy] Caddell [Patrick] Box 77, Chief of Staff (Jordan), Jimmy Carter Library.

119. "Presidential Election: The Male and Female Vote — A Gallup Analysis," *Gallup Poll* (October 26, 1980), p. 235; Schneider, "The November 4 Vote for President," pp. 237–38. Actually, while "women's issues" were not especially salient for the majority of the electorate, their salience for a minority was profound. The most striking demographic feature of the 1980 vote was the "gender gap." My own analysis of University of Michigan exit poll data shows almost an eight-point gap between men and women, with women favoring Carter by that margin. Among voters 27 to 34 years old, the cohort that had come of age at the height of feminism's cultural resurgence, the gender gap was an astonishing 18 percent. The increased gap in this age bracket, however, does not reflect increased female support for Carter but rather increased male support for Reagan, a fact that might be better accounted for by the Vietnam War than by a reaction to feminism (see n. 124 below). Even so, it is plausible that a number of the men from this cohort later became the "angry white males" of the 1990s, noted primarily for their op-

position to Affirmative Action. Despite this 1980 gender gap, however, women as a whole supported Reagan over Carter by 53 to 47 percent.

120. "Presidential Candidates — Election," *Gallup Poll*, Oct. 19, 1980, p. 209; Leo Ribuffo, "God and Jimmy Carter," in M. L. Bradbury and James B. Gilbert (eds.), *Transforming Faith: The Sacred and Secular in Modern American History* (Westport, Conn.: Greenwood, 1989).

121. Schneider, "The November 4 Vote for President," pp. 237–38; "Presidential Election," *Gallup Poll*, Dec. 7, 1980, p. 261.

122. This and the following interpretation of themes are drawn from Schneider, "The November 4 Vote for President."

123. Ibid.; "Presidential Election: The Male and Female Vote — A Gallup Analysis."

124. Ibid.; "Presidential Candidates — Election," p. 209. Perhaps suggestive of the continuing importance of the Vietnam War, my own analysis of University of Michigan exit poll data shows that male voters in the 27- to 34-year-old age bracket (and who would have turned 18, or draft age, between 1964 and 1971) voted for Reagan over Carter 70 to 30 percent — the largest Reagan advantage found in any age bracket.

125. "Presidential Trial Heat — Final Survey," *Gallup Poll*, Nov. 3, 1980, p. 240; Warren E. Miller and Santa A. Traugott, *American National Election Survey Data Sourcebook, 1952–1986* (Cambridge: Harvard University Press, 1989), p. 319; other polls cited in Kaufman, *The Presidency of James Earl Carter, Jr.*, p. 207.

126. Jordan, *Crisis*, pp. 346–50.

127. Ibid.

128. "Presidential Candidates — Election," p. 209.

129. Schneider, "The November 4 Vote for President."

CHAPTER 9: JIMMY CARTER AT SEVENTY

1. Ken Foskett, "'Working Man' Likeness Pleases Former President," *Atlanta Constitution*, June 8, 1994, p. D3.

2. Ken Foskett, "Tuesday Unveiling a Tribute in Shirt Sleeves," *Atlanta Constitution*, June 4, 1994, p. B1.

3. Foskett, "'Working Man' Likeness Pleases Former President."

4. Meg Greenfield, "Is Carter a Victim of an Unfair Fate?" reprinted in the *Atlanta Constitution*, Mar. 18, 1984, p. D6.

5. Associated Press, "Reagan Aides Say '84 Foe Tougher," *Atlanta Constitution*, Oct. 9, 1983, p. A3.

6. James J. Kilpatrick, "Weight of Jimmy Carter Lies Heavy on Mondale," *Atlanta Constitution*, Oct. 16, 1983, p. D3.

7. Quoted in ibid.

8. Jack Germond and Jules Witcover, "Carter's 'Endorsement' Should Help Mondale," *Atlanta Journal*, Sept. 2, 1983, p. A14; and "Will the 'Carter Connection' Hurt Mondale?" *Atlanta Journal*, Mar. 4, 1983, p. A10.

9. George C. Edwards III, *Presidential Approval: A Sourcebook* (Baltimore: Johns

Hopkins University Press, 1990), pp. 94–104; Seymour Martin Lipset and William Schneider, *The Confidence Gap: Business, Labor, and Government in the Public Mind*, rev. ed. (Baltimore: Johns Hopkins University Press, 1987), pp. 17, 48–49; Stanley B. Greenberg, *Middle Class Dreams: The Politics and Power of the New American Majority* (New York: Times Books, 1995), p. 286.

10. Mary McGrory, "Reagan's Image May Be All He Needs in '84," *Atlanta Constitution*, Sept. 29, 1983, p. A13.

11. One indicator of the effectiveness of the Reagan campaign's "morning in America" commercial came in 1995 when editors of *Advertising Age* selected it as one of the 50 "best" commercials of all times. Only one other political commercial, Lyndon Johnson's 1964 depiction of a girl picking petals from a daisy against a nuclear countdown, made the list. (See Stuart Elliott, "Advertising," *New York Times*, Mar. 14, 1995, p. C9.)

12. Susan Mackley-Kallis and Ian McDermott, "Bruce Springsteen, Ronald Reagan, and the American Dream," *Popular Music and Society* 16 (Winter 1992): 1–9.

13. Frederick Allen, "Carter Getting to Be Tiresome," *Atlanta Journal*, Oct. 18, 1983, p. B1.

14. Esther Bauer, "Bargain Hunters at Carter Auction Keep Bids on Low Side," *Atlanta Journal*, Oct. 7, 1983, p. A1.

15. Interview with Jimmy Carter, Miller Center Interviews, Carter Presidency Project, vol. 19, November 29, 1982, p. 1, Jimmy Carter Library.

16. Associated Press, "Carter's Public Approval Skyrockets to 60 Percent," *Athens Daily News/Banner Herald*, Oct. 1, 1994, p. A4.

17. Bill Shipp, "Jimmy Carter Is Hot Again after a Decade," *Athens Daily News*, Mar. 4, 1990, p. D1.

18. Elizabeth Kurylo, "Jimmy Carter at 70," *Atlanta Journal/Constitution*, Sept. 25, 1994, p. A1.

19. Martin Merzer (Knight-Ridder), "Carter Is Snubbed by Nobel Prize Committee," *Athens Daily News/Banner Herald*, Oct. 15, 1994, p. A1.

20. *New York Times*, June 27, 1994, p. A13, and Sept. 22, 1994, p. A19.

21. Murray Kempton, "The Carter Mission," *New York Review of Books*, Oct. 20, 1994, p. 71.

22. Ron Fournier, "Carter: 'Dupe' or Statesman?" *San Francisco Examiner*, June 21, 1994, p. A10; Richard Matthews, "Will Carter's Kind of Peace Really Save Lives?" *Atlanta Journal*, Sept. 22, 1994, p. A12.

23. Interview with John and Betty Pope, National Park Service Interviews, June 28, 1989, Jimmy Carter Library.

24. Ron Taylor, "Driven by Beliefs, an Ex-President Turns 'Mr. Fix-It,'" *Atlanta Constitution*, Sept. 9, 1984, p. A1.

25. Joe R. Feagin and Robert Parker, *Building American Cities: The Urban Real Estate Game*, 2d ed. (Englewood Cliffs, N.J.: Prentice-Hall, 1990).

26. Quoted in Bill Shipp, "Maybe Carter's Grandest Achievement," *Atlanta Journal/Constitution*, Aug. 10, 1986, p. C1.

27. Frederick Allen, "A 'Camp David South' within the Great Park?" *Atlanta Constitution*, June 19, 1984, p. A2.

28. Bill Shipp, "Jimmy Carter Fights for His 'Life,'" *Atlanta Constitution*, Nov. 13, 1985, p. A10.

29. Howard Pousner, "Reagan Lauds Political Foe for His Efforts," *Atlanta Journal*, Oct. 1, 1986, p. A1; "Carter Center a Gift to the Nation," *Atlanta Constitution*, Oct. 2, 1986, p. A18; Shipp, "Maybe Carter's Grandest Achievement."

30. Jane O. Hansen, "Biden Unabashedly Praises Carter, Seeks His Endorsement and Advice," *Atlanta Constitution*, June 13, 1987, p. A4.

31. Bruce Babbitt, "Citizen Carter Is Worthy of Honor," *Atlanta Constitution*, July 19, 1988, p. C2.

32. "Carter: Prophet without Honor in His Own Land," reprinted in the *Atlanta Constitution*, Dec. 5, 1987, p. A15.

33. Kevin Sack, "Carter Image Looms Large," *Atlanta Journal/Constitution*, Feb. 15, 1987, p. D1.

34. Raad Cawthon, "Carter Star Rising Again within Party," *Atlanta Constitution*, July 18, 1988, p. C1.

35. John W. Mashek, "Bush Paints Dukakis as a 'Jimmy Carter from Massachusetts,'" *Atlanta Constitution*, May 4, 1988, p. A1; Jimmy Carter, "We Do Not Fear Change. We Welcome It" (text of Carter's speech to the 1988 Democratic Convention), *Atlanta Constitution*, July 19, 1988, p. C15; "Alas, It's Still Open Season on Carter," *Atlanta Constitution*, Feb. 5, 1989, p. B5.

36. Bob Dart, "Letter from Carter Hits Hard at Bork," *Atlanta Constitution*, Oct. 1, 1987, p. A1; "Carter Says 'Moral Hunger' Growing after Arms Scandal," *Atlanta Constitution*, Nov. 22, 1987, p. A3 (reprinted from the *New York Times*); Jimmy Carter, "U.S. by Its Great Silence Is Accomplice to Human Rights Violations Worldwide," *Atlanta Constitution*, Dec. 16, 1987, p. A15; "Carter Says Amy Is Right about CIA," *Atlanta Constitution*, Apr. 17, 1987; Gustav Niebuhr and Mark Silk, "Carter Assails Pope, Baptists on Major Issues," *Atlanta Constitution*, Apr. 22, 1988, p. A4.

37. Colin Campbell, "Carter Sows Innovative Seeds on West African Farm Mission," *Atlanta Constitution*, Aug. 6, 1989, p. A11.

38. Associated Press, "Carter Finds Way to Help Former Nanny," *Athens Daily News/Banner Herald*, Aug. 28, 1994, p. A5.

39. Jimmy Carter, *Always a Reckoning, and Other Poems* (New York: Times Books, 1995).

40. Associated Press, "Carter Vows Action after Meeting a Crack Baby," *Athens Daily News*, Oct. 27, 1991.

41. Peter Scott, "Atlanta Project Contributions Top $32 Million," *Atlanta Constitution*, Apr. 5, 1993, p. C1.

42. Andrew L. Yarrow (*New York Times* News Service), "History Looking Kindly on Carter Presidency," *Athens Daily News*, Nov. 19, 1990; E. J. Dionne Jr., "Jimmy — Come Back! All Is Forgiven!" *Washington Post National Weekly Edition*, Nov. 26–Dec. 2, 1990, p. 15; "Jimmy Carter in '92?" *Atlanta Journal/Constitution*, Dec. 30, 1990 (reprinted from the *Economist*); Julia Malone, "Trailing Bush Tries Carter-Bashing, But It May Be Risky," *Atlanta Constitution*, Aug. 11, 1992.

43. Drew Jubera, "Carter's Fans Jam Bookstore for a Signature and a Smile," *Atlanta Constitution*, Dec. 18, 1992, p. F1; Joe Earle, "Luring Tourists Back to

Plains," *Atlanta Constitution*, July 12, 1993, p. C4; Elizabeth Kurylo, "The World Beats a Path to Door of Plains Church to Worship with Carter," *Atlanta Constitution*, Sept. 3, 1989, p. A4.

44. Peggy Noonan, *What I Saw at the Revolution: A Political Life in the Reagan Era* (New York: Random House, 1990), p. 311.

45. Rheta Grimsley Johnson, "Carter Shines Bright as Volunteer," *Atlanta Constitution*, April 28, 1992, p. A13.

46. Jimmy Carter, "We Do Not Fear Change. We Welcome It."

47. Richard L. Berke, "U.S. Voters Focus on Selves, Poll Says," *New York Times*, Sept. 21, 1994, p. A12.

48. Richard L. Berke, "Victories Were Captured by G.O.P. Candidates, Not the Party's Platform," *New York Times*, Nov. 10, 1994, p. B1; John B. Judis, "The New Era of Instability," *New York Times*, Nov. 10, 1994, p. A15; Stanley B. Greenberg, "Mistaking a Moment for a Mandate," *New York Times*, Mar. 9, 1995, p. A15; and Kevin Phillips, "Under the Electoral Volcano," *New York Times*, Nov. 7, 1994, p. A15.

49. B. Drummond Ayres Jr., "In Race for California Chief No Candidate Is Favorite," *New York Times*, Sept. 19, 1994, p. A1.

50. Caddell recalled: "The voters were alienated. They weren't strongly disposed to vote, and they were very turned off by negative campaigning. The fewer who voted, the better for Cranston [who, as an incumbent with better name recognition, would do better in a low-turnout race]. So I told them, 'Run the most negative campaign you can. Drive the voters away. Piss them off with politics.' It worked. Cranston just made it by two points. The day after, I realized what I had done and got out of the business." Quoted in Christopher Hitchens, "Voting in the Passive Voice: What Polling Has Done to American Democracy," *Harper's*, April 1992, p. 47.

51. B. Drummond Ayres Jr., "Ad Nauseam: Campaigns Take over California TV," *New York Times*, Oct. 14, 1994, p. A1.

52. Bob Dart, "Attack Ads' Negative Drumbeat Is Growing," *Atlanta Journal*, Oct. 11, 1994, p. A7.

53. Associated Press, "New Congress Members Resemble the Old Ones," *Athens Daily News/Banner Herald*, Nov. 13, 1994, p. A3; Stephen Labaton, "On the Money Trail, Most 'Insiders' Had the Advantage," *New York Times*, Nov. 9, 1994, p. B1.

54. Bill Shipp, "Is Sam Nunn out of Place in Capitol, and Will He Quit in '96?" *Athens Daily News*, June 11, 1995, p. D1.

55. Sharon Cohen (Associated Press), "Voters Get Tough on Crime, Illegal Aliens," *Athens Banner Herald*, Nov. 9, 1994, p. 18; Dirk Johnson, "Conspiracy Theories' Impact Reverberates in Legislatures," *New York Times*, July 6, 1995, p. A1.

56. Herbert L. Abrams, "If the Chief Can't Command," *New York Times*, Jan. 4, 1995; Martha A. Bethel, "Terror in Montana," *New York Times*, July 20, 1995, p. A13.

57. Dan Shaw, "Hints of Arrogant Greed Suggest an 80's Revival," *New York Times*, Oct. 3, 1994, p. B5; Pete Hamill, "End Game," *Esquire*, Dec. 1994, p. 86.

58. Berke, "U.S. Voters Focus on Selves, Poll Says."

59. Frederick R. Lynch, "Tales from an Oppressed Class," *Wall Street Journal*, Nov. 11, 1991, p. A12.

60. Berke, "U.S. Voters Focus on Selves, Poll Says."

61. David W. Dunlap, "Gay Politicians Say Losses Are Partly Offset by Gains," *New York Times*, Nov. 14, 1994, p. A9.

62. Fox Butterfield, "More in U.S. Are in Prison, Report Says," *New York Times*, Aug. 10, 1995, p. A7; D. Stanley Eitzen and Maxine Baca Zinn, *Social Problems*, 6th ed. (Boston: Allyn & Bacon, 1994), p. 215; Richard J. Herrnstein and Charles Murray, *The Bell Curve: Intelligence and Class Structure in American Life* (New York: Free Press, 1994).

63. Jason DeParle, "Census Report Sees Incomes in Decline and More Poverty," *New York Times*, Oct. 7, 1994, p. A1.

64. Tom Walker, "Prospect of Grim Economic Future Doesn't Seem to Faze Under-30 Crowd," *Atlanta Constitution*, July 3, 1992, p. E1.

65. Quoted in DeParle, "Census Report Sees Incomes in Decline and More Poverty."

66. Steven A. Holmes, "Census Finds Little Change in Income Gap between Races," *New York Times*, Feb. 23, 1995, p. A10.

67. A. M. Rosenthal, "Lean and Very Mean," *New York Times*, Dec. 16, 1994, p. A19; Tom Teepen, "Toxic Rhetoric Poisons America," *Atlanta Journal*, Jan. 3, 1995, p. A9; Katherine Q. Seelye, "Voters Disgusted with Politicians As Election Nears," *New York Times*, Nov. 3, 1994, p. A1; Associated Press, "Americans Anticipate Armageddon, Poll Shows," *Athens Daily News/Banner Herald*, Dec. 11, 1994, p. A3.

68. Charles A. Radin, "In 1990 America, Encouraging Word Is Seldom Heard," reprinted in *Atlanta Constitution*, July 4, 1990; Tanya Barrientos (Knight-Ridder Newspapers), "Like a Bad Dream, the '70s Recur," *Athens Daily News/Banner Herald*, Dec. 25, 1994, p. A5; Rufus Adair, "A Reflective Norwood Talks about Congress, Redistricting and Nunn," *Athens Daily News/Banner Herald*, July 9, 1995, p. A1.

69. Peter M. Nichols, "On Disney's Mountain of Video Sales, a Sighting of 'Forrest Gump,'" *New York Times*, May 22, 1995, p. C9.

70. William J. Bennett, *The Book of Virtues: A Treasury of Great Moral Stories* (New York: Simon & Schuster, 1993).

71. Gertrude Himmelfarb, *The De-Moralization of Society: From Victorian Virtues to Modern Values* (New York: Knopf, 1994).

72. Mary B. W. Tabor, "Of Grace, Damnation and Best Sellers," *New York Times*, July 31, 1995, p. C1.

73. "Best Sellers," *New York Times Book Review*, Dec. 25, 1994, p. 18.

74. Mireya Navarro, "Protester Is Convicted of Murder in Deaths of 2 at Abortion Clinic," *New York Times*, Nov. 3, 1994, p. A1.

75. Ralph Waldo Emerson, "Self-Reliance," in Emerson, *Essays and Lectures* (New York: Library of America, 1983), p. 256.

76. Johnson, "Carter Shines Bright as Volunteer."

77. Quoted in Norman Polmar and Thomas B. Allen, *Rickover* (New York: Simon & Schuster, 1982), pp. 666–67.

78. The popularity of Sade in intellectual circles has gone largely unnoticed

outside them. Anyone acquainted with trends in the academy during the 1980s and 1990s, however, will surely attest to the fact that Sade is at least as popular as Marx once was among avant garde intellectuals. The popularity of Sade — and the lessening popularity of Marx — is probably attributable in large part to the influence of Michel Foucault. For an examination of this Foucault-Sade influence, see Jim Miller, *The Passion of Michel Foucault* (Simon & Schuster, 1993). Of course, for thinkers like Rickover the influence of Sade or others with similarly libertarian ideas was inevitable, anyway.

79. Michiko Kakutani, "Jackie, Oh. Oh, Oh, Oh" (review of *Jackie under My Skin*, by Wayne Koestenbaum), *New York Times*, May 5, 1995.

80. John Gray, "Does Democracy Have a Future?" (review of *Democracy on Trial*, by Jean Bethke Elshtain; *The Revolt of the Elites and the Betrayal of Democracy*, by Christopher Lasch; and *Making Democracy Work*, by Robert D. Putnam), *New York Times Book Review*, Jan. 22, 1995, p. 25.

81. Jonathan Yardley, "Picking up Good Vibrations" (review of *What Really Matters*, by Tony Schwartz), *Washington Post National Weekly Edition*, March 20–26, 1995, p. 35.

82. Jimmy Carter, "A New Turning Point: America's Economically Fueled Segregation," *Los Angeles Times*, Jan. 3, 1993, p. M3; and "Society's at 'Turning Point' to Heal Itself," *Atlanta Journal/Constitution*, Mar. 21, 1993, p. G1.

83. Catherine Fox, "Critique: Bronze Sculpture Works as a Testimonial, Not Art," *Atlanta Constitution*, June 8, 1994, p. D3.

84. Jimmy Carter, *Always a Reckoning*, pp. 119, 121.

SELECTED BIBLIOGRAPHY

MAJOR BOOKS BY JIMMY CARTER

Always a Reckoning, and Other Poems. New York: Times Books, 1995.
The Blood of Abraham. Boston: Houghton Mifflin, 1985.
Everything to Gain: Making the Most of the Rest of Your Life (with Rosalynn Carter). New York: Ballantine, 1987.
Keeping Faith: Memoirs of a President. New York: Bantam, 1982.
An Outdoor Journal: Adventures and Reflections. New York: Bantam, 1988.
Turning Point: A Candidate, a State, and a Nation Come of Age. New York: Times Books, 1992.
Why Not the Best? Nashville: Broadman, 1975.

COMPILATIONS, MEMOIRS, AND REMINISCENCES

Brzezinski, Zbigniew, *Power and Principle: Memoirs of the National Security Advisor, 1977–1981.* New York: Farrar, Straus, Giroux, 1983.
Califano, Joseph A., Jr. *Governing America: An Insider's Report from the White House and the Cabinet.* New York: Simon and Schuster, 1981.
Carter, Billy. *Redneck Power: The Wit and Wisdom of Billy Carter.* Comp. and ed. Jeremy Rifkin and Ted Howard. New York: Bantam, 1977.
Carter, Hugh. *Cousin Beedie and Cousin Hot: My Life with the Carter Family of Plains, Georgia.* Englewood Cliffs, N.J.: Prentice-Hall, 1978.
Carter, Jimmy. *Addresses of Jimmy Carter (James Earl Carter), Governor of Georgia, 1971–1975.* Comp. Frank Daniel. Atlanta: Georgia Department of Archives and History, 1975.
———. *A Government as Good as Its People.* New York: Simon and Schuster, 1977.
———. *"I'll Never Lie to You": Jimmy Carter in His Own Words.* Comp. Robert W. Turner. New York: Ballantine, 1976.
———. *The Presidential Campaign, 1976.* 3 vols. Compiled under the direction of the Committee on House Administration, U.S. House of Representatives. Washington, D.C.: U.S. Government Printing Office, 1978–79.
———. *Public Papers of the Presidents of the United States, Jimmy Carter (1977–1981).* 9 vols. Washington, D.C.: U.S. Government Printing Office, 1977–1982.
———. *The Spiritual Journey of Jimmy Carter: In His Own Words.* Comp. Wesley G. Pippert. New York: Macmillan, 1978.
Carter, Lillian. As told to Beth Tartan and Rudy Hayes. *Miss Lillian and Friends: The Plains, Georgia, Family Philosophy and Recipe Book.* New York: A & W Publishers, 1977.
Carter, Rosalynn. *First Lady from Plains.* Boston: Houghton Mifflin, 1984.

Jordan, Hamilton. *Crisis: The Last Year of the Carter Presidency.* New York: G. P. Putnam's Sons, 1982.

Lance, Bert, with Bill Gilbert. *The Truth of the Matter: My Life in and out of Politics.* New York: Summit Books, 1991.

Lance, LaBelle. *This Too Shall Pass.* Chappaqua, N.Y.: Christian Herald Books, 1978.

Powell, Jody. *The Other Side of the Story.* New York: Morrow, 1984.

Stapleton, Ruth Carter. *Brother Billy.* New York: Harper & Row, 1978.

———. *The Gift of Inner Healing.* Waco, Tex.: Word Books, 1976.

Vance, Cyrus. *Hard Choices: Critical Years in America's Foreign Policy.* New York: Simon and Schuster, 1983.

SECONDARY SOURCES

Abernathey, M. Glenn, Dilys M. Hill, and Phil Williams, eds. *The Carter Years: The President and Policy Making.* New York: St. Martin's Press, 1984.

"Aftermath: Pollsters Assess the '78 Elections. A Conversation with Pat Caddell and Bob Teeter." *Public Opinion* 1 (Nov./Dec. 1978): 14–19.

Ambrose, Stephen E. "The Presidency and Foreign Policy." *Foreign Affairs* 70 (Winter 1991): 120–38.

Anderson, James E. "The Management of Wage-Price Policies in the Johnson and Carter Administrations." *Policy Studies Journal* 12 (1984): 733–45.

Anderson, Patrick. *Electing Jimmy Carter: The Campaign of 1976.* Baton Rouge: Louisiana State University Press, 1994.

Astiz, Carlos A. "Changing United States Policy in Latin America." *Current History* 81 (1982): 49–50, 88–92.

Baker, James T. *A Southern Baptist in the White House.* Philadelphia: Westminster Press, 1977.

Bartley, Numan V. *Jimmy Carter and the Politics of the New South.* St. Louis: Forum Press, 1979.

Beisel, David R. "Toward a Psychohistory of Jimmy Carter." *Journal of Psychohistory* 5 (1977): 202–38.

Bell, Coral. "From Carter to Reagan." *Foreign Affairs* 63 (1984): 490–510.

Bishop, Joseph W., Jr. "Carter's Last Capitulation." *Commentary* 71 (1981): 32–35.

Bitzer, Lloyd, and Theodore Rueter. *Carter vs. Ford: The Counterfeit Debates of 1976.* Madison: University of Wisconsin Press, 1980.

Blount, Roy, Jr. *Crackers.* New York: Knopf, 1980.

Bosworth, Barry P. "The Carter Administration's Anti-Inflation Program." *Proceedings of the Academy of Political Science* 33 (1979): 12–19.

Braestrup, Peter. "The American Military: The Changing Outlook." *Wilson Quarterly* 3 (1979): 124–30.

Brill, Steven. "Jimmy Carter's Pathetic Lies." *Harper's,* March 1976, 77–88.

Brown, Harold. *Thinking about National Security: Defense and Foreign Policy in a Dangerous World.* Boulder, Colo.: Westview Press, 1983.

Brummett, Barry. "Towards a Theory of Silence as a Political Strategy." *Quarterly Journal of Speech* 66 (1980): 289–303.

Caddell, Patrick H. "Trapped in a Downward Spiral." *Public Opinion* 2 (Oct./ Nov. 1979): 2–7, 52–55, 58–60.

Campbell, Colin. *Managing the Presidency: Carter, Reagan, and the Search for Executive Harmony.* Pittsburgh: University of Pittsburgh Press, 1986.

Carpenter, Ronald H., and William J. Jordan, "Style in Discourse as a Predictor of Political Personality for Mr. Carter and Other Twentieth-Century Presidents: Testing the Barber Paradigm." *Presidential Studies Quarterly* 8 (1978): 67–78.

Chaffee, Steven H., and Sun Yuel Choe. "Time of Decision and Media Use during the Ford-Carter Campaign." *Public Opinion Quarterly* 44 (1980): 53–69.

Christopher, Warren, et al. *American Hostages in Iran: The Conduct of a Crisis.* New Haven: Yale University Press, 1985.

Copeland, Ronald. "The Cuban Boatlift of 1980: Strategies in Federal Crisis Management." *Annals of the American Academy of Political and Social Science* 467 (1983): 138–50.

Crane, Philip M. *Surrender in Panama: The Case against the Treaty.* New York: Dale Books, 1978.

David, Paul T., and David H. Everson, eds. *The Presidential Election and Transition, 1980–1981.* Carbondale: Southern Illinois University Press, 1983.

Davis, Leslie K. "Camera Eye-Contact by the Candidates in the Presidential Debates of 1976." *Journalism Quarterly* 55 (1978): 431–37.

Dayan, Moshe. *Breakthrough: A Personal Account of the Egypt-Israel Peace Negotiations.* London: Weidenfeld and Nicolson, 1981.

deMause, Lloyd, and Henry Ebel. *Jimmy Carter and American Fantasy: Psychohistorical Explorations.* New York: Two Continents/Psychohistory Press, 1977.

Diskin, Martin. Editor. *Trouble in Our Backyard: Central America and the United States in the Eighties.* New York: Pantheon, 1983.

Dobriansky, Paula J. "Human Rights and Policy: The American Tradition." *Current* (July/Aug. 1989): 28–38.

Donovan, Hedley. *Roosevelt to Reagan: A Reporter's Encounters with Nine Presidents.* New York: Harper & Row, 1985.

Drew, Elizabeth. *American Journal: The Events of 1976.* New York: Random House, 1977.

———. *Portrait of an Election: The 1980 Presidential Campaign.* New York: Simon and Schuster, 1981.

Dye, Kenneth, Donald Rothchild, and Robert Lieber, eds. *Eagle Entangled: U.S. Foreign Policy in a Complex World.* New York: Longman, 1979.

Elovitz, Paul H. "Three Days in Plains." *Journal of Psychohistory* 5 (Fall 1977): 175–99.

Erickson, Keith V. "Jimmy Carter: The Rhetoric of Private and Civic Piety." *Western Journal of Speech Communication* 44 (Summer 1980): 221–35.

Etzioni, Amitai. "Mass Psychology in the White House." *Society* 18 (1980): 82–85.

"Face Off: A Conversation with the President's Pollsters Patrick Caddell and Richard Wirthlin." *Public Opinion* 3 (Dec./Jan. 1981): 2–12.

Fallows, James. "The Passionless Presidency: The Trouble with Jimmy Carter's Administration." *Atlantic* (May 1979): 33–48.

———. "The Passionless Presidency II: More from Inside Jimmy Carter's White House." *Atlantic* (June 1979): 75–81.

———. "The President and the Press." *Washington Monthly* 11 (1979): 9–17.

———. "The Seductions of Washington Society." *Washington Monthly* 8 (1976): 18–24.

Farer, Tom J. "Searching for Defeat." *Foreign Policy* 40 (1980): 155–74.

Feigenbaum, Edward D. "Staffing, Organization, and Decision-Making in the Ford and Carter White Houses." *Presidential Studies Quarterly* 10 (1980): 364–77.

Feinberg, Richard E. "Background to Crisis: U.S. Policies toward Central America in the 1970s." *Towson State Journal of International Affairs* 16 (1981): 29–40.

Ferguson, Thomas, and Joel Rogers. *The Hidden Election: Politics and Economics in the 1980 Presidential Campaign.* New York: Pantheon Books, 1981.

Fink, Gary M. *Prelude to the Presidency: The Political Character and Legislative Leadership Style of Governor Jimmy Carter.* Westport, Conn.: Greenwood, 1980.

Fleisher, Richard, and Jon R. Bond. "Assessing Presidential Support in the House: Lessons from Reagan and Carter." *Journal of Politics* 45 (August 1983): 745–58.

Flowers, Ronald B. "President Jimmy Carter, Evangelicalism, Church-State Relations, and Civil Religion." *Journal of Church and State* 25 (1983): 113–32.

Ford, Gerald R. *A Time to Heal: The Autobiography of Gerald R. Ford.* New York: Harper & Row, 1979.

Forsythe, David P. "Human Rights in U.S. Foreign Policy: Retrospect and Prospect." *Political Science Quarterly* 105 (Fall 1990): 435–55.

Francis, Samuel T. "Conflict in the Horn of Africa." *Journal of Social and Political Studies* 2 (1978): 155–68.

Gaver, Jessyca. *The Faith of Jimmy Carter.* New York: Manor Books, 1977.

Gergen, David. "A Report from the Editors on the 'Crisis of Confidence,'" *Public Opinion* 2 (Aug./Sept. 1979): 2–3, 54.

Germond, Jack, and Jules Witcover. *Blue Smoke and Mirrors: How Reagan Won and Why Carter Lost the Election of 1980.* New York: Viking, 1981.

Geyer, Anne E., and Robert Y. Shapiro. "Human Rights." *Public Opinion Quarterly* 52 (Fall 1988): 386–99.

Gillon, Steven M. *The Democrats' Dilemma: Walter F. Mondale and the Liberal Legacy.* New York: Columbia University Press, 1992.

Glad, Betty. *Jimmy Carter, In Search of the Great White House.* New York: Norton, 1980.

Grover, William F. *The President as Prisoner: A Structural Critique of the Carter and Reagan Years.* Albany: SUNY Press, 1989.

Gulliver, Hal. *A Friendly Tongue.* Macon, Ga.: Mercer University Press, 1984.

Haas, Garland A. *Jimmy Carter and the Politics of Frustration*. Jefferson, N.C.: McFarland & Co., 1992.

Hahn, Don F. "Flailing the Profligate: Carter's Energy Sermon of 1979." *Presidential Studies Quarterly* 11 (1980): 583–87.

———. "The Rhetoric of Jimmy Carter, 1976–1980." *Presidential Studies Quarterly* 14 (1984): 265–88.

Hargrove, Erwin C. *Jimmy Carter as President: Leadership and the Politics of the Public Good*. Baton Rouge: Louisiana State University Press, 1988.

Hefley, James C., and Marti Hefley. *The Church That Produced a President*. New York: Wyden Books, 1977.

Helicher, Karl. "The Response of the Soviet Government and Press to Carter's Human Rights Policies." *Presidential Studies Quarterly* 13 (1983): 296–304.

Hill, Alette. "The Carter Campaign in Retrospect: Decoding the Cartoons." *Semiotica* 23 (1978): 307–32.

Hoffmann, Stanley. "Foreign Policy Transition: Requiem." *Foreign Policy* 42 (1981): 3–26.

Holifield, E. Brooks. "The Three Strands of Jimmy Carter's Religion." *New Republic*, June 5, 1976.

Holland, J. William. "The Great Gamble: Jimmy Carter and the 1979 Energy Crisis." *Prologue: Quarterly Journal of the National Archives* 22 (Spring 1990): 63–79.

Howell, John M. "The Carter Human Rights Policy as Applied to the Soviet Union." *Presidential Studies Quarterly* 13 (1983): 286–95.

Hoxie, R. Gordon. "Staffing the Ford and Carter Presidencies." *Presidential Studies Quarterly* 19 (1980): 378–401.

Huddleston, Mark W. "The Carter Civil Service Reforms: Some Implications for Political Theory and Public Administration." *Political Science Quarterly* 96 (Winter 1981–82): 607–21.

Hughes, Arthur J. "Amazin' Jimmy and a Mighty Fortress Was Our Teddy: Theodore Roosevelt and Jimmy Carter, the Religious Link." *Presidential Studies Quarterly* 9 (1979): 8–83.

Humphrey, Robert. *The Carters of Kings Langley: The President's Roots: A Family History and Guide to the Parish of Kings Langley*. Kings Langley: John Bourne, 1978.

Hyatt, Richard. *The Carters of Plains*. Huntsville, Ala.: Strode Publishers, 1977.

Jackson, John S., III, Jesse C. Brown, and Barbara L. Brown. "Recruitment, Representation, and Political Values: The 1976 Democratic National Convention Delegates." *American Political Quarterly* 6 (1978): 187–212.

Jennings, Genelle. *Into the Jaws of Politics: The Charge of the Peanut Brigade*. Huntsville, Ala.: Strode Publishers, 1979.

Jimmy Carter, 1962–1976: A Comprehensive Newsfile on Microfiche. In Cooperation with the *Atlanta Constitution*. Glen Rock, N.J.: Microfilming Corporation of America, 1976.

Johnson, Haynes. *In the Absence of Power: Governing America*. New York: Viking Press, 1980.

Johnstone, Christopher Lyle. "Electing Ourselves in 1976: Jimmy Carter and the American Faith." *Western Journal of Speech Communication* 42 (1978): 241–49.

Jones, Charles O. *The Trusteeship Presidency: Jimmy Carter and the United States Congress*. Baton Rouge: Louisiana State University Press, 1988.

Jorden, William J. *Panama Odyssey*. Austin: University of Texas Press, 1984.

Kantowicz, Edward R. "The Limits of Incrementalism: Carter's Efforts at Tax Reform." *Journal of Policy Analysis and Management* 4 (1985): 217–33.

———. "Reminiscences of a Fated Presidency: Themes from the Carter Memoirs." *Presidential Studies Quarterly* 16 (1986): 651–65.

Kaufman, Burton I. *The Presidency of James Earl Carter, Jr.* Lawrence: University Press of Kansas, 1993.

Kellerman, Barbara. "Introversion in the Oval Office." *Presidential Studies Quarterly* 13 (1983): 383–99.

———. *The Political Presidency: Practice of Leadership*. New York: Oxford University Press, 1984.

Kessel, John H. "The Structures of the Carter White House." *American Journal of Political Science* 27 (1983): 431–63.

Kirkpatrick, Jeane J. "Establishing a Viable Human Rights Policy." *World Affairs* 143 (1981): 323–34.

———. "U.S. Security and Latin America." *Commentary* 71 (1981): 29–40.

Kohut, Andrew. "Public Attitudes on Domestic Issues, 1981." *Public Opinion* 4 (Dec./Jan. 1982): 41–43.

Kraus, Jon. "American Foreign Policy in Africa." *Current History* 80 (1981): 97–100, 129, 138.

Kraus, Sidney, ed. *The Great Debates: Carter vs. Ford, 1976*. Bloomington: Indiana University Press, 1979.

Krukones, Michael G. "The Campaign Promises of Jimmy Carter: Accomplishments and Failures." *Presidential Studies Quarterly* 15 (1985): 136–44.

Kucharsky, David. *The Man from Plains: The Mind and Spirit of Jimmy Carter*. New York: Harper & Row, 1976.

LaFeber, Walter. *Inevitable Revolutions: The United States in Central America*. New York: Norton, 1983.

Lang, Gladys Engel, and Kurt Lang. "The First Debate and the Coverage Gap." *Journal of Communication* 28 (1978): 93–98.

———. "Immediate and Delayed Responses to a Carter–Ford Debate: Assessing Public Opinion." *Public Opinion Quarterly* (1978): 322–41.

Langford, Edna, and Linda Maddox. *Rosalynn, Friend and First Lady*. Old Tappan, N.J.: Revell, 1980.

Lasky, Victor. *Jimmy Carter: The Man and the Myth*. New York: R. Marek, 1979.

Lee, David D. "The Politics of Less: The Trials of Herbert Hoover and Jimmy Carter." *Presidential Studies Quarterly* 13 (1983): 305–12.

———. "The South and the American Mainstream: The Election of Jimmy Carter." *Georgia Historical Quarterly* 61 (1977): 7–12.

Lemann, Nicholas. "Jordan, Georgia, and the Establishment." *Washington Monthly* 10 (1978): 36–47.

————. "Why Carter Fails: Taking the Politics out of Government." *Washington Monthly* 10 (1978): 12–23.

Levantrosser, William F. "Financing Presidential Campaigns: The Impact of Reform Campaign Finance Laws on the Democratic Presidential Nomination of 1976." *Presidential Studies Quarterly* 11 (1981): 280–88.

Lewis, Finlay. *Mondale: Portrait of an American Politician*. rev. ed. New York: Harper & Row, 1984.

Lipset, Seymour Martin, and William Schneider. "Carter vs. Israel: What the Polls Reveal." *Commentary* 64 (1977): 21–29.

Locander, Robert. "Carter and the Press: The First Two Years." *Presidential Studies Quarterly* 10 (1980): 106–20.

Lynn, Laurence E., Jr., and David deF. Whitman. *The President as Policymaker: Jimmy Carter and Welfare Reform*. Philadelphia: Temple University Press, 1983.

Maddox, Robert L. *Preacher at the White House*. Nashville: Broadman Press, 1984.

Markus, Gregory B. "Political Attitudes during an Election Year: A Report on the 1980 NES Panel Study." *American Political Science Review* (Sept. 1982).

Martin, Martha Anna. "Ideologues, Ideographs, and 'The Best Man': From Carter to Reagan." *Southern Speech Communication Journal* 49 (1983): 12–25.

Mazlish, Bruce, and Edwin Diamond. *Jimmy Carter: A Character Portrait*. New York: Simon and Schuster, 1979.

Mead, Walter J. "The National Energy Program Evaluated." *Current History* 75 (1978): 9–12, 31–33.

Melusky, Joseph A. "A Comparative Analysis of the Regional Strength of Major Party Presidential Candidates in 1976 and 1980: Some Tactical Prescriptions for 1984 in View of Electoral Vote Shifts." *Presidential Studies Quarterly* 13 (1983): 482–89.

Menendez, Albert J. "How Carter Won." *Church and State* 29 (Dec. 1976): 9–14.

————. "Religion at the Polls, 1980." *Church and State* 33 (Dec. 1980): 15–18.

Metzgar, Jack. "Public Policy and Steel." *Dissent* 29 (1982): 325–29.

Miller, Warren E. "Learning about the Candidates: The 1976 Presidential Debates." *Public Opinion Quarterly* 43 (Fall 1979): 326–46.

————. "Misreading the Public Pulse." *Public Opinion* 2 (Oct./Nov. 1979): 9–15, 60.

Miller, William L. *Yankee from Georgia: The Emergence of Jimmy Carter*. New York: Harper & Row, 1978.

Mintz, Alex. "Guns versus Butter: A Disaggregated Analysis." *American Political Science Review* 83 (Dec. 1989): 1285–94.

Mitofsky, Warren J., and Kathleen A. Frankovic. "Don't Count Jimmy Carter Out." *Public Opinion* 2 (Aug./Sept. 1979): 5–8.

Moens, Alexander. *Foreign Policy under Carter: Testing Multiple Advocacy Decision Making*. Boulder, Colo.: Westview Press, 1990.

————. "President Carter's Advisers and the Fall of the Shah." *Political Science Quarterly* 106 (Summer 1991): 211–38.

Moffett, George D., III. *The Limits of Victory: The Ratification of the Panama Canal Treaties*. Ithaca, N.Y.: Cornell University Press, 1985.

Mollenhoff, Clark R. *The President Who Failed: Carter out of Control.* New York: Macmillan, 1980.

Mullen, William F. "Perceptions of Carter's Legislative Successes and Failures: Views from the Hill and the Liaison Staff." *Presidential Studies Quarterly* 12 (1982): 522–33.

Muravchik, Joshua. *The Uncertain Crusade: Jimmy Carter and the Dilemmas of Human Rights Policy.* Lanham, Md.: Hamilton, 1986.

Nathan, James A. "Zbigscam: U.S. Foreign Policy, 1976–80." *Virginia Quarterly Review* 57 (1981): 210–26.

Naveh, David, and A. Paul Hare. "On the Mountain." *Policy Studies Journal* 18 (Summer 1990): 827–47.

Neyland, James. *The Carter Family Scrapbook: An Intimate Close-Up of America's First Family.* New York: Grosset & Dunlap, 1977.

Nielsen, Niels C., Jr. *The Religion of President Carter.* Nashville: T. Nelson, 1977.

Nincic, Miroslav. "The United States, the Soviet Union, and the Politics of Opposites." *World Politics* 40 (July 1988): 452–76.

Norton, Howard Melvin. *Rosalynn.* Plainfield, N.J.: Logos International, 1977.

Orman, John. *Comparing Presidential Behavior: Carter, Reagan, and the Macho Presidential Style.* Westport, Conn.: Greenwood, 1987.

Paletz, David L., and Robert M. Entman. "Presidents, Power, and the Press." *Presidential Studies Quarterly* 10 (1980): 416–26.

Patton, John H. "A Government as Good as Its People: Jimmy Carter and the Restoration of Transcendence to Politics." *Quarterly Journal of Speech* 63 (Oct. 1977): 249–57.

Peters, Charles. "Concerns about Carter: And His Chief Courtier." *Washington Monthly* 8 (1976): 2–8.

Pfluger, Friedbert. "Human Rights Unbound: Carter's Human Rights Policy Reassessed." *Presidential Studies Quarterly* 19 (Fall 1989): 705–17.

Podhoretz, Norman. "The New American Majority." *Commentary* 71 (1981): 19–28.

Poe, Steven C. "Human Rights and Economic Aid Allocation under Ronald Reagan and Jimmy Carter." *American Journal of Political Science* 36 (Feb. 1992): 147–68.

Powell, Jody. "Trial by Media: The Studio 54 Scandal." *Rolling Stone,* March 29, 1984, 49–55.

President Carter. Washington, D.C.: Congressional Quarterly, 1977.

President Carter, 1978. Washington, D.C.: Congressional Quarterly, 1979.

President Carter, 1979. Washington, D.C.: Congressional Quarterly, 1980.

President Carter, 1980. Washington, D.C.: Congressional Quarterly, 1981.

Puddington, Arch. "Voices in the Wilderness: The Western Heroes of Eastern Europe." *Policy Review* 53 (Summer 1990): 34–40.

Ranney, Austin, ed. *The American Elections of 1980.* Washington, D.C.: American Enterprise Institute, 1981.

Rarick, David L., Mary B. Duncan, David G. Lee, and Laurinda W. Porter. "The Carter Persona: An Empirical Analysis of the Rhetorical Visions of Campaign '76." *Quarterly Journal of Speech* 63 (Oct. 1977): 258–73.

Reichard, Gary W. "Early Returns: Assessing Jimmy Carter." *Presidential Studies Quarterly* 20 (Summer 1990): 603–21.

Ribuffo, Leo P. "God and Jimmy Carter." In *Transforming Faith: The Sacred and Secular in Modern American History*, edited by M. L. Bradbury and James B. Gilbert, 141–59. Westport, Conn.: Greenwood, 1989.

———. "Is Poland a Soviet Satellite? Gerald Ford, the Sonnenfeldt Doctrine, and the Election of 1976." *Diplomatic History* 14 (Summer 1990): 385–403.

———. "Jimmy Carter and the Ironies of American Liberalism." *Gettysburg Review* (Autumn 1988): 738–49.

Richman, Alvin. "Public Attitudes on Military Power, 1981." *Public Opinion* 4 (Dec./Jan. 1982): 44–46.

Rosati, Jerel A. *The Carter Administration's Quest for Global Community: Beliefs and Their Impact on Behavior.* Columbia, S.C.: University of South Carolina Press, 1987.

Rose, Douglas D. "Citizen Uses of the Ford–Carter Debates." *Journal of Politics* 41 (1979): 214–21.

Rowland, Robert. "The Substance of the 1980 Carter–Reagan Debate." *Southern Speech Communication Journal* 51 (1986): 142–65.

Rozell, Mark J. *The Press and the Carter Presidency.* Boulder, Colo.: Westview, 1989.

Safty, Adel. "Sadat's Negotiations with the United States and Israel: From Sinai to Camp David." *American Journal of Economics and Sociology* 50 (July 1991): 285–99.

Scheele, Paul E. "President Carter and the Water Projects: A Case Study in Presidential and Congressional Decision-Making." *Presidential Studies Quarterly* 8 (1978): 348–64.

Schlesinger, Arthur M., Jr. "Human Rights and the American Tradition." *Foreign Affairs* 57 (1979): 503–26.

Schram, Martin. *Running for President, 1976: The Carter Campaign.* New York: Stein and Day, 1977.

Shapiro, Walter. "The Triumph and the Trivia: Inside the Carter Headquarters in Pennsylvania." *Washington Monthly* 8 (1976): 31–39.

Shichor, David, and Donald R. Ranish. "President Carter's Vietnam Amnesty: An Analysis of a Public Policy Decision." *Presidential Studies Quarterly* 10 (1980): 443–50.

Shogan, Robert. *Promises to Keep: Carter's First Hundred Days.* New York: Crowell, 1977.

Shoup, Laurence H. *The Carter Presidency, and Beyond: Power and Politics in the 1980s.* Palo Alto, Calif.: Ramparts, 1980.

Sick, Gary. *All Fall Down: America's Tragic Encounter with Iran.* New York: Random House, 1985.

———. *October Surprise: America's Hostages in Iran and the Election of Ronald Reagan.* New York: Random House, 1991.

Sigelman, Lee, and Carol K. Sigelman. "Judgments of the Carter–Reagan Debate: The Eyes of the Beholders." *Public Opinion Quarterly* 48 (1984): 624–28.

Simmons, Dawn Langley. *Rosalynn Carter: Her Life Story*. New York: F. Fell, 1979.

Smith, Craig Allen. "Leadership, Orientation, and Rhetorical Vision: Jimmy Carter, the 'New Right,' and the Panama Canal." *Presidential Studies Quarterly* 16 (1986): 317–28.

Smith, Gaddis. *Morality, Reason, and Power: American Diplomacy in the Carter Years*. New York: Hill & Wang, 1986.

Solomon, Martha. "Jimmy Carter and *Playboy:* A Sociolinguistic Perspective on Style." *Quarterly Journal of Speech* 64 (1978): 173–82.

Spaulding, Phinizy. "Georgia and the Election of Jimmy Carter." *Georgia Historical Quarterly* 61 (1977): 13–22.

Stacks, John F., Jack Germond, and Jules Witcover. "How the Democrats Gave Us Reagan: The Ten Key Moments of the 1980 Campaign." *Washington Monthly* 13 (1982): 8–20.

Stephens, David. "President Carter, Congress, and NEH: Creating the Department of Education." *Political Science Quarterly* 98 (1983–84): 641–63.

Stockman, David A. "The Wrong War? The Case against a National Energy Policy." *Public Interest* 53 (1978): 3–44.

Strong, Robert A. "Jimmy Carter and the Panama Canal Treaties." *Presidential Studies Quarterly* 21 (Spring 1991): 269–87.

———. "Recapturing Leadership: The Carter Administration and the Crisis of Confidence." *Presidential Studies Quarterly* 16 (1986): 636–50.

Stroud, Kandy. *How Jimmy Won: The Victory Campaign from Plains to the White House*. New York: Morrow, 1977.

Sudol, Ronald A. "The Rhetoric of Strategic Retreat: Carter and the Panama Canal Debate." *Quarterly Journal of Speech* 65 (1979): 379–91.

Sundquist, James L. "The Crisis of Competence in Our National Government." *Political Science Quarterly* 95 (1980): 183–208.

Swanson, David L. "And That's the Way It Was? Television Coverage of the 1976 Presidential Campaign." *Quarterly Journal of Speech* 63 (1977): 239–48.

Talbott, Strobe. *Endgame: The Inside Story of SALT II*. New York: Harper & Row, 1979.

Thomas, Dan B., and Larry A. Bass. "Presidential Identification and Mass-Public Compliance with Official Policy: The Case of the Carter Energy Program." *Policy Studies Journal* 10 (1982): 448–65.

Thompson, Hunter S. "Jimmy Carter and the Great Leap of Faith." In *The Great Shark Hunt*. New York: Summit Books, 1979.

Thornton, Richard C. *The Carter Years: Toward a New Global Order*. New York: Paragon House, 1991.

Tucker, Robert W. "America in Decline: The Foreign Policy of 'Maturity.'" *Foreign Affairs* 58 (1980): 449–84.

Turner, Stansfield. *Secrecy and Democracy: The CIA in Transition*. Boston: Houghton Mifflin, 1985.

Vance, Cyrus. "The Human Rights Imperative." *Foreign Policy* (Summer 1986): 3–20.

Viguerie, Richard A. *The New Right: We're Ready to Lead*. rev. ed. Falls Church, Va.: Viguerie Co., 1981.

Wheeler, Leslie. *Jimmy Who?: An Examination of Presidential Candidate Jimmy Carter: The Man, His Career, His Stands on the Issues.* Woodbury, New York: Barron's, 1976.

Witcover, Jules. *Marathon: The Pursuit of the Presidency, 1972–1976.* New York: Viking, 1977.

Wolfe, James S. "Exclusion, Fusion, or Dialogue: How Should Religion and Politics Relate?" *Journal of Church and State* 22 (1980): 89–105.

Wooten, James. *Dasher: The Roots and Rising of Jimmy Carter.* New York: Summit Books, 1978.

OTHER WORKS CONSULTED

Adams, David S. "Ronald Reagan's 'Revival': Voluntarism as a Theme in Reagan's Civil Religion." *Sociological Analysis* 48 (1987): 17–29.

Barber, James David. *The Presidential Character: Predicting Performance in the White House.* 3d ed. Englewood Cliffs, N.J.: Prentice-Hall, 1985.

Barone, Michael. *Our Country: The Shaping of America from Roosevelt to Reagan.* New York: Free Press, 1990.

Bartley, Numan V. *The Creation of Modern Georgia.* Athens: University of Georgia Press, 1983.

Bell, Daniel. *The Cultural Contradictions of Capitalism.* New York: Basic Books, 1976.

Bellah, Robert N. *Beyond Belief: Essays on Religion in a Post-Traditional World.* New York: Harper & Row, 1970.

———. *The Broken Covenant: American Civil Religion in a Time of Trial.* New York: Seabury Press, 1975.

———. "Religion and Legitimation in the American Republic." *Society* 15 (May/June 1978): 6–23.

Bellah, Robert N., Richard Madsen, William M. Sullivan, Ann Swindler, and Steven M. Tipton. *Habits of the Heart: Individualism and Commitment in American Life.* Berkeley: University of California Press, 1985.

Black, Earl, and Merle Black. *Politics and Society in the South.* Cambridge: Harvard University Press, 1987.

Bloom, Harold. *The American Religion: The Emergence of the Post-Christian Nation.* New York: Simon and Schuster, 1992.

Boszormenyi-Nagy, Ivan, and Geraldine M. Spark. *Invisible Loyalties: Reciprocity in Intergenerational Family Therapy.* New York: Harper & Row, 1973.

Burns, James MacGregor. *Leadership.* New York: Harper Colophon, 1978.

———. *The Power to Lead: The Crisis of the American Presidency.* New York: Simon and Schuster, 1984.

Cannon, Lou. *President Reagan: The Role of a Lifetime.* New York: Simon and Schuster, 1991.

Capps, Walter. *The New Religious Right: Piety, Patriotism, and Politics.* Columbia: University of South Carolina Press, 1990.

Cherry, Conrad. *God's New Israel: Religious Interpretations of American Destiny.* Englewood Cliffs, N.J.: Prentice-Hall, 1971.

Coleman, Kenneth, ed. *A History of Georgia.* Athens: University of Georgia Press, 1977.

Davis, Fred I. "Decade Labeling: The Play of Collective Memory and Narrative Plot." *Symbolic Interaction* 7 (1984): 15–24.

Donahue, Barnard F. "The Political Use of Religious Symbols." *Review of Politics* (January 1974): 48–59.

Edwards, George C., III, with Alec M. Gallup. *Presidential Approval: A Sourcebook.* Baltimore: Johns Hopkins University Press, 1990.

Erickson, Paul D. *Reagan Speaks: The Making of an American Myth.* New York: New York University Press, 1985.

Fairbanks, James David. "The Priestly Functions of the Presidency: A Discussion of the Literature on Civil Religion and Its Implications for the Study of Presidential Leadership." *Presidential Studies Quarterly* 11 (Spring 1981): 214–32.

Flowers, Ronald B. *Religion in Strange Times: The 1960s and 1970s.* Macon, Ga.: Mercer University Press, 1984.

Galphin, Bruce. *The Riddle of Lester Maddox.* Atlanta: Camelot, 1968.

Garment, Suzanne. *Scandal: The Crisis of Mistrust in American Politics.* New York: Times Books, 1991.

Gehrig, Gail. *American Civil Religion: An Assessment.* Storrs, Conn.: Society for the Scientific Study of Religion, 1979.

Goffman, Erving. *The Presentation of Self in Everyday Life.* Garden City, N.Y.: Doubleday, 1959.

Greenberg, Stanley B. *Middle Class Dreams: The Politics and Power of the New American Majority.* New York: Times Books, 1995.

Hadden, Jeffrey, and Anson Shupe. *Televangelism, Power, and Politics on God's Frontier.* New York: Henry Holt, 1988.

———, eds. *Prophetic Religions and Politics.* New York, Paragon, 1986.

Harris, Louis. *Inside America.* New York: Vintage, 1987.

Henderson, Charles P., Jr. *The Nixon Theology.* New York: Harper & Row, 1972.

Henderson, Harold P., and Gary L. Roberts, eds. *Georgia Governors in an Age of Change: From Ellis Arnall to George Busbee.* Athens: University of Georgia Press, 1988.

Hepburn, Lawrence R., ed. *Contemporary Georgia.* Athens, Ga.: Carl Vinson Institute of Government, University of Georgia, 1987

Horney, Karen. *Neurosis and Human Growth: The Struggle toward Self-Realization.* New York: Norton, 1950.

Hunter, James Davison. *Culture Wars: The Struggle to Define America.* New York: Basic Books, 1991.

Inglehart, Ronald. *Culture Shift in Advanced Industrial Society.* Princeton: Princeton University Press, 1990.

Jewett, Robert. *The Captain America Complex: The Dilemma of Zealous Nationalism.* Philadelphia: Westminster Press, 1973.

Kelly, George Armstrong. *Politics and Religious Consciousness in America.* New Brunswick, N.J.: Transaction, 1984.

Kernberg, Otto. *Borderline Conditions and Pathological Narcissism.* New York: J. Aronson, 1975.

Key, V. O., Jr. *Southern Politics in State and Nation.* New York: Knopf, 1949.

Kirby, Jack Temple. *Media-Made Dixie: The South in the American Imagination.* rev. ed. Athens, Ga.: University of Georgia Press, 1986.

Klapp, Orin E. *Symbolic Leaders: Public Dramas and Public Men.* Chicago: Aldine, 1964.

Knutson, Jeanne, ed. *Handbook of Political Psychology.* San Francisco: Jossey-Bass, 1973.

Kohut, Heinz. *The Analysis of the Self.* New York: International Universities Press, 1971.

Ladd, Everett Carll, Jr., and Seymour Martin Lipset. "Anatomy of a Decade." *Public Opinion* 3 (Dec./Jan. 1980): 2–9.

Lasch, Christopher. *The Culture of Narcissism: American Life in an Age of Diminishing Expectations.* New York: Norton, 1979.

Lemann, Nicholas. "How the Seventies Changed America." *American Heritage* 42 (July/Aug. 1991): 39–49.

Lipset, Seymour Martin, and William Schneider. *The Confidence Gap: Business, Labor, and Government in the Public Mind.* rev. ed. Baltimore: Johns Hopkins University Press, 1987.

Maddox, Lester. *Speaking Out: The Autobiography of Lester Garfield Maddox.* New York: Doubleday, 1975.

Marty, Martin E. *Religion and Republic: The American Circumstance.* Boston: Beacon, 1987.

Mathisen, James A. "Twenty Years after Bellah: Whatever Happened to Civil Religion?" *Sociological Analysis* 50 (Summer 1989): 129–46.

Mayer, William G. *The Changing American Mind: How and Why American Public Opinion Changed between 1960 and 1988.* Ann Arbor: University of Michigan Press, 1992.

Mead, George Herbert. *Mind, Self, and Society from the Standpoint of a Social Behaviorist.* Vol. 1. Ed. Charles W. Morris. Chicago: University of Chicago Press, 1934.

Miller, Warren E., and Santa A. Traugott. *American National Election Studies Data Sourcebook, 1952–1986.* Cambridge: Harvard University Press, 1989.

Neustadt, Richard E. *Presidential Power: The Politics of Leadership from FDR to Carter.* New York: Wiley, 1980.

Novak, Michael. *Choosing Our King: Powerful Symbols in Presidential Politics.* 2d ed. New Brunswick, N.J.: Transaction, 1991.

Pierard, Richard V., and Robert D. Linder. *Civil Religion and the Presidency.* Grand Rapids, Mich.: Zondervan, 1988.

Quebedeaux, Richard. *The Worldly Evangelicals.* New York: Harper & Row, 1978.

Reichley, A. James. *Religion in American Public Life.* Washington, D.C.: Brookings Institution, 1985.

Richey, Russell E., and Donald G. Jones, eds. *American Civil Religion.* New York: Harper & Row, 1974.

Rockwell, Theodore. *The Rickover Effect: How One Man Made a Difference.* Annapolis: Naval Institute Press, 1992.

Rossiter, Clinton. *The American Presidency.* rev. ed. New York: Harcourt, Brace, & World, 1960.

Rouner, Leroy S., ed. *Civil Religion and Political Theology.* Notre Dame, Ind.: University of Notre Dame Press, 1986.

Schwartz, Barry. "Emerson, Cooley, and the American Heroic Vision." *Symbolic Interactionism* 8 (1985): 103–20.

Stein, Arthur. *Seeds of the Seventies: Values, Work, and Commitment in Post-Vietnam America.* Hanover, N.H.: University Press of New England, 1985.

Sutherland, John. *Bestsellers: Popular Fiction of the 1970s.* London: Routledge & Kegan Paul, 1981.

Tipton, Steven M. "Religion and the Moral Rhetoric of Presidential Politics." *Christian Century* 101 (1984): 1010–13.

Tulis, Jeffrey K. *The Rhetorical Presidency.* Princeton: Princeton University Press, 1987.

Weber, Max. *The Sociology of Religion.* Trans. Epheraim Fischoff. Boston: Beacon, 1963.

White, Theodore H. *America in Search of Itself: The Making of the President, 1956–1980.* New York: Harper & Row, 1982.

Wicker, Tom. *One of Us: Richard Nixon and the American Dream.* New York: Random House, 1991.

Wilkinson, Rupert. *American Tough: The Tough-Guy Tradition and American Character.* New York: Harper & Row, 1984.

Wills, Garry. *Reagan's America: Innocents at Home.* Garden City, N.Y.: Doubleday, 1987.

———. *Under God: Religion and American Politics.* New York: Simon and Schuster, 1990.

Wilson, John F. *Public Religion in American Culture.* Philadelphia: Temple University Press, 1979.

Wolfe, Tom. *The Purple Decades: A Reader.* New York: Berkley Books, 1983.

Wood, Robin. *Hollywood from Vietnam to Reagan.* New York: Columbia University Press, 1986.

Wuthnow, Robert. *The Restructuring of American Religion: Society and Faith Since World War II.* Princeton: Princeton University Press, 1988.

Yergin, Daniel. *The Prize: The Epic Quest for Oil, Money, and Power.* New York: Simon & Schuster, 1991.

INDEX

Abedi, Agha Hasan, 304–5
Afghanistan, Soviet invasion of, 273–74, 275
Agnew, Spiro, 214
Allen, Frederick, 293, 299
Allen, Woody, 353 (n. 112)
Allman Brothers, 205
Altamont, 167
Altizer, Thomas J. J., 151, 155, 351 (n. 83)
America (band), 205, 207
America Project, 304
Anderson, John, 286
Andrews, Joe, 54
Aristide, Jean-Bertrand, 302
Aristotle, 200
Arnall, Ellis, 137, 138, 146, 149, 150
Askew, Reuben, 192
Atlanta Project, 304, 319, 320

Babbitt, Bruce, 301
Bacon, Joe A., 191
Ball, Steve, 189
Barber, James David, 242
Barrett, James, 316
Bartlett, Robert, 268
Begin, Menachem, 273
Bell, Daniel, 237
Bellah, Robert, 3–4, 9, 19, 261–62, 326 (n. 21)
Bennett, William, 315
Berke, Richard, 309
Bestsellers, 11, 14–16, 292, 315–16, 326 (n. 28)
Bicentennial, 203, 206, 224
Biden, Joseph, 300–301
Black Panthers, 148
Bode, Ken, 265
Bolton, Arthur, 198
Bond, Julian, 197
Booker T. and the MGs, 126
Bork, Robert, 301–2

Born again, Carter's experience of being, 156–58, 171
Bourbonism, 33, 35, 40–41, 331 (n. 48)
Bourne, Peter, 54, 55, 56, 57, 102, 157, 169, 171, 172, 173, 175, 191, 193, 200, 336 (n. 19)
Boyd, Eva, 126
Brezhnev, Leonid, 273
Britton, John, 316
Brown, Edmund G. (Jerry), 228, 231–34, 235, 237, 250, 278–79, 363 (n. 77)
Brown, Edmund G. (Pat), 148
Bryan, William Jennings, 34
Brzezinski, Zbigniew, 69–70, 78, 241, 263, 367 (n. 66)
Buchanan, Patrick, 18
Buckley, William F., 265, 266, 267
Bush, George, 18, 269, 301, 305, 306, 307, 308, 309, 317
Butler, Landon, 173, 176, 193
Byrd, Garland, 97

Caddell, Patrick, 3–4, 5, 6, 12, 37, 56, 171, 173, 192, 200, 226, 234, 238, 247, 249–52, 256, 258, 259, 260, 261, 284, 286, 287, 310, 327 (n. 7), 374 (n. 50)
Caldwell, Erskine, 27
Califano, Joseph, 245, 246, 249, 257
Calley, William, 219–20
Calloway, Howard ("Bo"), 144, 145, 146, 149, 150, 151, 189
Cambodia, bombing of, 216
Capote, Truman, 167
Capricorn Records, 205
Carpenters (band), 204
Carson, Johnny, 305
Carson, Rachel, 125
Carter, Alton (Buddy), 23–26, 30, 33, 50, 66, 117

391

Hurst, Joe, 136–41, 145
Hyperbole, Carter's habit of, 20, 30, 53, 69–70, 75, 104, 108, 198, 214, 355 (n. 19)

Individualism, 19, 130, 132, 156, 162, 164, 166, 168, 169, 306–8, 309, 311–12, 314–21
International Negotiating Network (INN), 302
Iran: revolution in, 16, 260, 276, 279–80; hostages taken, 259, 264–65, 275, 276–78, 286, 287, 293, 299

Jackson, Brooks, 275
Jackson, Henry ("Scoop"), 192, 193, 220, 228, 231
Jackson, Jesse, 310
James, William, 254
Jamieson, Kathleen Hall, 310
Jesus, Carter compared to, 214
Jesus Christ Superstar, 15, 204
Johnson, Bishop William, 39–40, 85–86, 88
Johnson, LeRoy, 143
Johnson, Lyndon, 39, 41, 109, 120, 144, 146, 147, 165, 210, 217, 242, 308
Johnson, Rheta Grimsley, 317
Jones, Jim, 16
Jones, Thad, 134, 136
Jordan, Clarence, 297
Jordan, Hamilton, 5, 50, 69, 150, 169, 172, 173, 174, 175, 176, 177, 178, 179, 189, 192, 193, 194, 195, 197, 199, 200, 211, 213, 220, 230, 238, 241, 243, 244, 245, 247, 249, 270, 277
Jova, Henri, V, 297
Judis, John B., 309

Kempton, Murray, 295
Kennedy, Edward, 6, 56, 167, 210, 213, 242, 245, 254, 259, 277, 278, 279, 280
Kennedy, John, 39, 120, 125, 133, 193, 242, 282

Kent State shootings, 216, 217
Kerrey, Robert, 305
Kierkegaard, Søren, 151, 155, 156
Killer rabbit story, 274–76, 284
Kilpatrick, James, 290
King, C. B., 187–88
King, Carole, 126
King, Martin Luther, Sr., 251, 252
King, Martin Luther, Jr., 124, 148, 230, 264
Kirbo, Charles, 54, 139, 145, 172, 173, 174, 175, 176, 177, 178, 187, 191, 200, 230, 249, 288
Kirkpatrick, Jeane, 262, 263
Kissinger, Henry, 109, 221
Koinonia Farm, 119, 297
Kopechne, Mary Jo, 167
Korca, negotiations with, 294–96
Kuhn, Thomas, 125

Laing, R. D., 15
Lalor, Bill, 113
Lance, Bert, 6, 172, 173, 174, 175, 176, 177, 178, 191, 197, 200, 242, 249, 255, 258, 305
Lasch, Christopher, 3, 4, 5, 283, 324 (n. 8)
Law Day speech, 152, 221
Laxalt, Paul, 272
Leddick, Roth, 107
Led Zeppelin, 15, 328 (n. 37)
Lennon, John, 206
Leno, Jay, 305
Letterman, David, 305
Lincoln, Abraham, 6, 264
Lindsey, Hal, 16
Lions Club, 117, 135, 152, 156
Lipshutz, Robert, 173, 196
Logan (physician), 25
Logan, Bobby, 97
Louis, Joe, 86, 88
Lynn, James, 249
Maddox, Lester, 145–50, 178, 184, 185, 186, 189, 190
Mailer, Norman, 54, 55, 56, 57, 155
"Malaise" speech, 1–7, 16, 18, 163,

218, 261–62, 314, 318, 324 (nn. 13, 15)
Manson, Charles, 15, 167
Maranatha Baptist Church, 132, 305
Marcuse, Herbert, 353 (n. 112)
Marquez, Gabriel Garcia, 14
Marx, Karl, 4, 283, 317, 348 (n. 26)
Matthews, Richard, 295
McCartney, Paul, 206
McGovern, George, 3, 191–92, 193–94, 210, 211, 212, 213, 215–16, 217, 219, 220
McGrory, Mary, 291
McLean, Don, 205
McLuhan, Marshall, 125
Meany, George, 245, 246
Menil, Dominique de, 303
Merritt, Janet S., 191
Middle East, 240, 259, 260, 264, 273, 295, 297, 298, 299, 302. *See also* Iran
Miller, William Lee, 54, 67
Moffett, George, 262
Mondale, Walter, 2, 3, 4, 17, 225, 226, 241, 250, 256, 283, 290, 291
Moon, Sun Myung, 14
Moore, Homer, 133–37, 139–40
Moyers, Bill, 155, 160, 168
Mudd, Roger, 277
Murphy, Reg, 141, 143, 152, 182, 189
Murray, Charles, 312–13
Music, popular, 15, 126, 148, 204–7, 217, 292, 328 (n. 37), 359 (n. 9). *See also under specific artists*
Muskie, Edmund, 219, 227
Myers, J. Frank, 33
My Lai massacre, 167, 219

Nader, Ralph, 211, 256
Narcissism (diagnosis of Carter), 8, 57–58, 77, 336 (n. 21)
National Organization of Women, 166
New Deal, 35, 234, 244
New Right, 14, 259, 267–68, 269, 270, 284, 315
Niebuhr, H. Richard, 158

Niebuhr, Reinhold, 75, 151, 160–61
Nietzsche, Friedrich, 9, 171
Nixon, Richard, 17, 148, 165, 185, 194, 200, 208, 210, 211, 212, 213, 214, 221, 224, 225, 243, 276, 279, 280, 281, 308, 309, 352 (n. 110), 360 (n. 28); as moral leader, 214–19, 361 (n. 33); theology of, 217–18
Noonan, Peggy, 305, 306
Noriega, Manuel, 302
Norwood, Charlie, 314
Novak, Robert, 275
Nunn, Sam, 144, 188, 272, 310

Ochs, Phil, 168
O'Neill, Tip, 243–44, 254–55

Pace, Stephen, 72
Panama Canal treaties, 222, 235, 264–72, 273, 283, 293, 314, 315
Particularism, 128–31, 163, 348 (n. 23). *See also* Universalism
Patton, John H., 236–37
Peale, Norman Vincent, 5
Peanut Brigade, 181, 227, 238
Pennington, Brooks, 142, 145
Pennington, John, 139
People's Temple, 16
Perot, Ross, 18, 308, 311
Peters, Thomas J., 292
Pfander, Bruce, 314
Phillips, Kevin, 209, 309
Pippert, Wesley, 162
Pirsig, Robert M., 14
Plains Baptist Church, 25, 30–31, 32, 41, 43, 51, 118, 132
Pluralism, 131
Pope, Betty, 116, 294, 296
Pope, Bill, 180, 196
Pope, John, 116, 117, 118, 122, 137, 138, 238, 294, 347 (n. 104)
Pope, Marjorie, 116
Pope Paul II, 316
Populism, 4, 5, 8, 33–41, 112, 147–48, 175, 177, 178, 180, 181, 182, 194, 195, 198, 210, 211, 220, 221–22,

Populism (continued)
232, 233, 234–35, 236–37, 241,
248, 259, 275, 323 (n. 7), 346
(n. 87)
Port Huron Statement, 126, 167, 168
Powell, Jody, 69, 172, 173, 174, 175,
176, 177, 178, 179, 195, 200, 230,
249, 275, 286
Prohibition, 44
Proposition 13, 210, 212, 246, 259

Quayle, Dan, 301, 305

Rabhan, David, 179
Rafshoon, Gerald, 143, 173, 180, 182,
188, 189, 192, 193, 194, 195, 197,
198, 200, 246, 250
Randolph, Cecil, 290
Reading, Carter's habit of, 46, 50, 72
Reagan, Ronald, 6, 10, 17, 148, 224,
231, 234–35, 237, 246, 247,
268–69, 274, 280, 281, 282, 284,
285, 286, 287, 290, 291, 292, 298,
299–300, 301, 305, 306, 307, 308
Redfield, James, 316
Reich, Robert, 313
Reston, James, 226
Rhodes, Annie Mae, 303
Rhodes scholarship, 95–96, 103–4
Ribicoff, Abraham, 256
Rick Dees and His Cast of Idiots, 206
Rickover, Hyman, 108–13, 177, 317
Robbins, Tom, 14
Robinson, John A. T., 125
Rogers, Carl, 15
Rolling Stones, 167
Ronstadt, Linda, 205, 206
Roosevelt, Eleanor, 36
Roosevelt, Franklin D., 6, 27, 35, 36,
39, 115, 285, 290
Rosenthal, A. A., 313
Ross, Diana, 206
Rostenkowski, Dan, 243
Royster, Vermont, 266
Rozell, Mark, 275
Rubin, Jerry, 165, 352 (n. 111)
Rusher, Albert, 101

Russell, Richard, 36, 172, 186, 188,
356 (n. 51)

Sadat, Anwar, 273
Sade, Marquis de, 317–18, 375 (n. 78)
Safire, William, 295
Sakharov, Andrei, 273
SALT II, 240, 264, 270, 273–74
Sanders, Carl, 124, 125, 129, 142,
181, 182, 183, 184, 185, 186, 187,
188, 189, 356 (n. 57)
Scharfenberg, Kirk, 276
Schmeling, Max, 86, 88
Schmidt, Helmut, 272
Schroeder, Patricia, 284
Schuller, Robert H., 14, 292
Schultze, Charles, 281–82
Sebastian, John, 206
Sexual revolution, 165–66, 353
(nn. 112, 114)
Sheffield (school principal), 51, 52, 68
Shipp, Bill, 141, 152, 180, 182, 187,
200, 299, 300, 310
Shirelles, 126
Simon, Carly, 206
Simon and Garfunkel, 206
Singer, Sam, 133
Slappey, Jack, 26
Slappey, Willard, 26, 45, 46, 66, 76, 84
Smile, Carter's, 17, 69–70, 75, 98, 101,
103, 113, 121, 289
Smith, Allie, 66
Smith, Edgar, 66, 78
Smith, George L., 197
Smith, Hedrick, 272
Smith, Hoke, 34
Smith, Rosalynn. See Carter, Rosalynn
Soviet Union, 125, 240, 263, 264,
273–74, 307, 319, 367 (n. 66)
Spann, Gloria Carter. See Carter,
Gloria
Spann, Walter, 60
Spann, Willie Carter, 60, 121–22
Speck, Richard, 166
Springsteen, Bruce, 292
Stallone, Sylvester, 248
Stapleton, Ruth Carter, 28, 32, 36, 44,